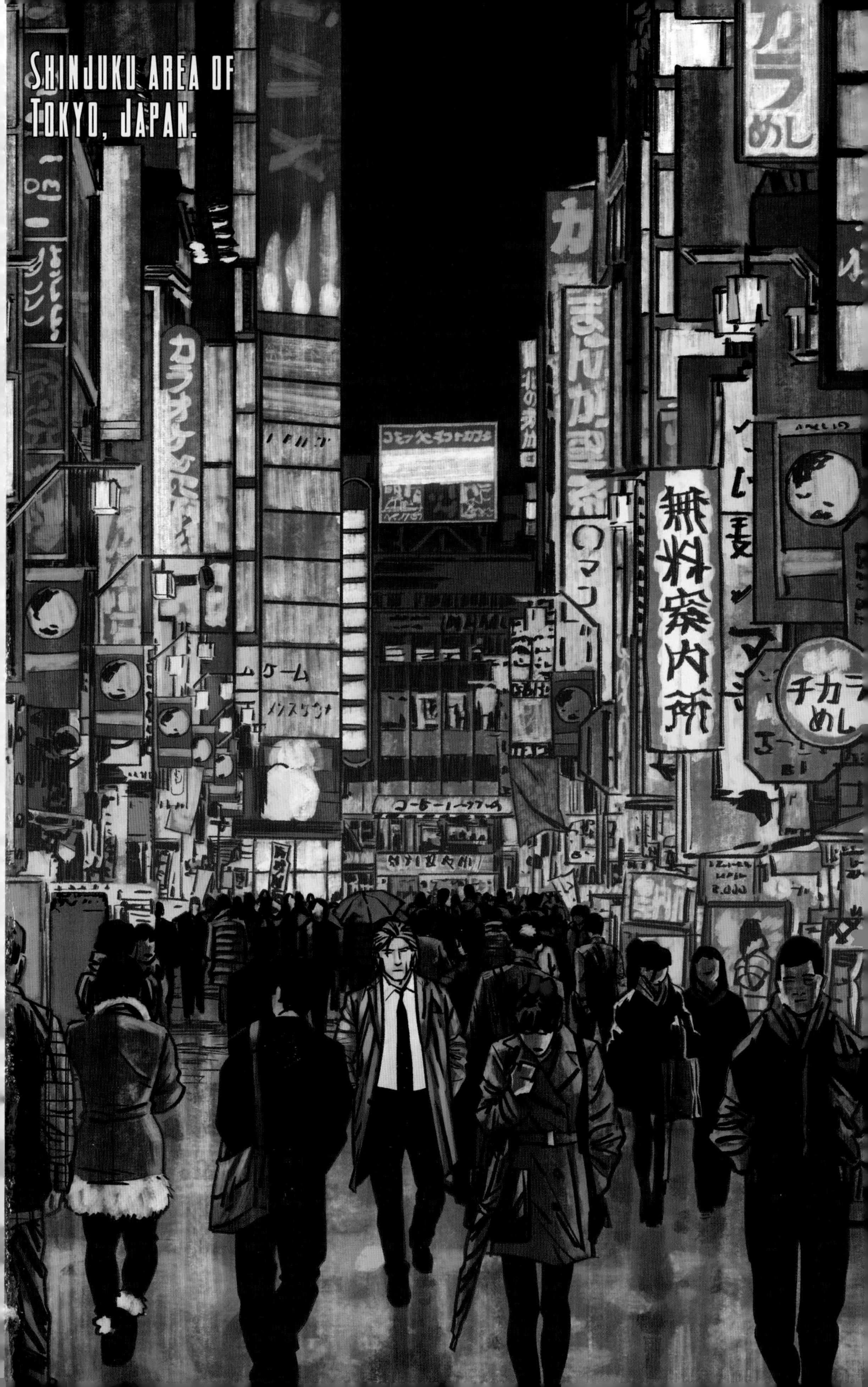
SHINJUKU AREA OF TOKYO, JAPAN.
無料案内所
チカラめし

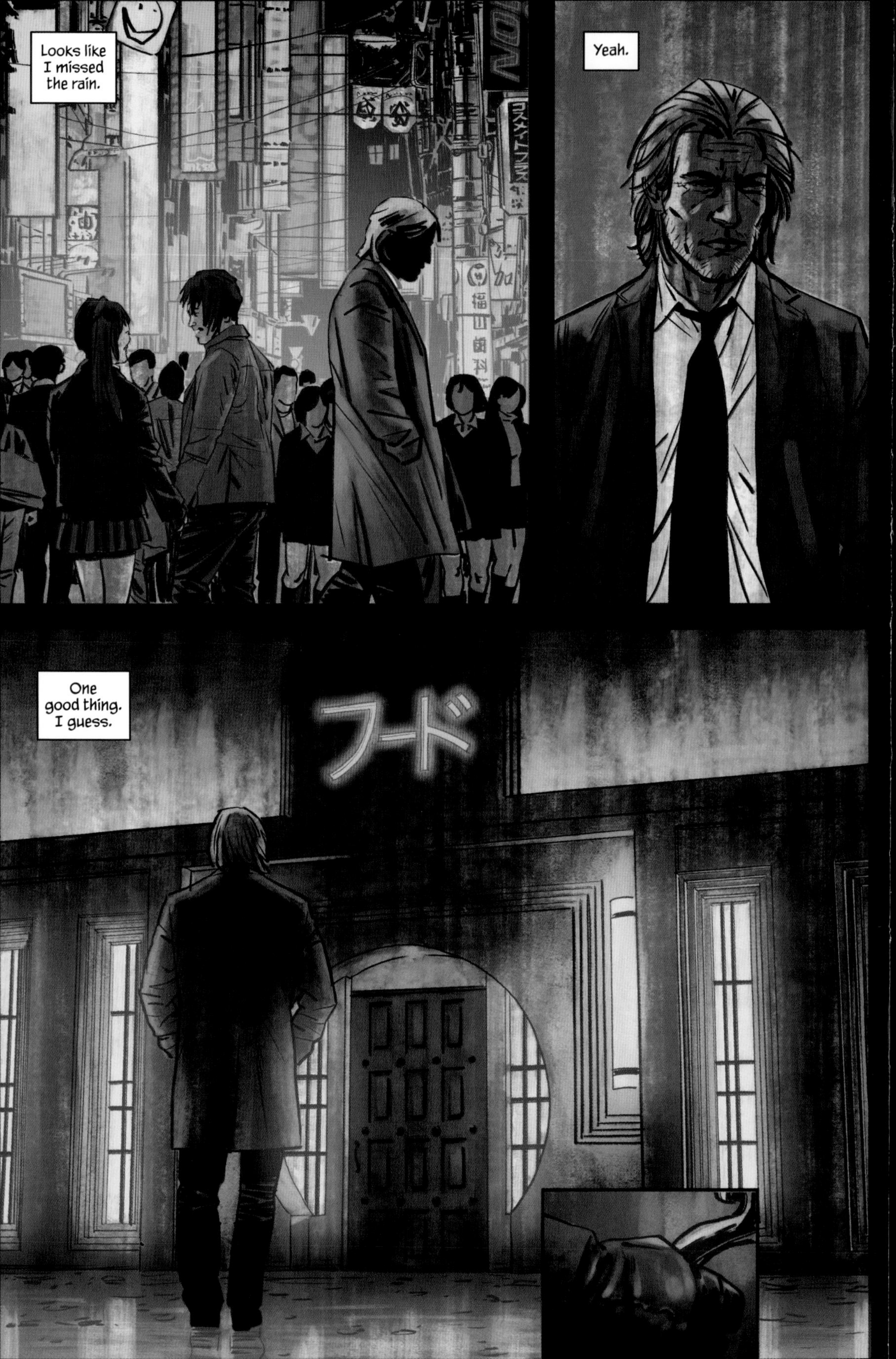
Looks like I missed the rain.
Yeah.
One good thing. I guess.
フード

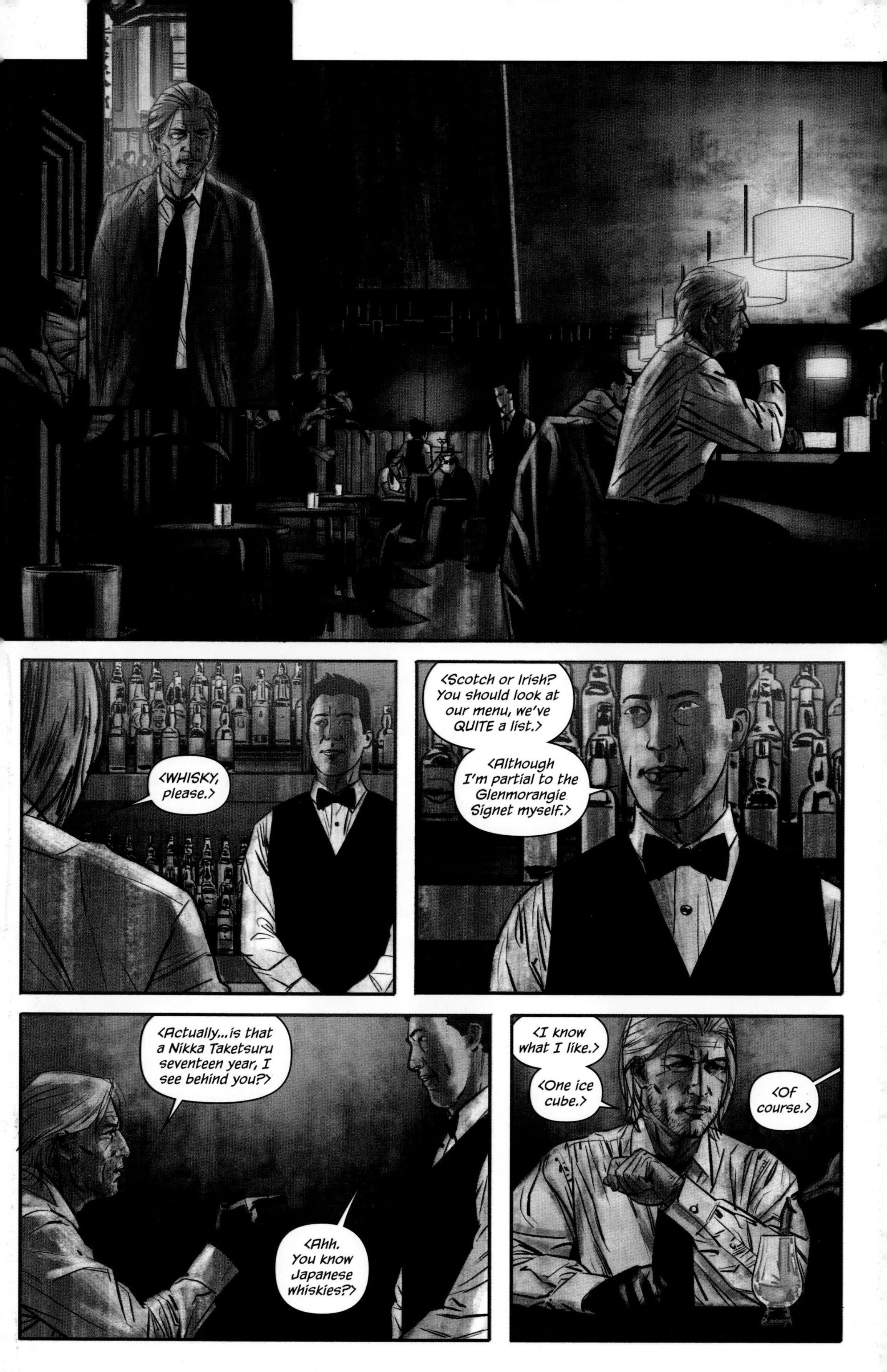
<WHISKY, please.>
<Scotch or Irish? You should look at our menu, we've QUITE a list.>
<Although I'm partial to the Glenmorangie Signet myself.>
<Actually...is that a Nikka Taketsuru seventeen year, I see behind you?>
<Ahh. You know Japanese whiskies?>
<I know what I like.>
<One ice cube.>
<Of course.>

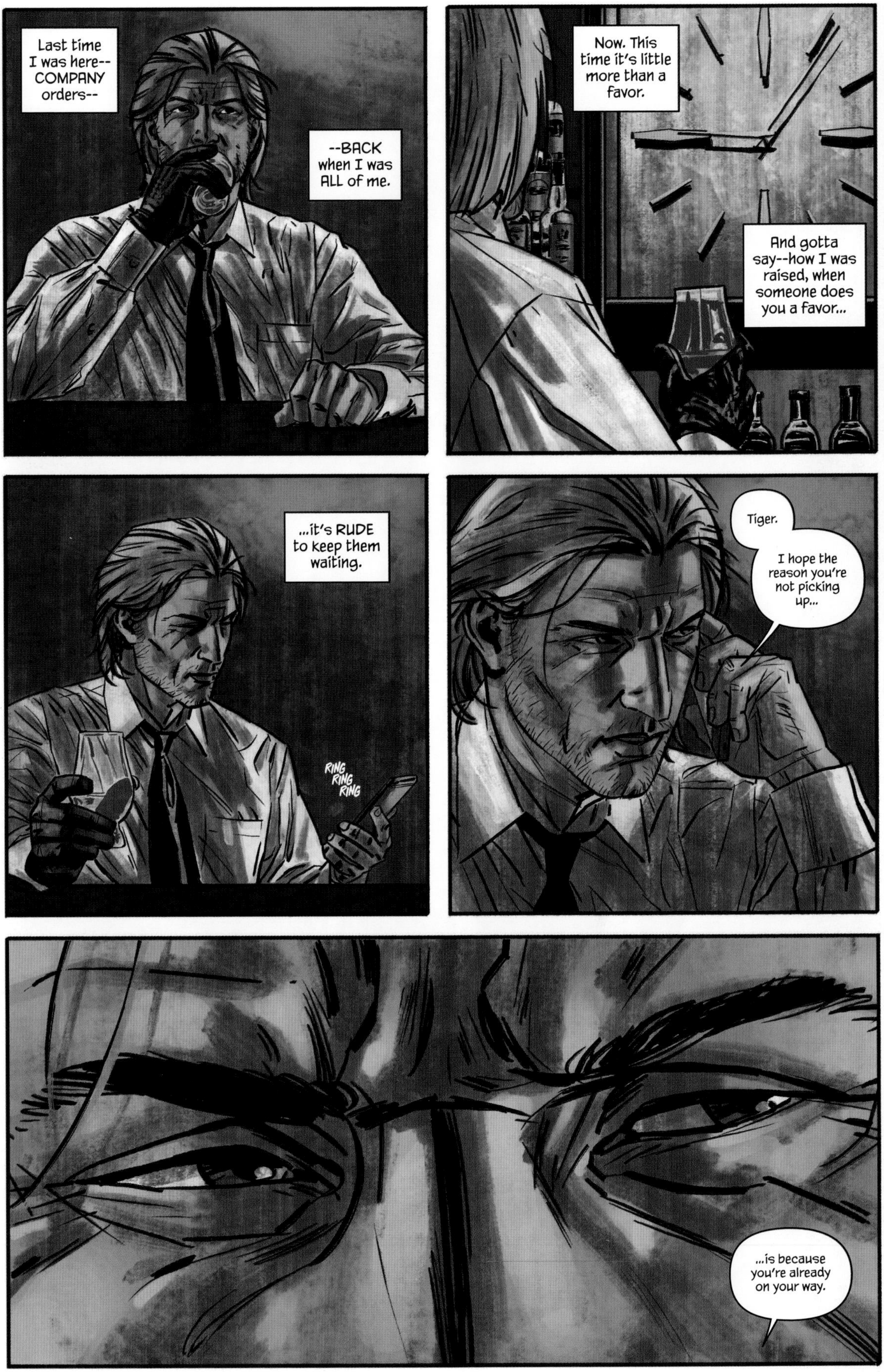
Last time I was here--COMPANY orders--
--BACK when I was ALL of me.
Now. This time it's little more than a favor.
And gotta say--how I was raised, when someone does you a favor...
...it's RUDE to keep them waiting.
RING RING RING
Tiger.
I hope the reason you're not picking up...
...is because you're already on your way.

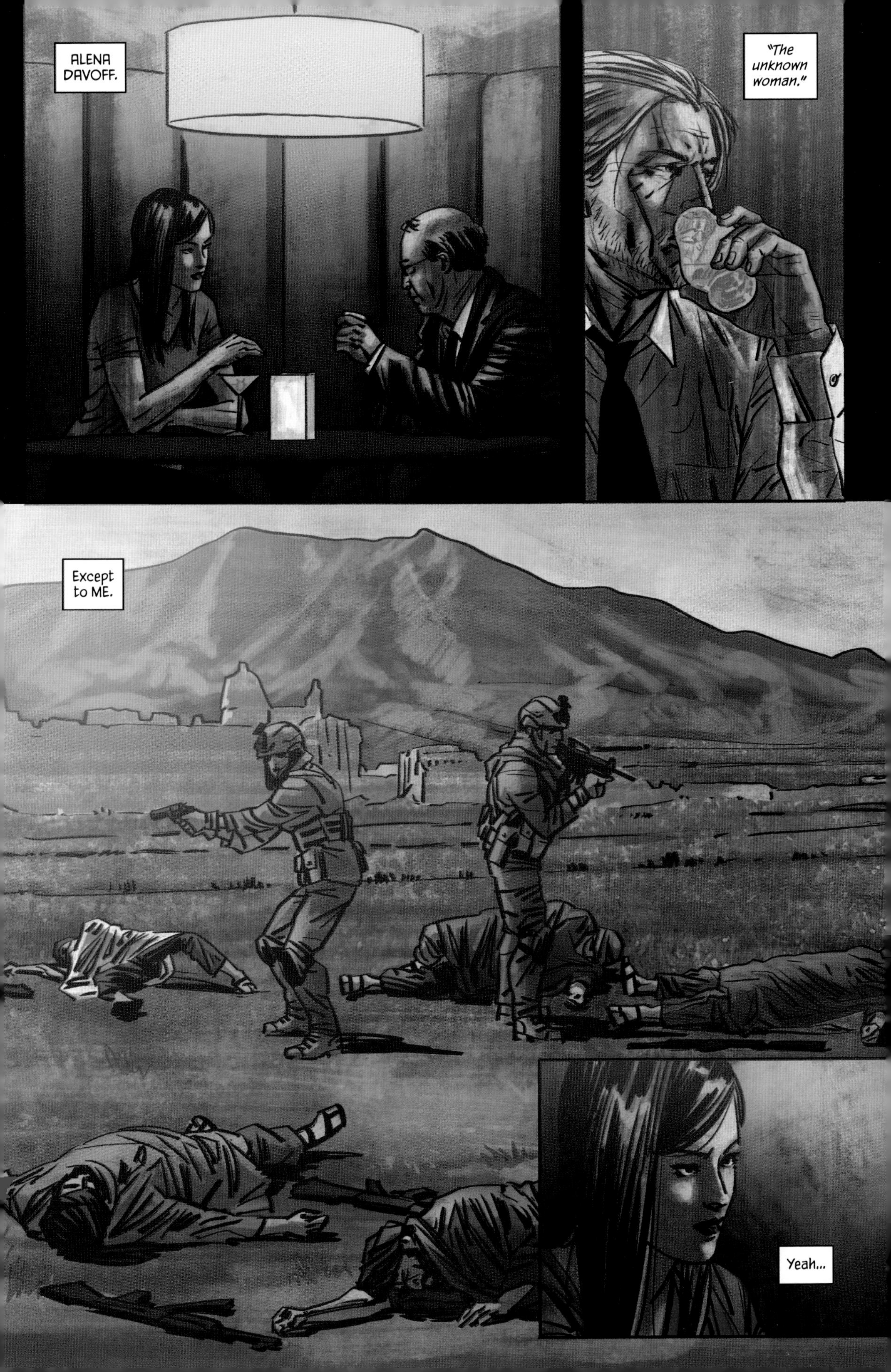
ALENA DAVOFF.
"The unknown woman."
Except to ME.
Yeah...

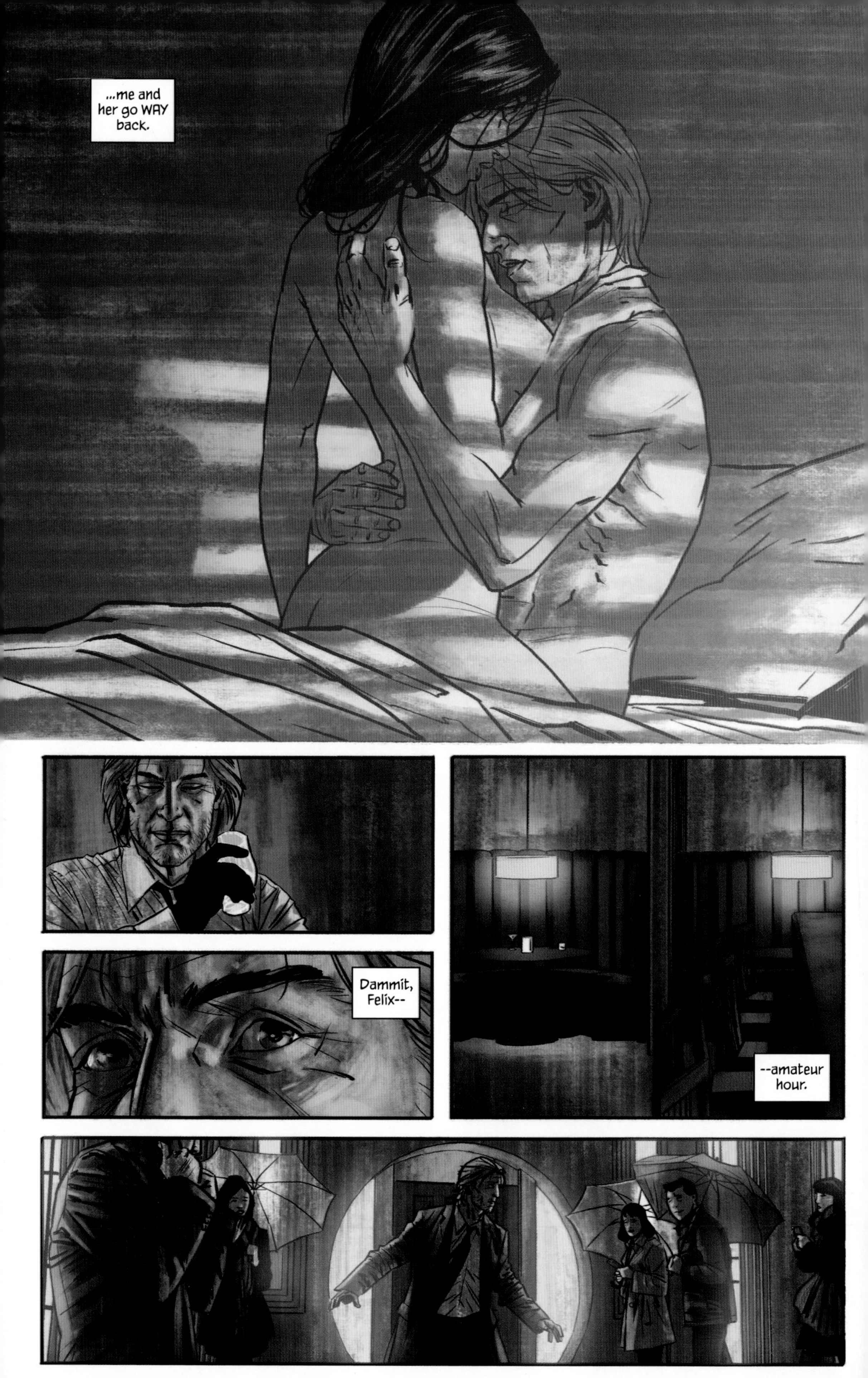
...me and her go WAY back.
Dammit, Felix--
--amateur hour.

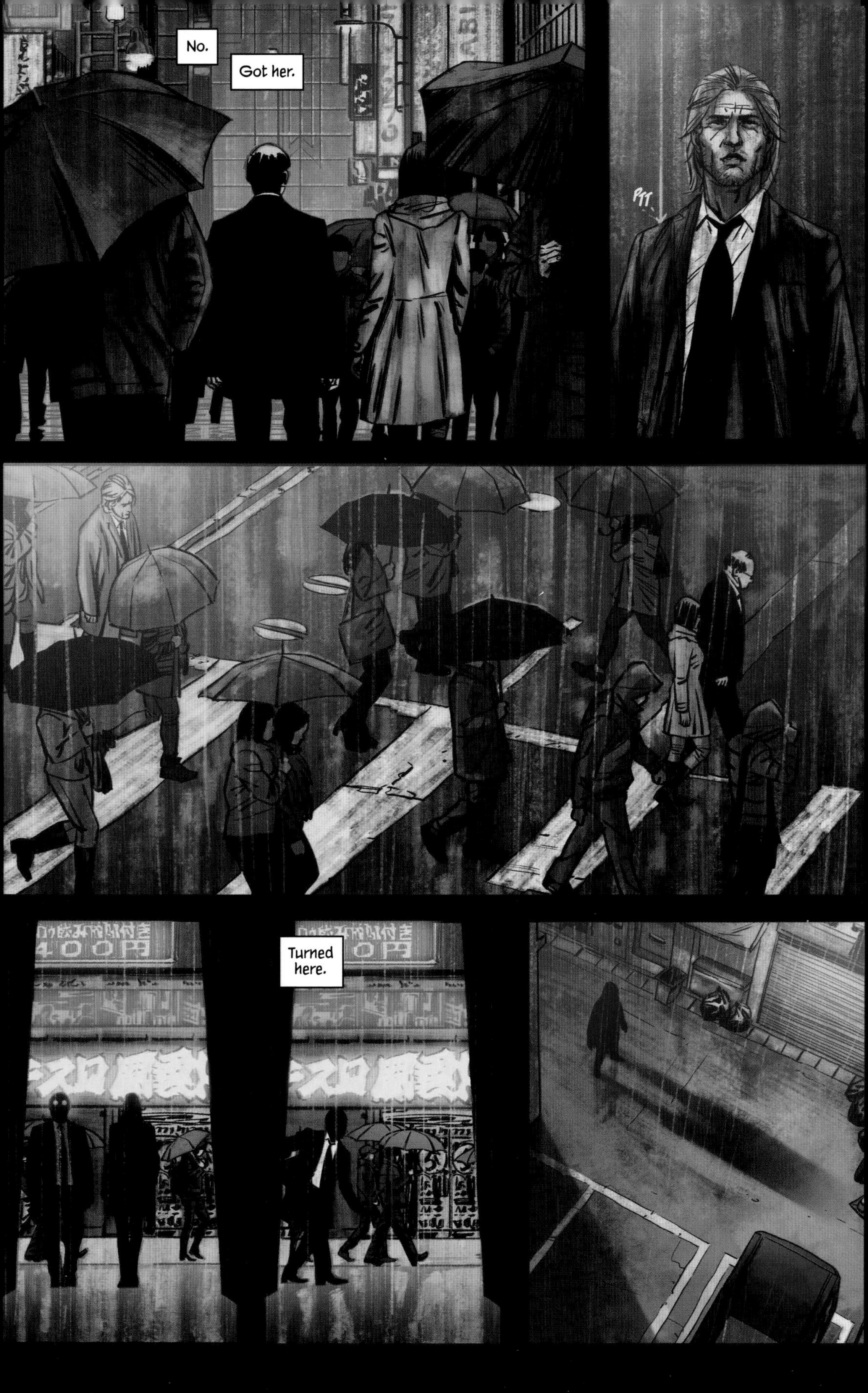
No.
Got her.
PTT
Turned here.

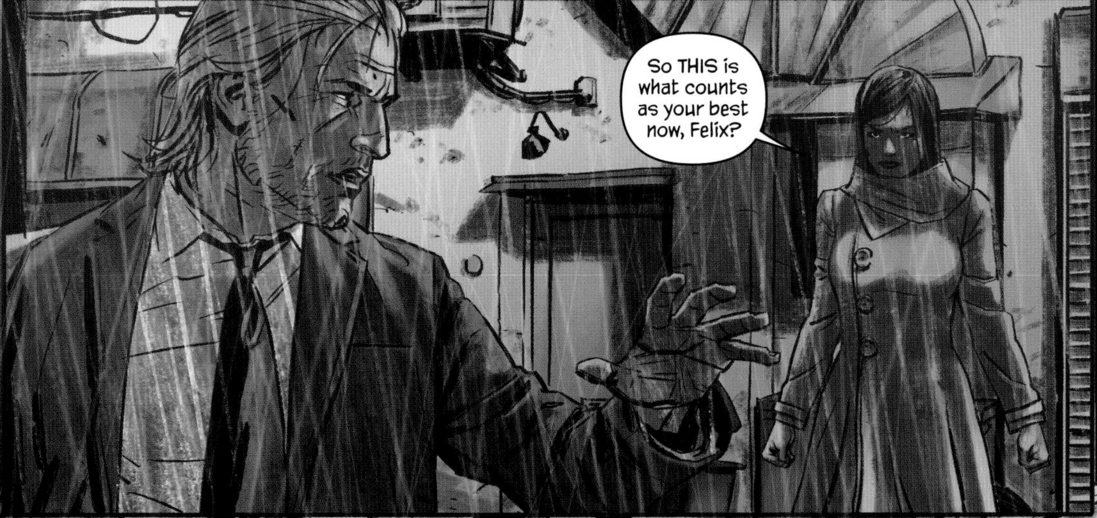
So THIS is what counts as your best now, Felix?

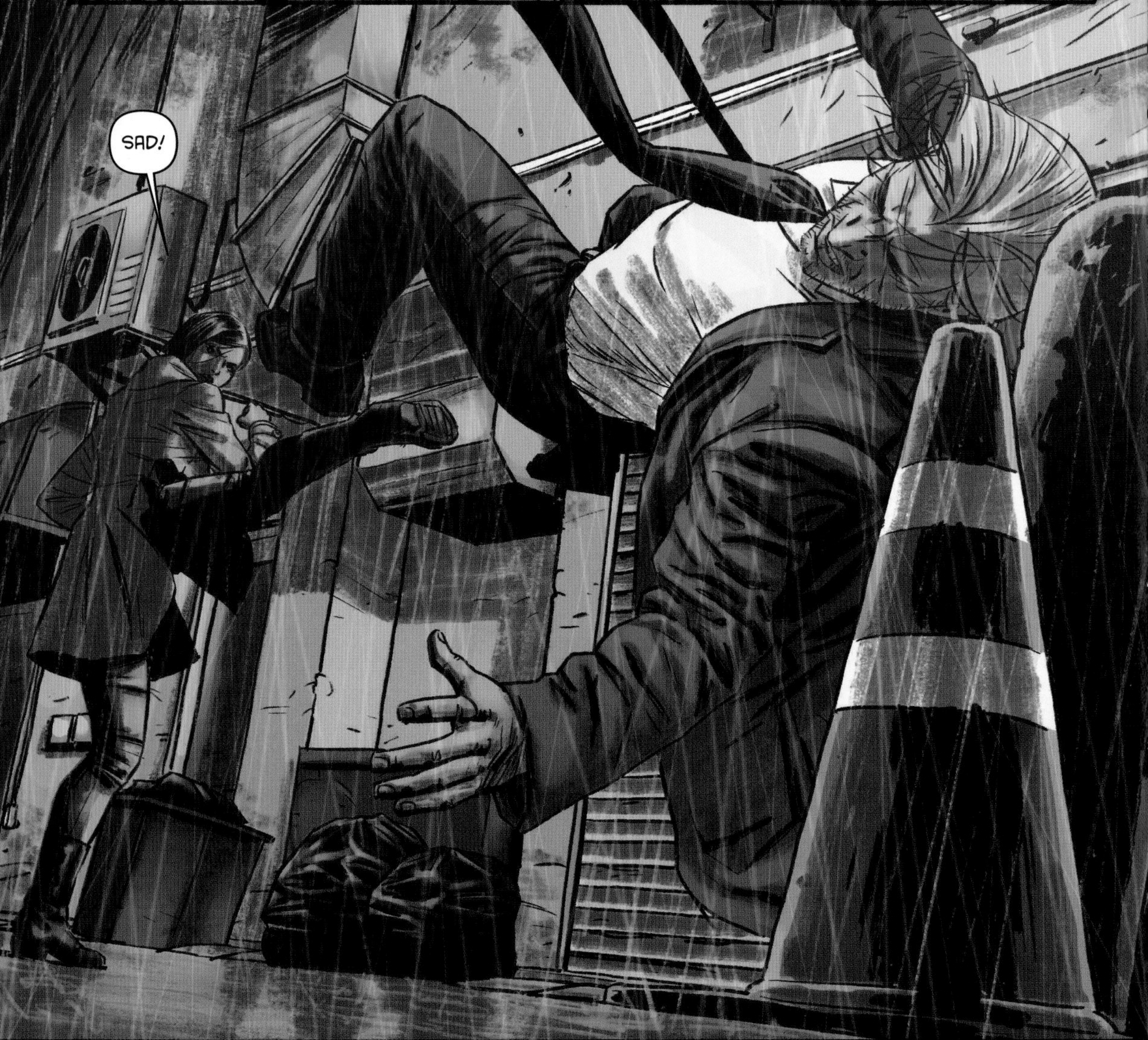
SAD!

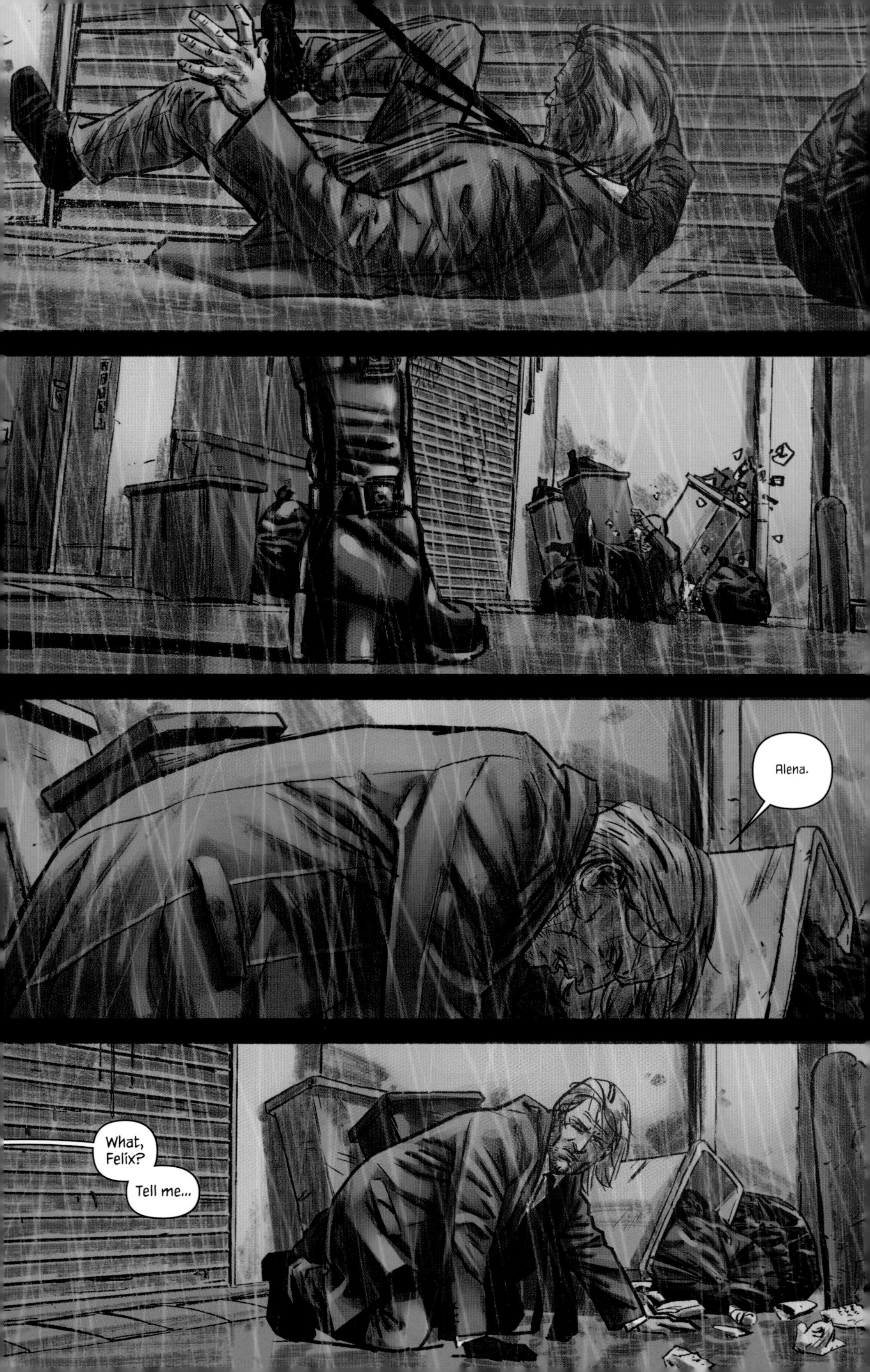
Alena.
What, Felix?
Tell me...

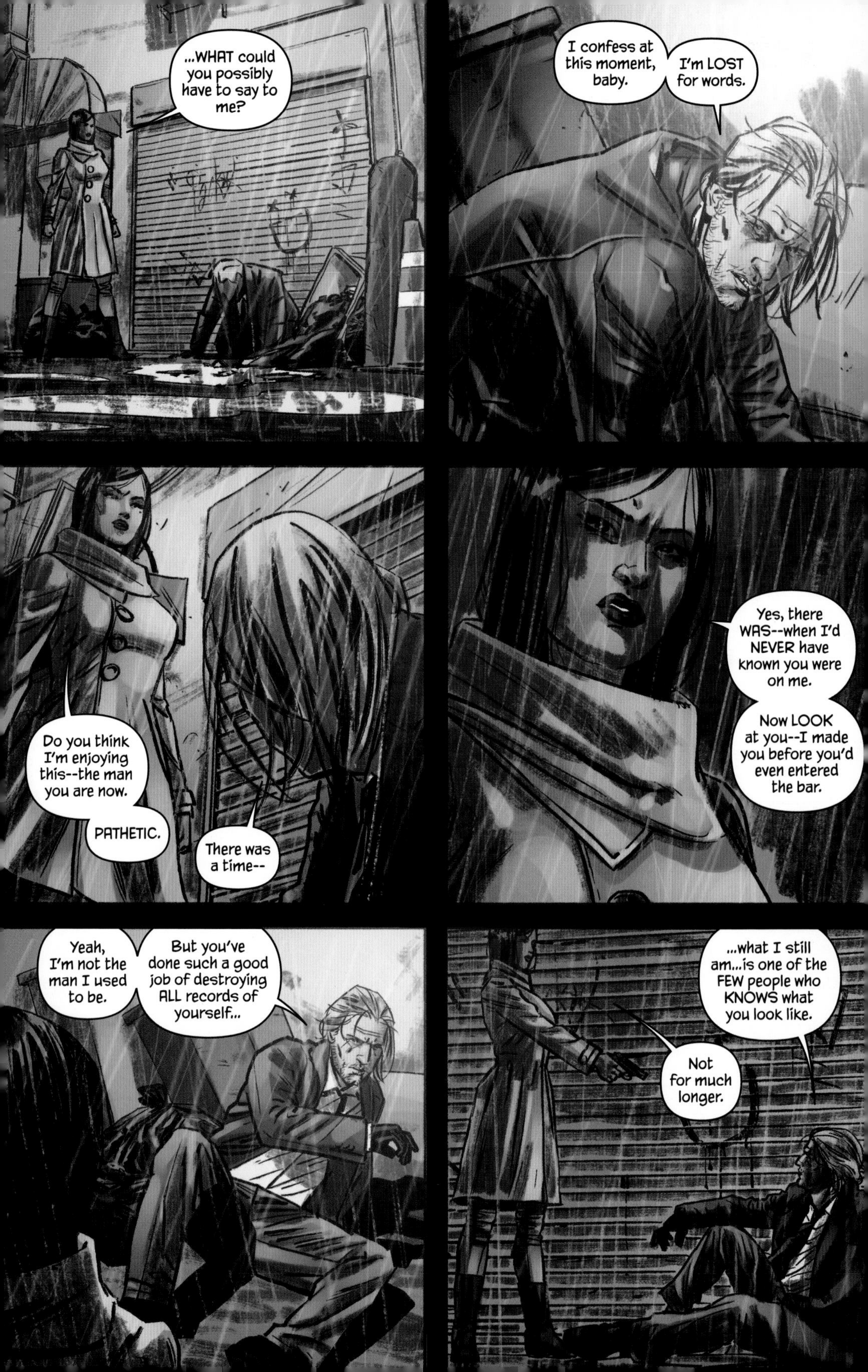
...WHAT could you possibly have to say to me?
I confess at this moment, baby.
I'm LOST for words.
Do you think I'm enjoying this--the man you are now.
PATHETIC.
There was a time--
Yes, there WAS--when I'd NEVER have known you were on me.
Now LOOK at you--I made you before you'd even entered the bar.
Yeah, I'm not the man I used to be.
But you've done such a good job of destroying ALL records of yourself...
...what I still am...is one of the FEW people who KNOWS what you look like.
Not for much longer.

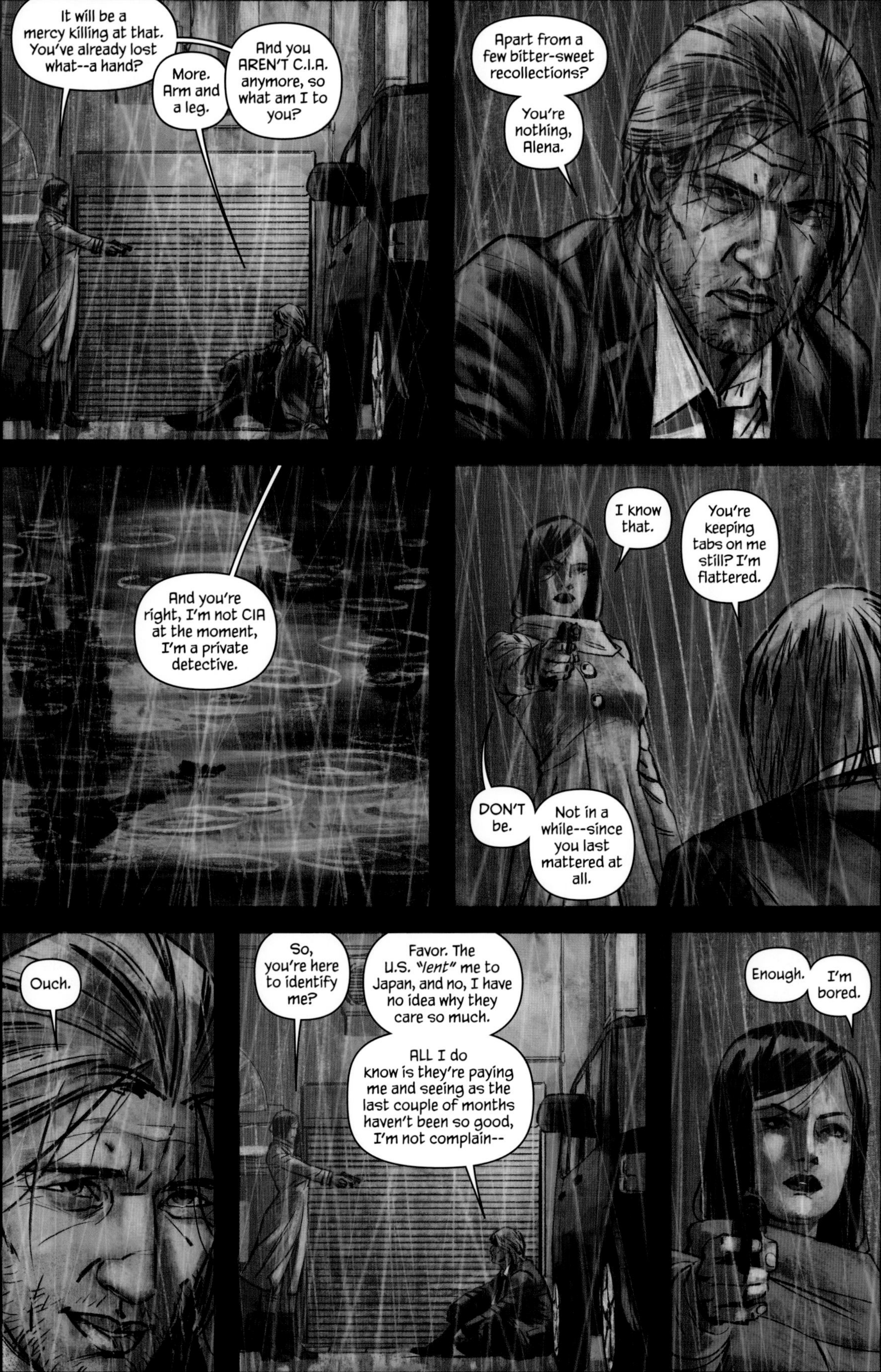
It will be a mercy killing at that. You've already lost what--a hand?
More. Arm and a leg.
And you AREN'T C.I.A. anymore, so what am I to you?
Apart from a few bitter-sweet recollections?
You're nothing, Alena.
And you're right, I'm not CIA at the moment, I'm a private detective.
I know that.
You're keeping tabs on me still? I'm flattered.
DON'T be.
Not in a while--since you last mattered at all.
Ouch.
So, you're here to identify me?
Favor. The U.S. *"lent"* me to Japan, and no, I have no idea why they care so much.
ALL I do know is they're paying me and seeing as the last couple of months haven't been so good, I'm not complain--
Enough.
I'm bored.

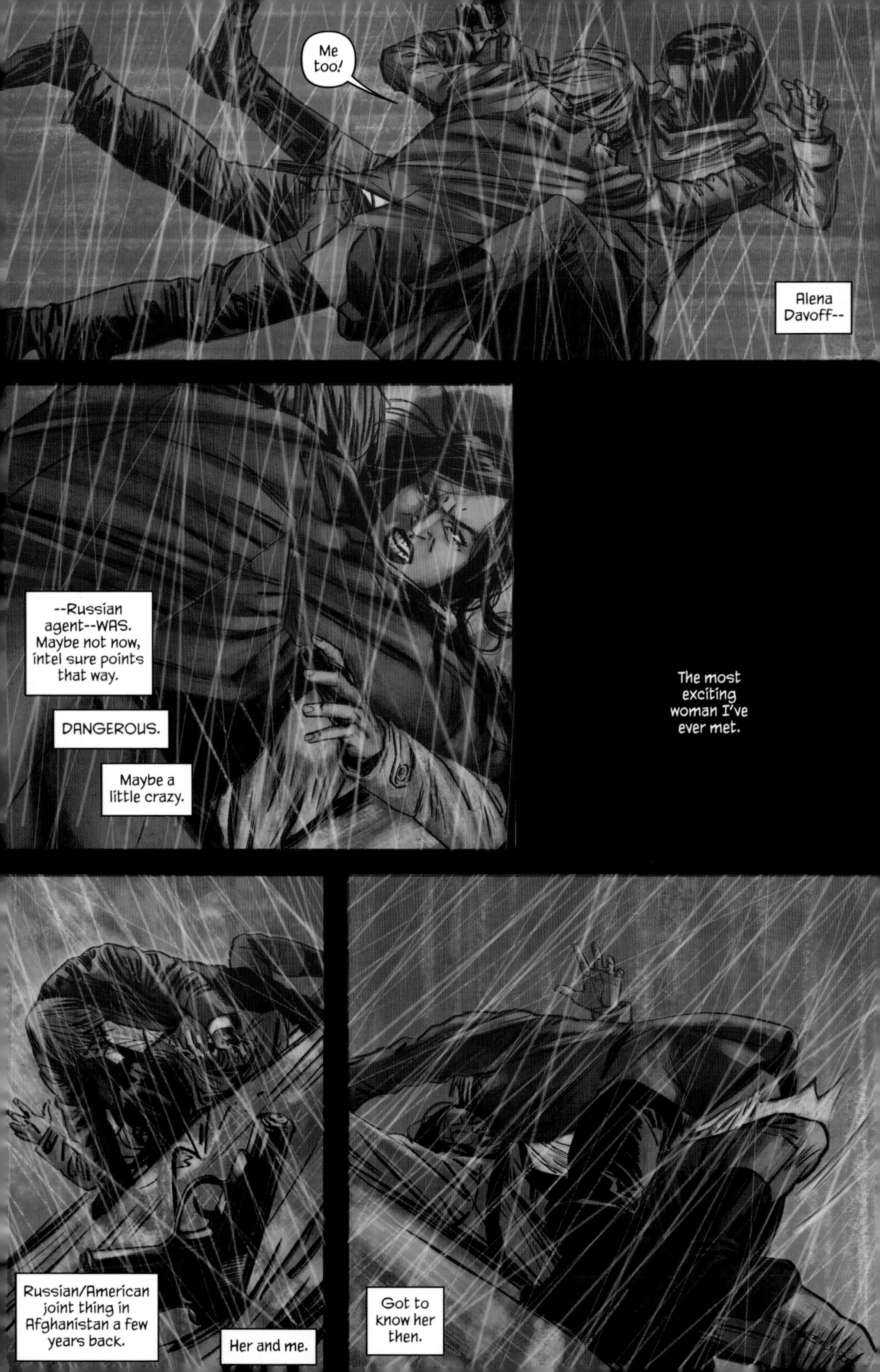
Me too!
Alena Davoff--
--Russian agent--WAS. Maybe not now, intel sure points that way.
DANGEROUS.
Maybe a little crazy.
The most exciting woman I've ever met.
Russian/American joint thing in Afghanistan a few years back.
Her and me.
Got to know her then.

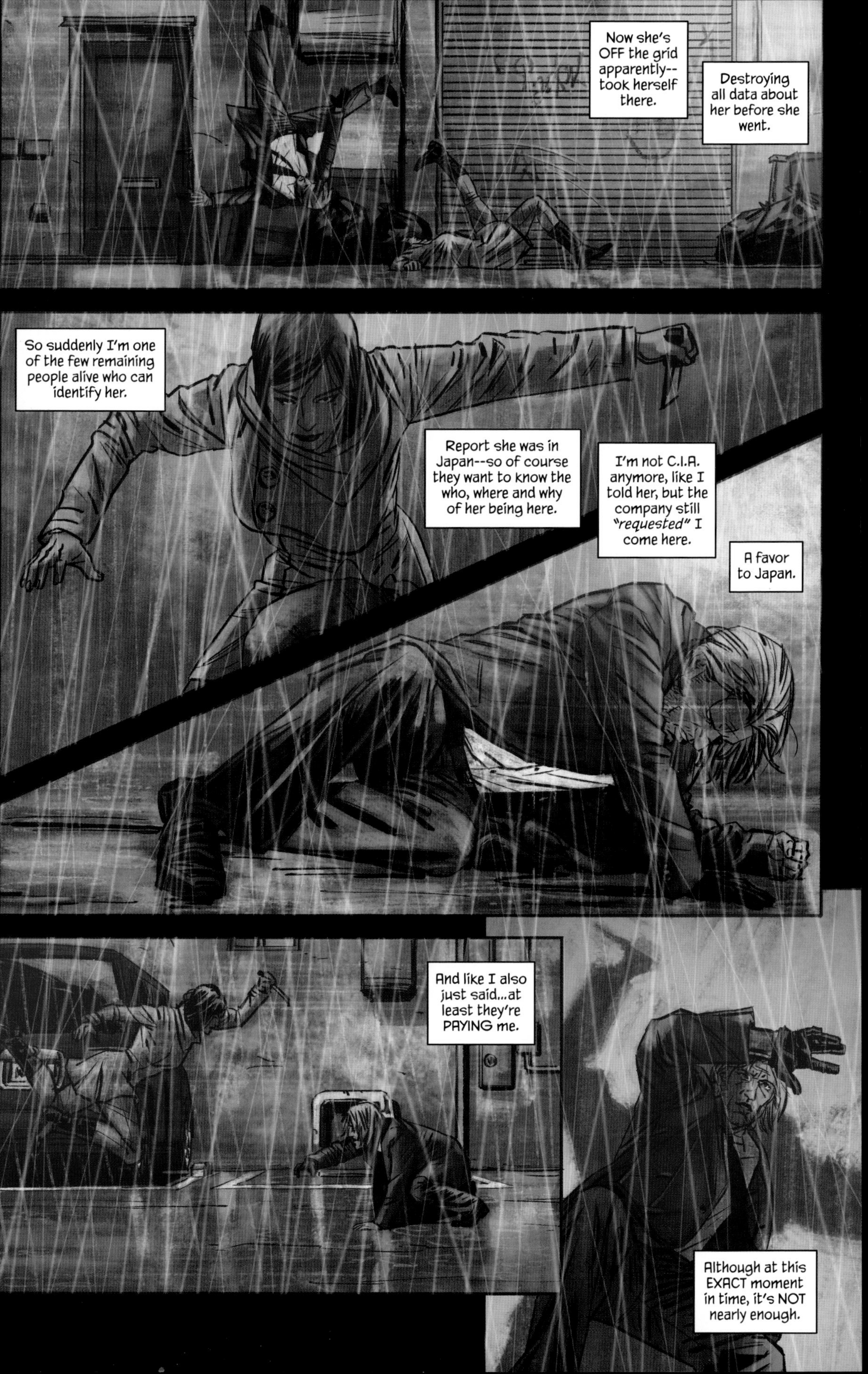
Now she's OFF the grid apparently--took herself there.
Destroying all data about her before she went.
So suddenly I'm one of the few remaining people alive who can identify her.
Report she was in Japan--so of course they want to know the who, where and why of her being here.
I'm not C.I.A. anymore, like I told her, but the company still "requested" I come here.
A favor to Japan.
And like I also just said...at least they're PAYING me.
Although at this EXACT moment in time, it's NOT nearly enough.

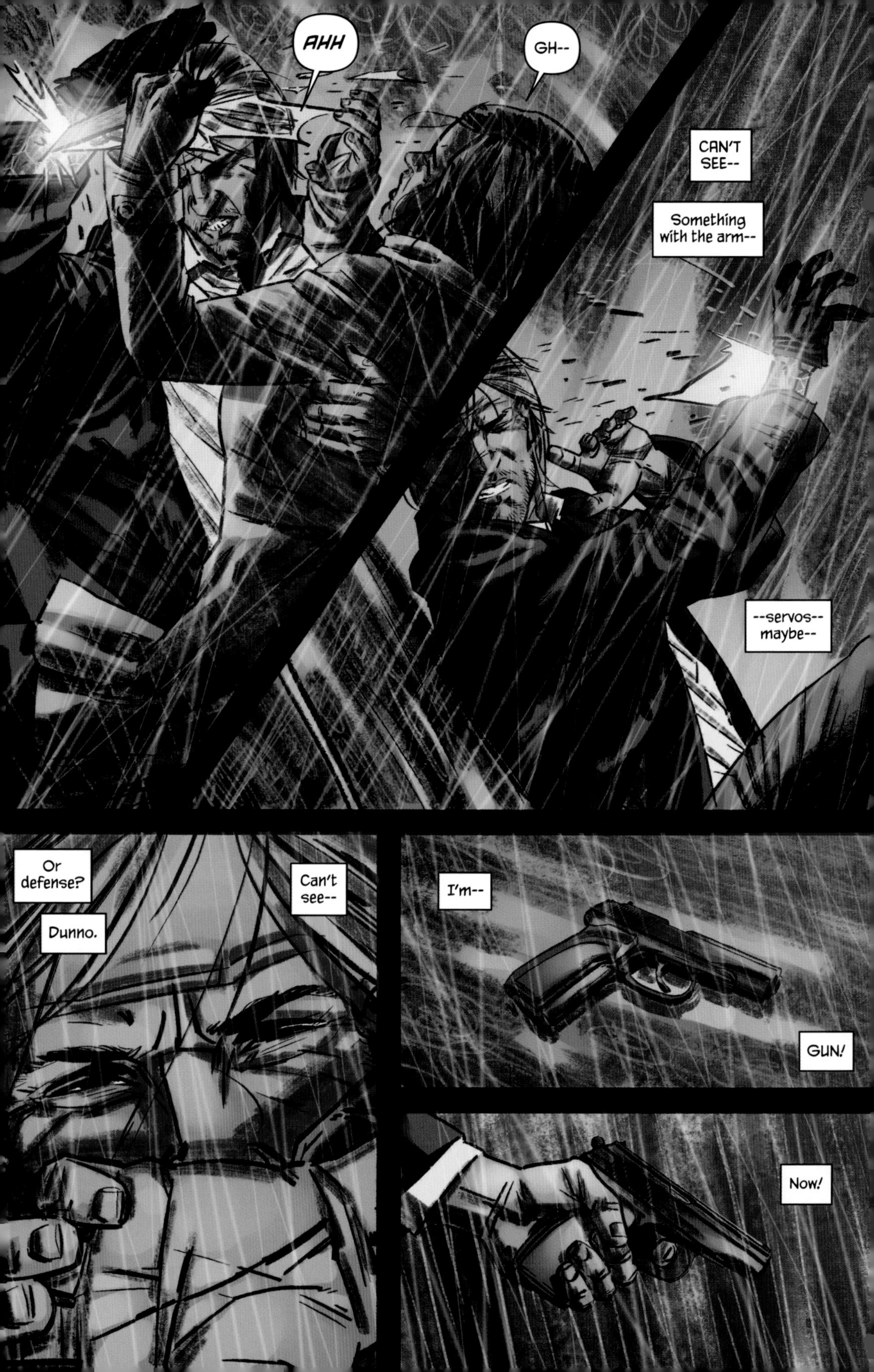

AHH
GH--
CAN'T SEE--
Something with the arm--
--servos-- maybe--
Or defense?
Dunno.
Can't see--
I'm--
GUN!
Now!

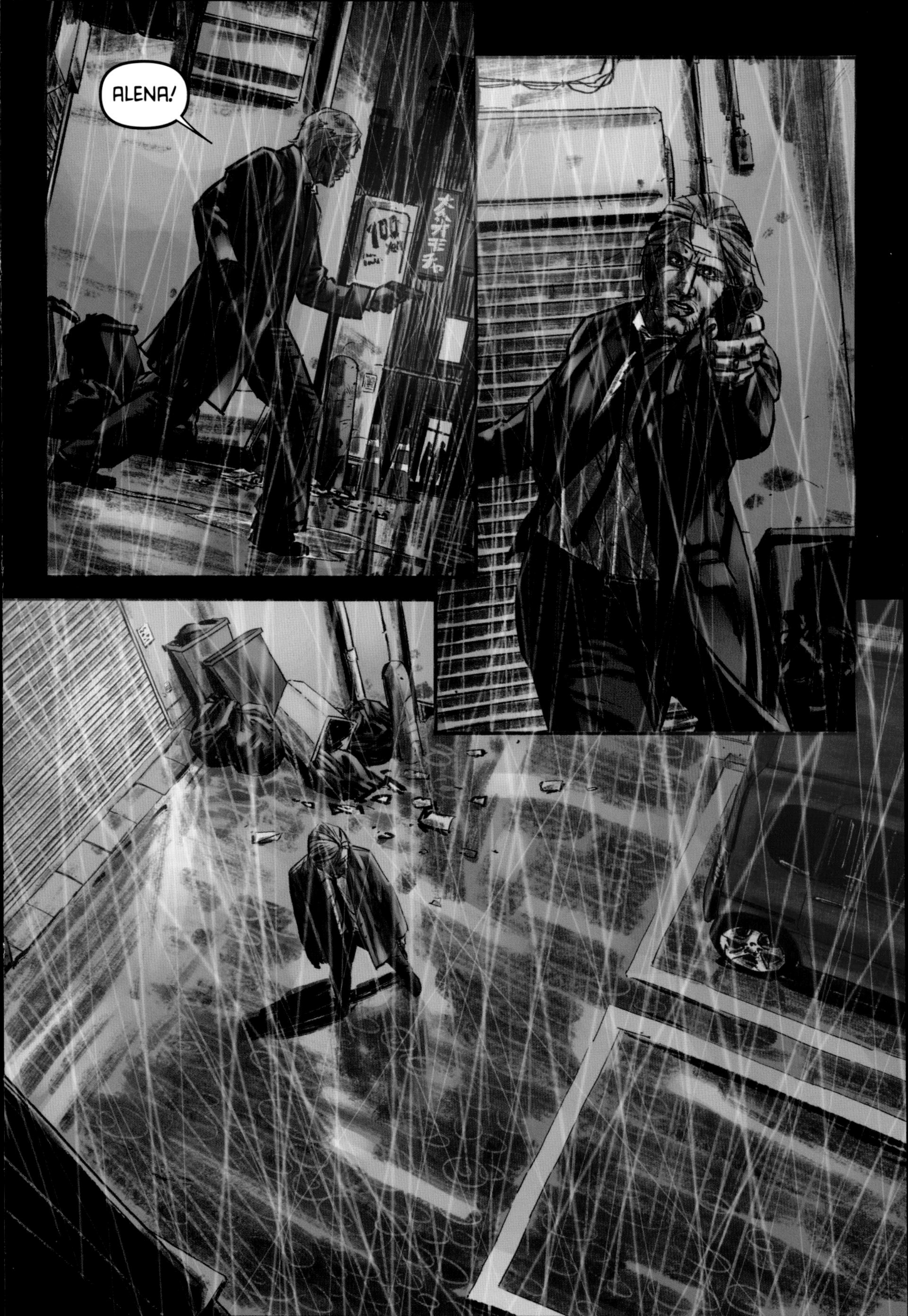
ALENA!

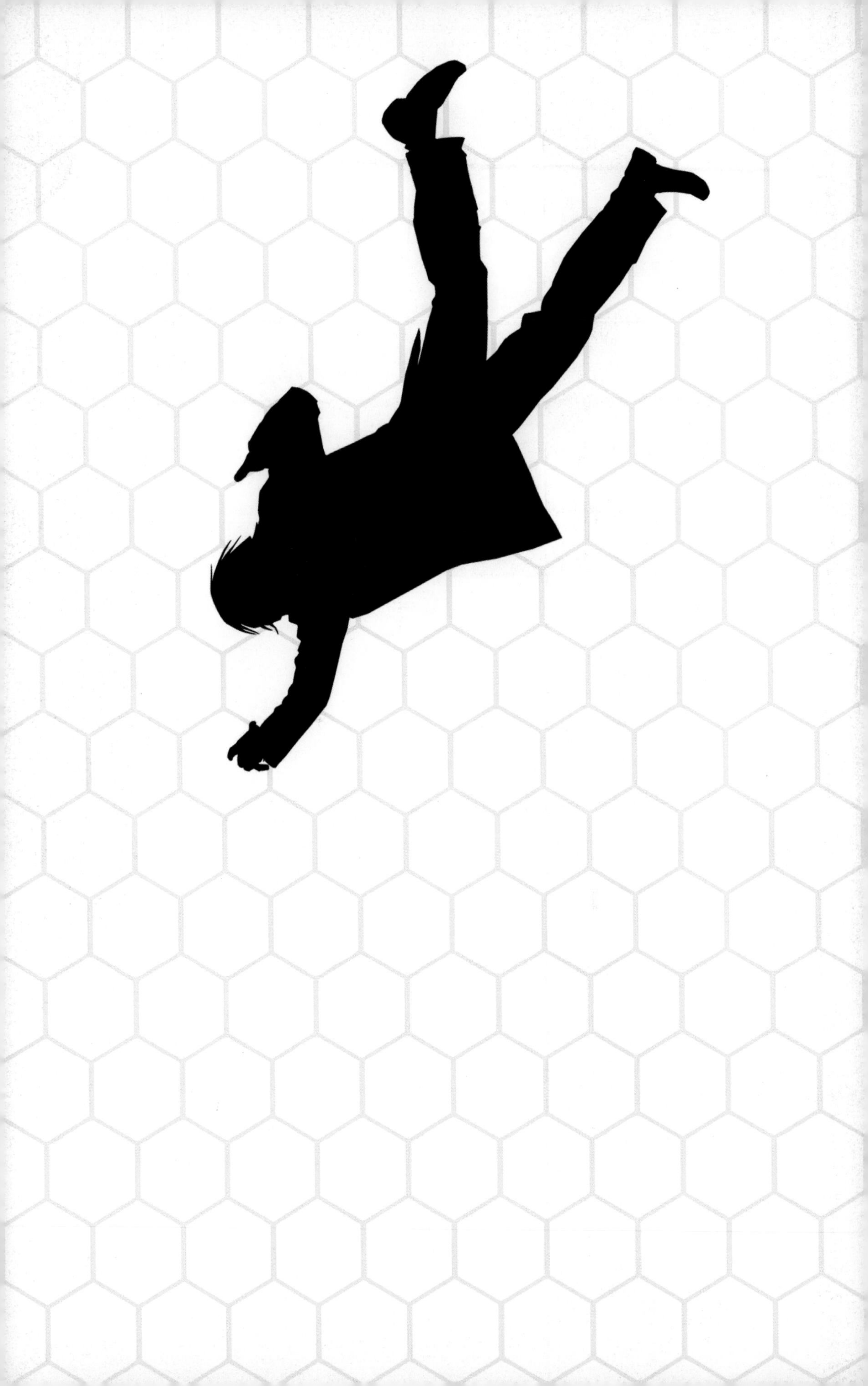

IAN FLEMING'S

JAMES BOND 007™

FELIX LEITER

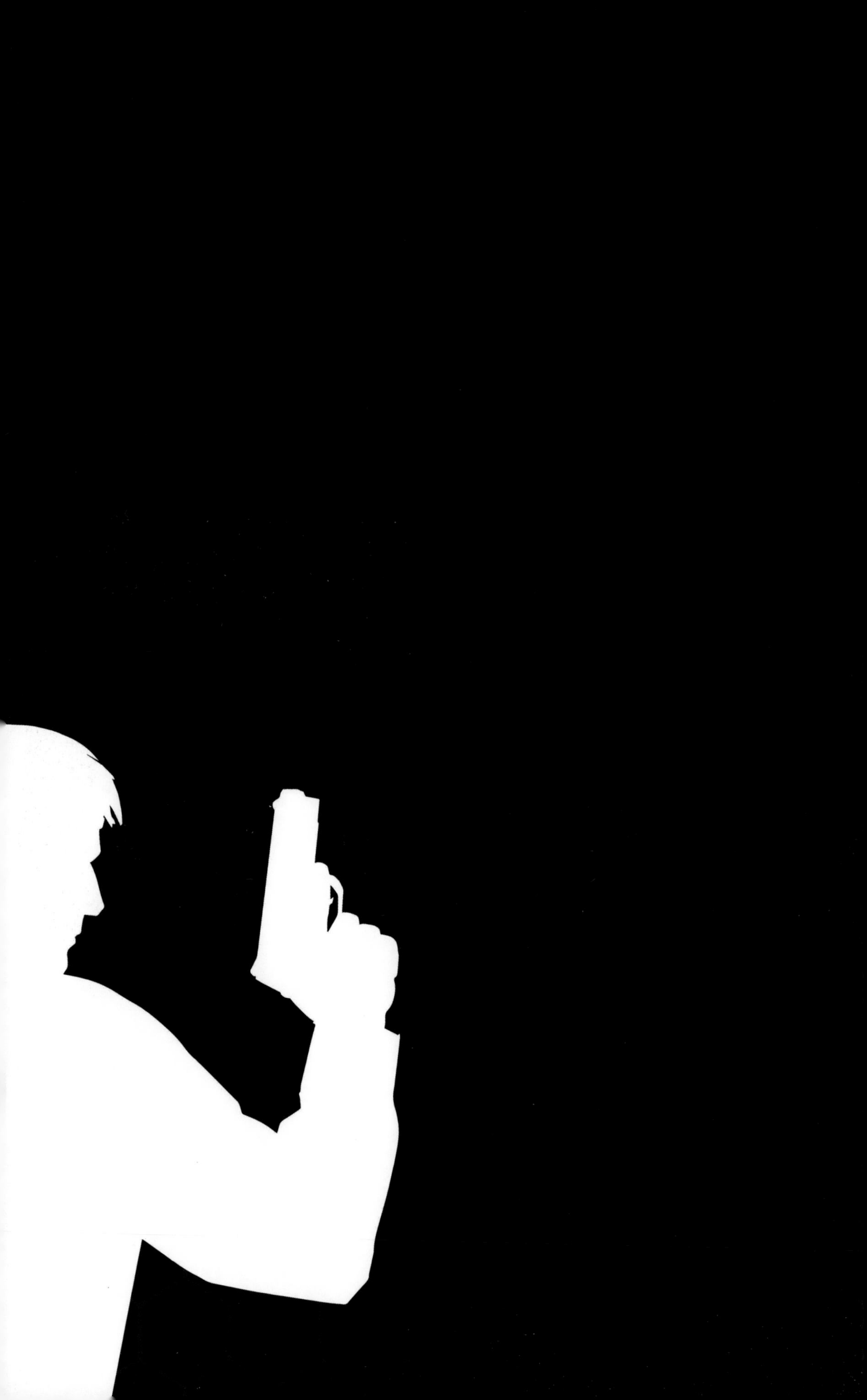

JAMES ROBINSON | WRITER

AARON CAMPBELL | ARTIST

SALVATORE AIALA | COLORS

SIMON BOWLAND | LETTERS

MIKE PERKINS & **ANDY TROY** | COVER

GEOFF HARKINS | DESIGNER

JOSEPH RYBANDT | EXECUTIVE EDITOR
ANTHONY MARQUES | ASSOCIATE EDITOR
MICHAEL LAKE | EDITORIAL CONSULTANT
RIAN HUGHES | JAMES BOND LOGO DESIGNER

SPECIAL THANKS TO **JOSEPHINE LANE,**
JONNY DAVIDSON, CORINNE TURNER
& **DIGGORY LAYCOCK** AT
IAN FLEMING PUBLICATIONS LTD.
& **JONNY GELLER** AT CURTIS BROWN

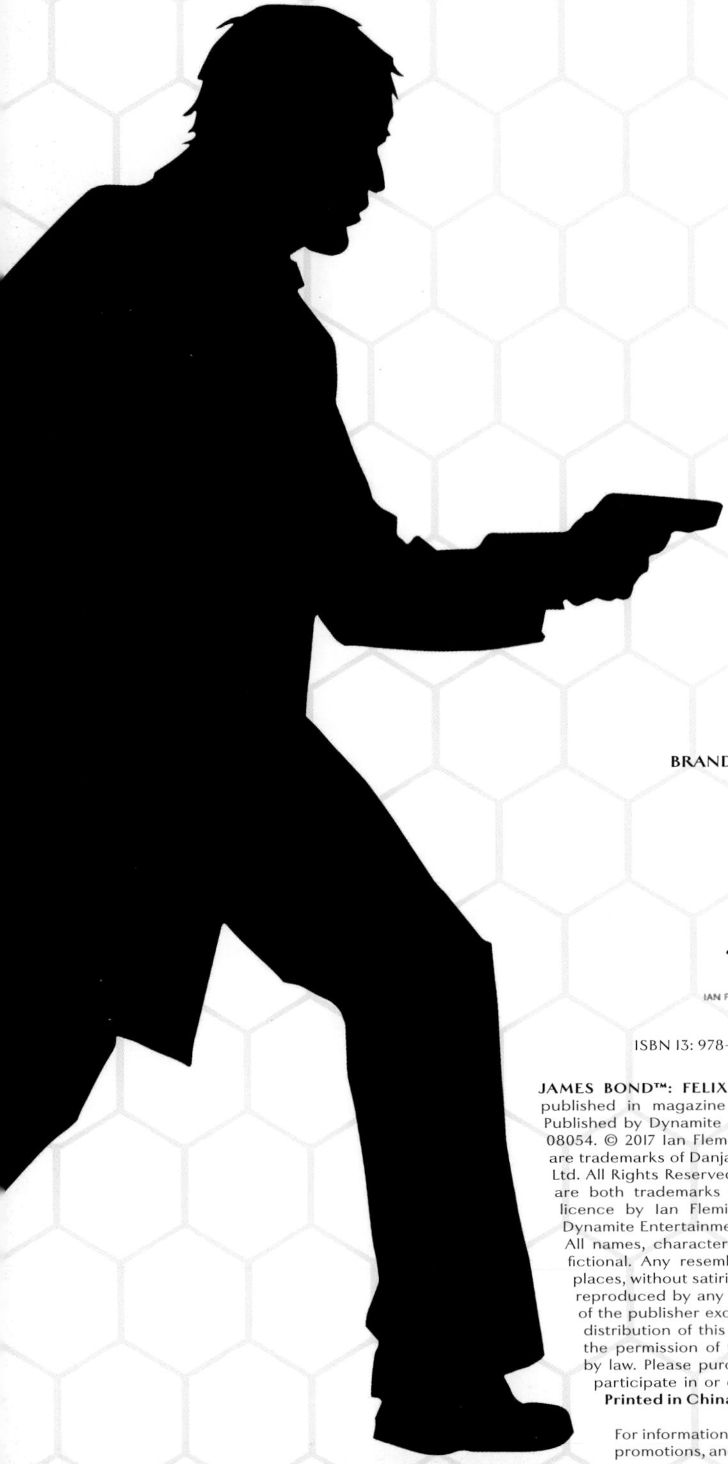

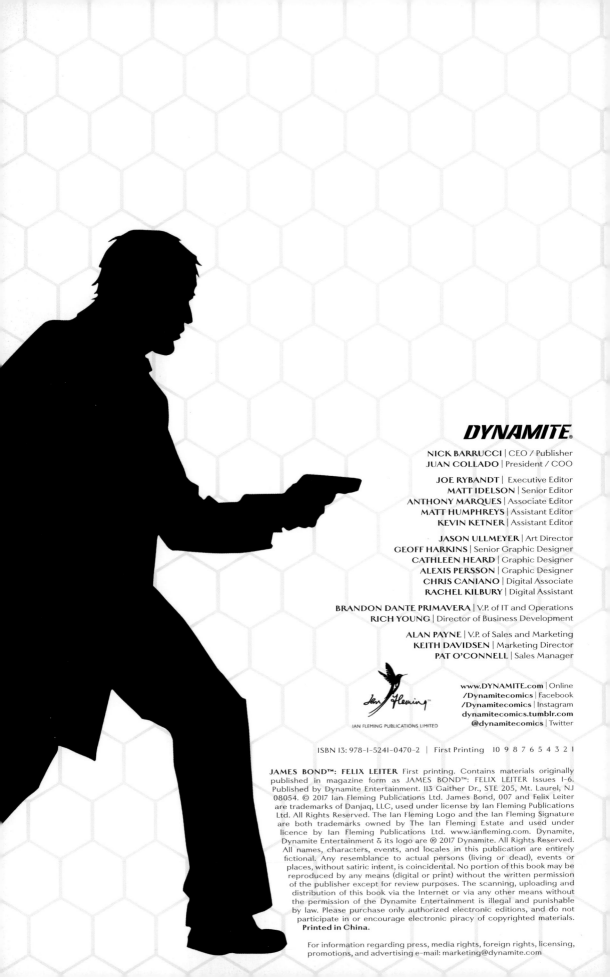

DYNAMITE

NICK BARRUCCI | CEO / Publisher
JUAN COLLADO | President / COO

JOE RYBANDT | Executive Editor
MATT IDELSON | Senior Editor
ANTHONY MARQUES | Associate Editor
MATT HUMPHREYS | Assistant Editor
KEVIN KETNER | Assistant Editor

JASON ULLMEYER | Art Director
GEOFF HARKINS | Senior Graphic Designer
CATHLEEN HEARD | Graphic Designer
ALEXIS PERSSON | Graphic Designer
CHRIS CANIANO | Digital Associate
RACHEL KILBURY | Digital Assistant

BRANDON DANTE PRIMAVERA | V.P. of IT and Operations
RICH YOUNG | Director of Business Development

ALAN PAYNE | V.P. of Sales and Marketing
KEITH DAVIDSEN | Marketing Director
PAT O'CONNELL | Sales Manager

Ian Fleming
IAN FLEMING PUBLICATIONS LIMITED

www.DYNAMITE.com | Online
/Dynamitecomics | Facebook
/Dynamitecomics | Instagram
dynamitecomics.tumblr.com
@dynamitecomics | Twitter

ISBN 13: 978-1-5241-0470-2 | First Printing 10 9 8 7 6 5 4 3 2 1

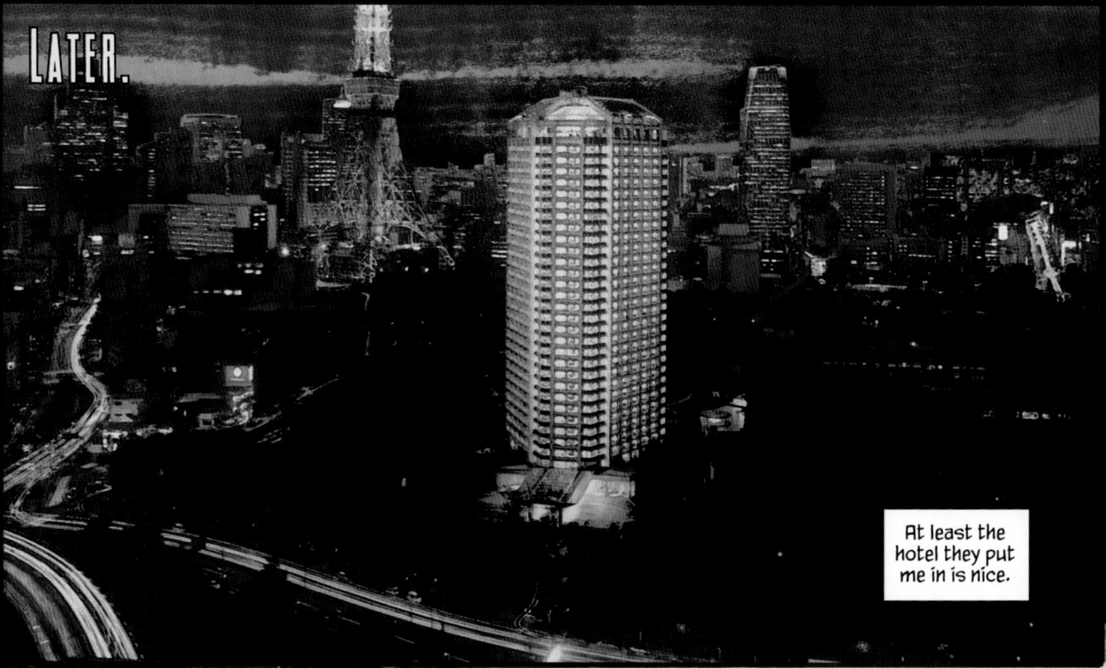
LATER.
At least the hotel they put me in is nice.

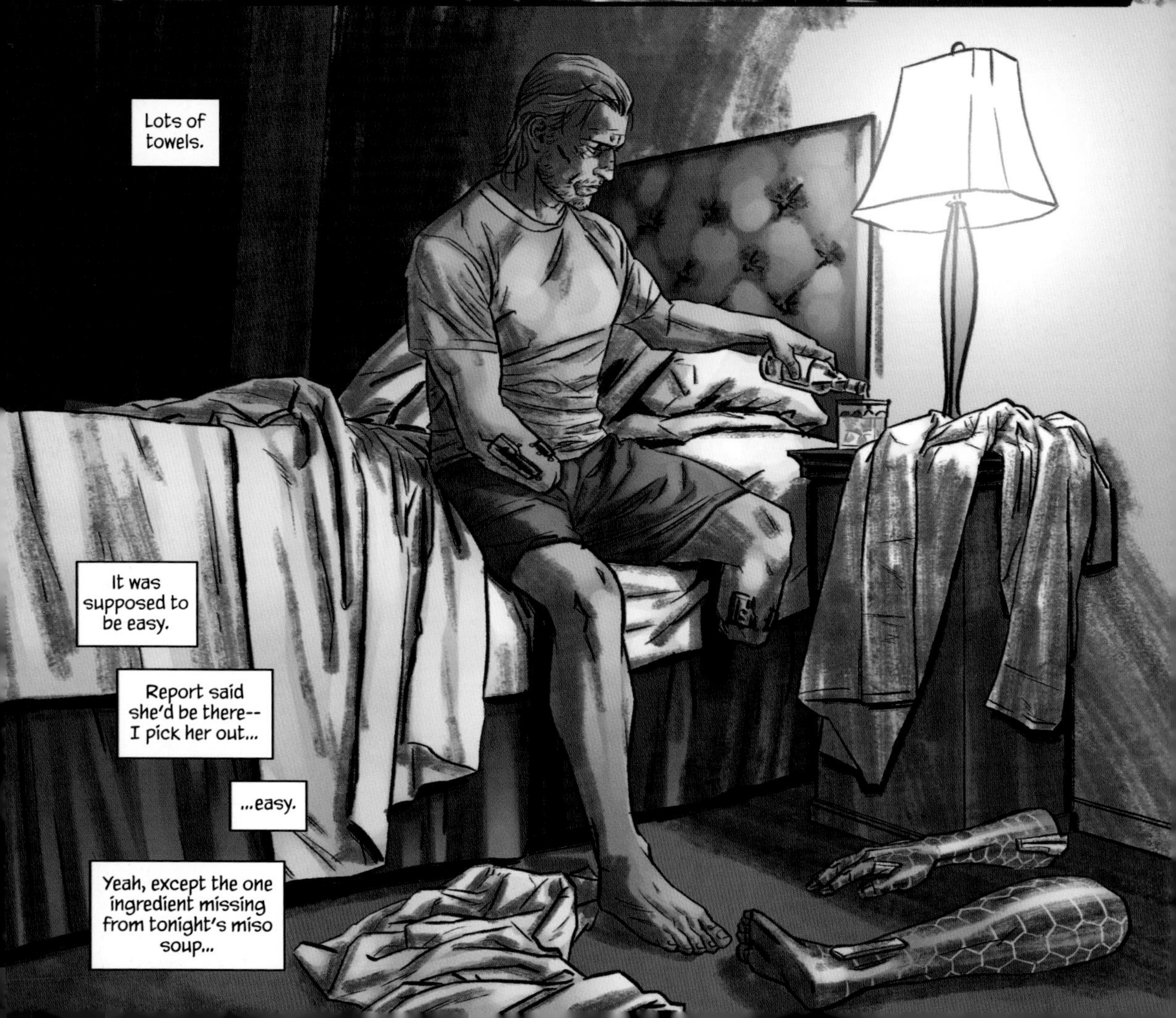
Lots of towels.
It was supposed to be easy.
Report said she'd be there-- I pick her out...
...easy.
Yeah, except the one ingredient missing from tonight's miso soup...

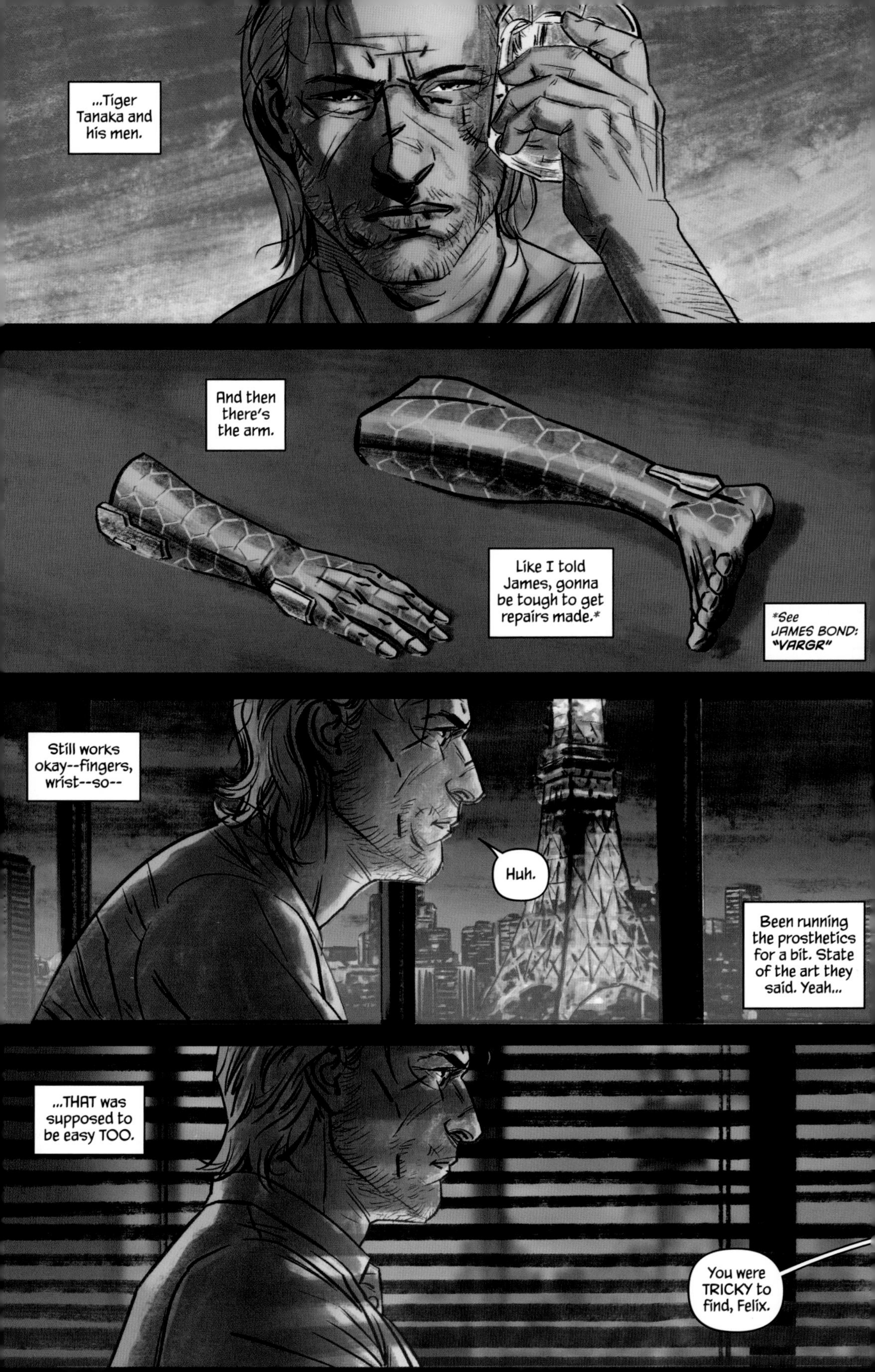

...Tiger Tanaka and his men.
And then there's the arm.
Like I told James, gonna be tough to get repairs made.*
*See JAMES BOND: "VARGR"
Still works okay--fingers, wrist--so--
Huh.
Been running the prosthetics for a bit. State of the art they said. Yeah...
...THAT was supposed to be easy TOO.
You were TRICKY to find, Felix.

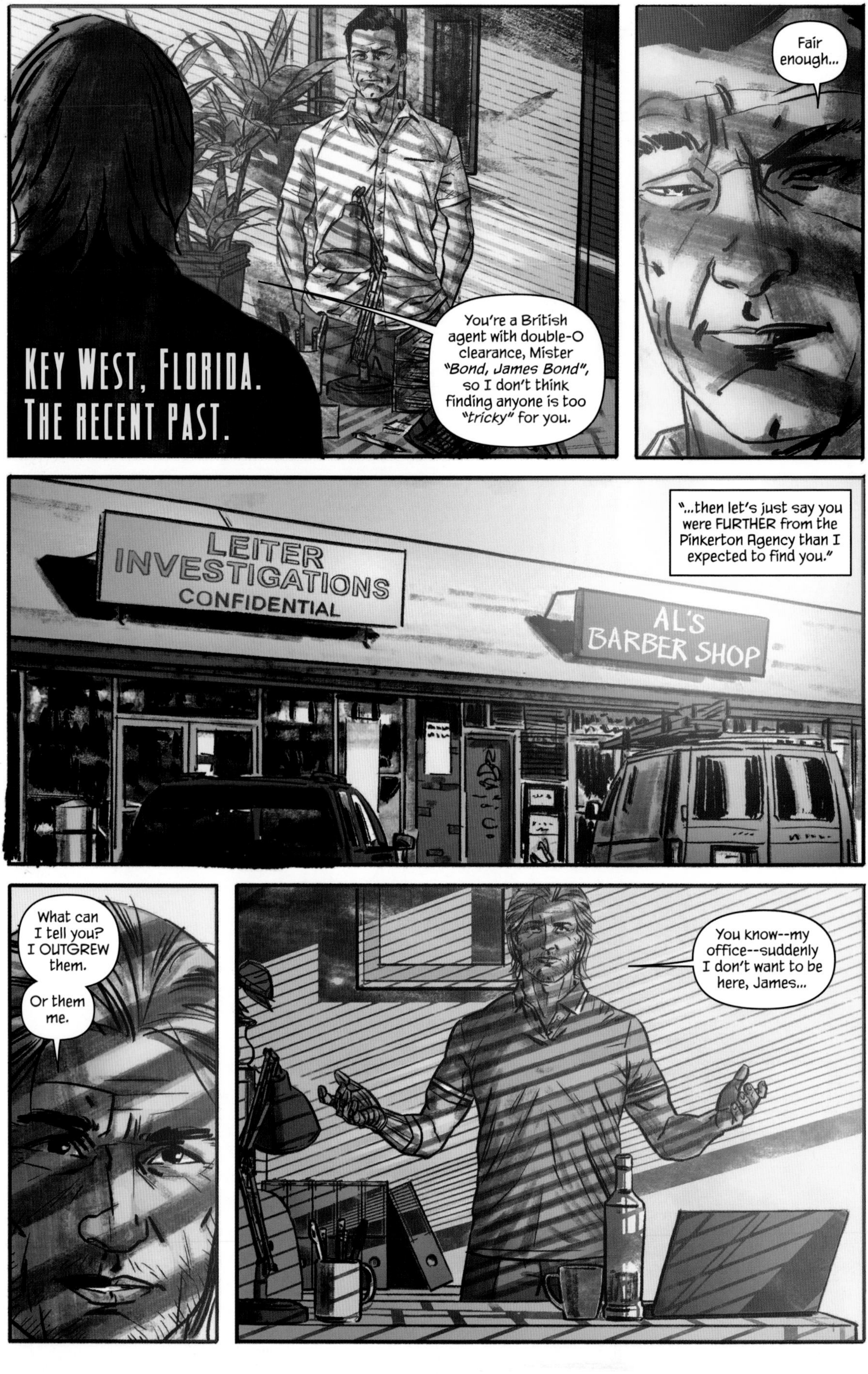
KEY WEST, FLORIDA.
THE RECENT PAST.
You're a British agent with double-O clearance, Mister "Bond, James Bond", so I don't think finding anyone is too "tricky" for you.
Fair enough...
"...then let's just say you were FURTHER from the Pinkerton Agency than I expected to find you."
LEITER INVESTIGATIONS CONFIDENTIAL
AL'S BARBER SHOP
What can I tell you? I OUTGREW them.
Or them me.
You know--my office--suddenly I don't want to be here, James...

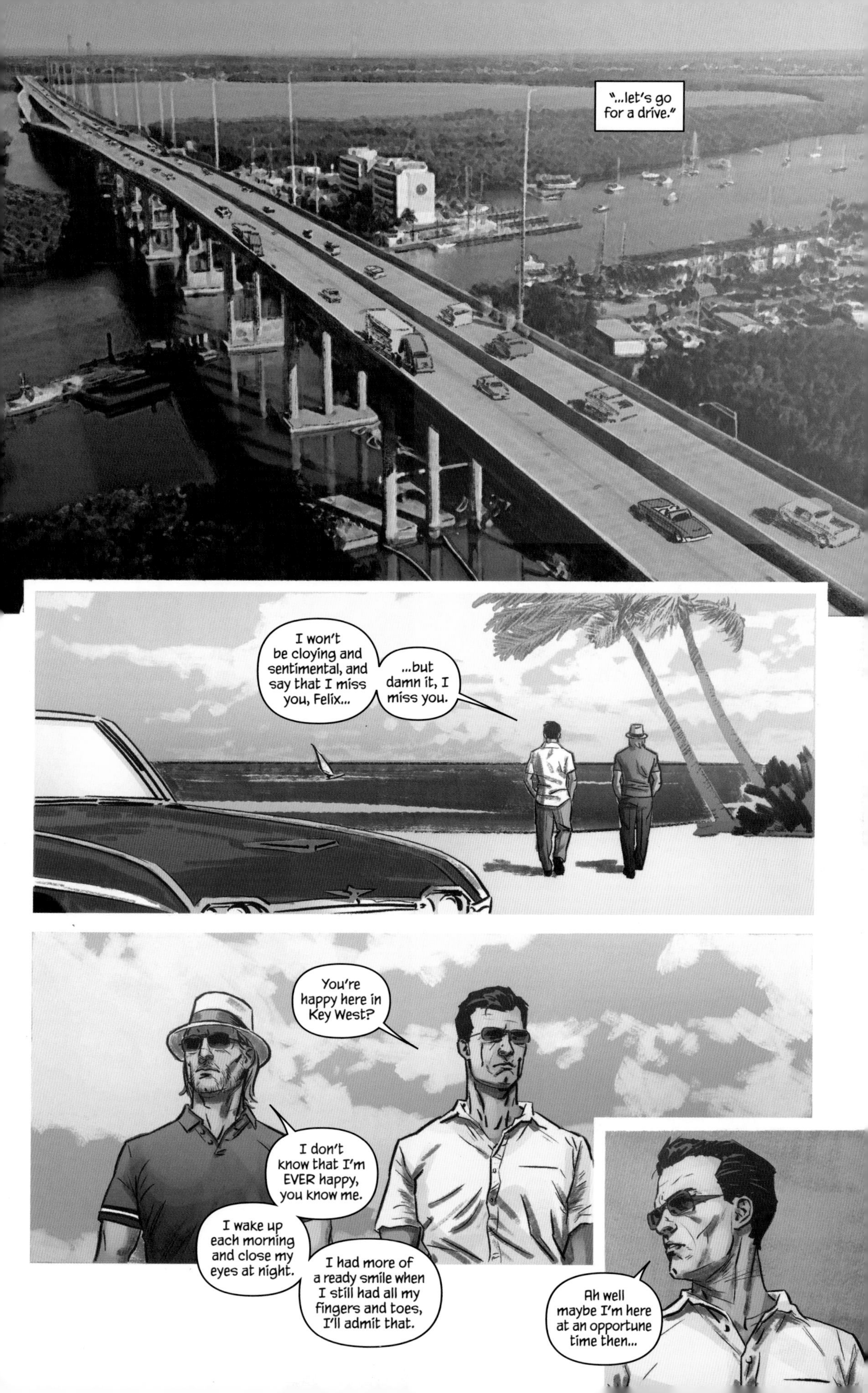
"...let's go for a drive."
I won't be cloying and sentimental, and say that I miss you, Felix...
...but damn it, I miss you.
You're happy here in Key West?
I don't know that I'm EVER happy, you know me.
I wake up each morning and close my eyes at night.
I had more of a ready smile when I still had all my fingers and toes, I'll admit that.
Ah well maybe I'm here at an opportune time then...

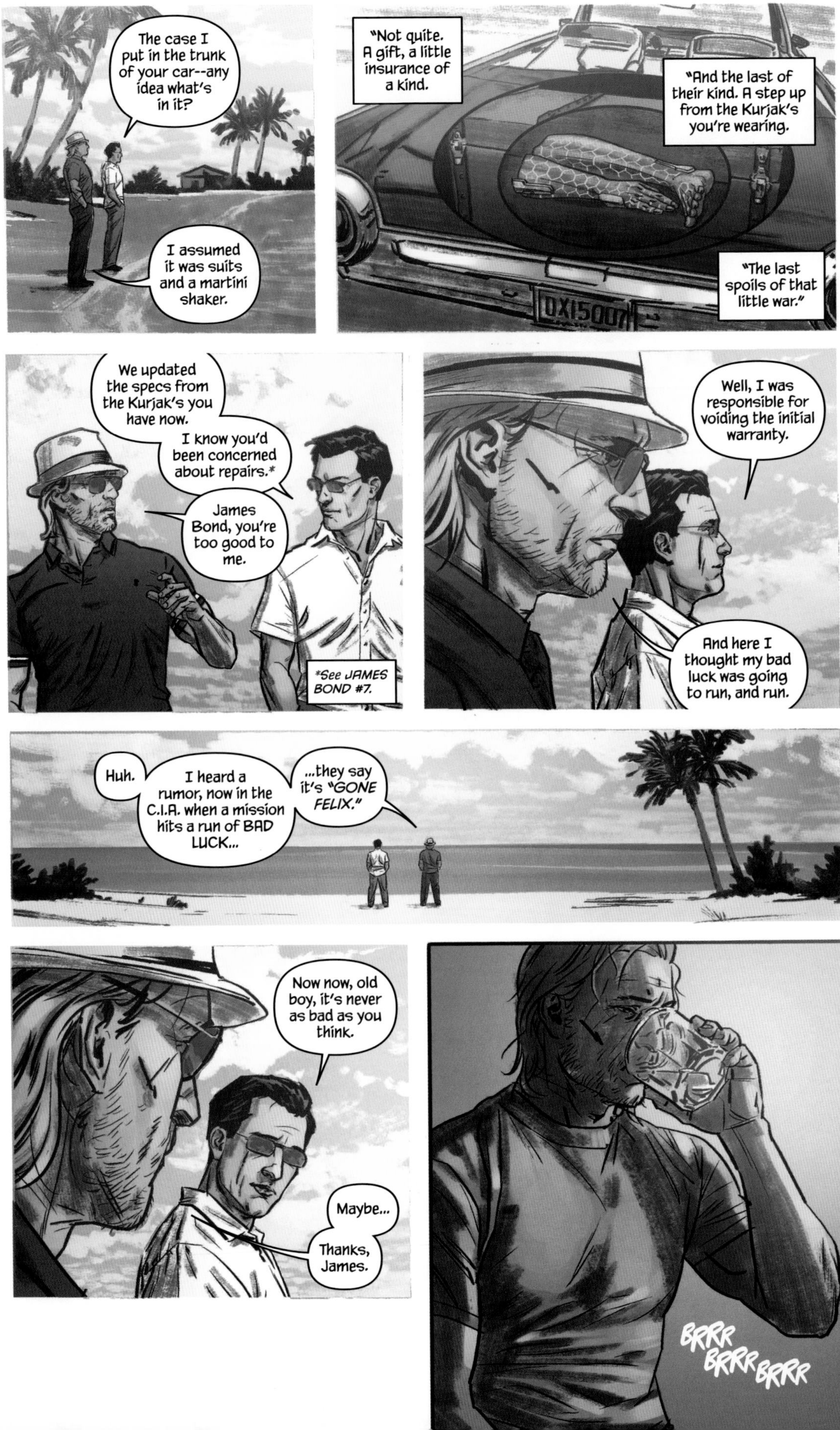
The case I put in the trunk of your car--any idea what's in it?
I assumed it was suits and a martini shaker.
"Not quite. A gift, a little insurance of a kind.
"And the last of their kind. A step up from the Kurjak's you're wearing.
"The last spoils of that little war."
DX15007
We updated the specs from the Kurjak's you have now.
I know you'd been concerned about repairs.*
James Bond, you're too good to me.
*See JAMES BOND #7.
Well, I was responsible for voiding the initial warranty.
And here I thought my bad luck was going to run, and run.
Huh.
I heard a rumor, now in the C.I.A. when a mission hits a run of BAD LUCK...
...they say it's "GONE FELIX."
Now now, old boy, it's never as bad as you think.
Maybe...
Thanks, James.
BRRR BRRR BRRR

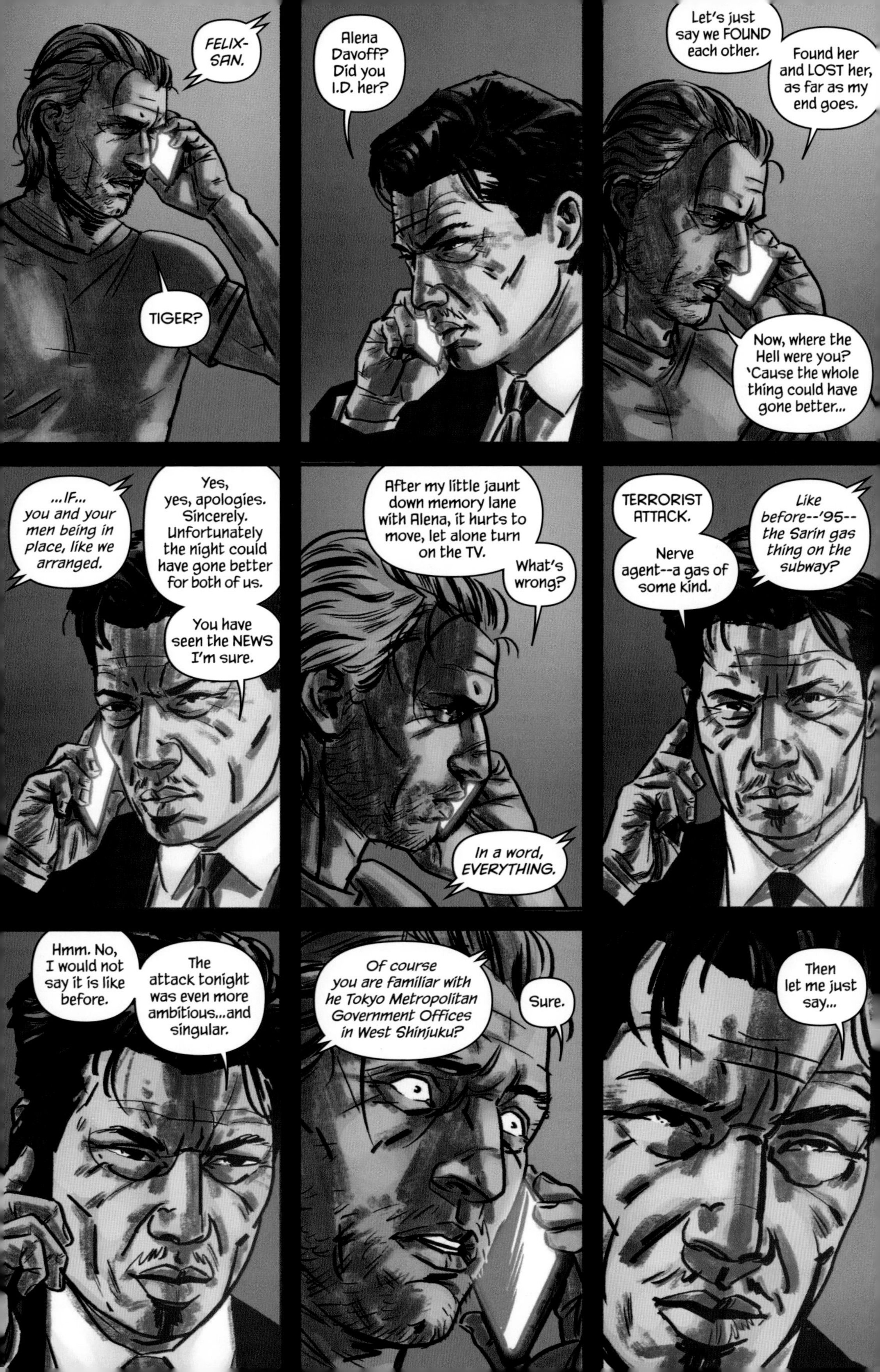
FELIX-SAN.
TIGER?
Alena Davoff? Did you I.D. her?
Let's just say we FOUND each other.
Found her and LOST her, as far as my end goes.
Now, where the Hell were you? 'Cause the whole thing could have gone better...
...IF... you and your men being in place, like we arranged.
Yes, yes, apologies. Sincerely. Unfortunately the night could have gone better for both of us.
You have seen the NEWS I'm sure.
After my little jaunt down memory lane with Alena, it hurts to move, let alone turn on the TV.
What's wrong?
In a word, EVERYTHING.
TERRORIST ATTACK.
Nerve agent--a gas of some kind.
Like before--'95--the Sarin gas thing on the subway?
Hmm. No, I would not say it is like before.
The attack tonight was even more ambitious...and singular.
Of course you are familiar with he Tokyo Metropolitan Government Offices in West Shinjuku?
Sure.
Then let me just say...

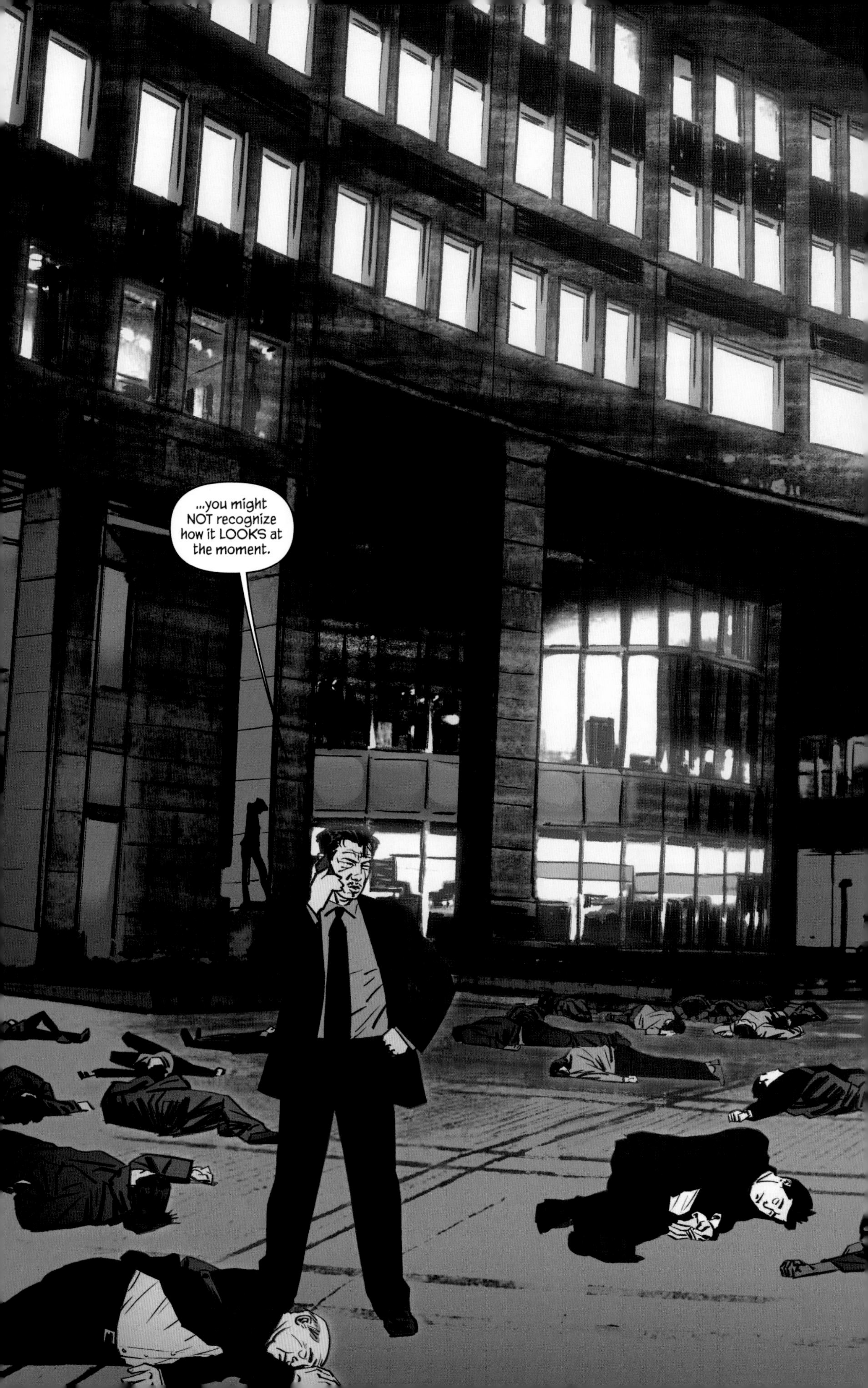
...you might NOT recognize how it LOOKS at the moment.

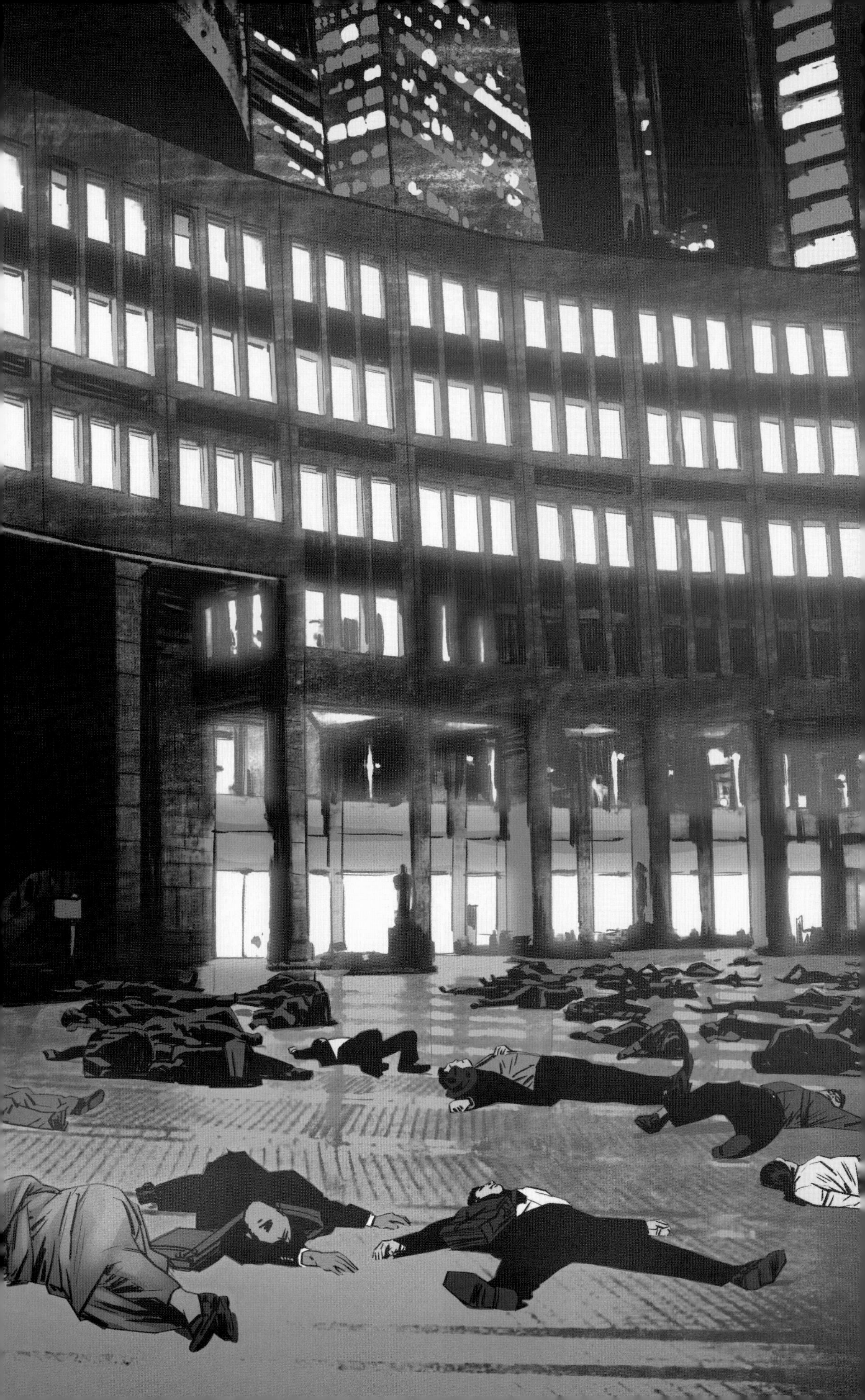

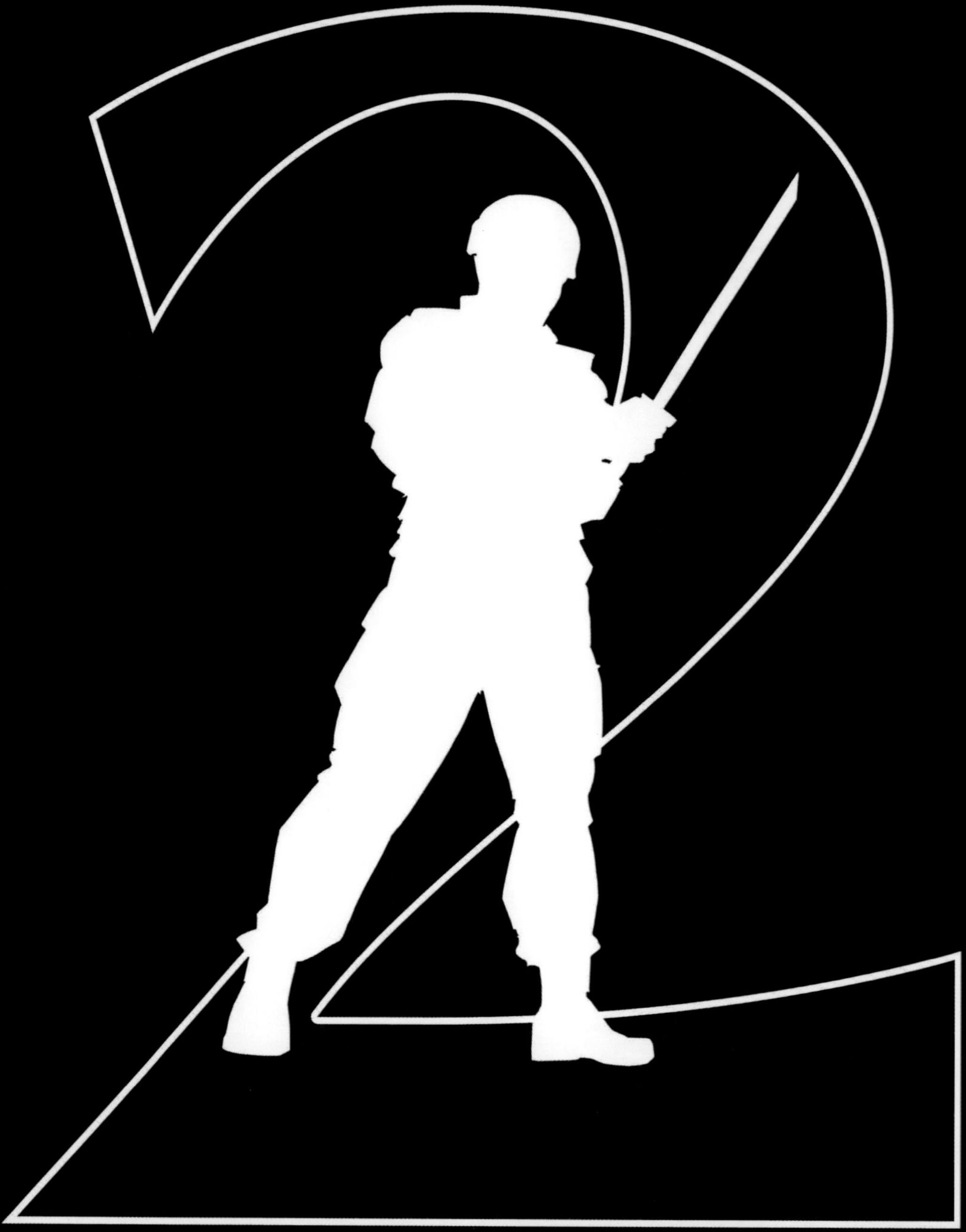

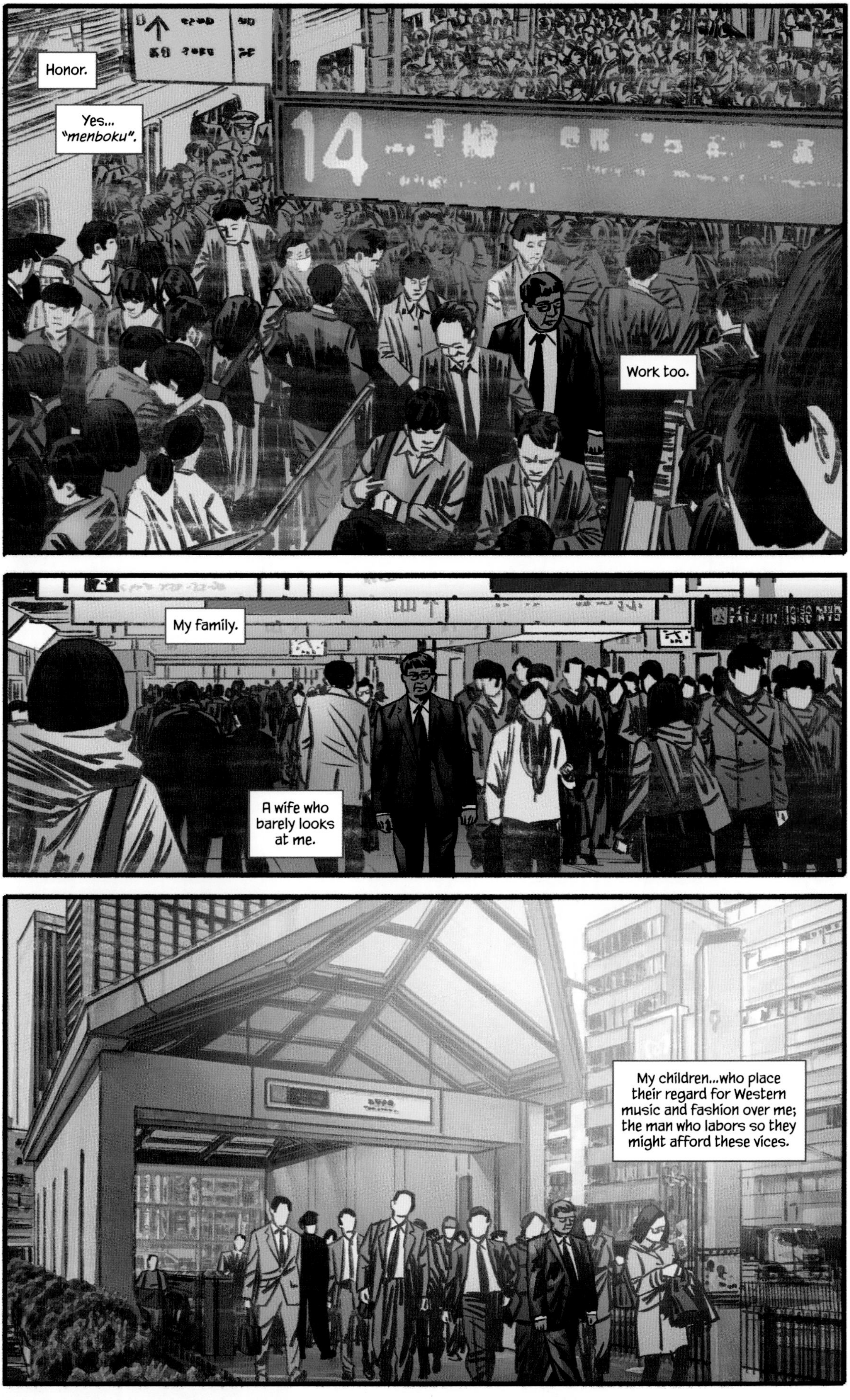
Honor.
Yes... *"menboku"*.
Work too.
My family.
A wife who barely looks at me.
My children...who place their regard for Western music and fashion over me; the man who labors so they might afford these vices.

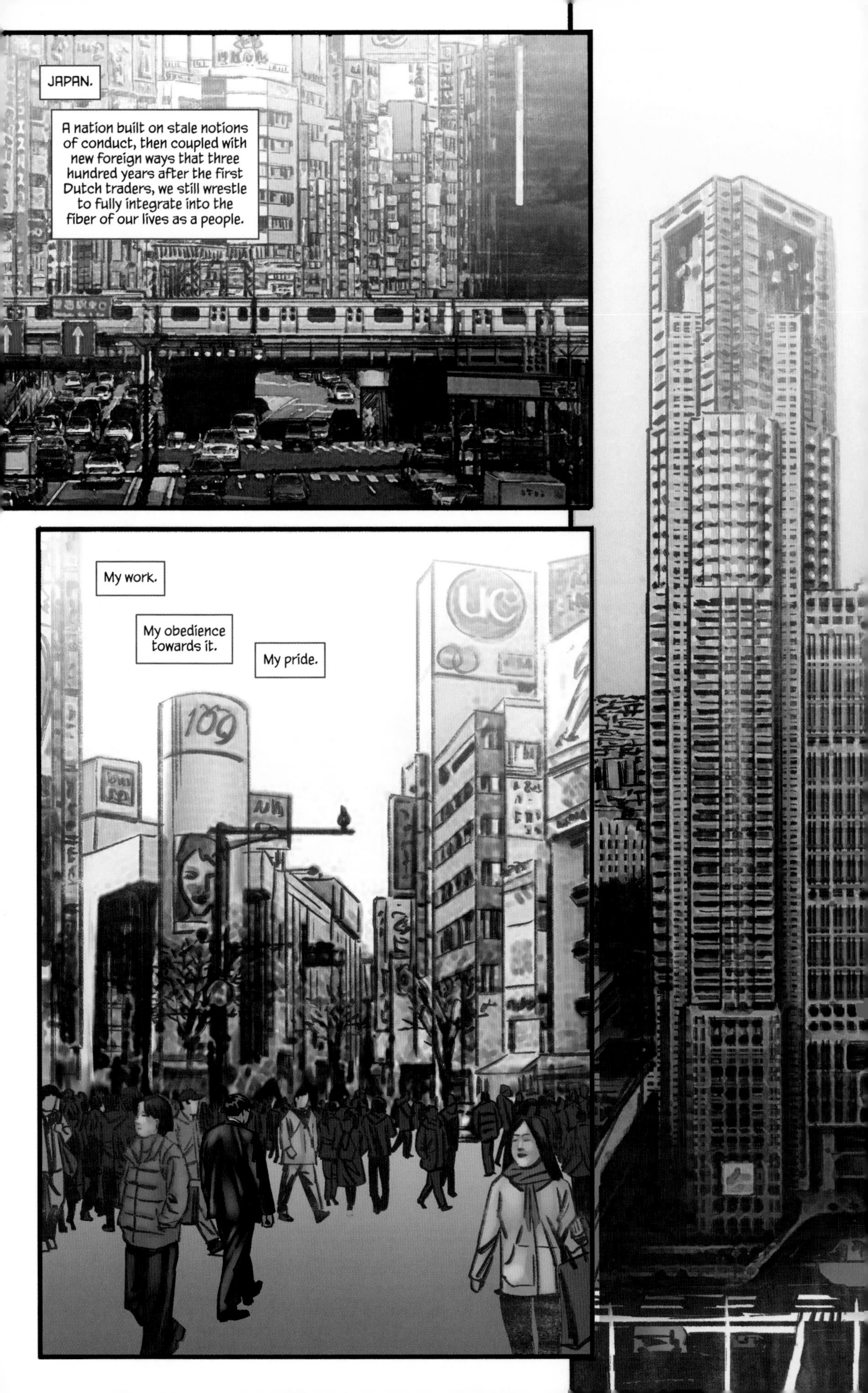
JAPAN.
A nation built on stale notions of conduct, then coupled with new foreign ways that three hundred years after the first Dutch traders, we still wrestle to fully integrate into the fiber of our lives as a people.
My work.
My obedience towards it.
My pride.

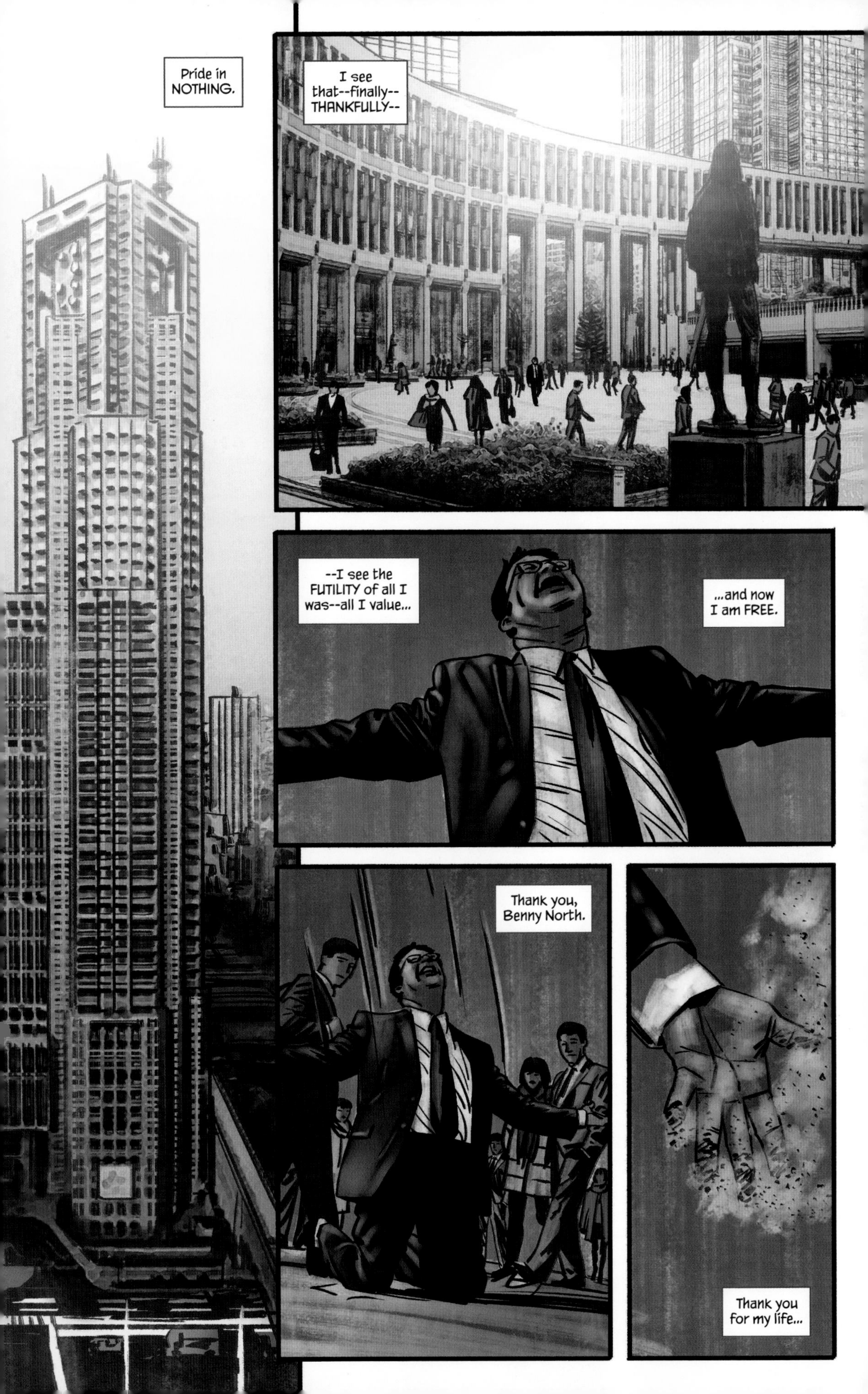
Pride in NOTHING.
I see that--finally--THANKFULLY--
--I see the FUTILITY of all I was--all I value...
...and now I am FREE.
Thank you, Benny North.
Thank you for my life...

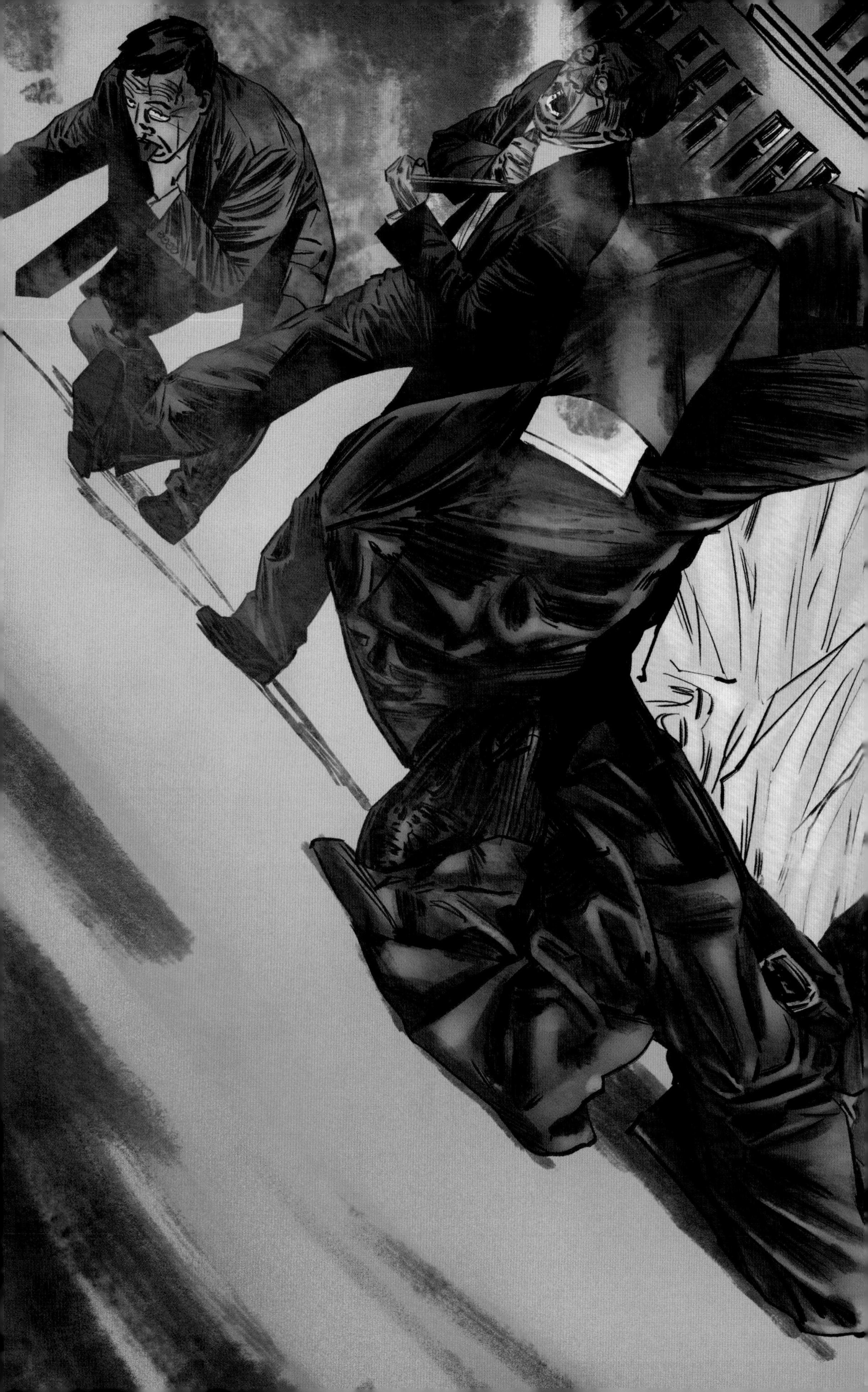

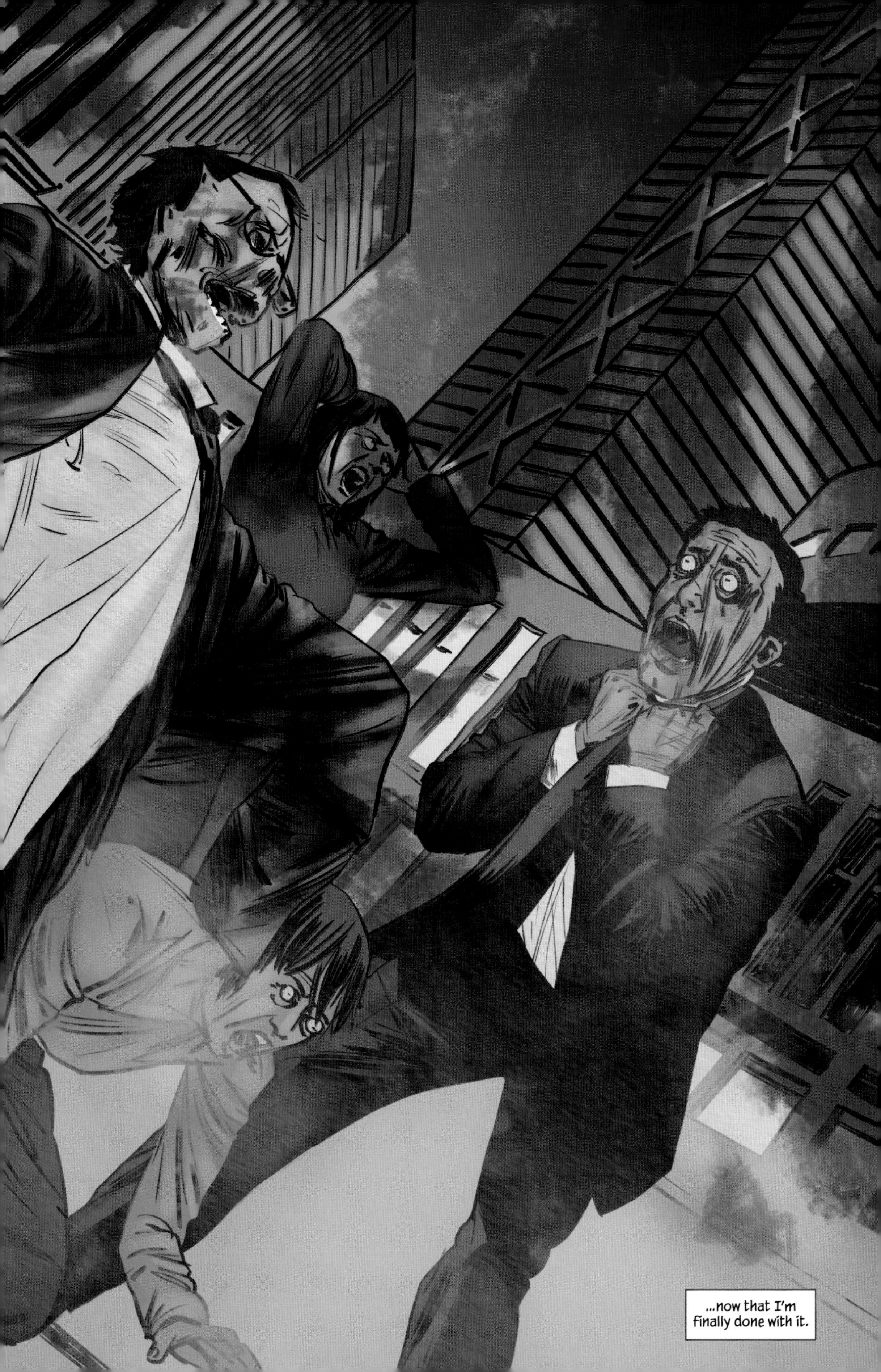
...now that I'm
finally done with it.

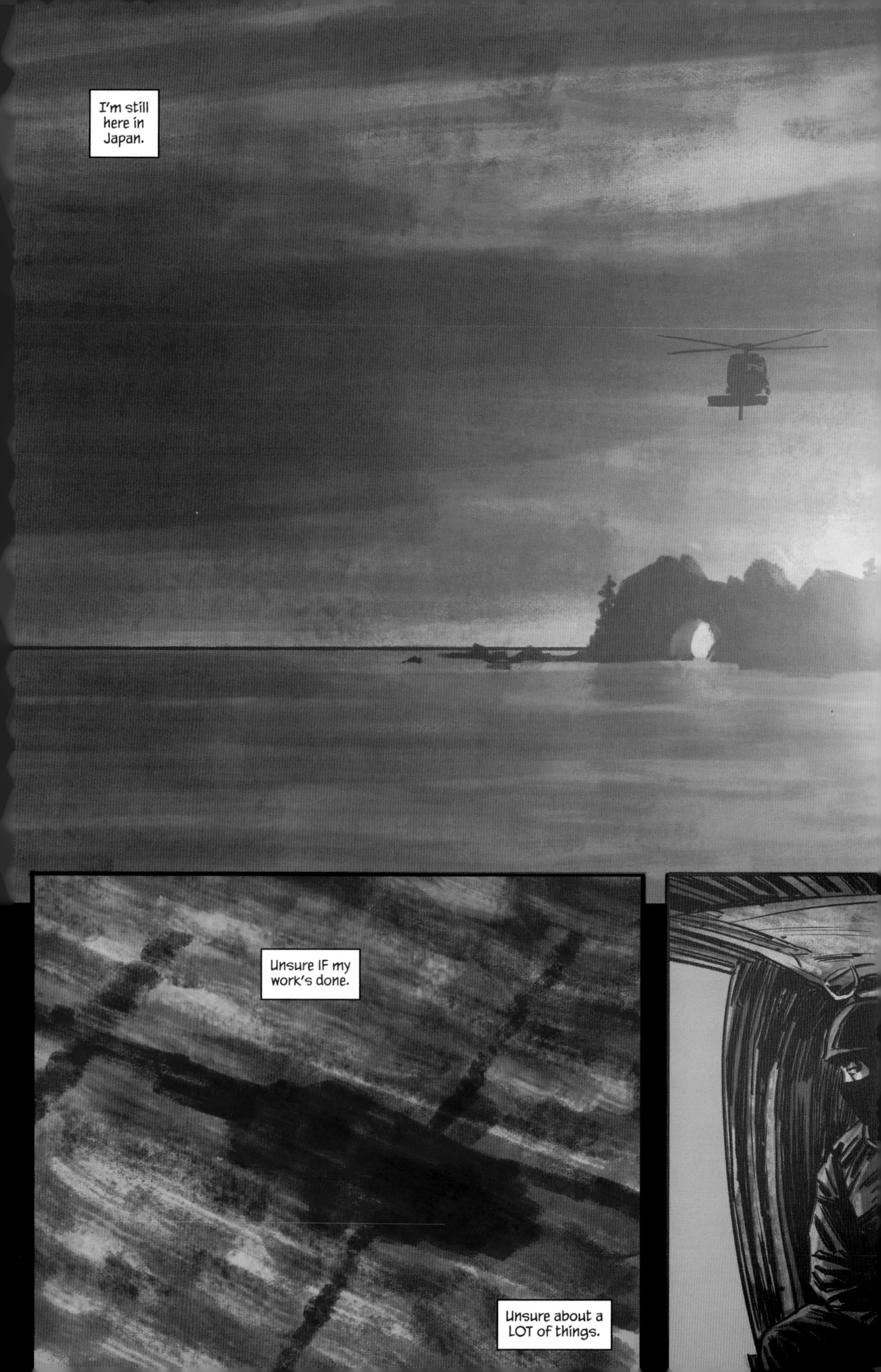
I'm still here in Japan.
Unsure IF my work's done.
Unsure about a LOT of things.

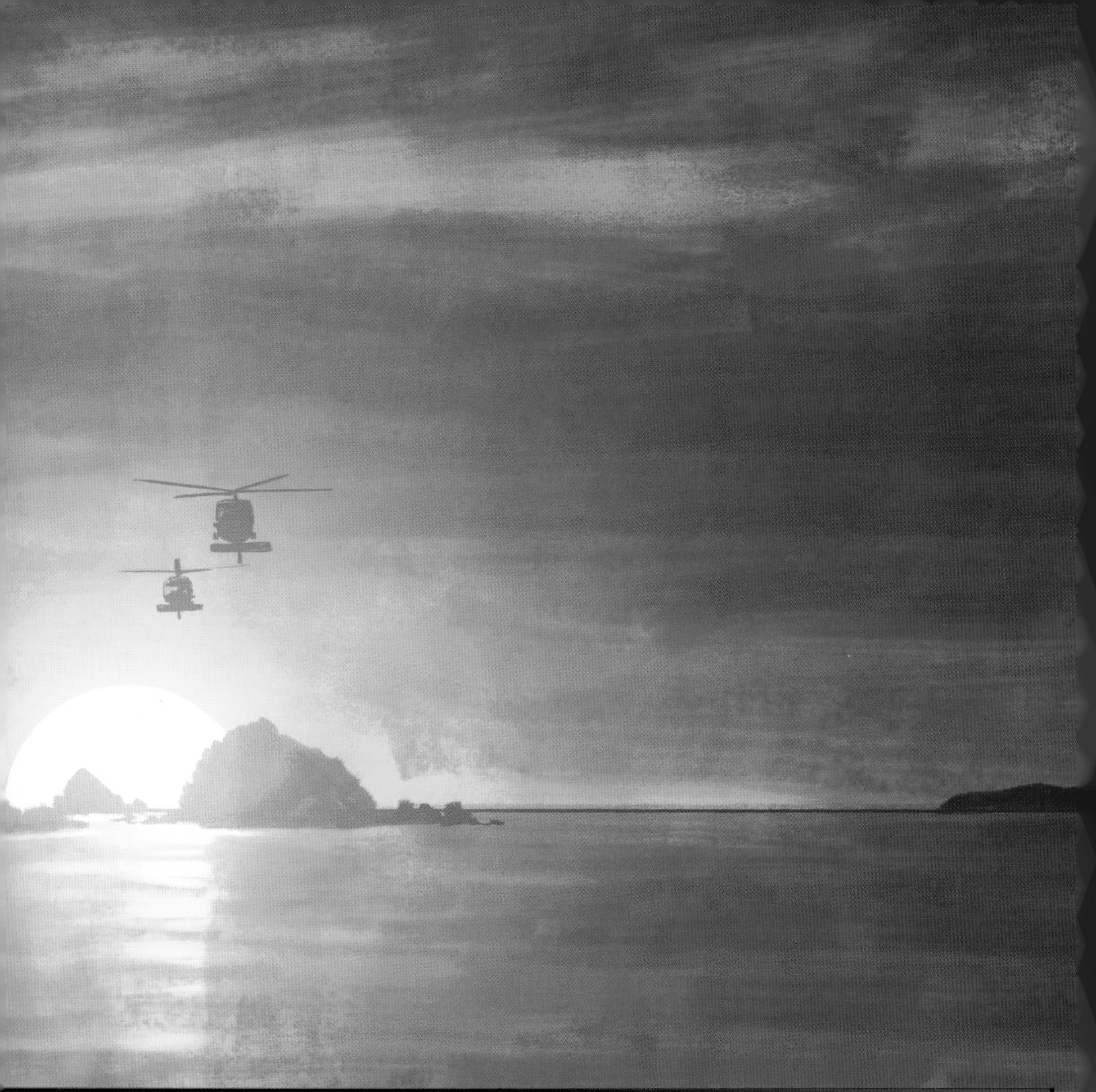

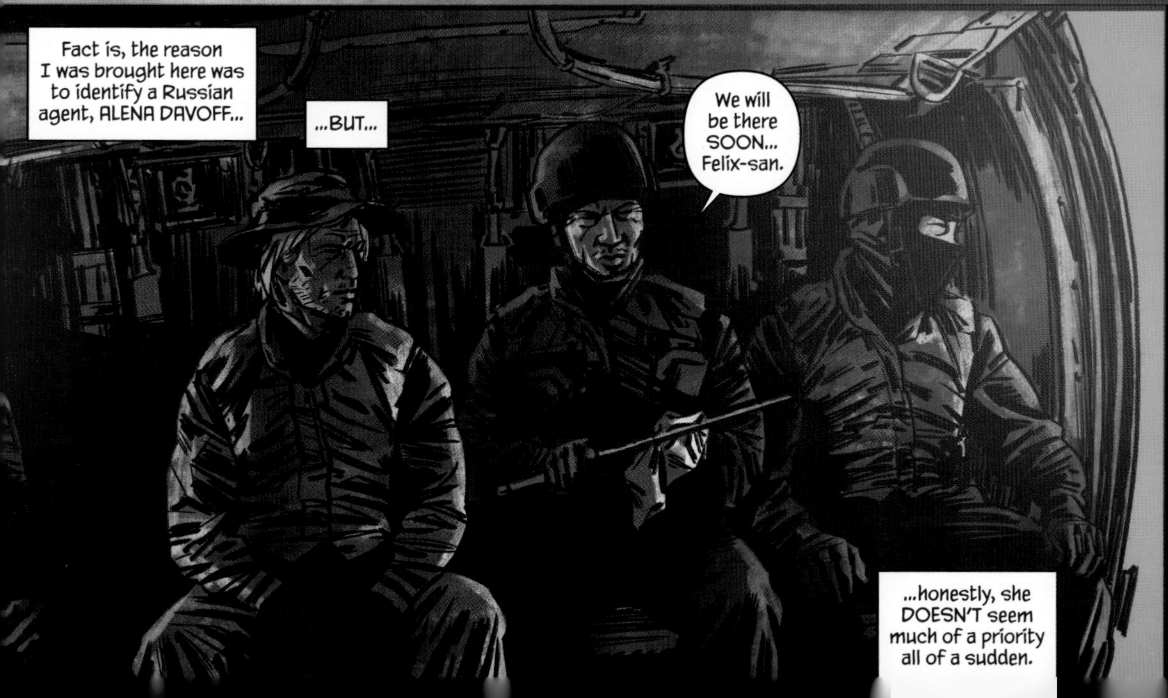

Fact is, the reason I was brought here was to identify a Russian agent, ALENA DAVOFF...
...BUT...
We will be there SOON... Felix-san.
...honestly, she DOESN'T seem much of a priority all of a sudden.

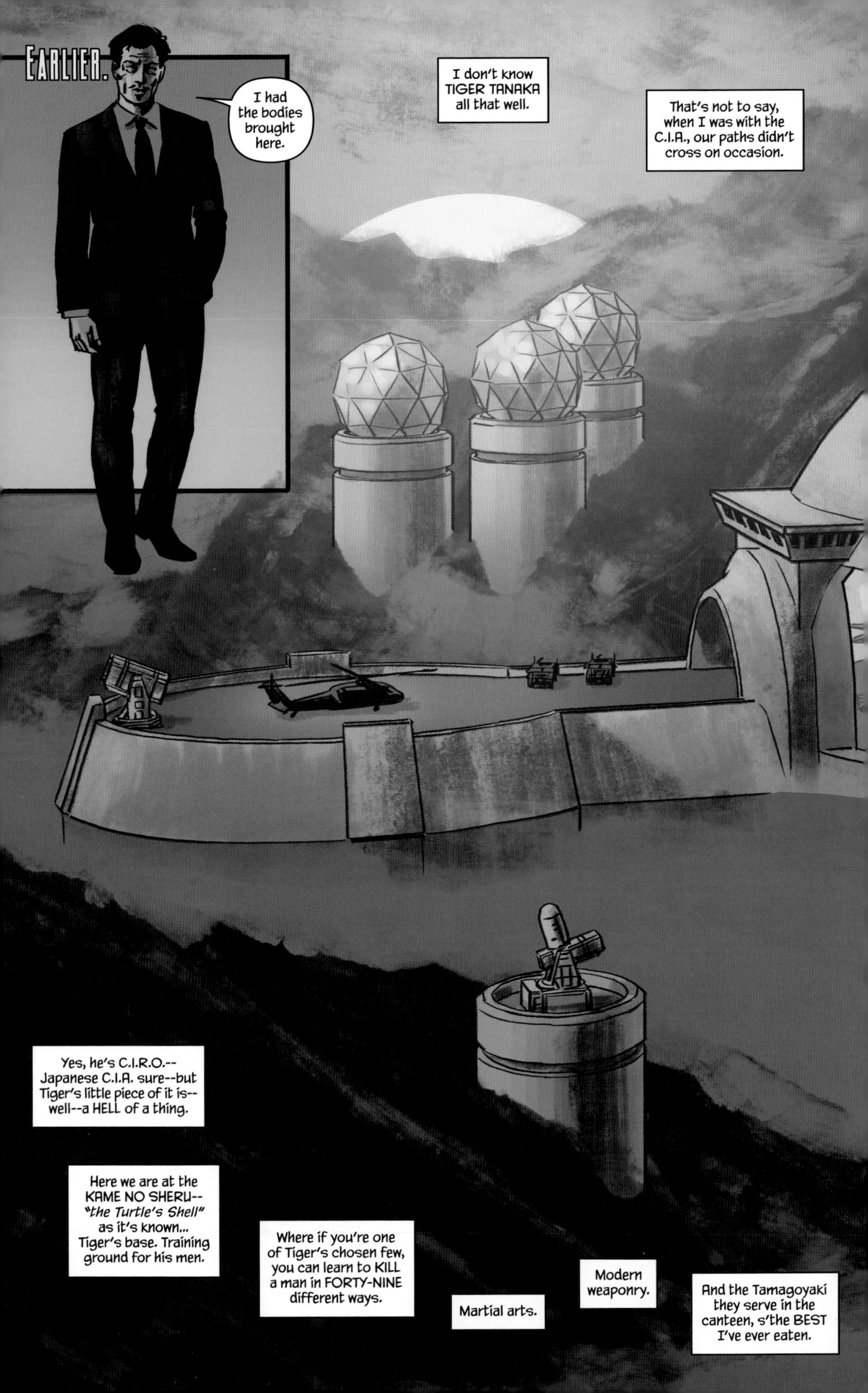
EARLIER.
I had the bodies brought here.
I don't know TIGER TANAKA all that well.
That's not to say, when I was with the C.I.A., our paths didn't cross on occasion.
Yes, he's C.I.R.O.--Japanese C.I.A. sure--but Tiger's little piece of it is--well--a HELL of a thing.
Here we are at the KAME NO SHERU--*"the Turtle's Shell"* as it's known... Tiger's base. Training ground for his men.
Where if you're one of Tiger's chosen few, you can learn to KILL a man in FORTY-NINE different ways.
Martial arts.
Modern weaponry.
And the Tamagoyaki they serve in the canteen, s'the BEST I've ever eaten.

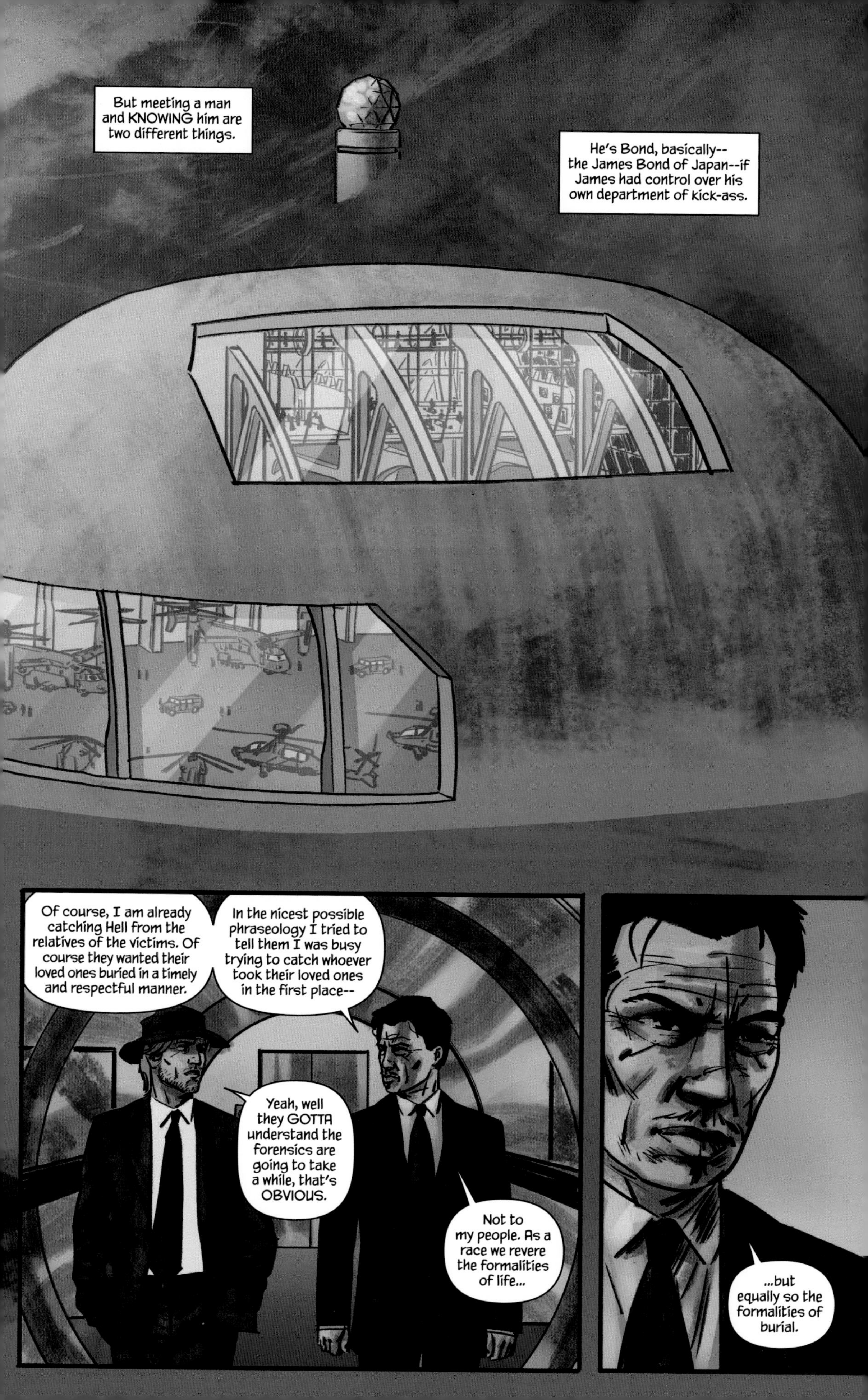
But meeting a man and KNOWING him are two different things.
He's Bond, basically-- the James Bond of Japan--if James had control over his own department of kick-ass.
Of course, I am already catching Hell from the relatives of the victims. Of course they wanted their loved ones buried in a timely and respectful manner.
In the nicest possible phraseology I tried to tell them I was busy trying to catch whoever took their loved ones in the first place--
Yeah, well they GOTTA understand the forensics are going to take a while, that's OBVIOUS.
Not to my people. As a race we revere the formalities of life...
...but equally so the formalities of burial.

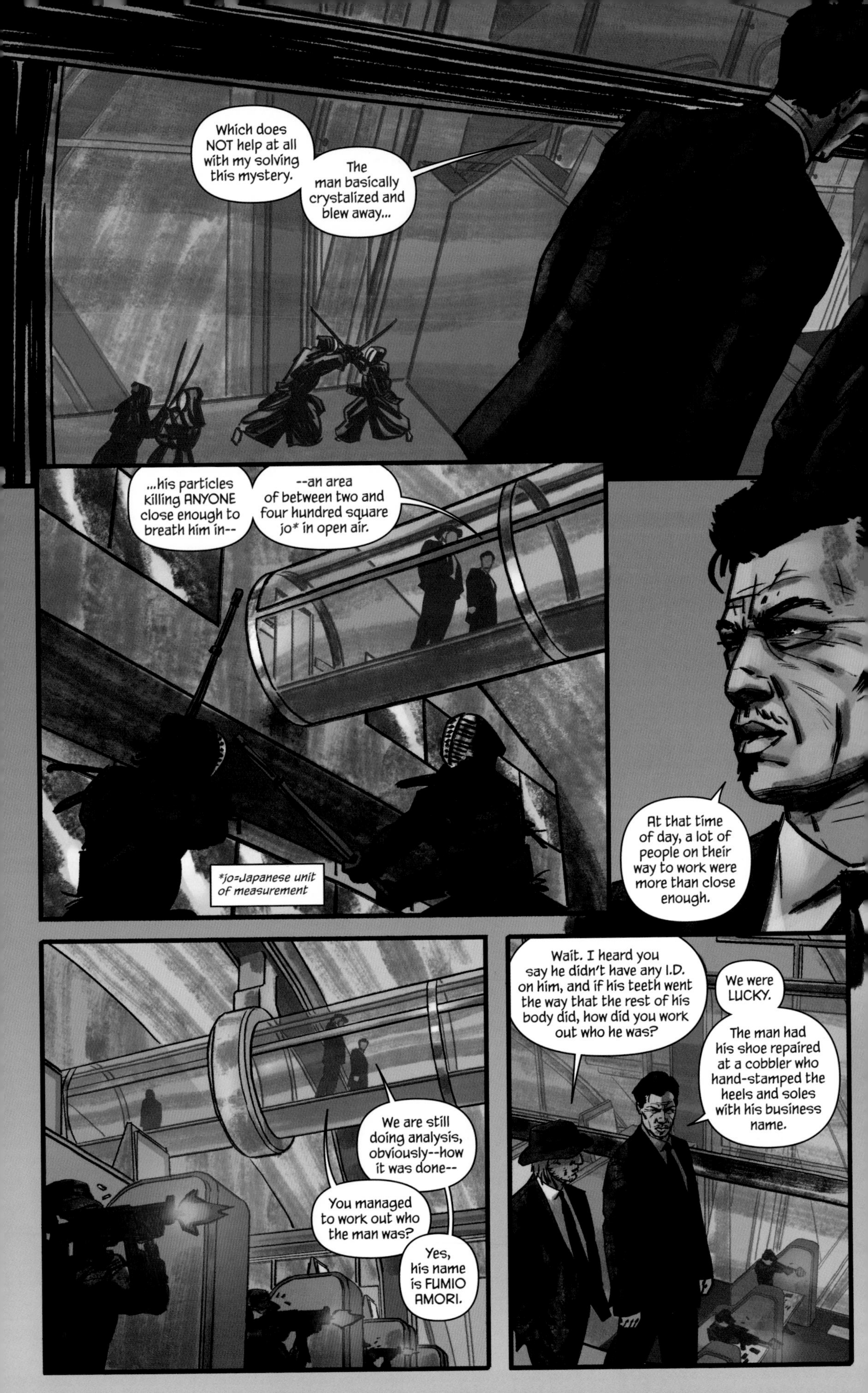
Which does NOT help at all with my solving this mystery.
The man basically crystalized and blew away...
...his particles killing ANYONE close enough to breath him in--
--an area of between two and four hundred square jo* in open air.
*jo=Japanese unit of measurement
At that time of day, a lot of people on their way to work were more than close enough.
We are still doing analysis, obviously--how it was done--
You managed to work out who the man was?
Yes, his name is FUMIO AMORI.
Wait. I heard you say he didn't have any I.D. on him, and if his teeth went the way that the rest of his body did, how did you work out who he was?
We were LUCKY.
The man had his shoe repaired at a cobbler who hand-stamped the heels and soles with his business name.

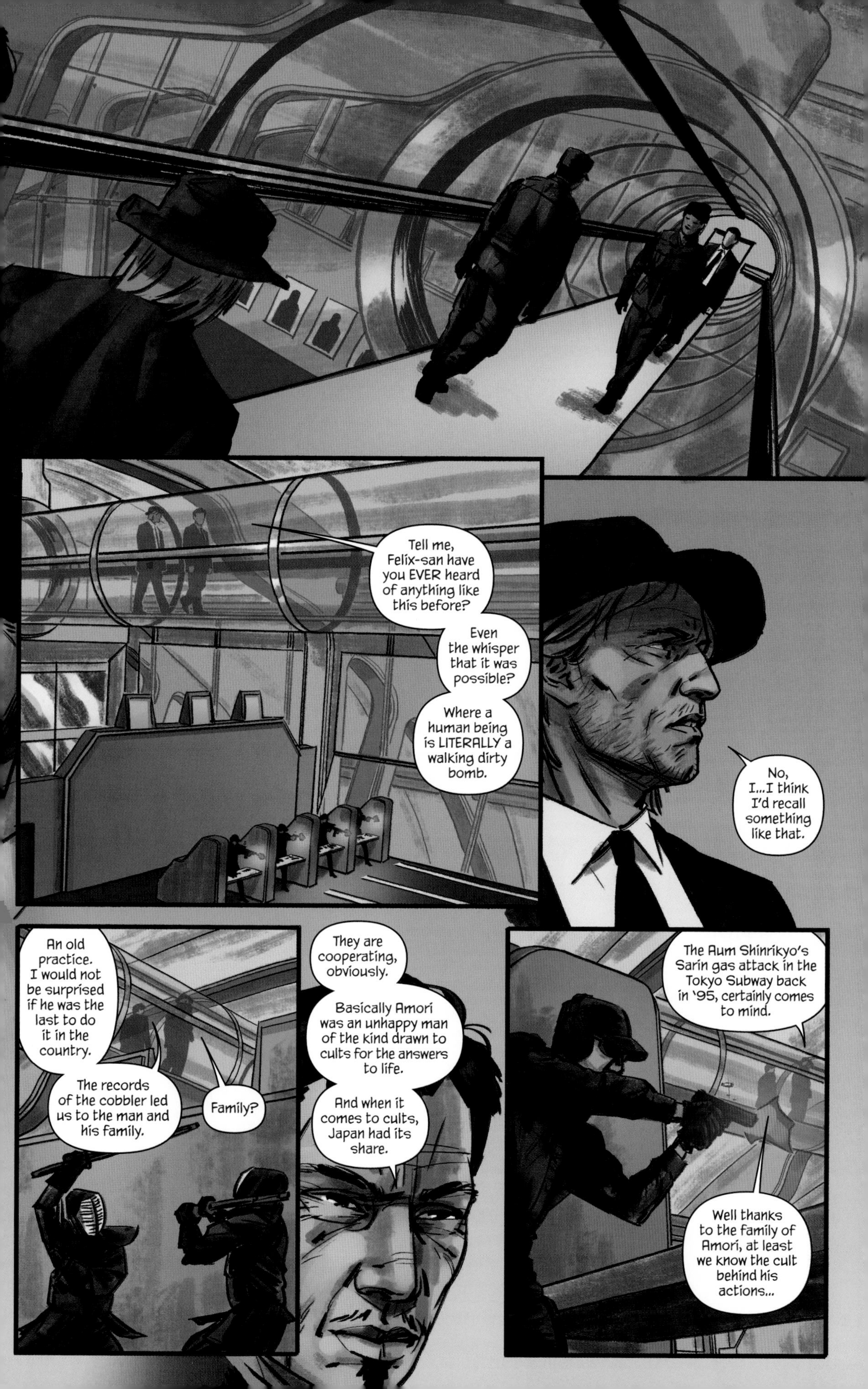
Tell me, Felix-san have you EVER heard of anything like this before?
Even the whisper that it was possible?
Where a human being is LITERALLY a walking dirty bomb.
No, I...I think I'd recall something like that.
An old practice. I would not be surprised if he was the last to do it in the country.
The records of the cobbler led us to the man and his family.
Family?
They are cooperating, obviously.
Basically Amori was an unhappy man of the kind drawn to cults for the answers to life.
And when it comes to cults, Japan had its share.
The Aum Shinrikyo's Sarin gas attack in the Tokyo Subway back in '95, certainly comes to mind.
Well thanks to the family of Amori, at least we know the cult behind his actions...

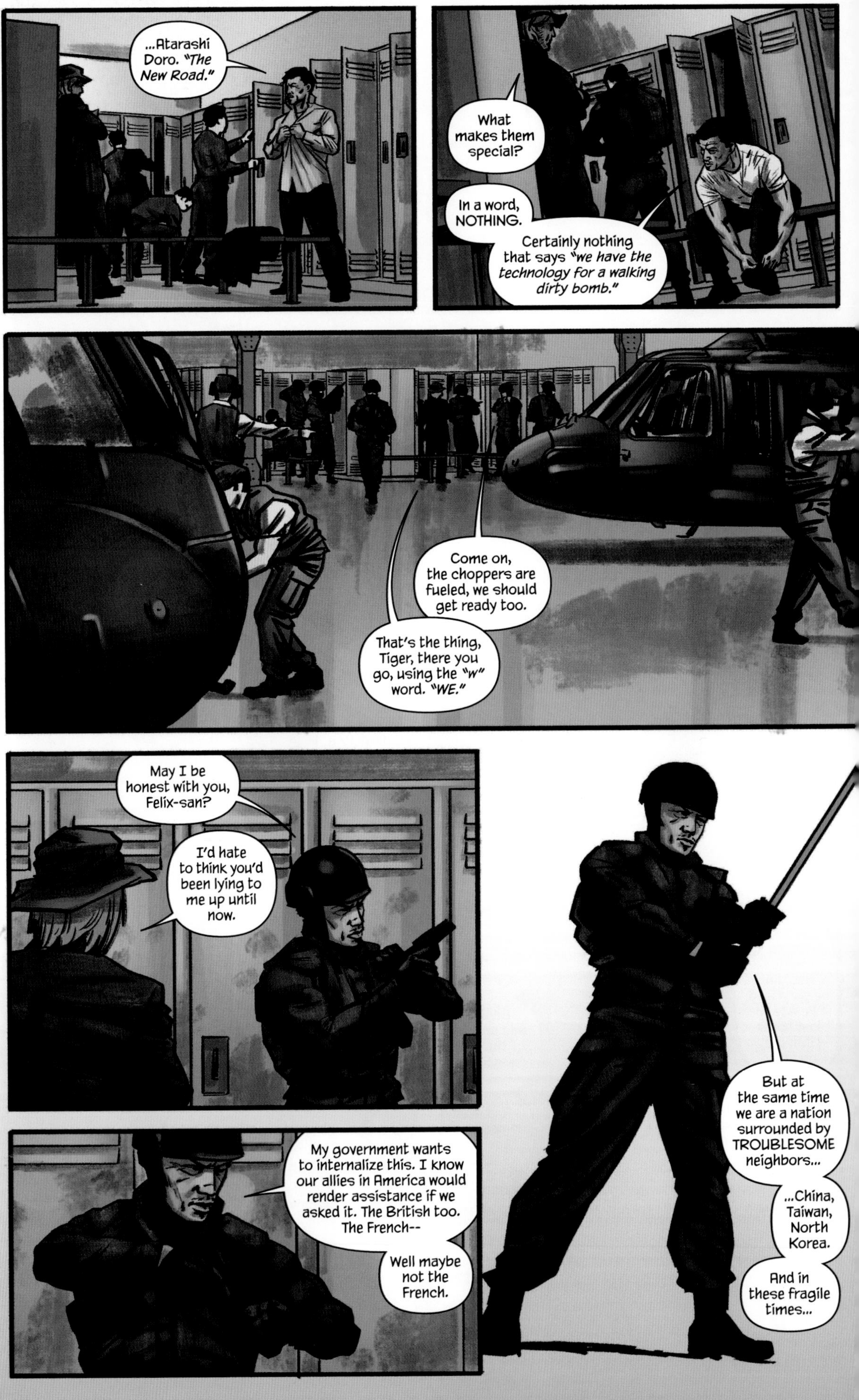
...Atarashi Doro. "The New Road."
What makes them special?
In a word, NOTHING.
Certainly nothing that says "we have the technology for a walking dirty bomb."
Come on, the choppers are fueled, we should get ready too.
That's the thing, Tiger, there you go, using the "w" word. "WE."
May I be honest with you, Felix-san?
I'd hate to think you'd been lying to me up until now.
My government wants to internalize this. I know our allies in America would render assistance if we asked it. The British too. The French--
Well maybe not the French.
But at the same time we are a nation surrounded by TROUBLESOME neighbors...
...China, Taiwan, North Korea.
And in these fragile times...

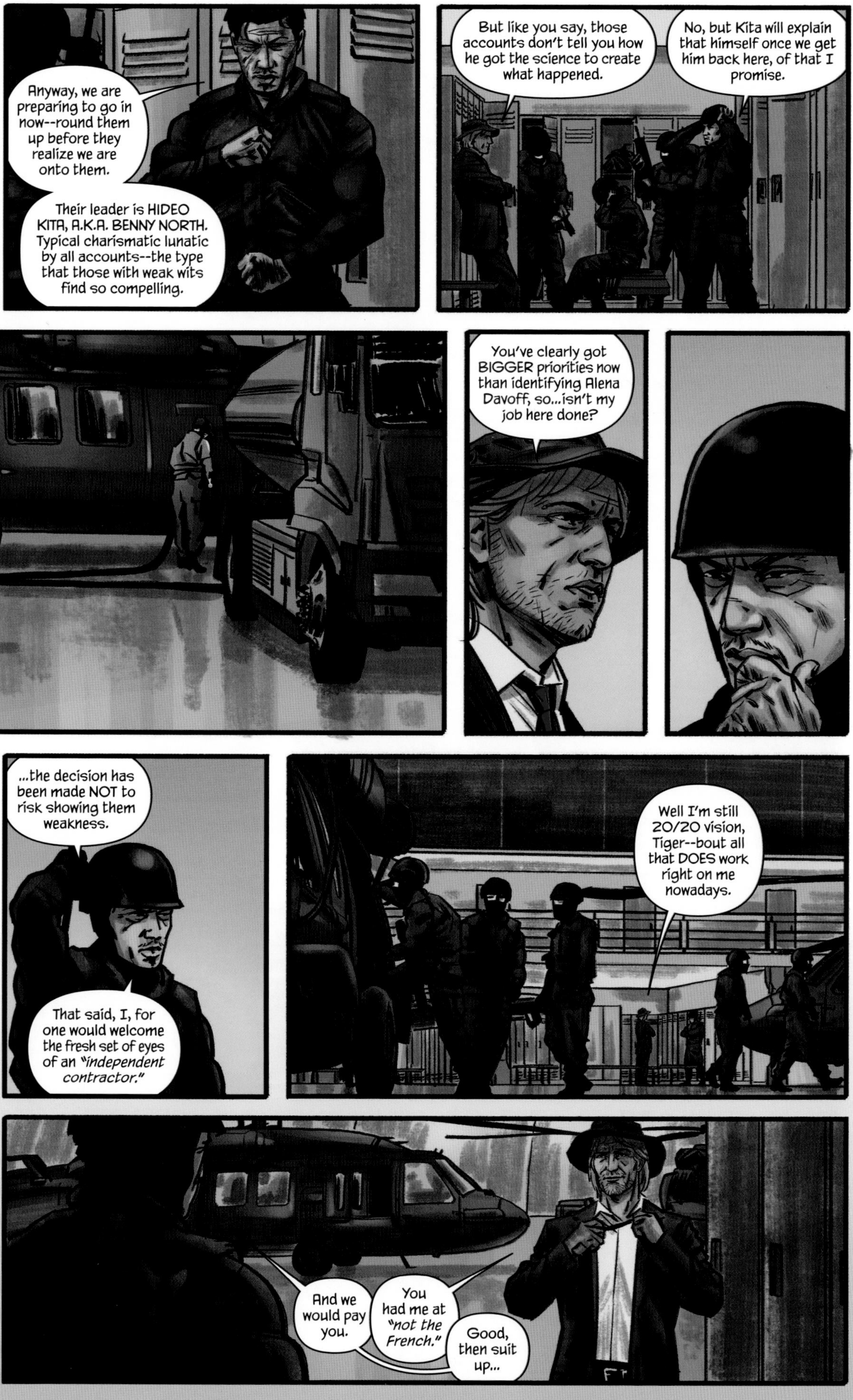
Anyway, we are preparing to go in now--round them up before they realize we are onto them.
Their leader is HIDEO KITA, A.K.A. BENNY NORTH. Typical charismatic lunatic by all accounts--the type that those with weak wits find so compelling.
But like you say, those accounts don't tell you how he got the science to create what happened.
No, but Kita will explain that himself once we get him back here, of that I promise.
You've clearly got BIGGER priorities now than identifying Alena Davoff, so...isn't my job here done?
...the decision has been made NOT to risk showing them weakness.
That said, I, for one would welcome the fresh set of eyes of an *"independent contractor."*
Well I'm still 20/20 vision, Tiger--bout all that DOES work right on me nowadays.
And we would pay you.
You had me at *"not the French."*
Good, then suit up...

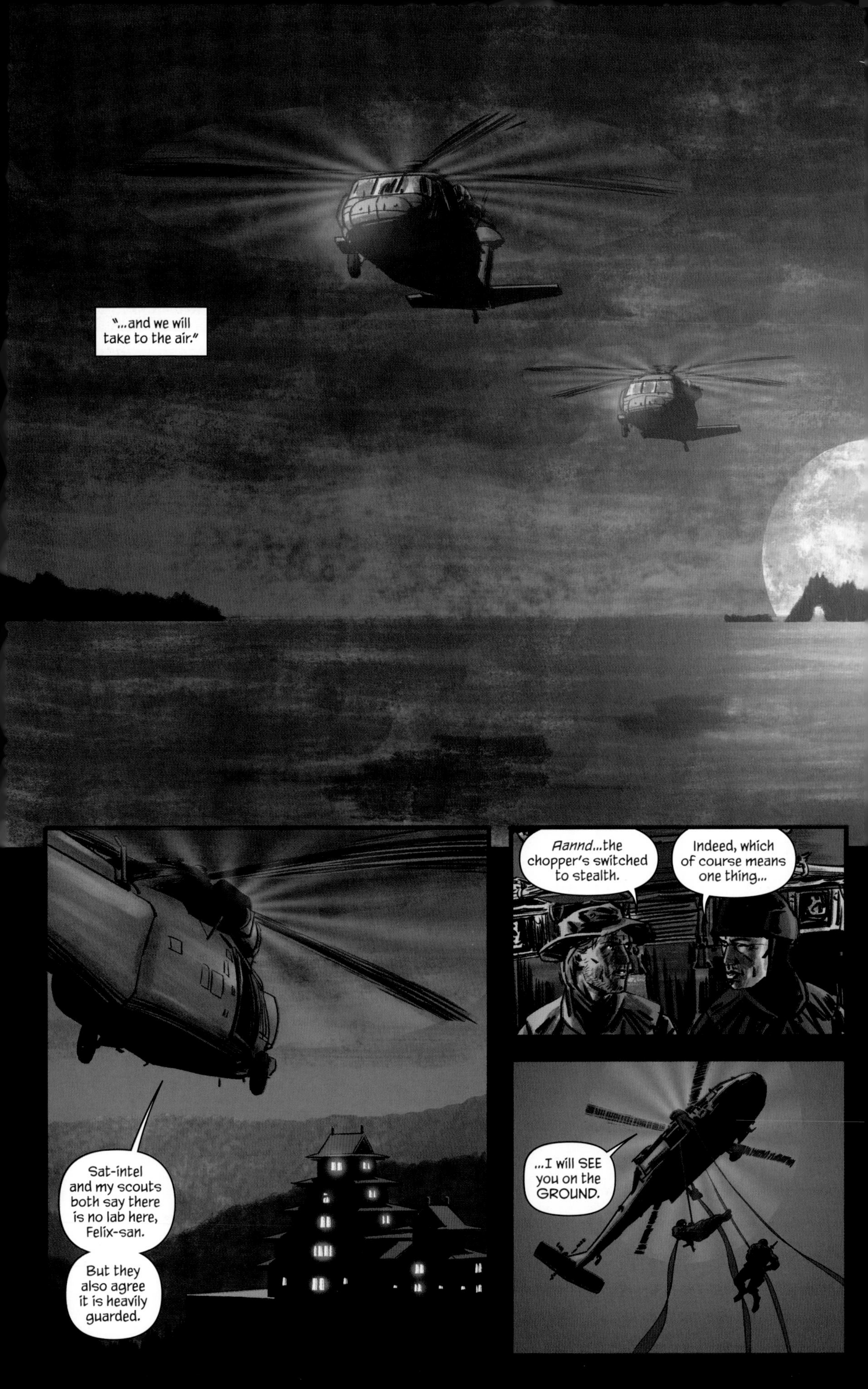
"...and we will take to the air."
Sat-intel and my scouts both say there is no lab here, Felix-san.
But they also agree it is heavily guarded.
Aannd...the chopper's switched to stealth.
Indeed, which of course means one thing...
...I will SEE you on the GROUND.

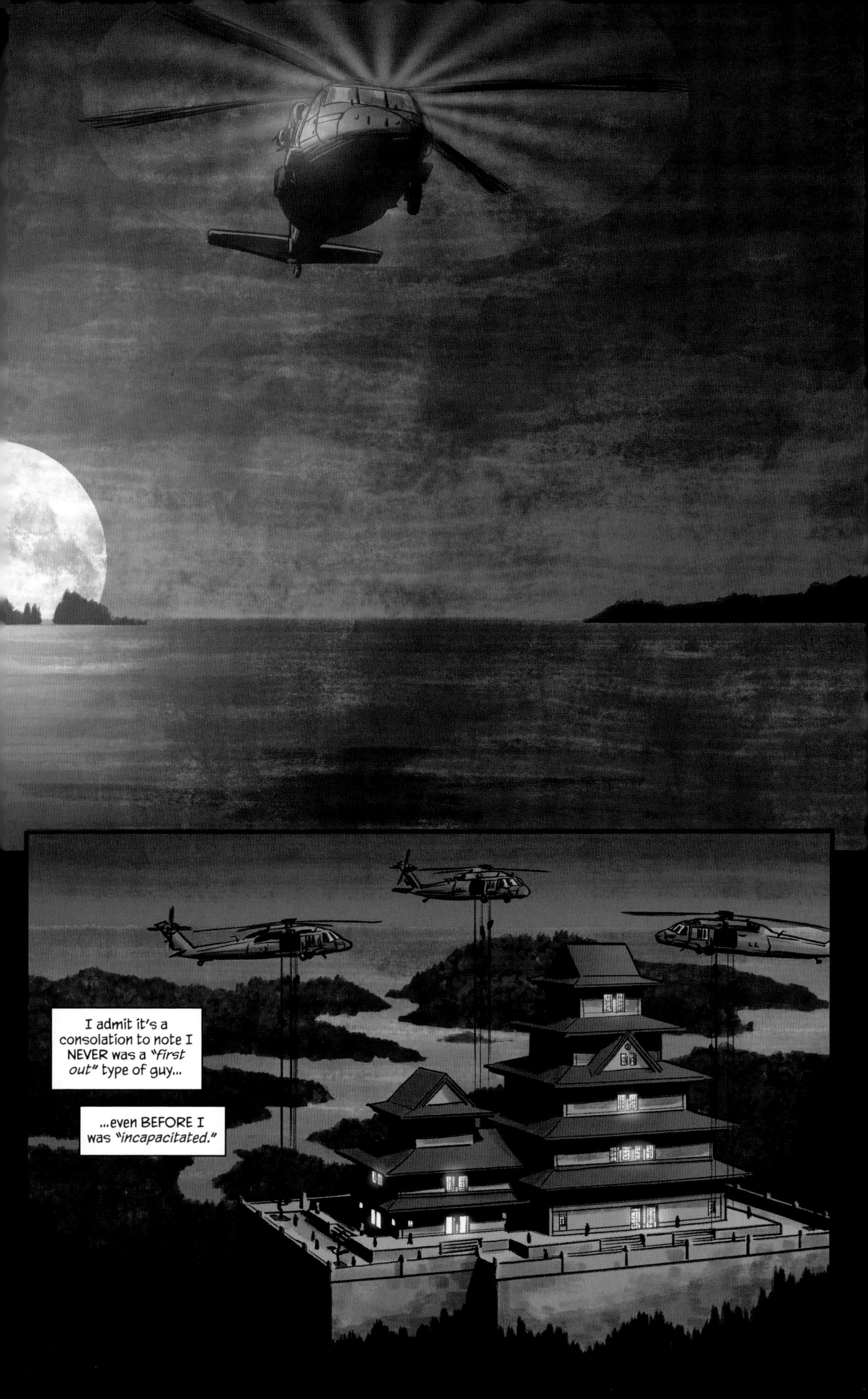
I admit it's a consolation to note I NEVER was a *"first out"* type of guy...
...even BEFORE I was *"incapacitated."*

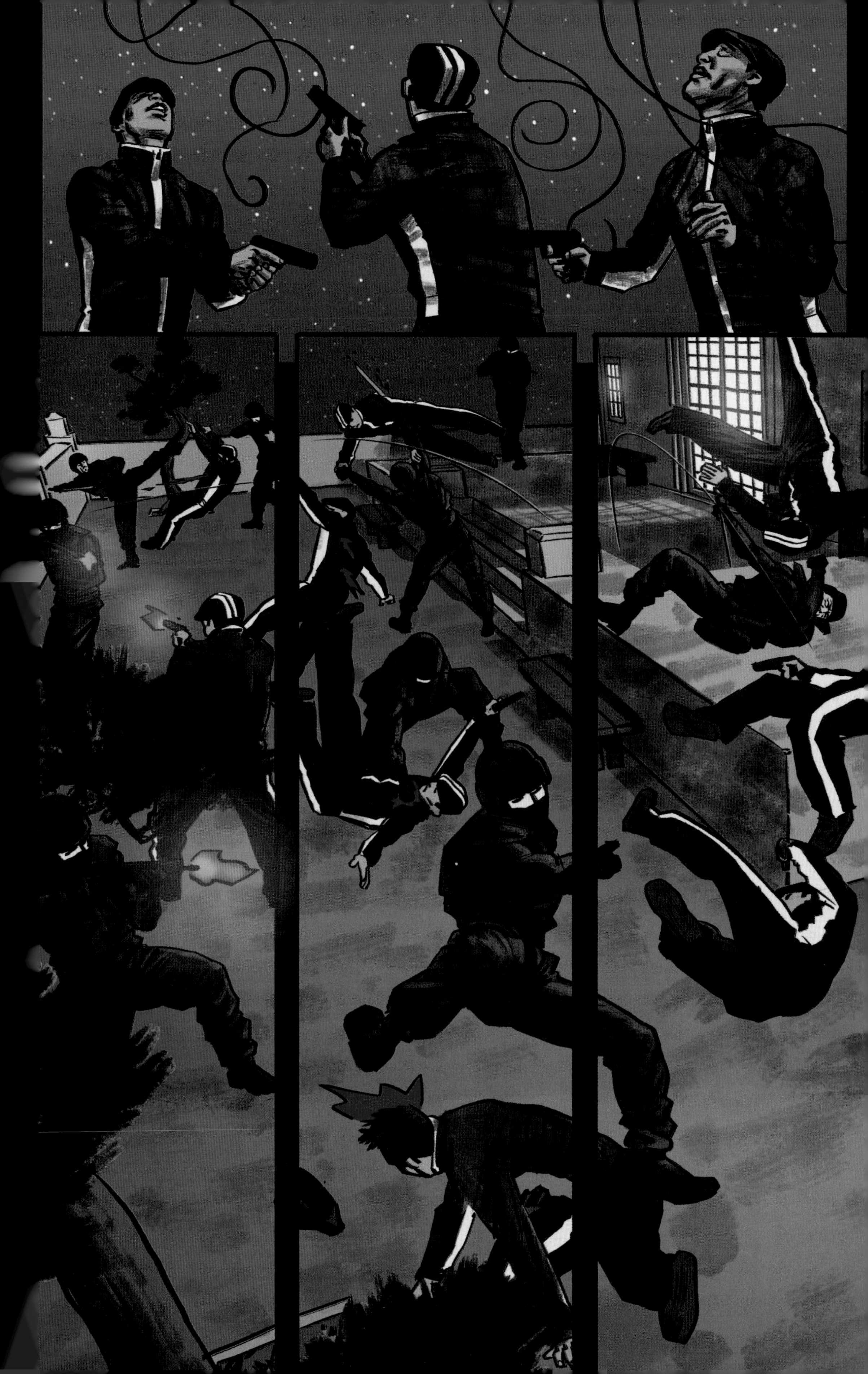

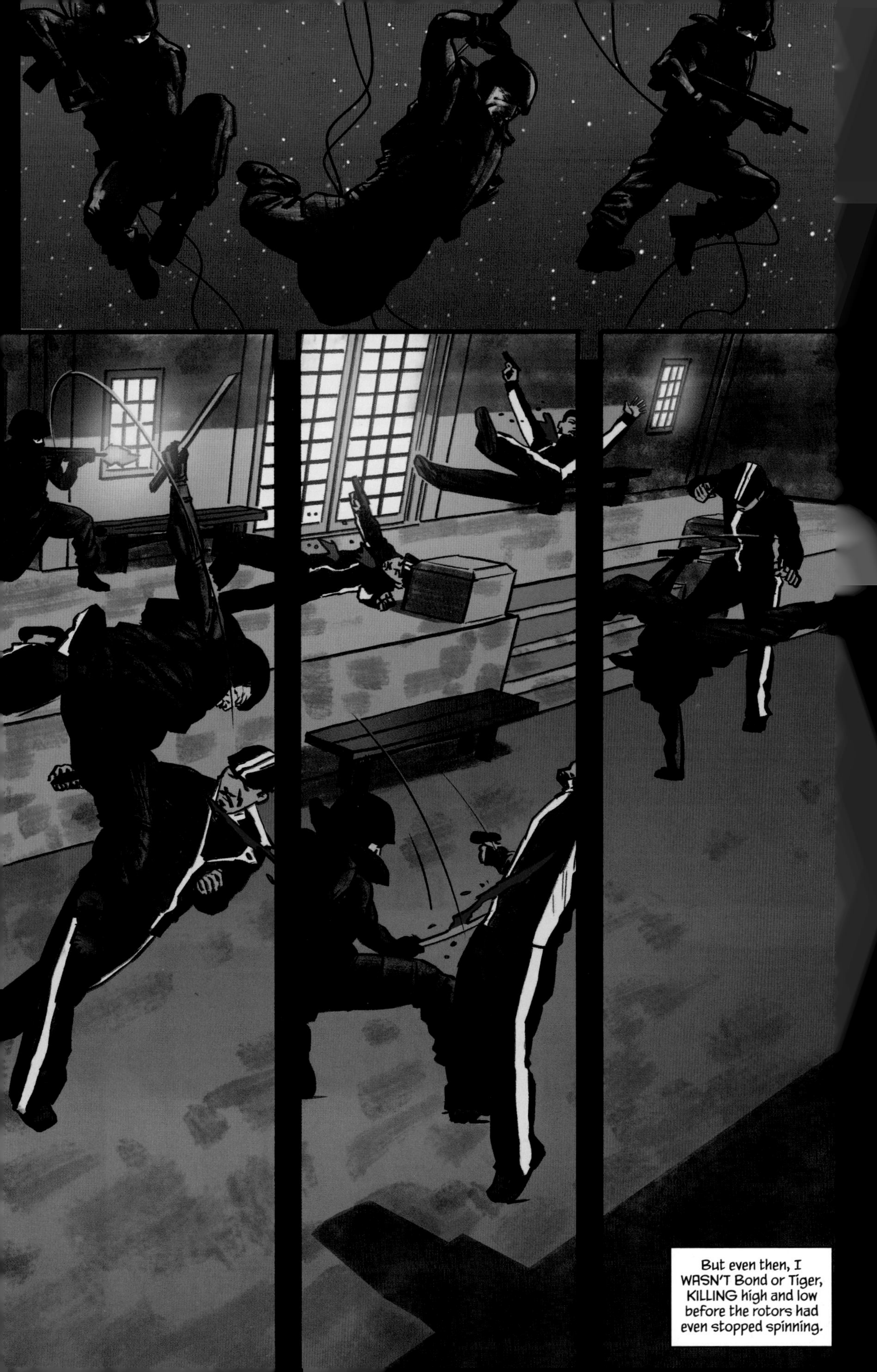
But even then, I WASN'T Bond or Tiger, KILLING high and low before the rotors had even stopped spinning.

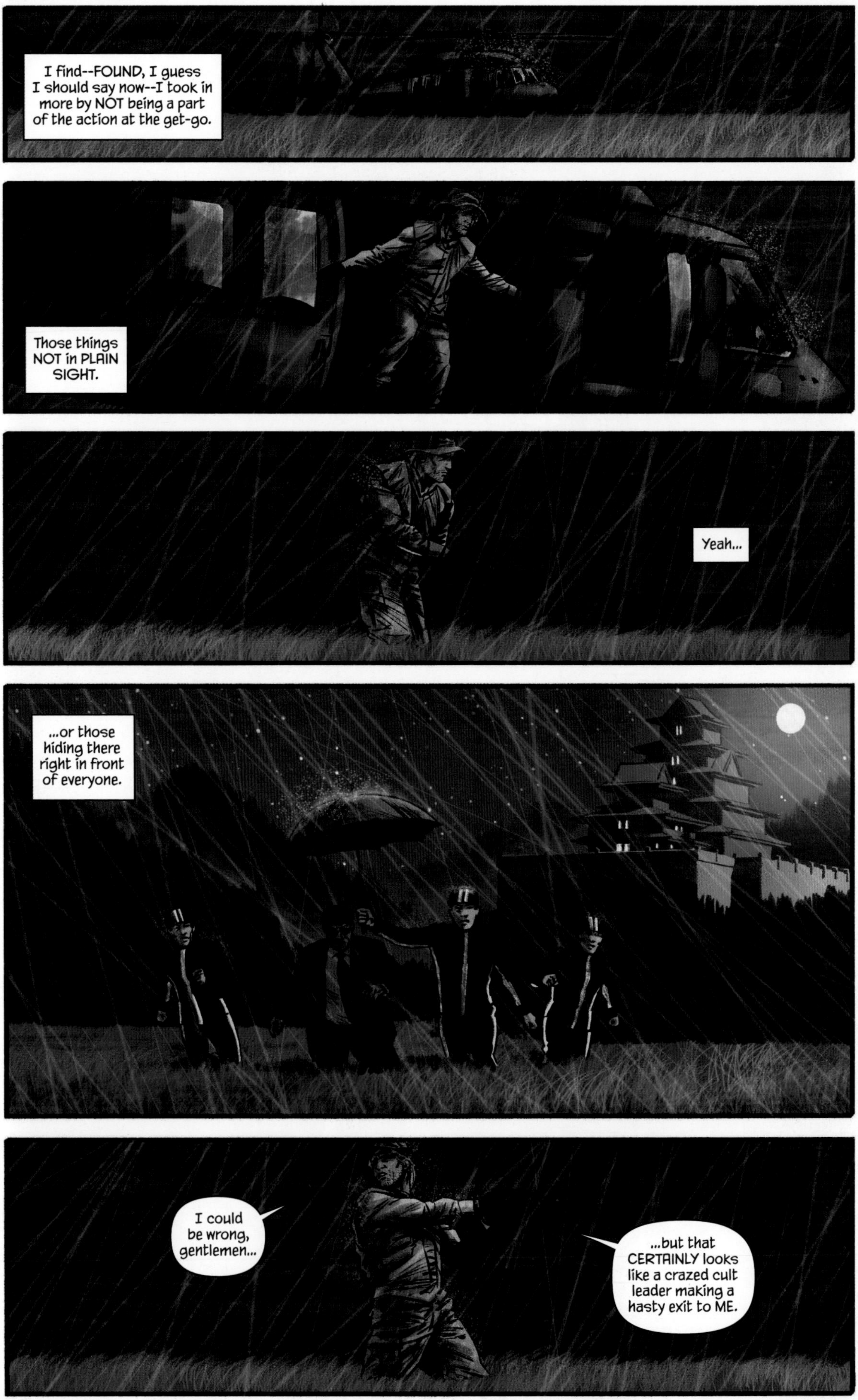
I find--FOUND, I guess I should say now--I took in more by NOT being a part of the action at the get-go.
Those things NOT in PLAIN SIGHT.
Yeah...
...or those hiding there right in front of everyone.
I could be wrong, gentlemen...
...but that CERTAINLY looks like a crazed cult leader making a hasty exit to ME.

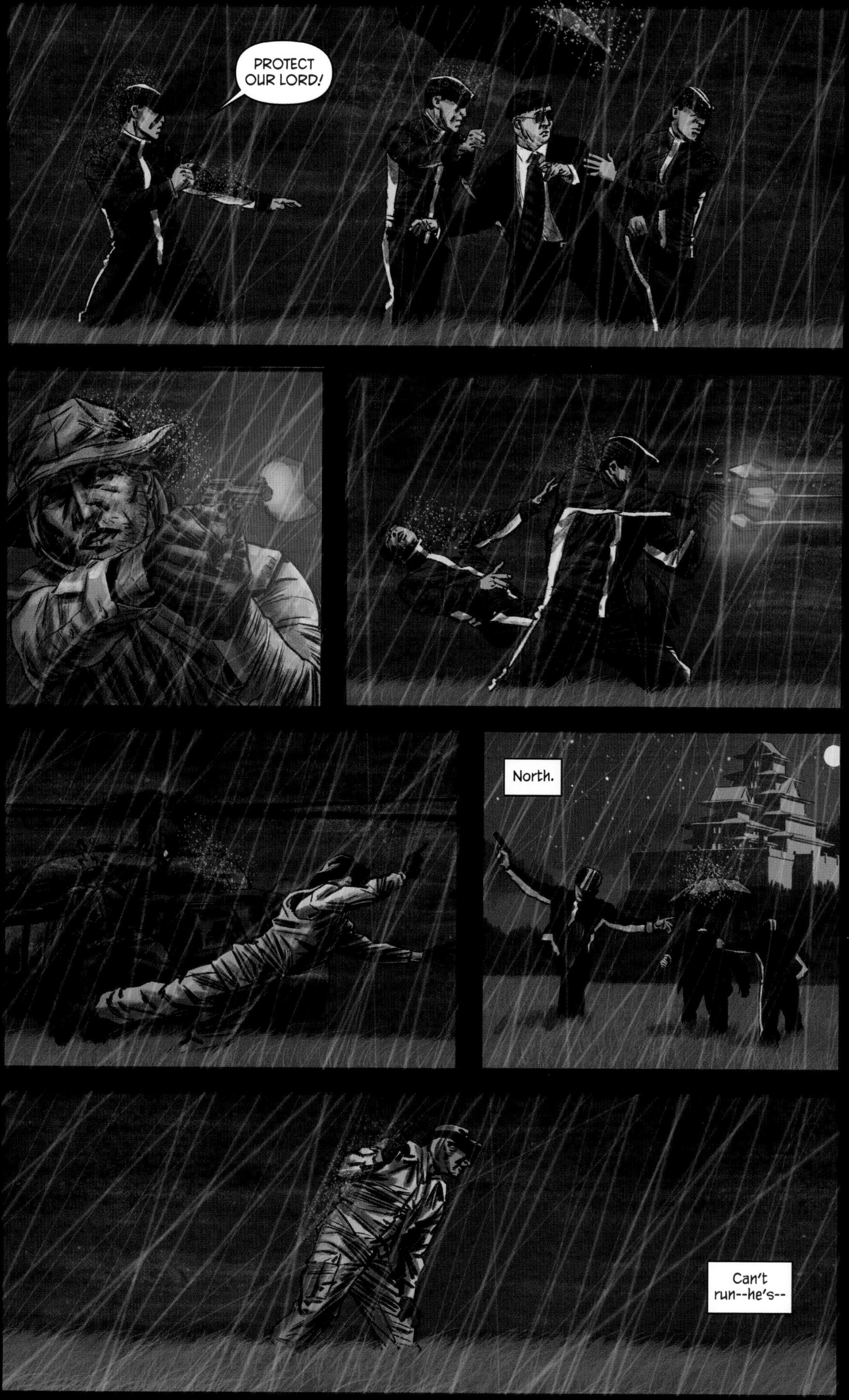
PROTECT OUR LORD!
North.
Can't run--he's--

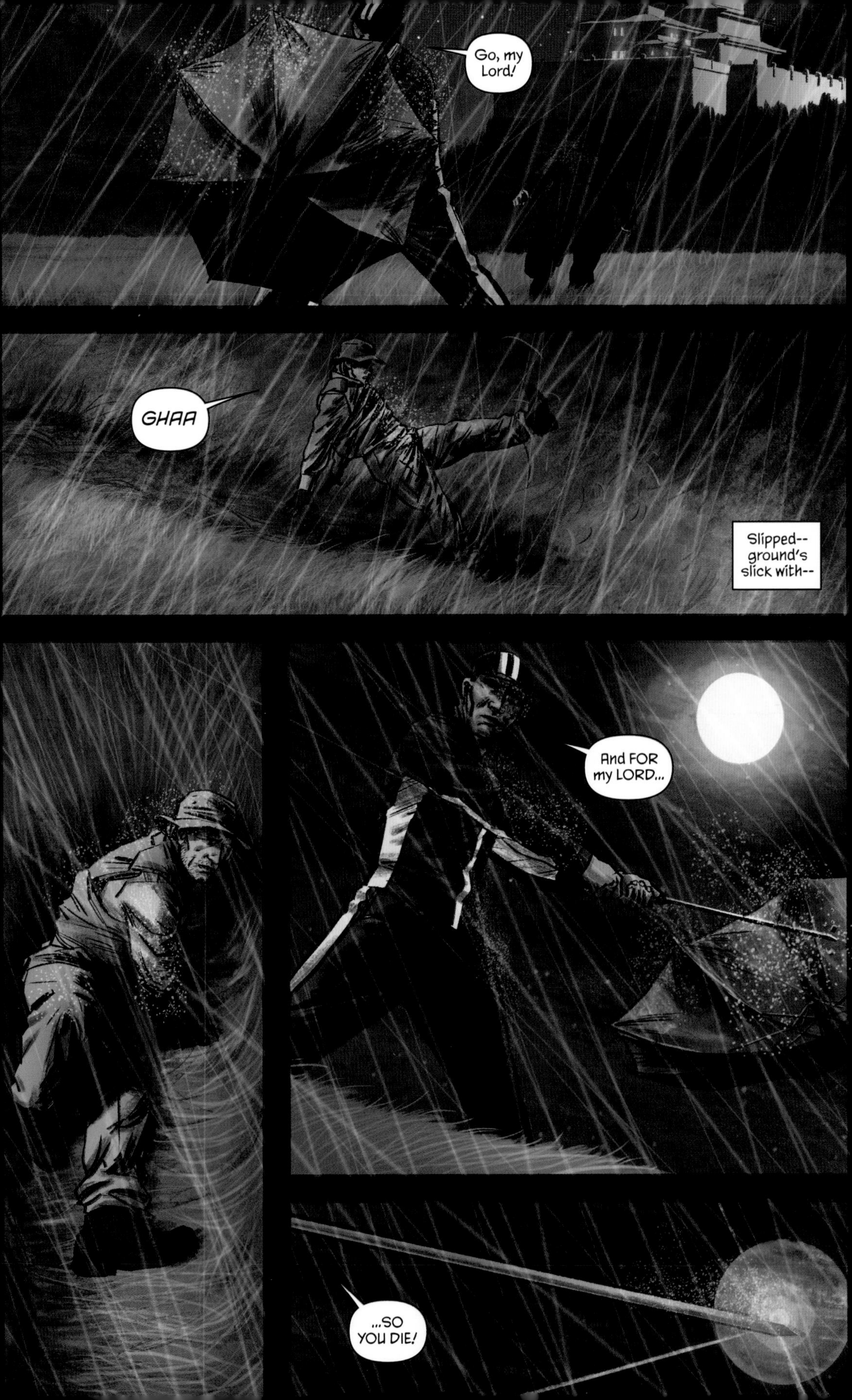
Go, my Lord!
GHAA
Slipped--ground's slick with--
And FOR my LORD...
...SO YOU DIE!

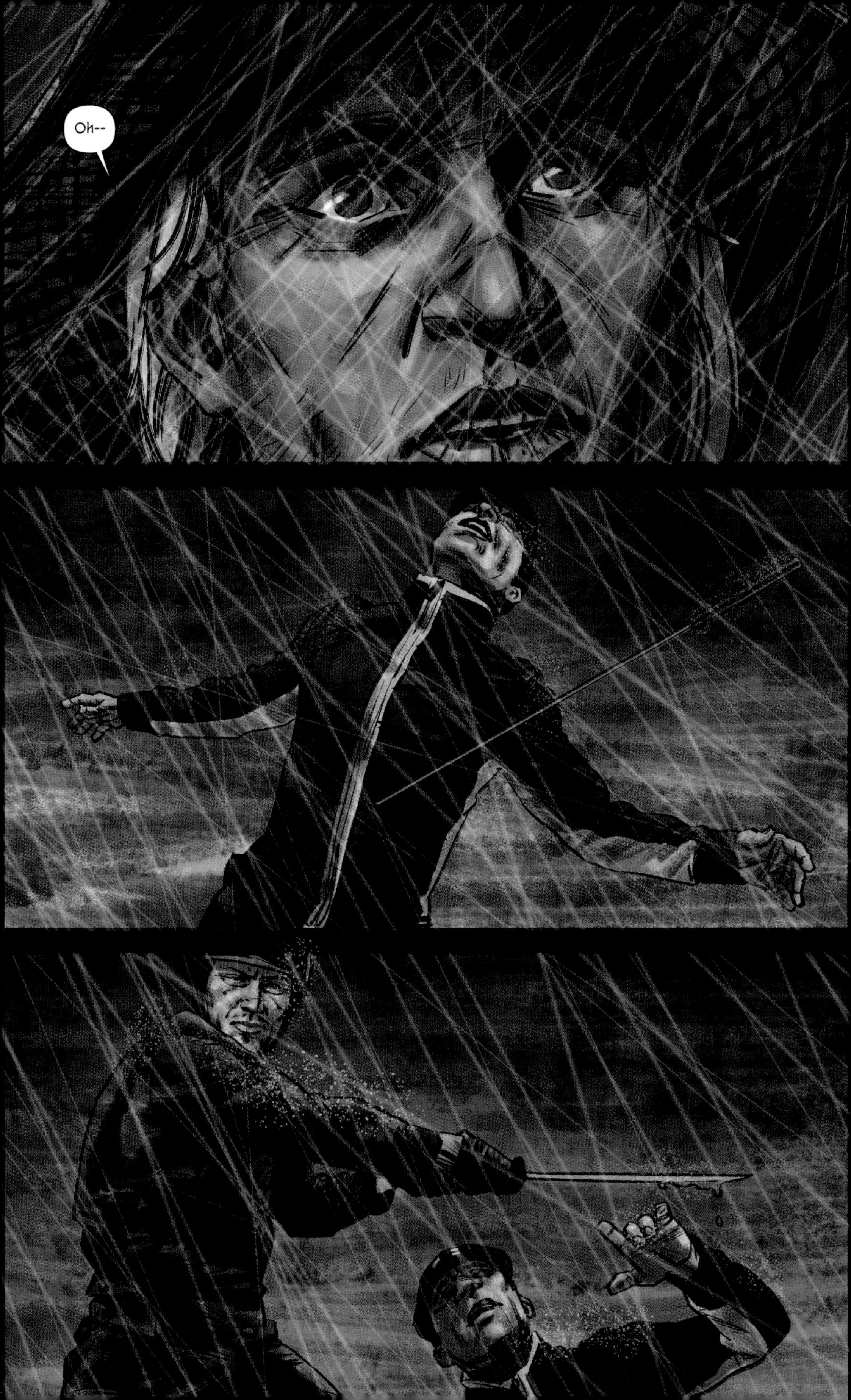
Oh--

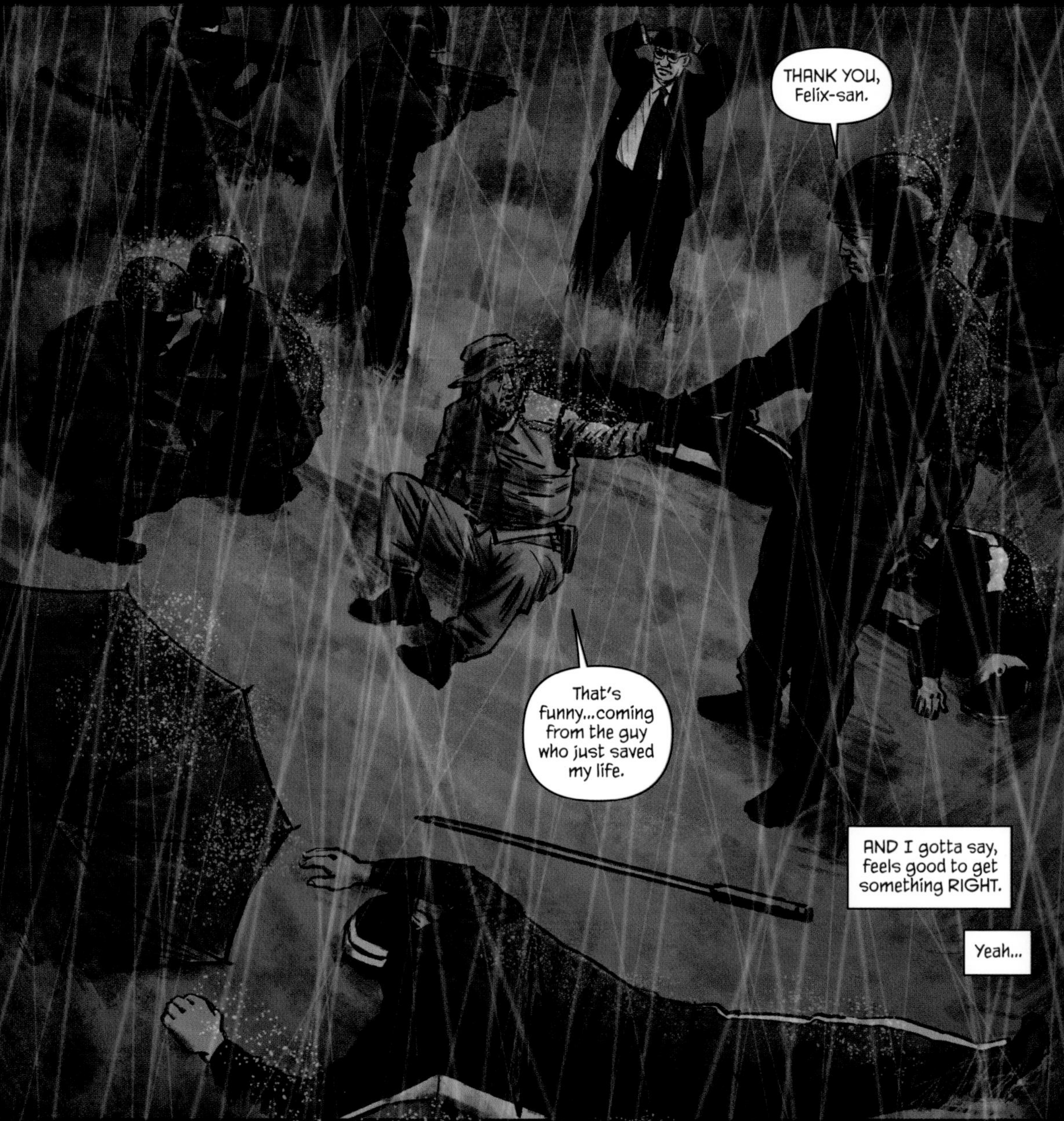
THANK YOU, Felíx-san.
That's funny...coming from the guy who just saved my life.
AND I gotta say, feels good to get something RIGHT.
Yeah...
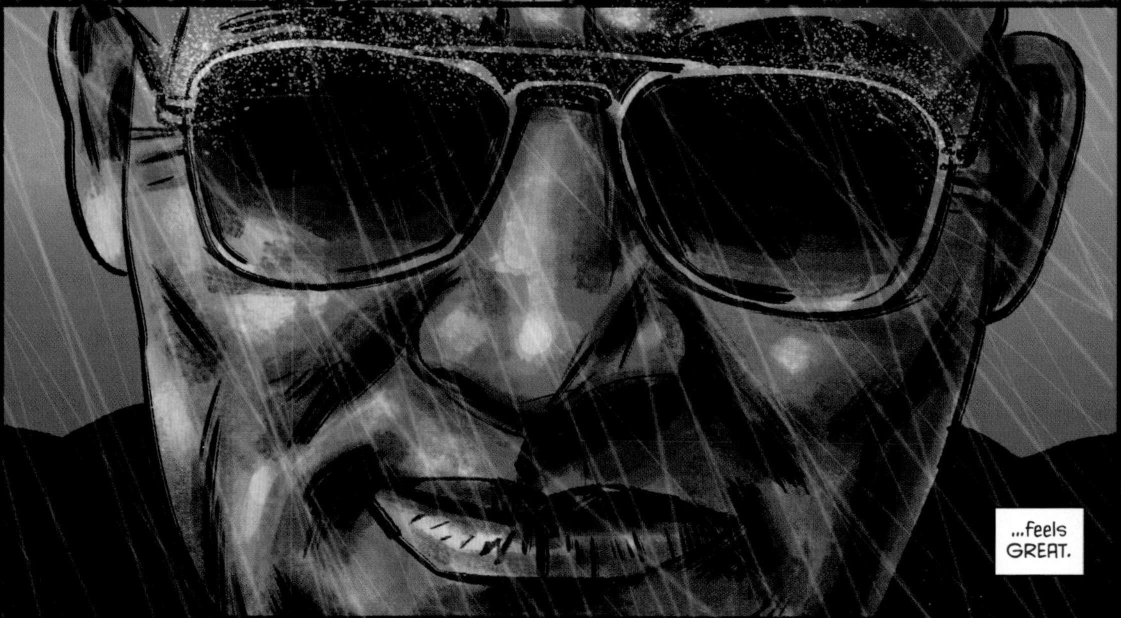
...feels GREAT.

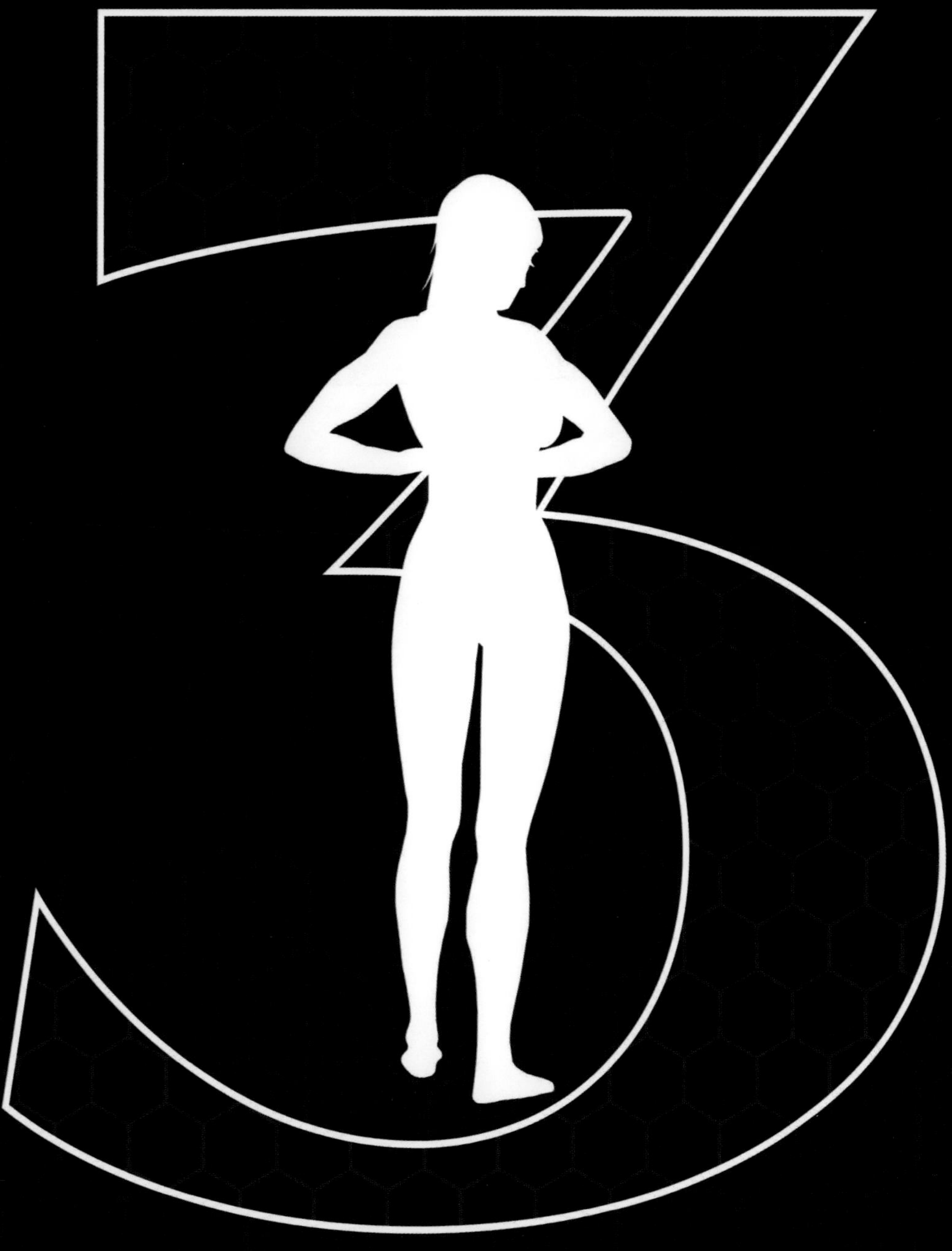
3

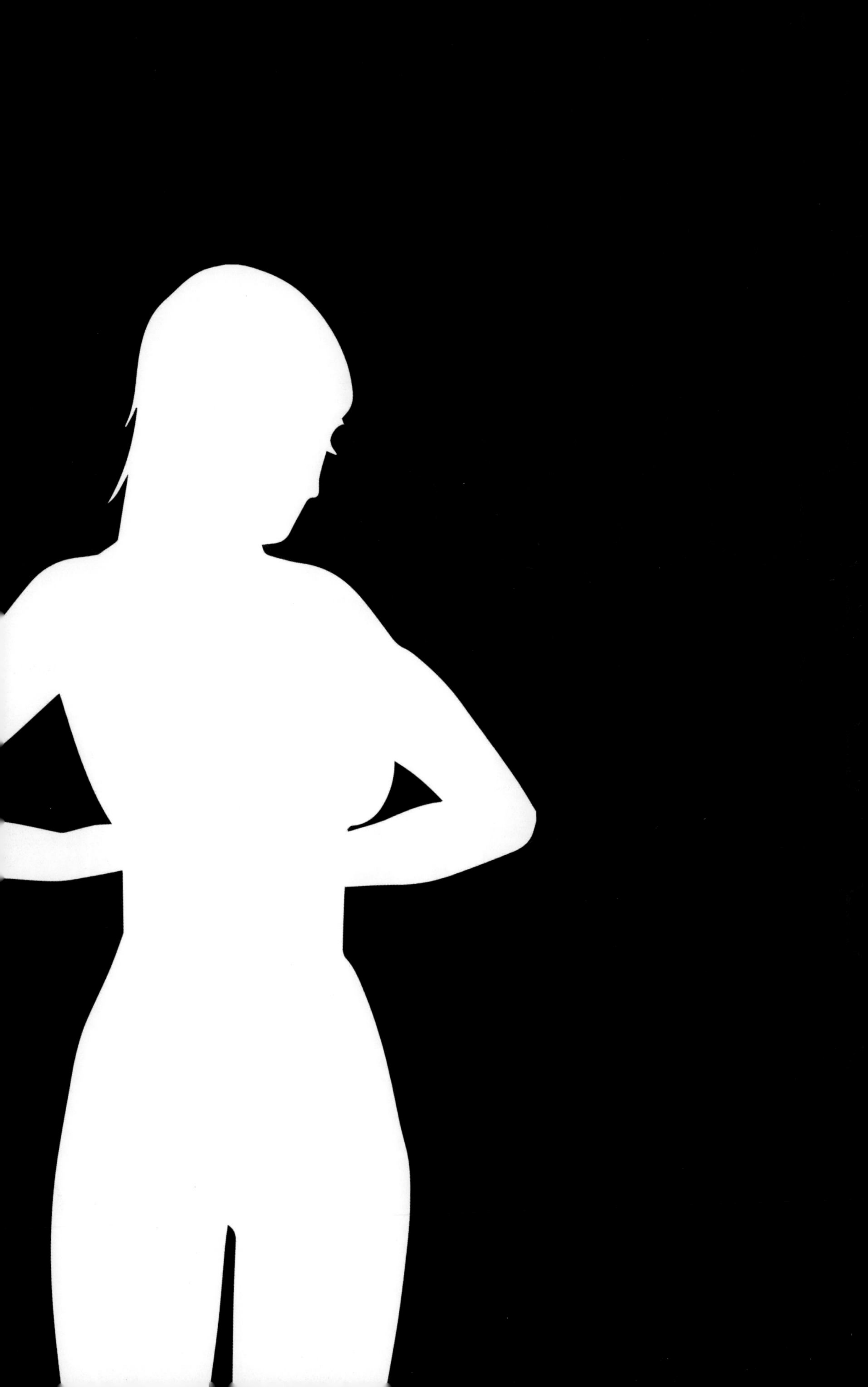

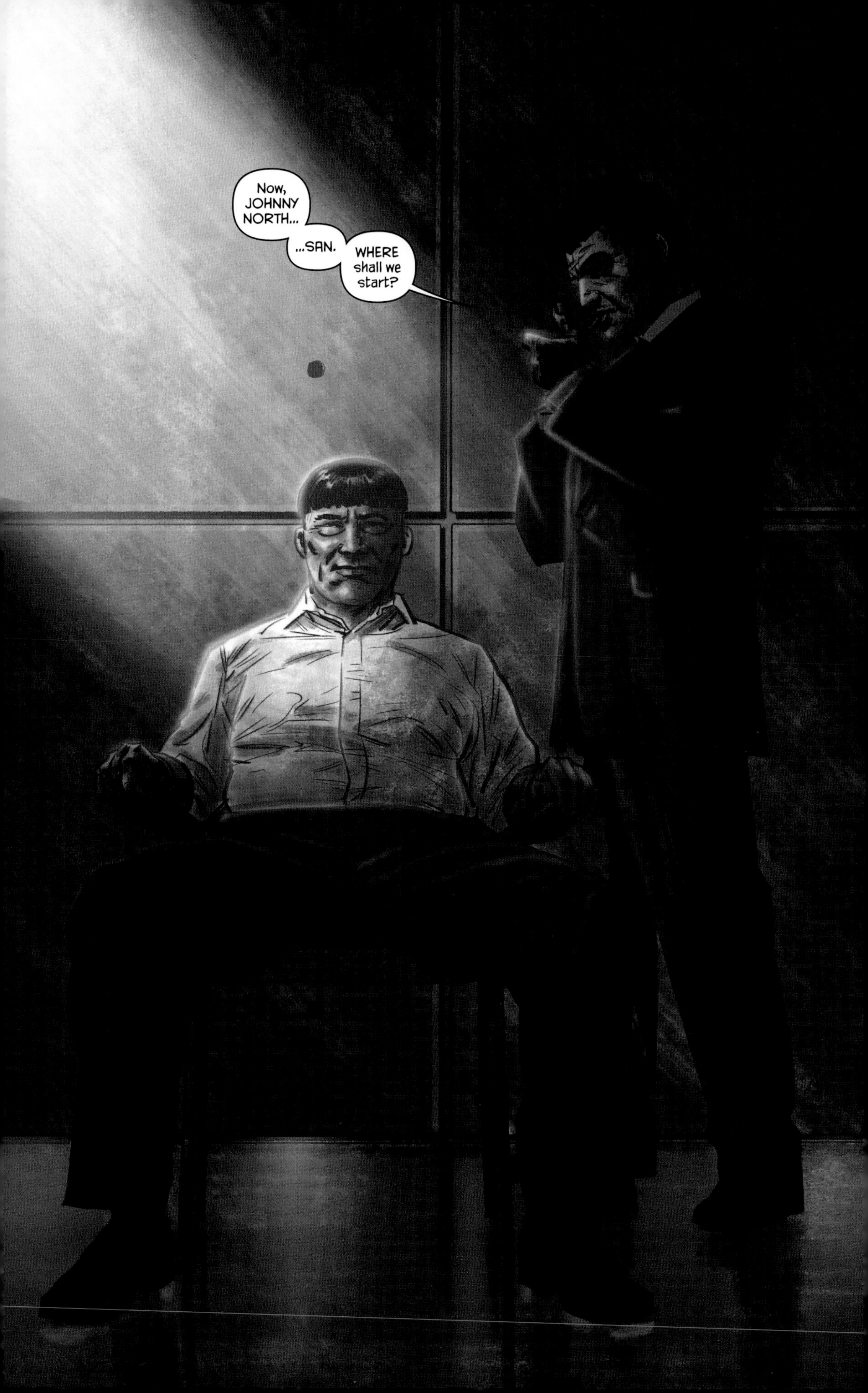
Now, JOHNNY NORTH...
...SAN.
WHERE shall we start?

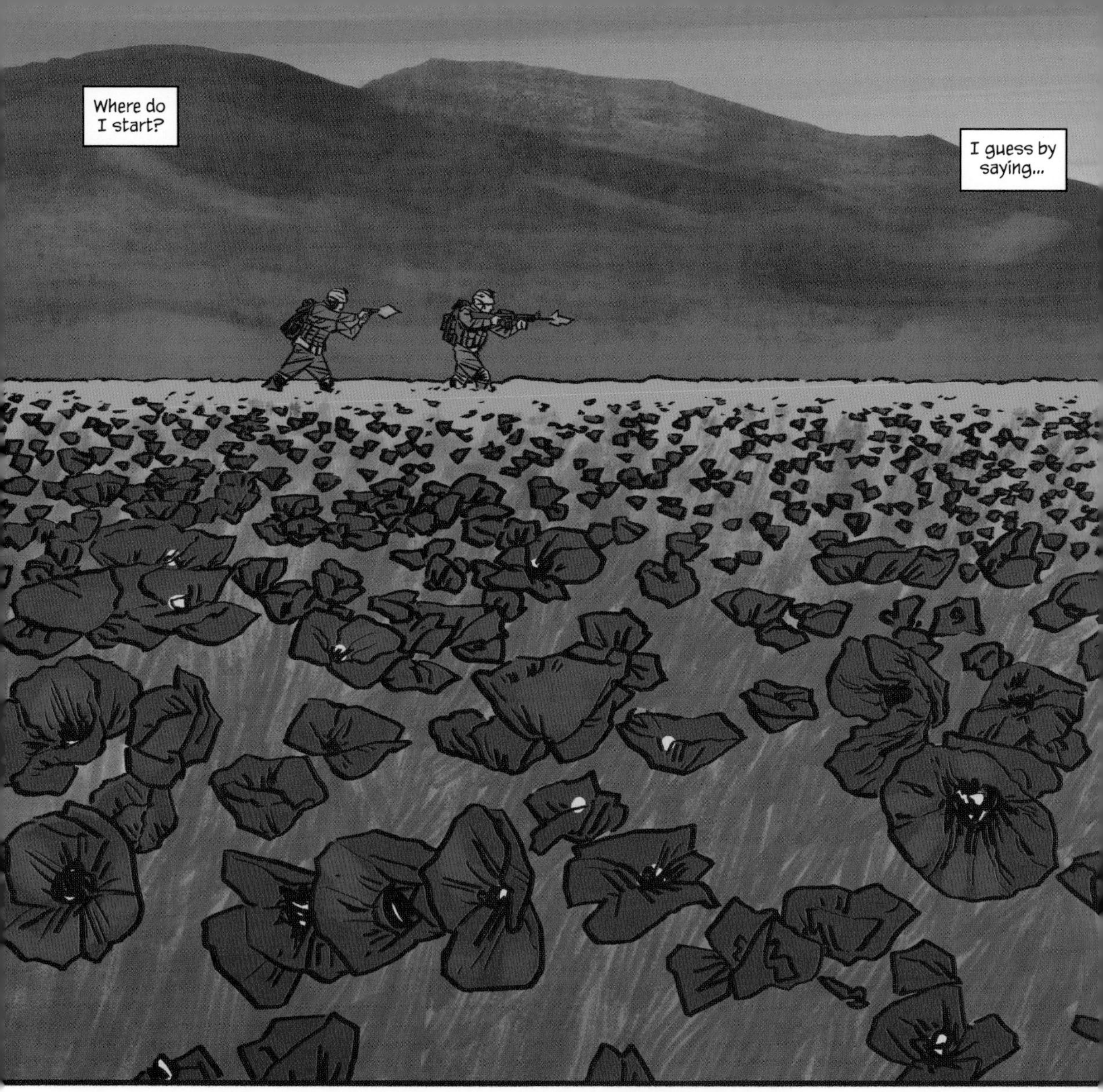
Where do I start?
I guess by saying...

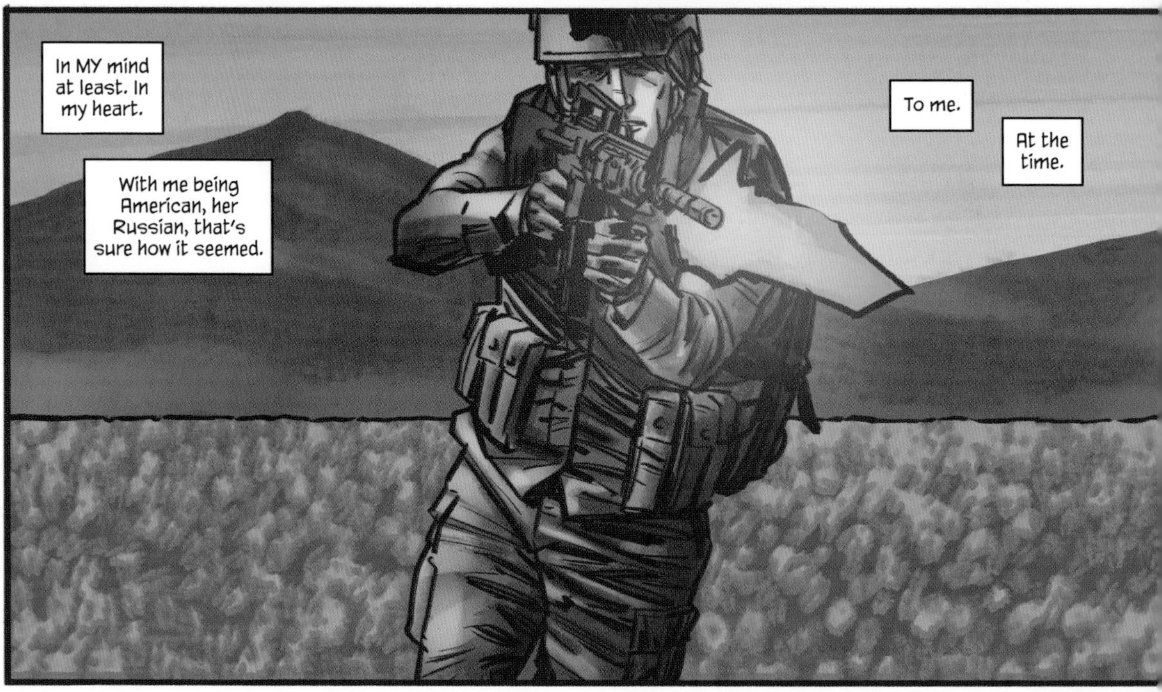
In MY mind at least. In my heart.
With me being American, her Russian, that's sure how it seemed.
To me.
At the time.

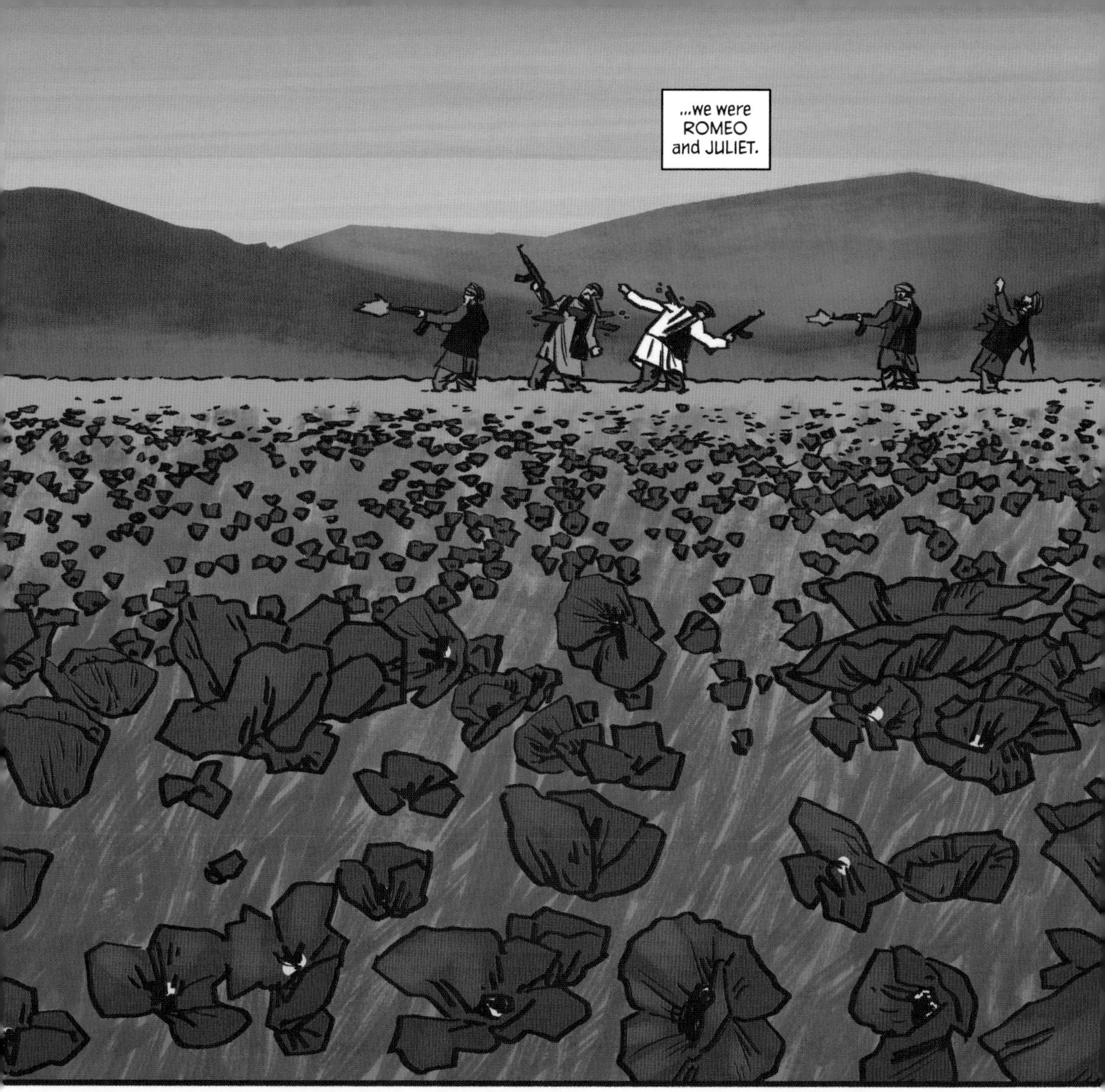
...we were ROMEO and JULIET.

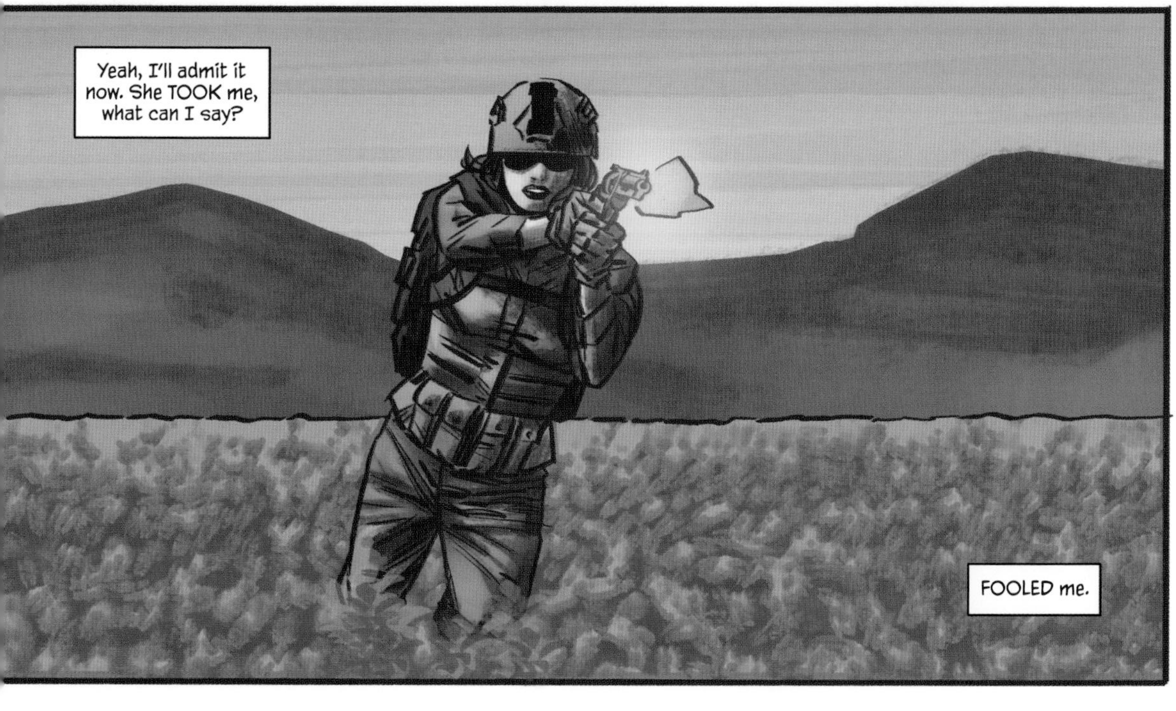
Yeah, I'll admit it now. She TOOK me, what can I say?
FOOLED me.

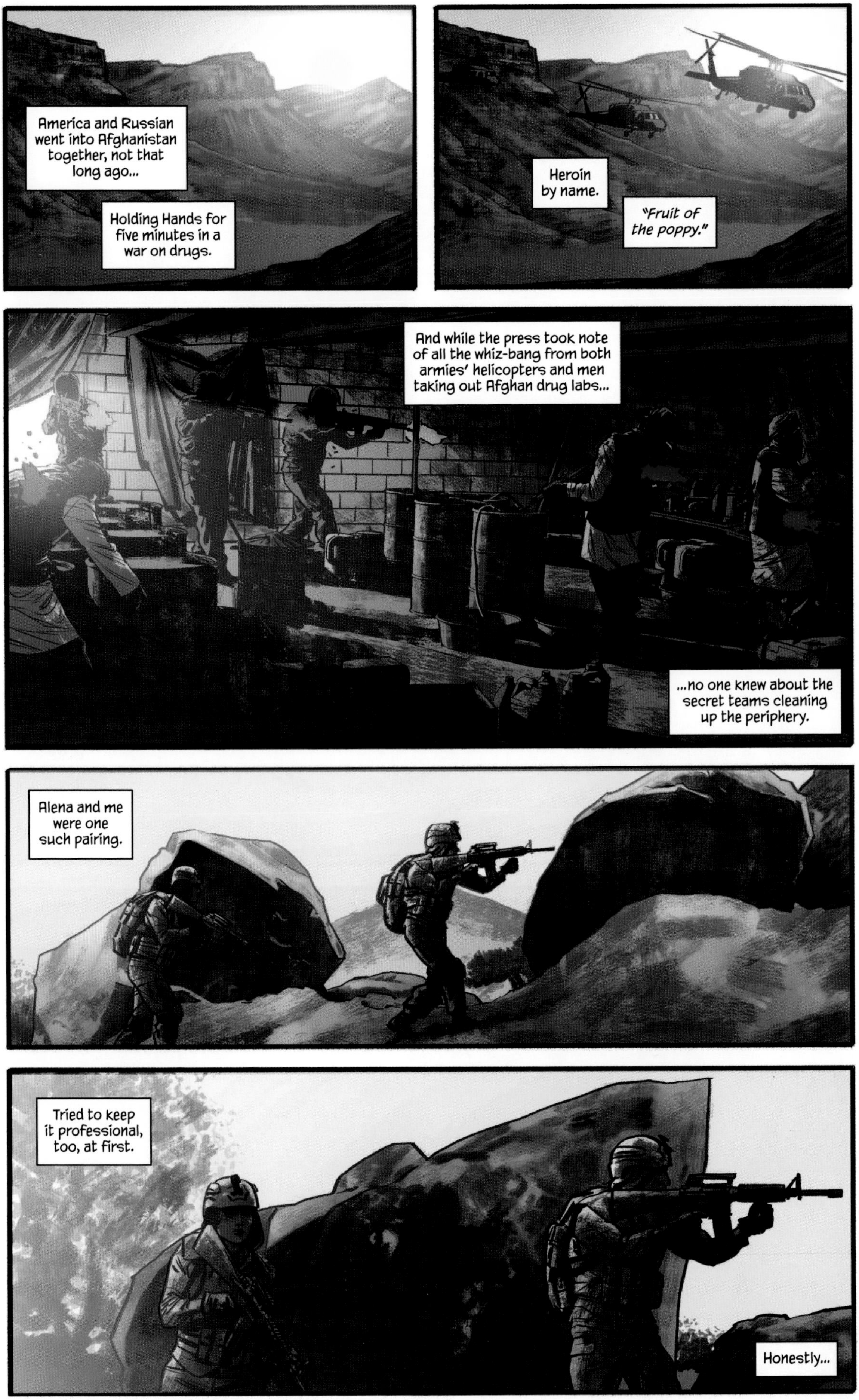
America and Russian went into Afghanistan together, not that long ago...
Holding Hands for five minutes in a war on drugs.
Heroin by name.
"Fruit of the poppy."
And while the press took note of all the whiz-bang from both armies' helicopters and men taking out Afghan drug labs...
...no one knew about the secret teams cleaning up the periphery.
Alena and me were one such pairing.
Tried to keep it professional, too, at first.
Honestly...

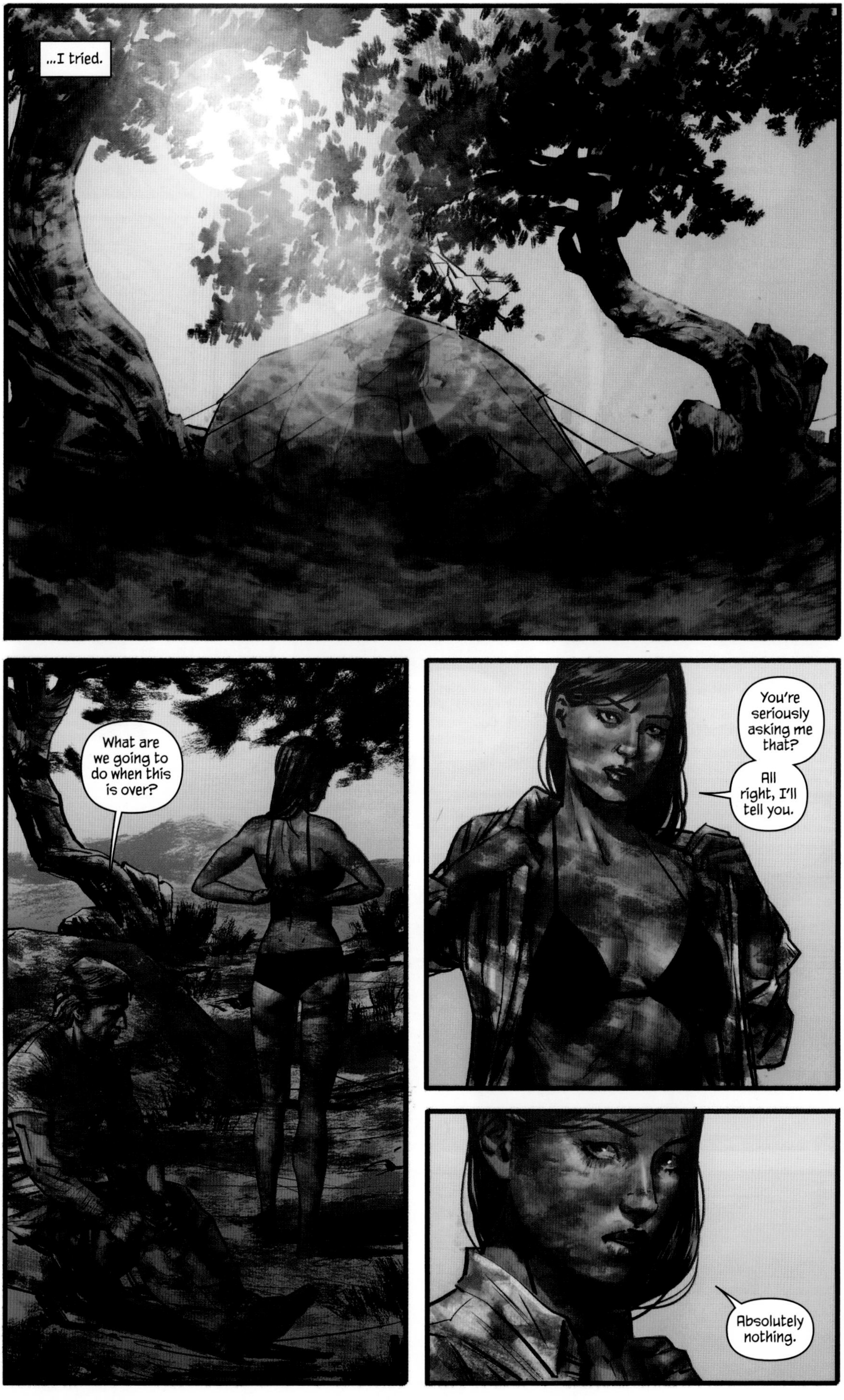
...I tried.
What are we going to do when this is over?
You're seriously asking me that?
All right, I'll tell you.
Absolutely nothing.

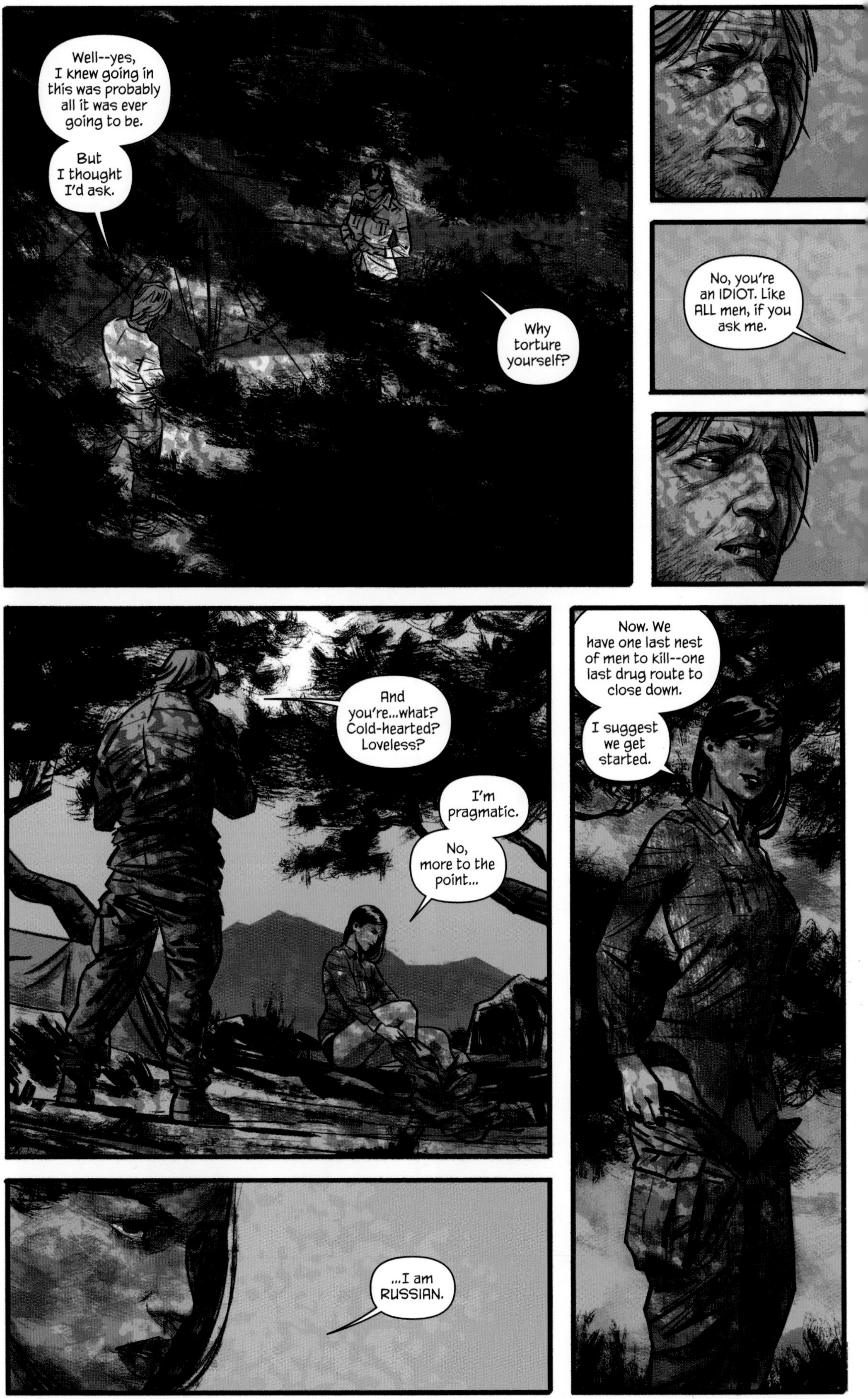

Well--yes, I knew going in this was probably all it was ever going to be.
But I thought I'd ask.
Why torture yourself?
No, you're an IDIOT. Like ALL men, if you ask me.
And you're...what? Cold-hearted? Loveless?
I'm pragmatic.
No, more to the point...
...I am RUSSIAN.
Now. We have one last nest of men to kill--one last drug route to close down.
I suggest we get started.

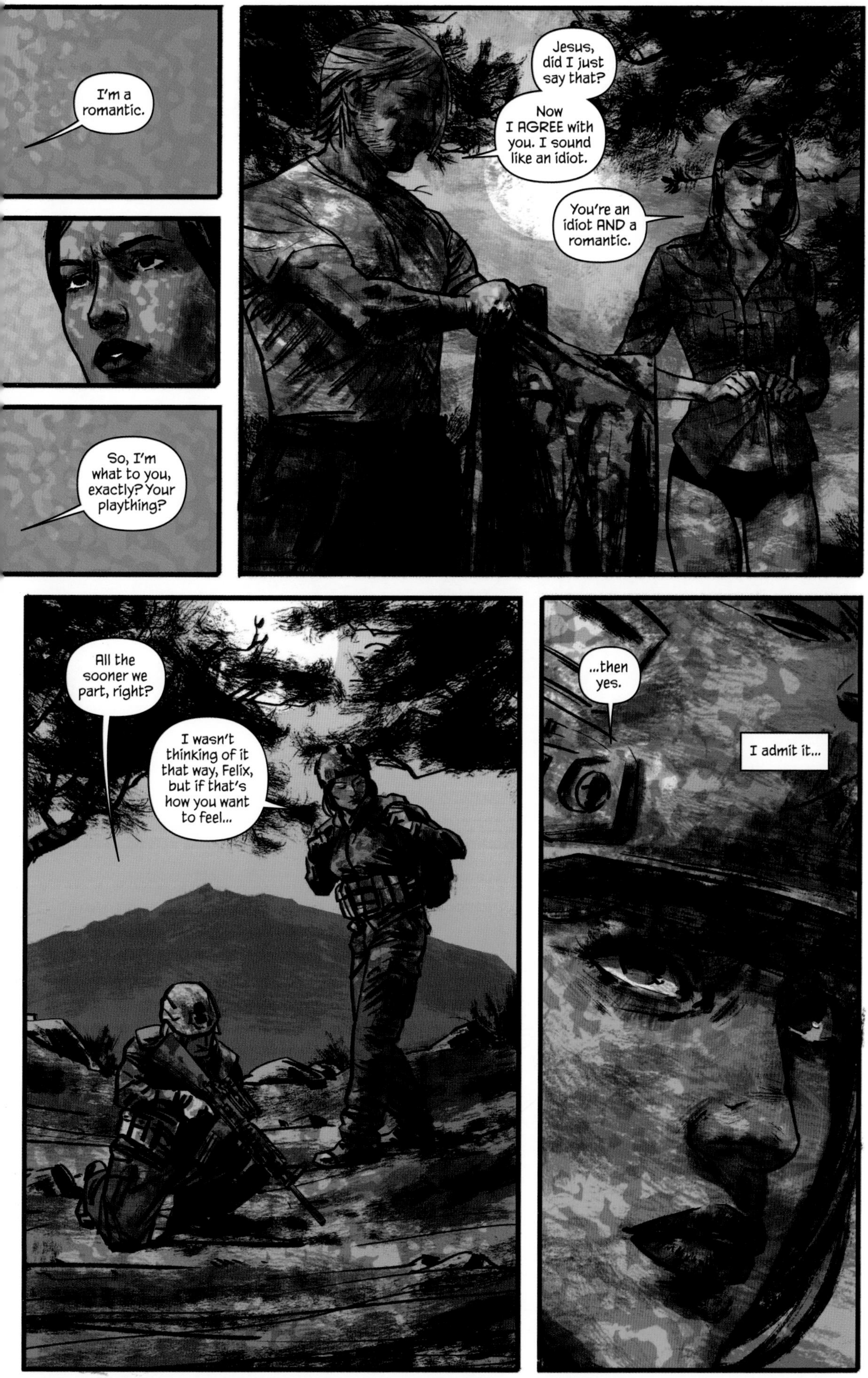
I'm a romantic.
Jesus, did I just say that?
Now I AGREE with you. I sound like an idiot.
You're an idiot AND a romantic.
So, I'm what to you, exactly? Your plaything?
All the sooner we part, right?
I wasn't thinking of it that way, Felix, but if that's how you want to feel...
I admit it...
...then yes.

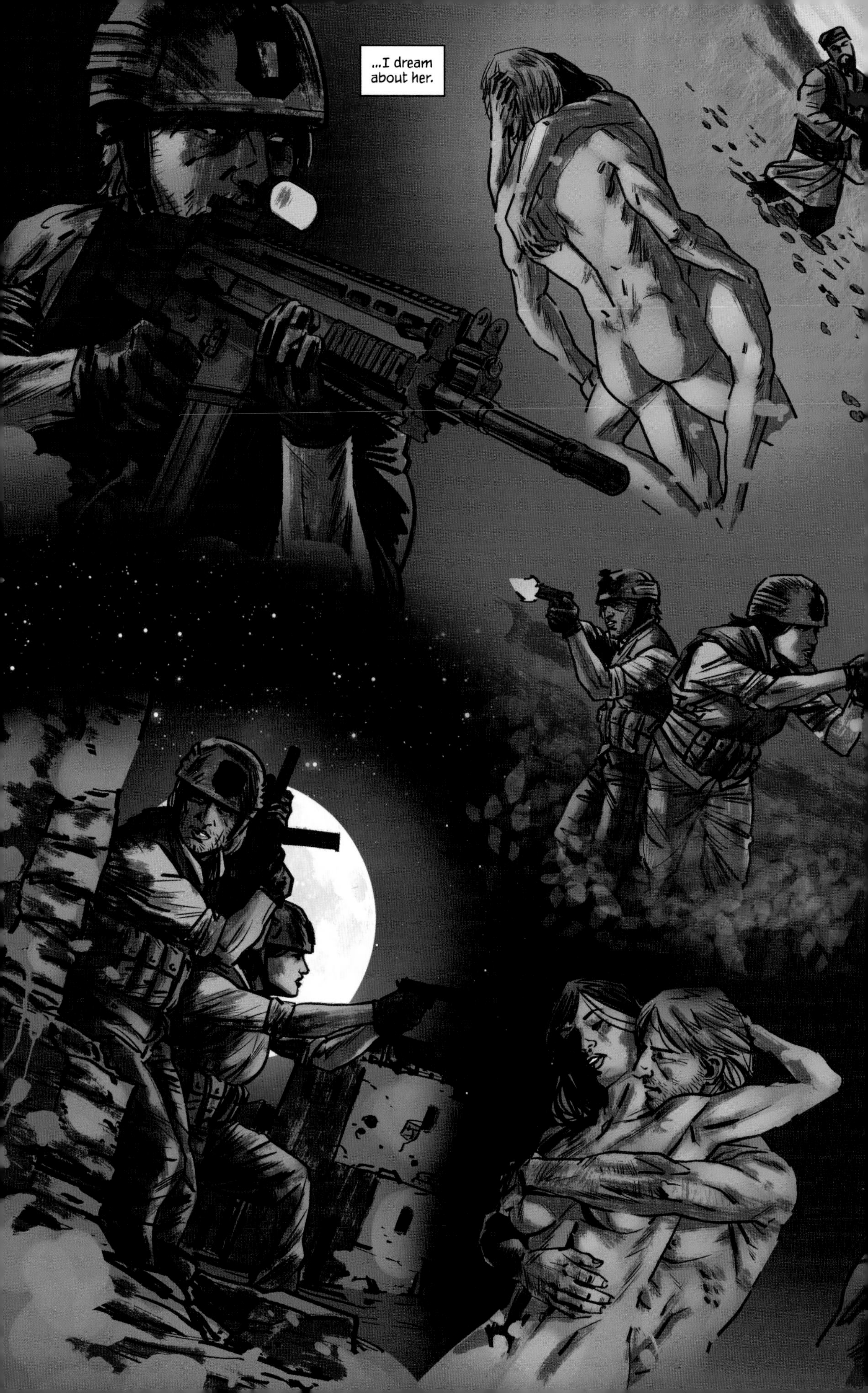
...I dream about her.

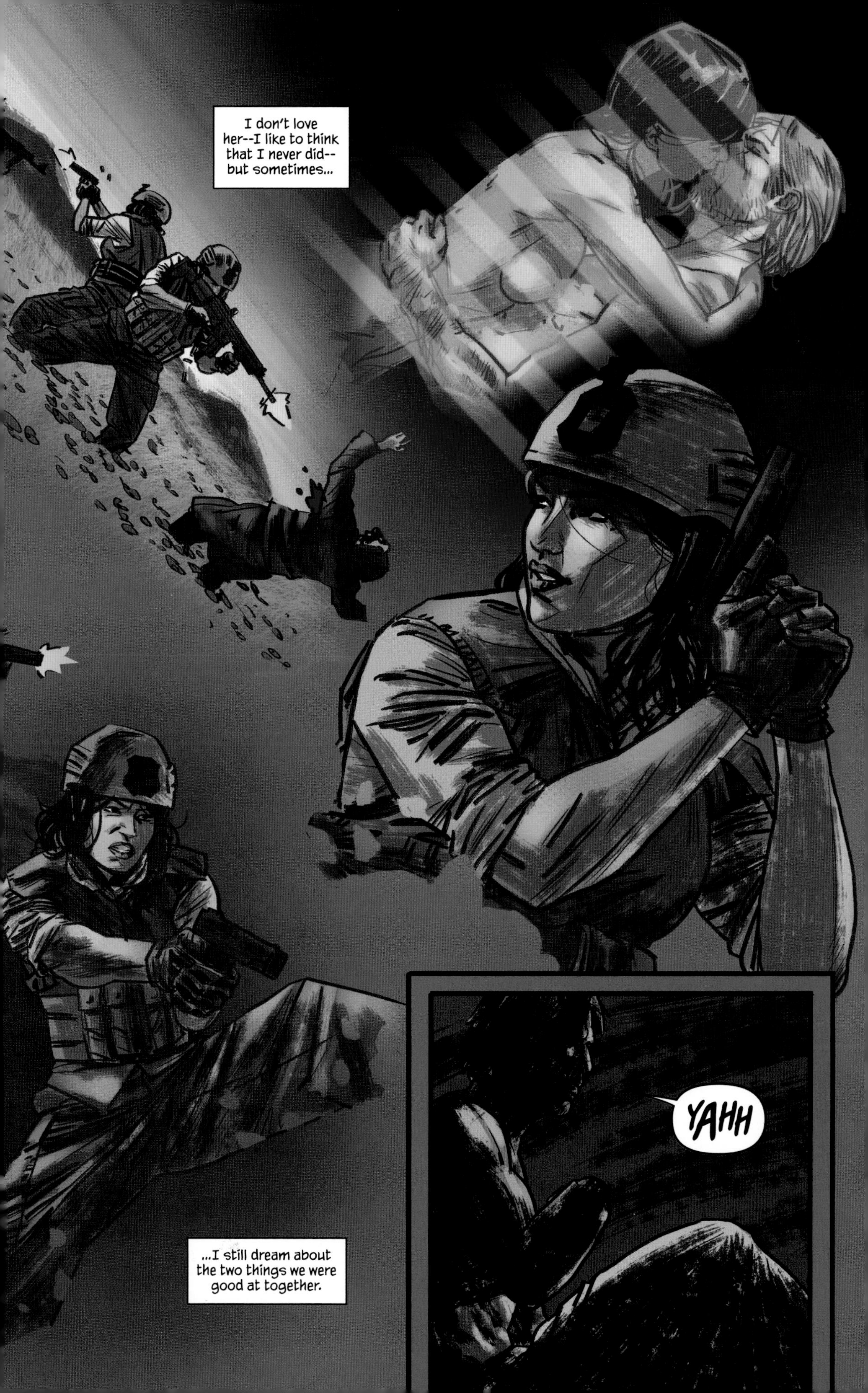
I don't love her--I like to think that I never did--but sometimes...
...I still dream about the two things we were good at together.
YAHH

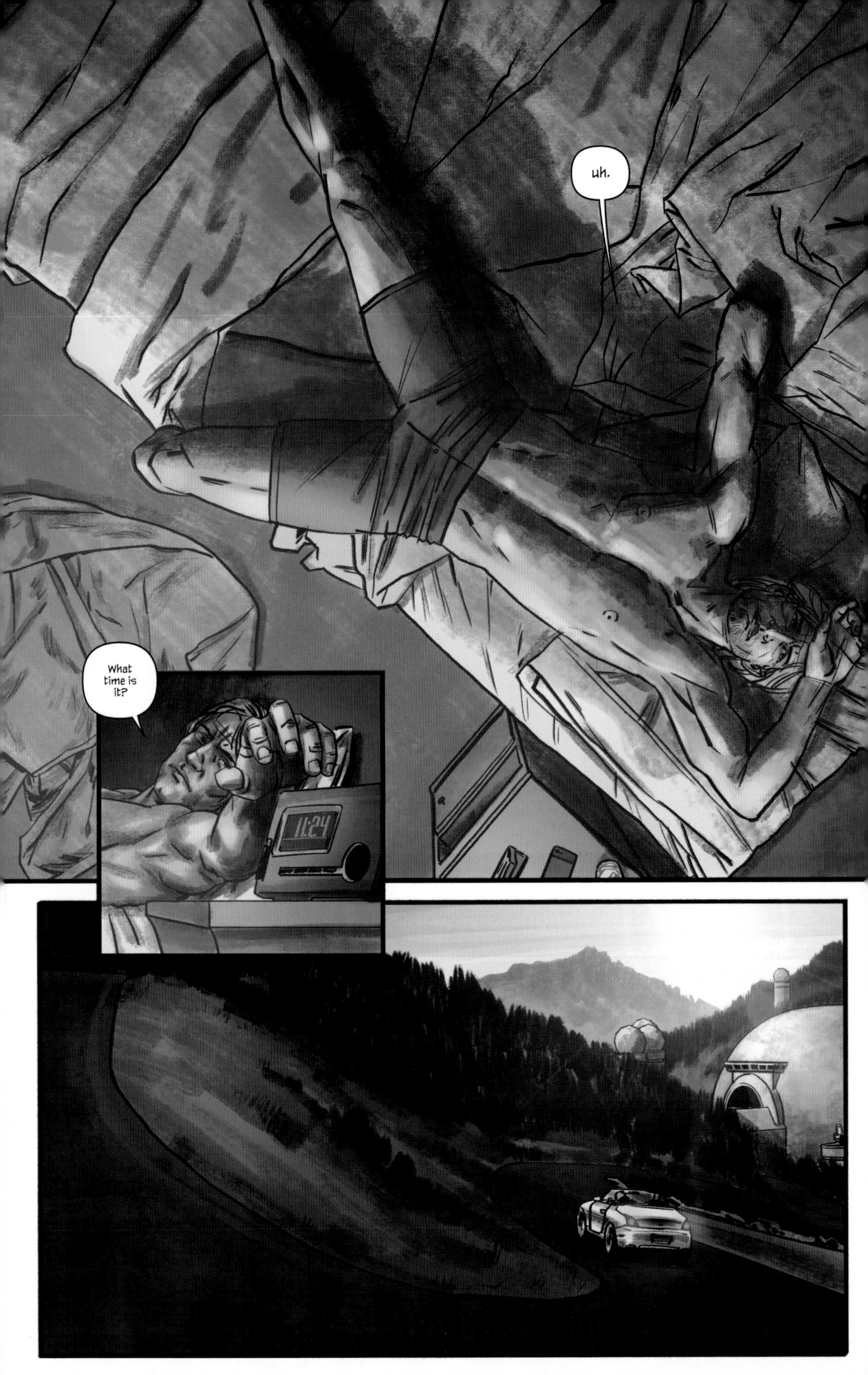
uh.
What time is it?
11:24

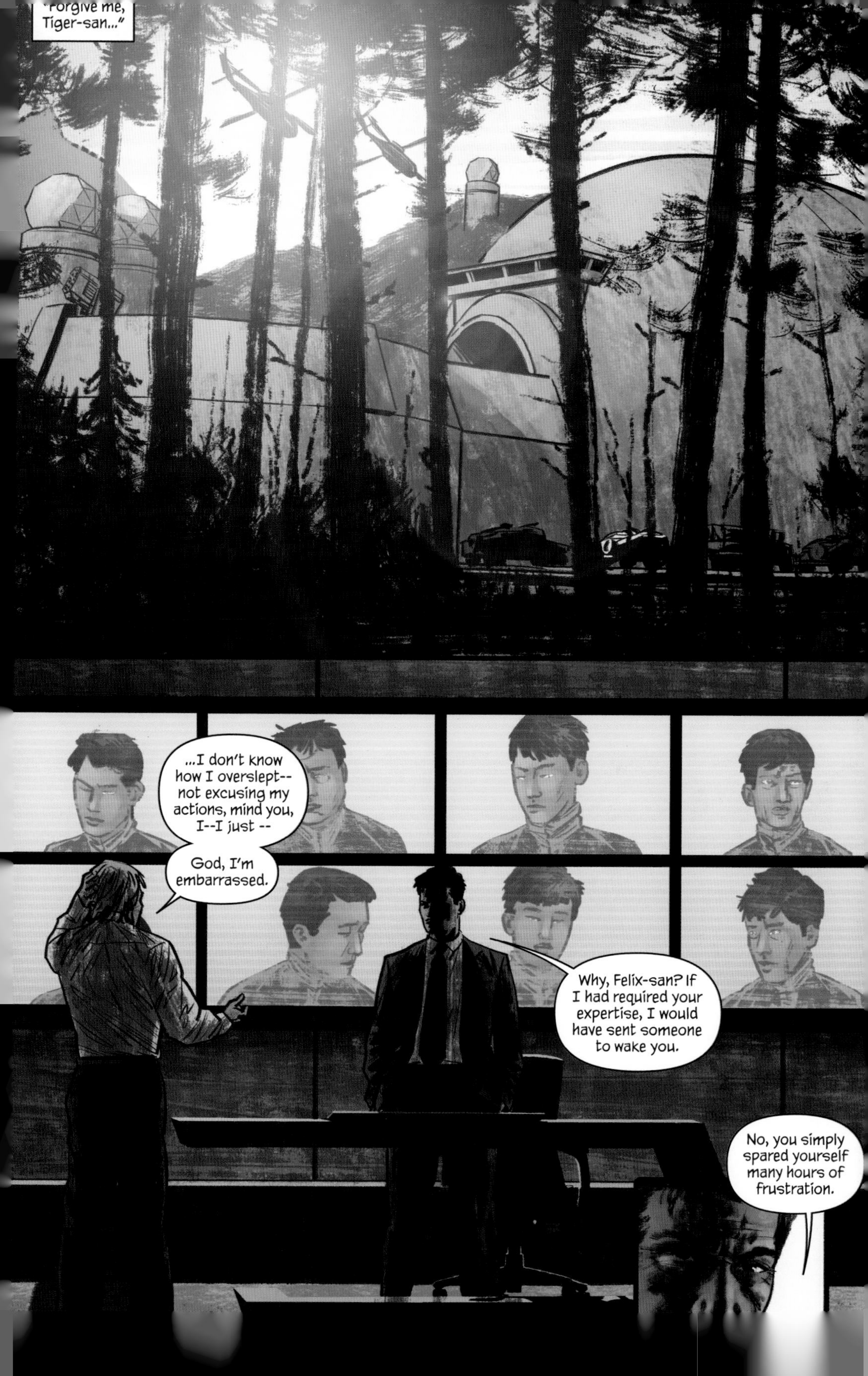

"Forgive me, Tiger-san..."
...I don't know how I overslept--not excusing my actions, mind you, I--I just --
God, I'm embarrassed.
Why, Felix-san? If I had required your expertise, I would have sent someone to wake you.
No, you simply spared yourself many hours of frustration.

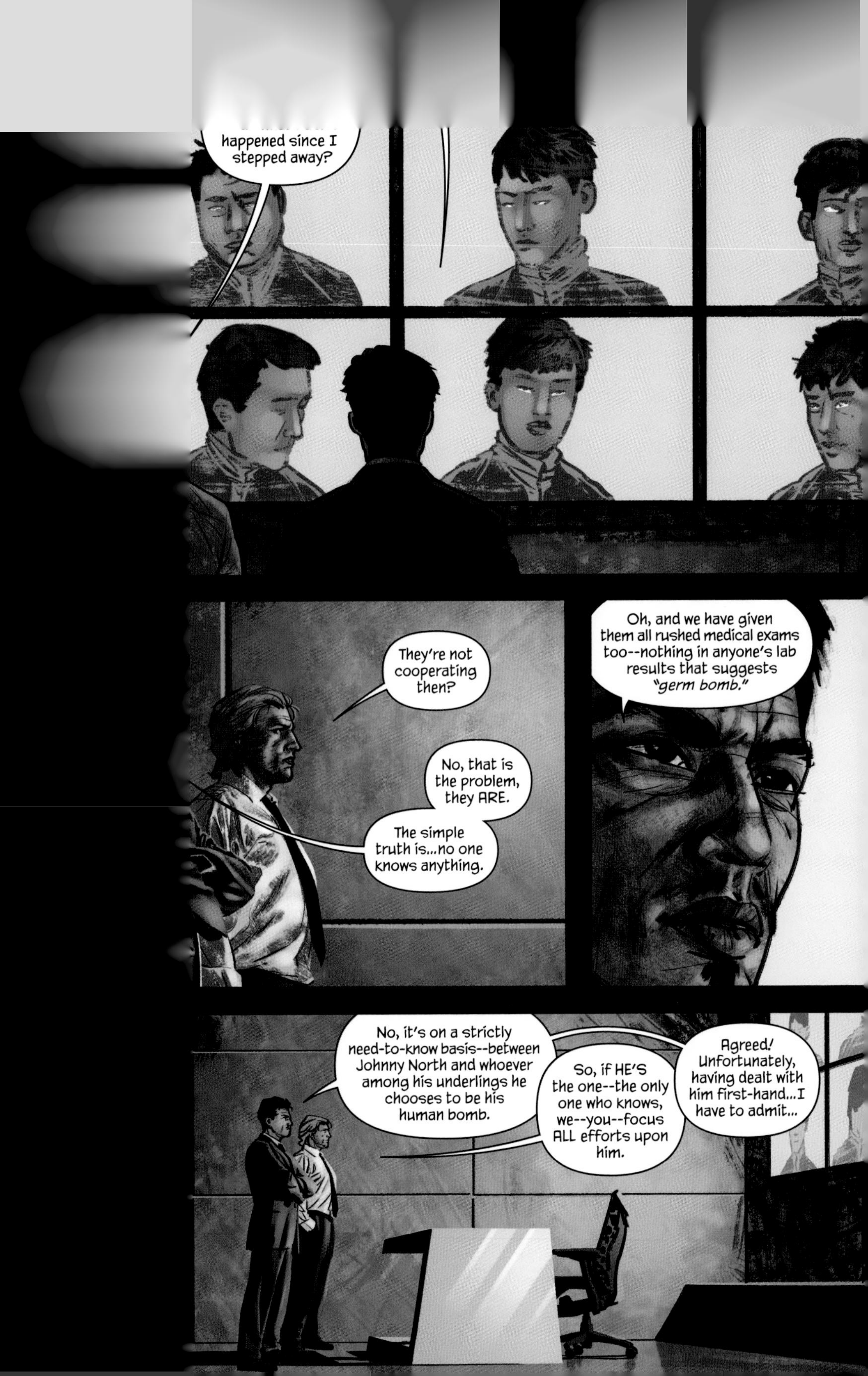
happened since I stepped away?
They're not cooperating then?
No, that is the problem, they ARE.
The simple truth is...no one knows anything.
Oh, and we have given them all rushed medical exams too--nothing in anyone's lab results that suggests *"germ bomb."*
No, it's on a strictly need-to-know basis--between Johnny North and whoever among his underlings he chooses to be his human bomb.
So, if HE'S the one--the only one who knows, we--you--focus ALL efforts upon him.
Agreed! Unfortunately, having dealt with him first-hand...I have to admit...

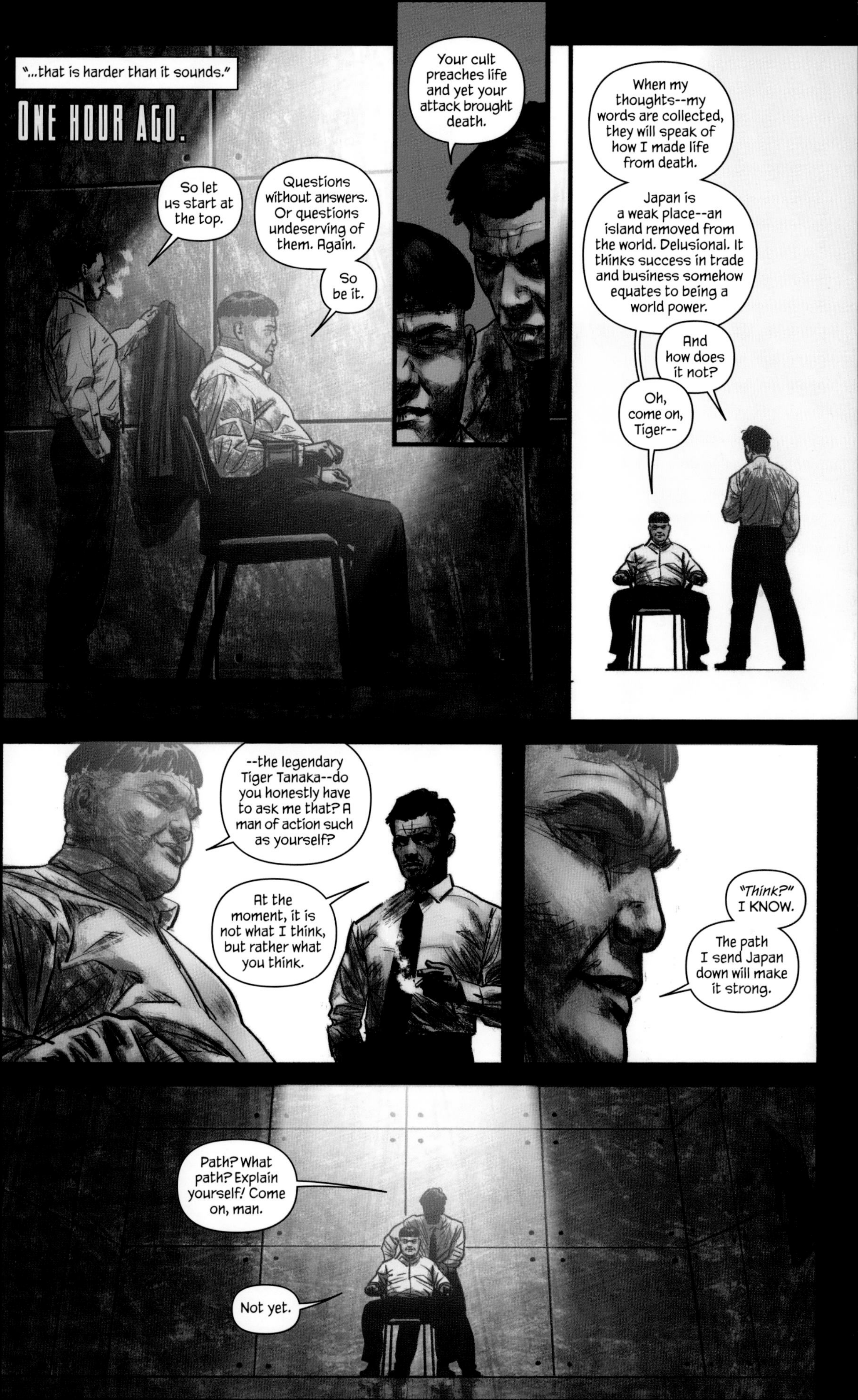
"...that is harder than it sounds."
ONE HOUR AGO.
So let us start at the top.
Questions without answers. Or questions undeserving of them. Again.
So be it.
Your cult preaches life and yet your attack brought death.
When my thoughts--my words are collected, they will speak of how I made life from death.
Japan is a weak place--an island removed from the world. Delusional. It thinks success in trade and business somehow equates to being a world power.
And how does it not?
Oh, come on, Tiger--
--the legendary Tiger Tanaka--do you honestly have to ask me that? A man of action such as yourself?
At the moment, it is not what I think, but rather what you think.
"Think?" I KNOW.
The path I send Japan down will make it strong.
Path? What path? Explain yourself! Come on, man.
Not yet.

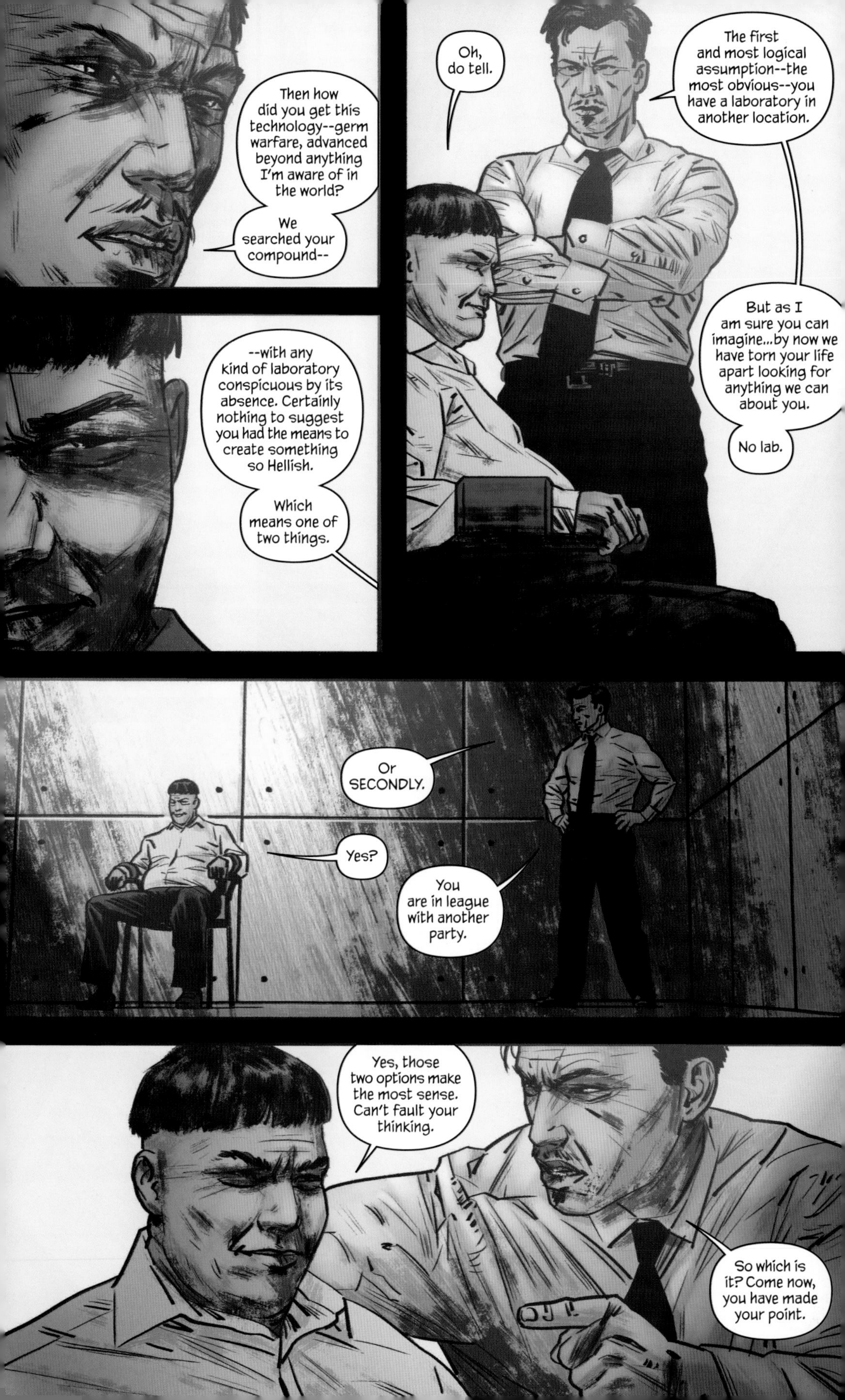
Then how did you get this technology--germ warfare, advanced beyond anything I'm aware of in the world?
We searched your compound--
--with any kind of laboratory conspicuous by its absence. Certainly nothing to suggest you had the means to create something so Hellish.
Which means one of two things.
Oh, do tell.
The first and most logical assumption--the most obvious--you have a laboratory in another location.
But as I am sure you can imagine...by now we have torn your life apart looking for anything we can about you.
No lab.
Or SECONDLY.
Yes?
You are in league with another party.
Yes, those two options make the most sense. Can't fault your thinking.
So which is it? Come now, you have made your point.

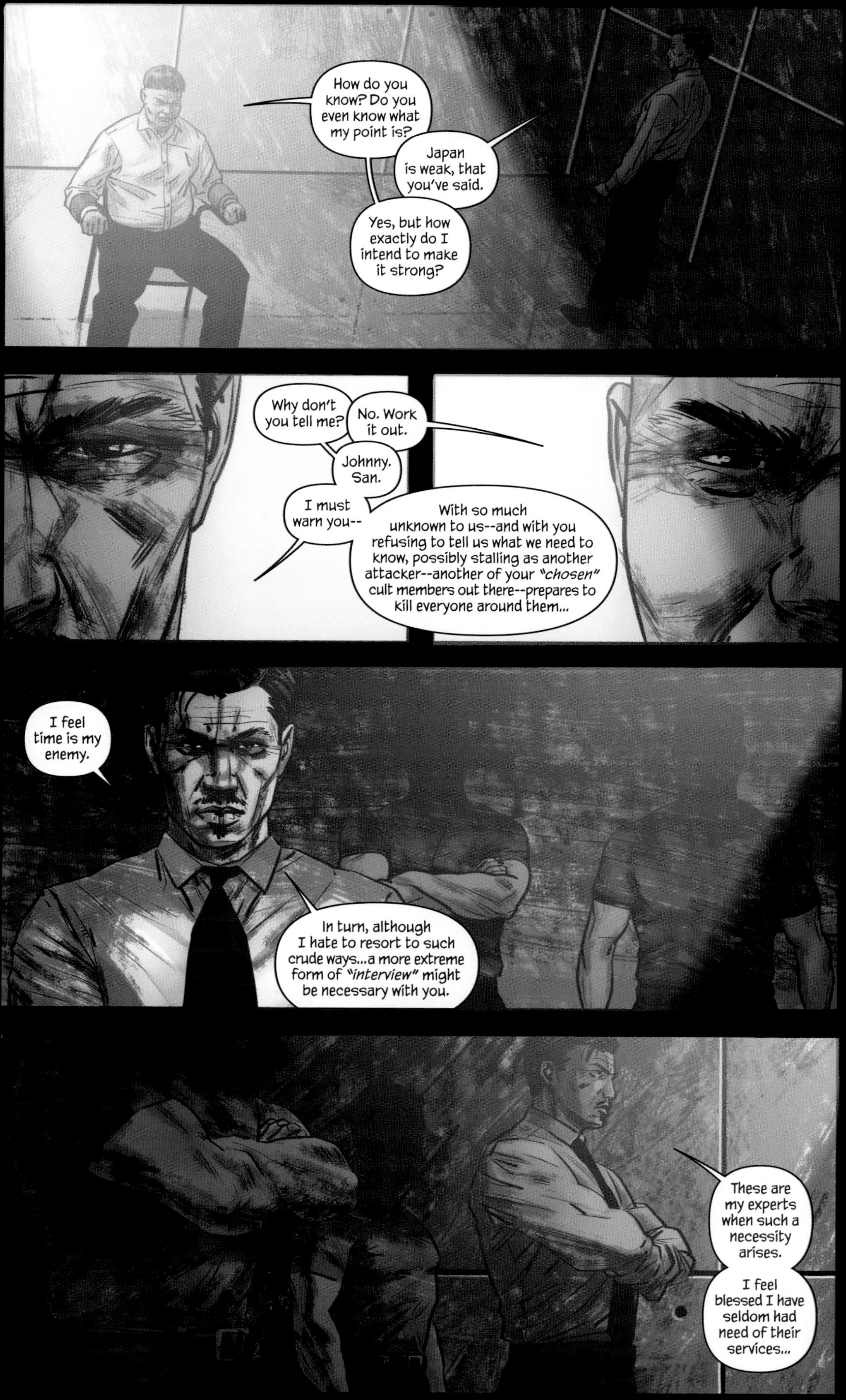
How do you know? Do you even know what my point is?
Japan is weak, that you've said.
Yes, but how exactly do I intend to make it strong?
Why don't you tell me?
No. Work it out.
Johnny. San.
I must warn you--
With so much unknown to us--and with you refusing to tell us what we need to know, possibly stalling as another attacker--another of your "chosen" cult members out there--prepares to kill everyone around them...
I feel time is my enemy.
In turn, although I hate to resort to such crude ways...a more extreme form of "interview" might be necessary with you.
These are my experts when such a necessity arises.
I feel blessed I have seldom had need of their services...

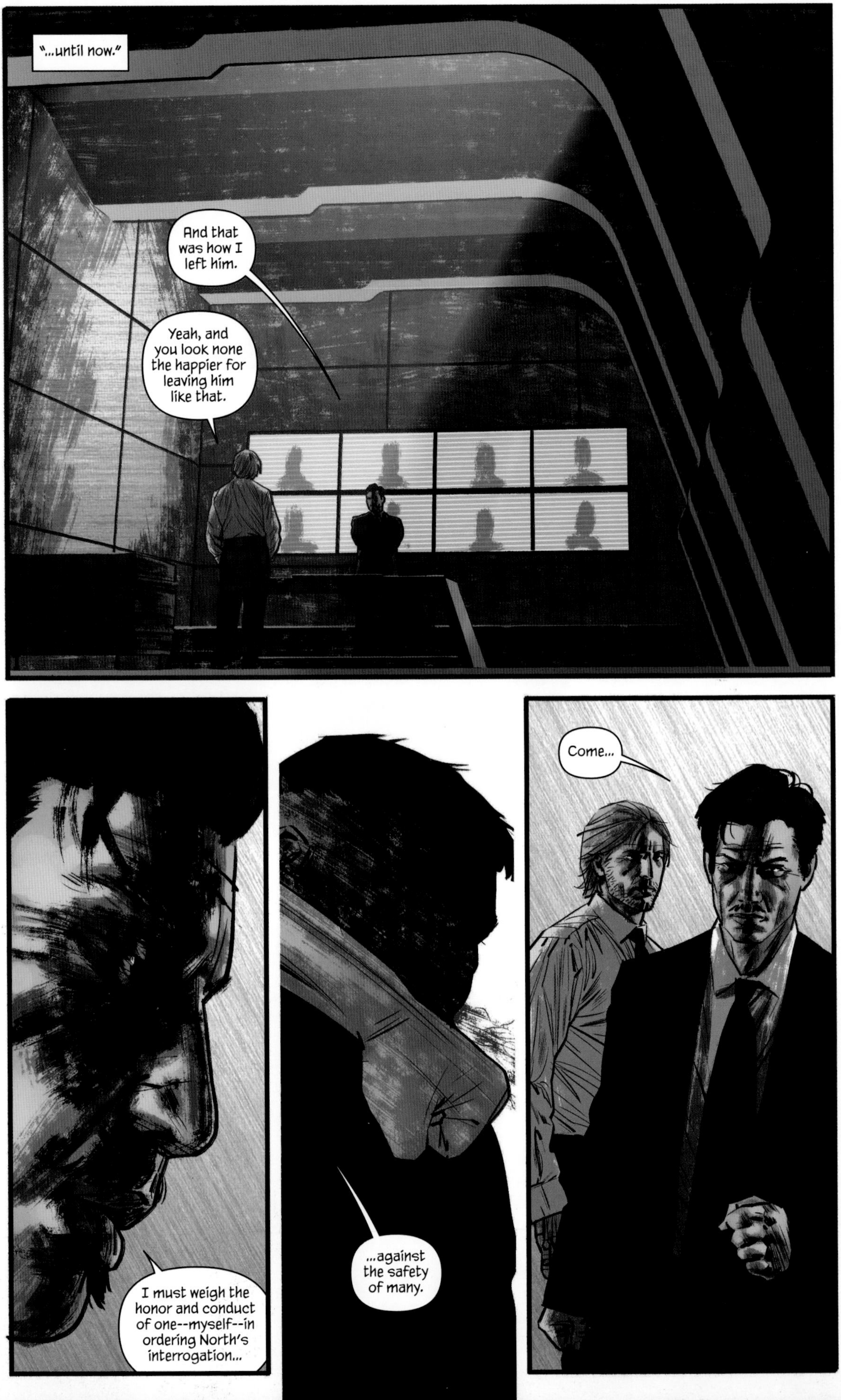
"...until now."
And that was how I left him.
Yeah, and you look none the happier for leaving him like that.
I must weigh the honor and conduct of one--myself--in ordering North's interrogation...
...against the safety of many.
Come...

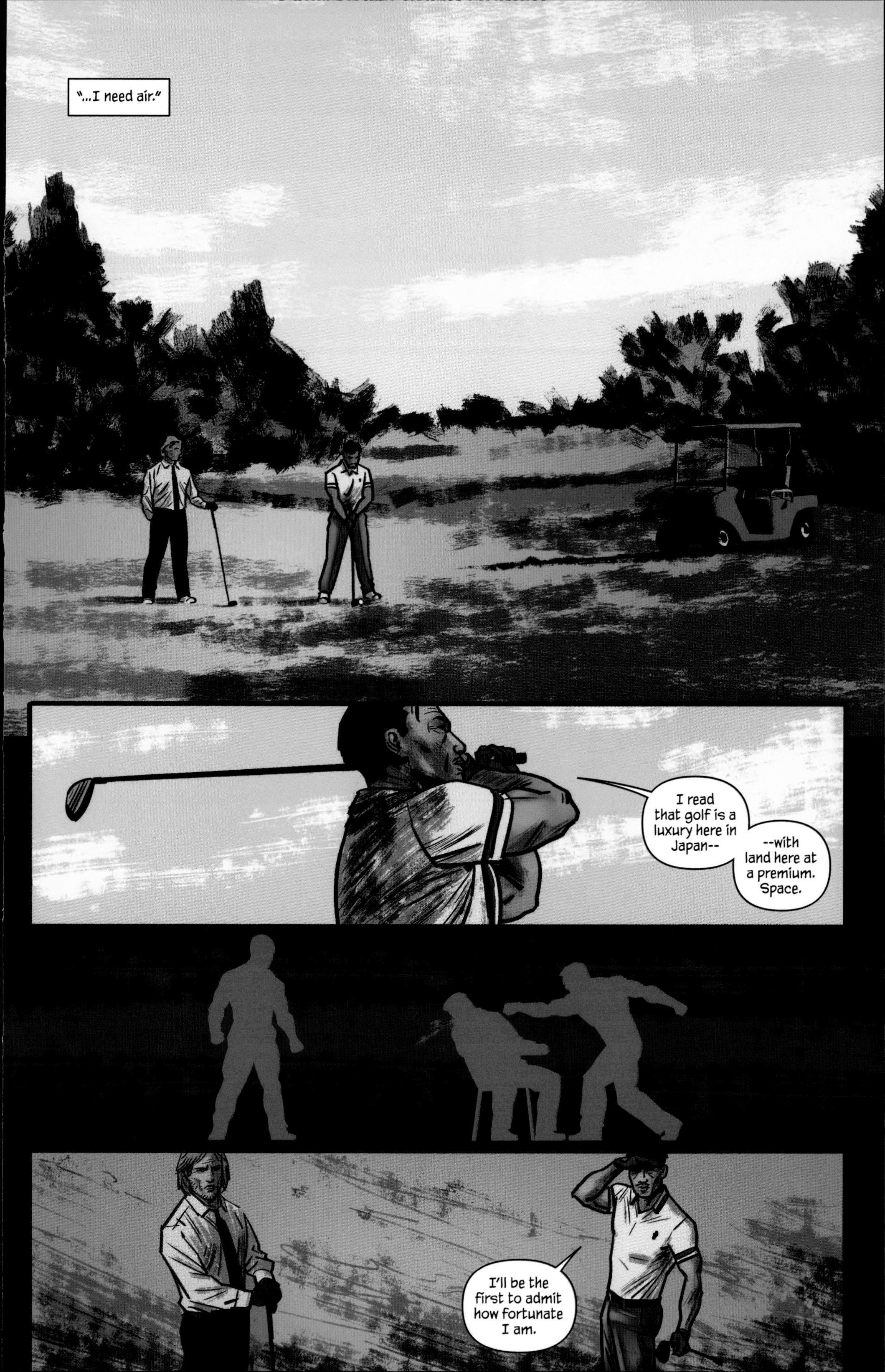
"...I need air."
I read that golf is a luxury here in Japan--
--with land here at a premium. Space.
I'll be the first to admit how fortunate I am.

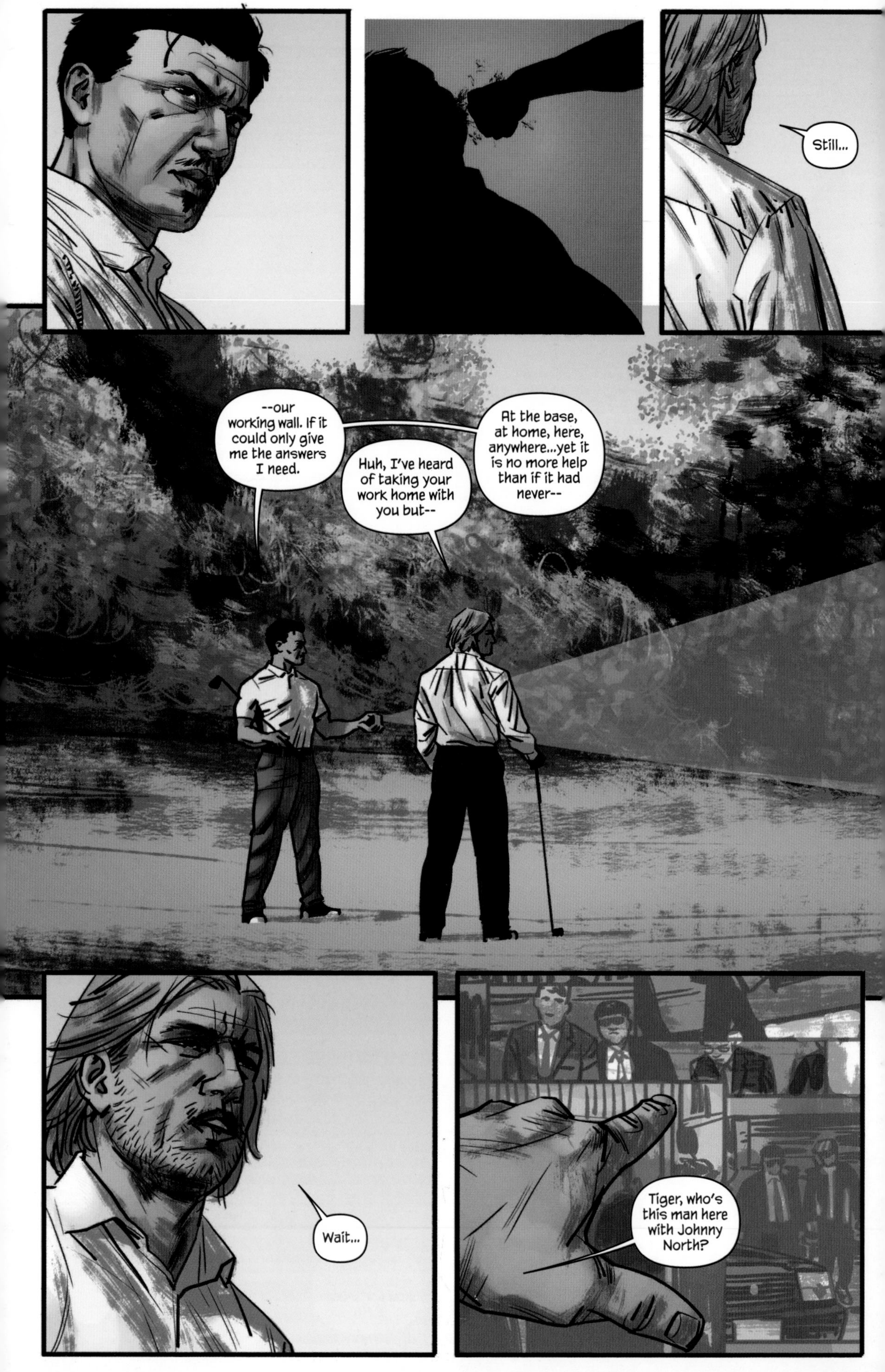
Still...
--our working wall. If it could only give me the answers I need.
Huh, I've heard of taking your work home with you but--
At the base, at home, here, anywhere...yet it is no more help than if it had never--
Wait...
Tiger, who's this man here with Johnny North?

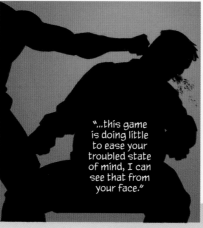

"...this game is doing little to ease your troubled state of mind, I can see that from your face."

Well if you are so good at seeing, look this way--

I do not know.

One of the few faces we are still working to identify. Why? Do you know him?

Not a clue. All I DO know is...

"...I saw this same guy yesterday with Alena Davoff."

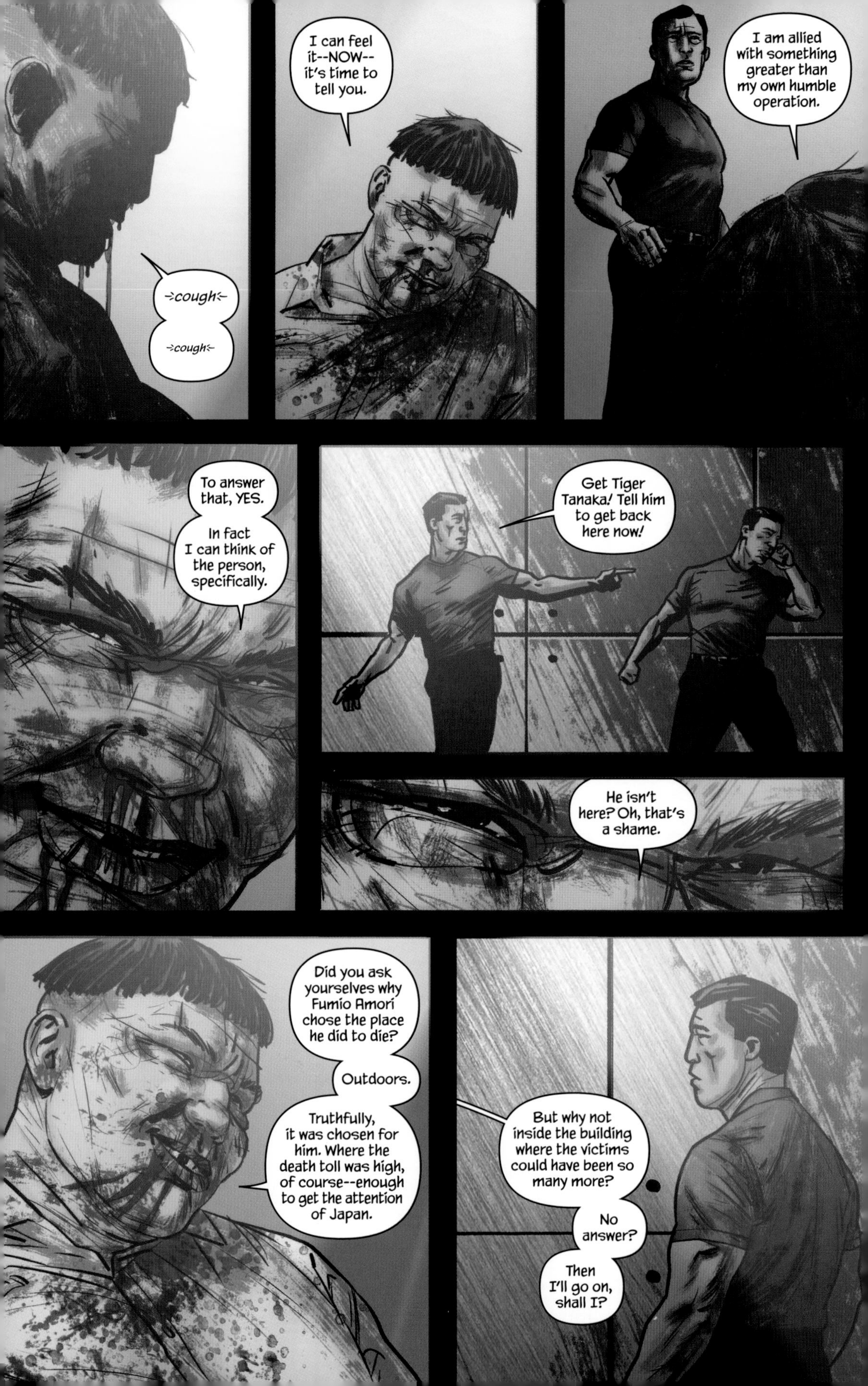

>cough<
>cough<
I can feel it--NOW-- it's time to tell you.
I am allied with something greater than my own humble operation.
To answer that, YES.
In fact I can think of the person, specifically.
Get Tiger Tanaka! Tell him to get back here now!
He isn't here? Oh, that's a shame.
Did you ask yourselves why Fumio Amori chose the place he did to die?
Outdoors.
Truthfully, it was chosen for him. Where the death toll was high, of course--enough to get the attention of Japan.
But why not inside the building where the victims could have been so many more?
No answer?
Then I'll go on, shall I?

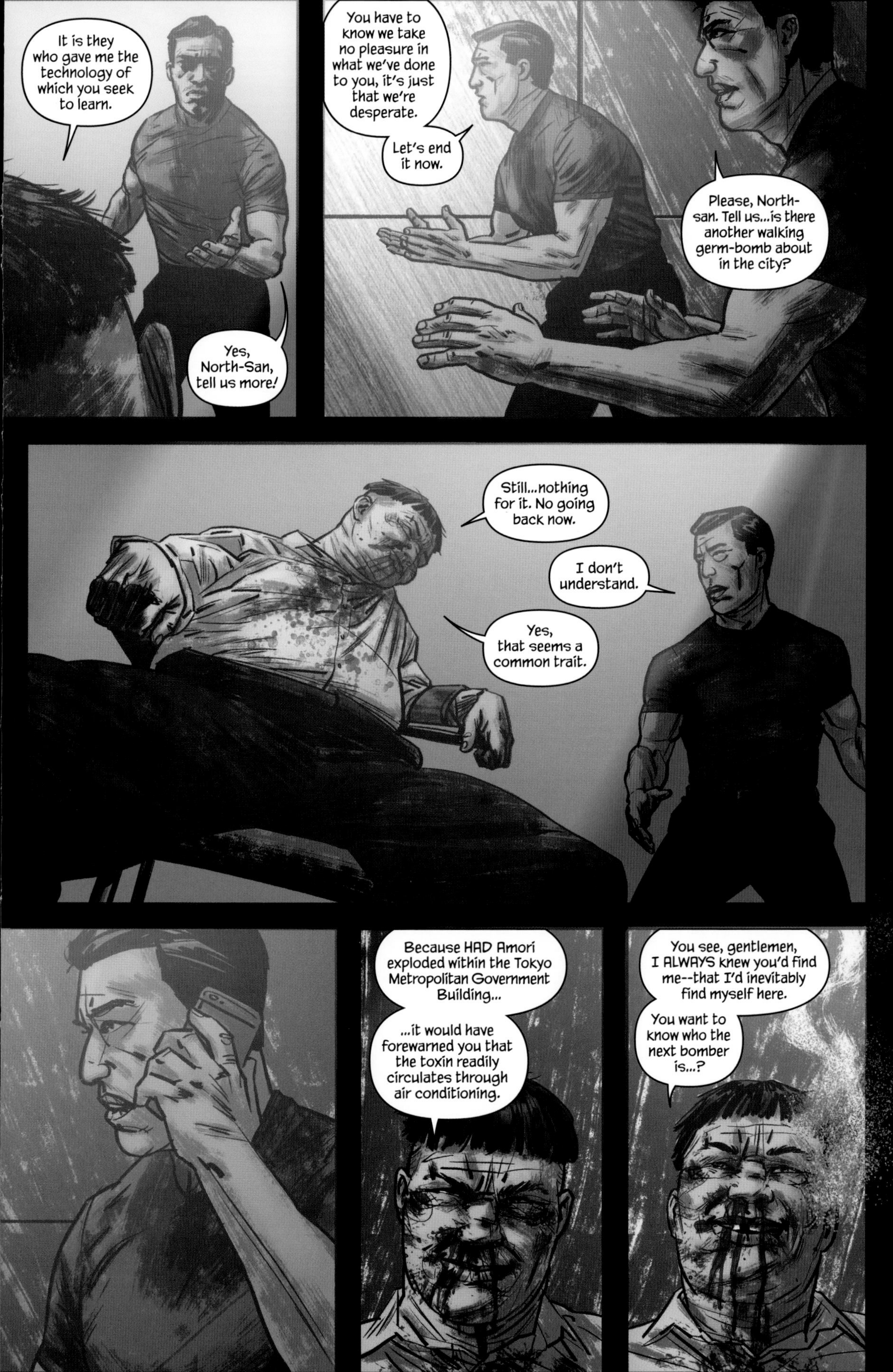
It is they who gave me the technology of which you seek to learn.
Yes, North-San, tell us more!
You have to know we take no pleasure in what we've done to you, it's just that we're desperate.
Let's end it now.
Please, North-san. Tell us...is there another walking germ-bomb about in the city?
Still...nothing for it. No going back now.
I don't understand.
Yes, that seems a common trait.
Because HAD Amori exploded within the Tokyo Metropolitan Government Building...
...it would have forewarned you that the toxin readily circulates through air conditioning.
You see, gentlemen, I ALWAYS knew you'd find me--that I'd inevitably find myself here.
You want to know who the next bomber is...?

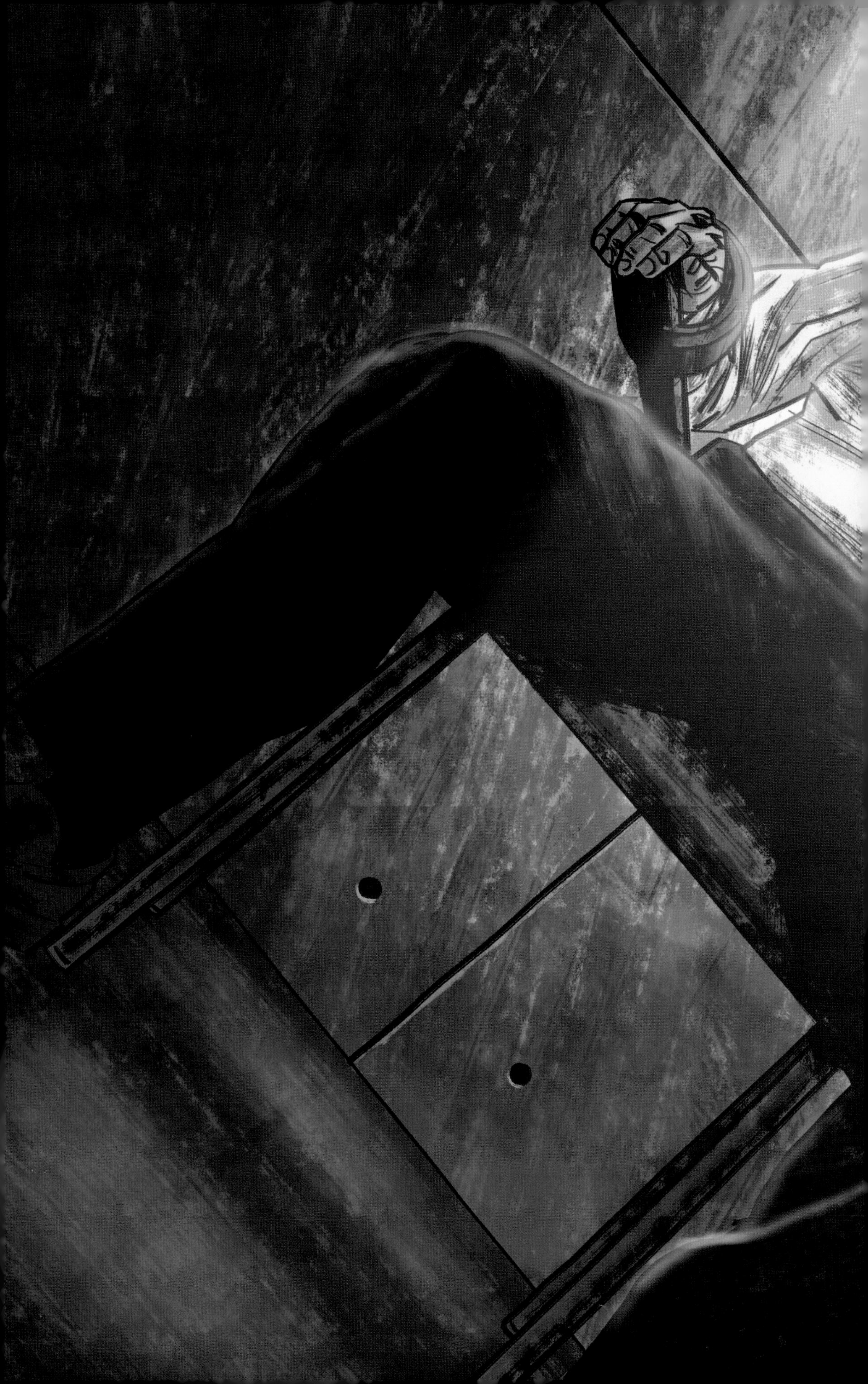

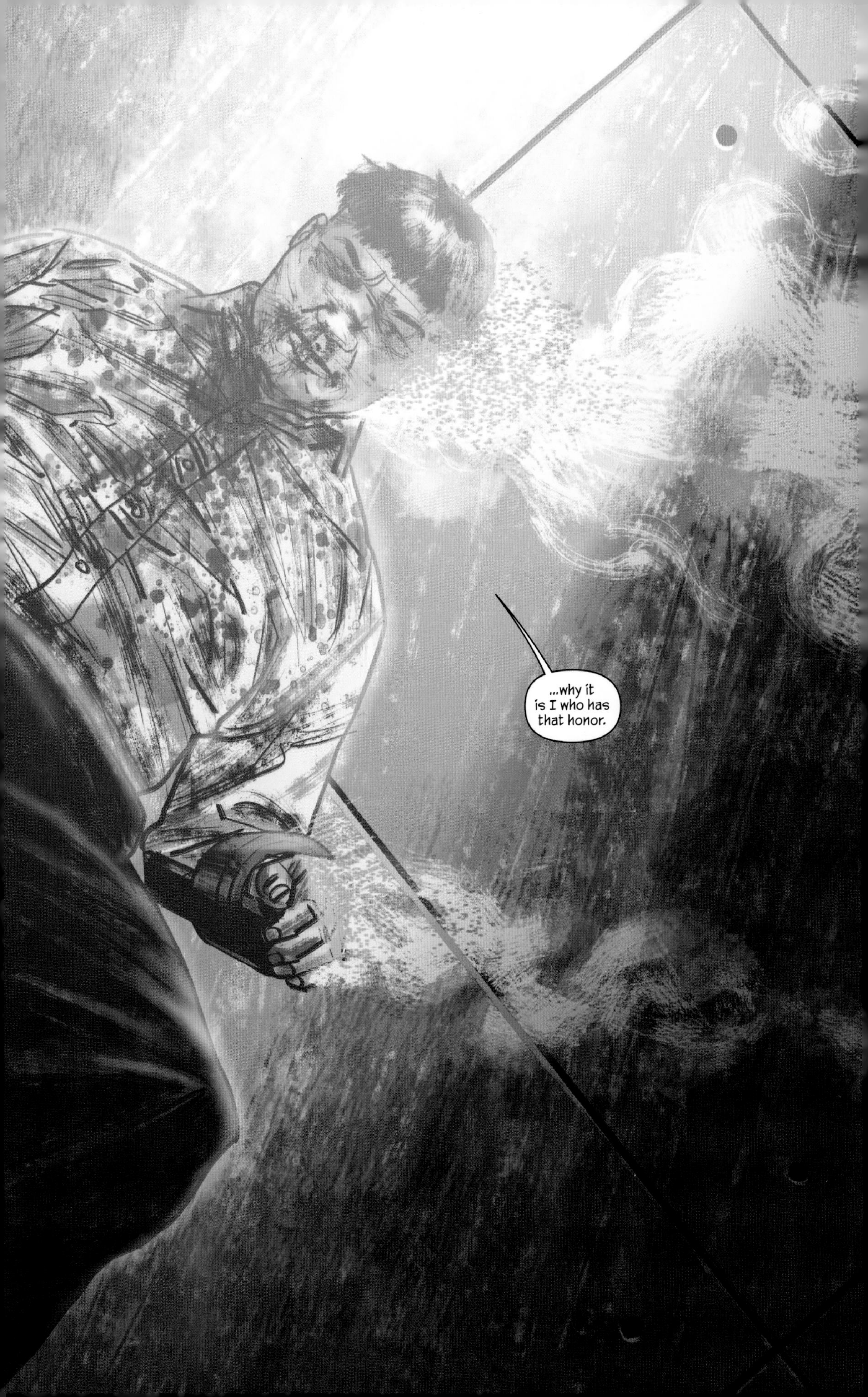
...why it is I who has that honor.

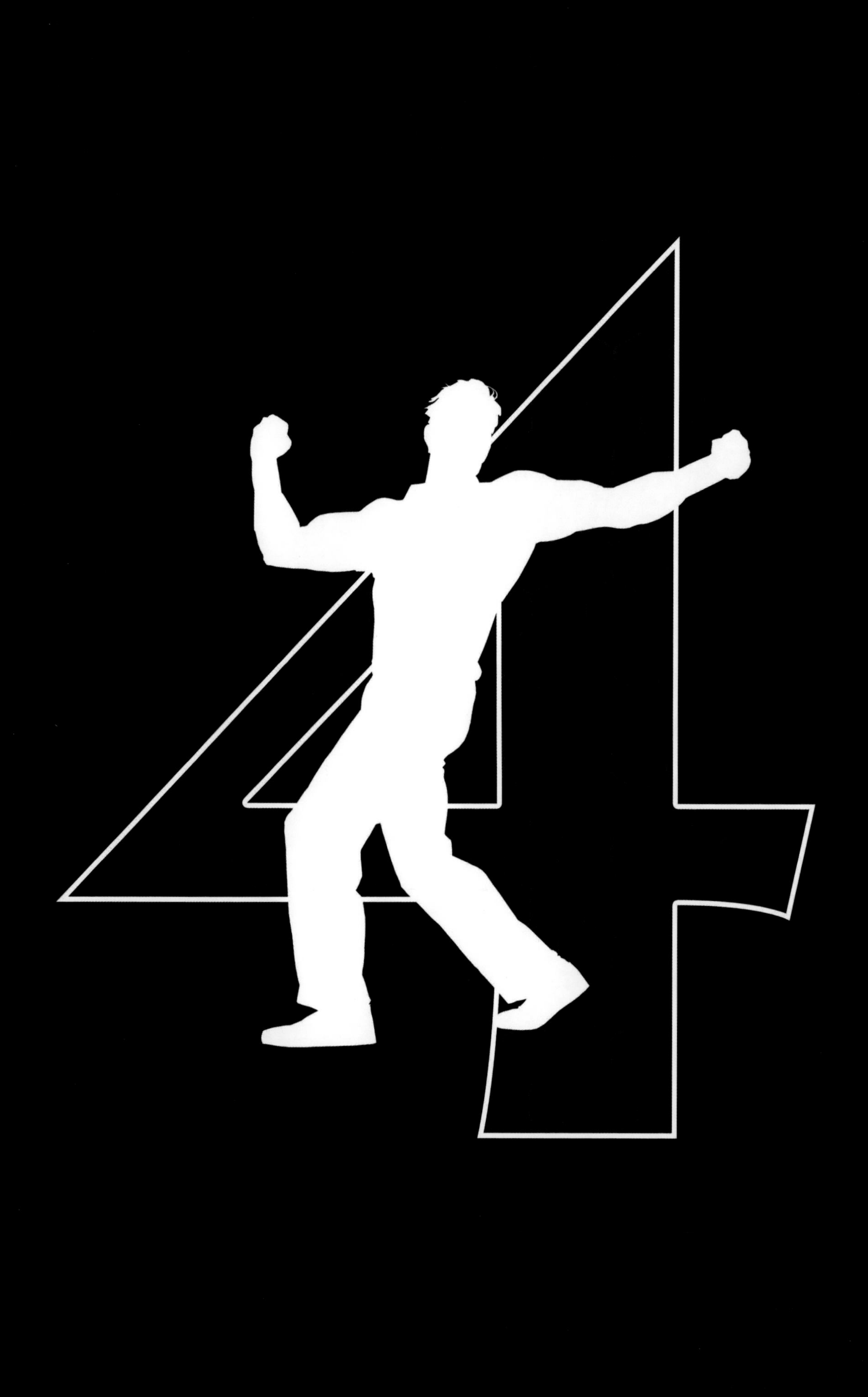

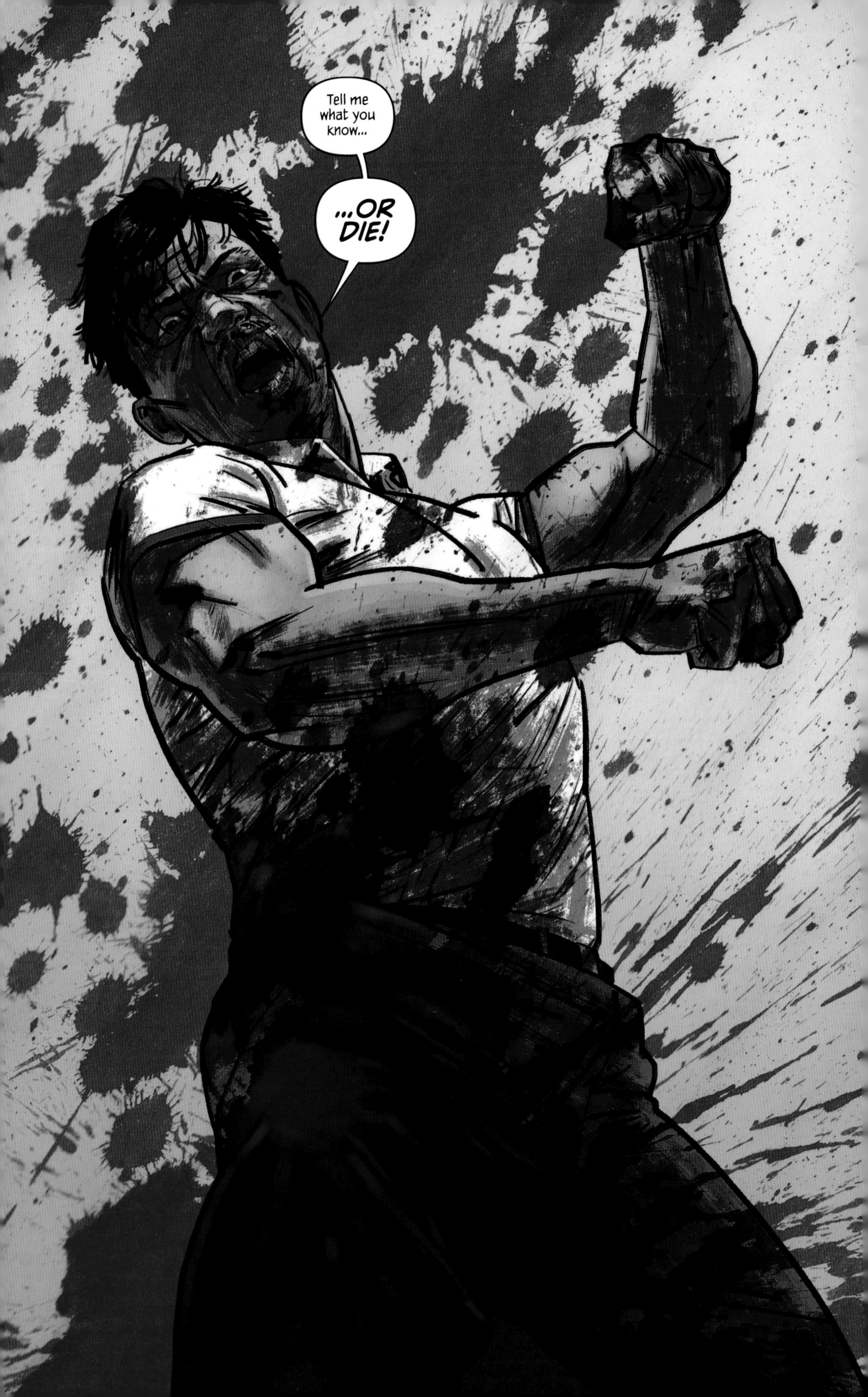
Tell me what you know...
...OR DIE!

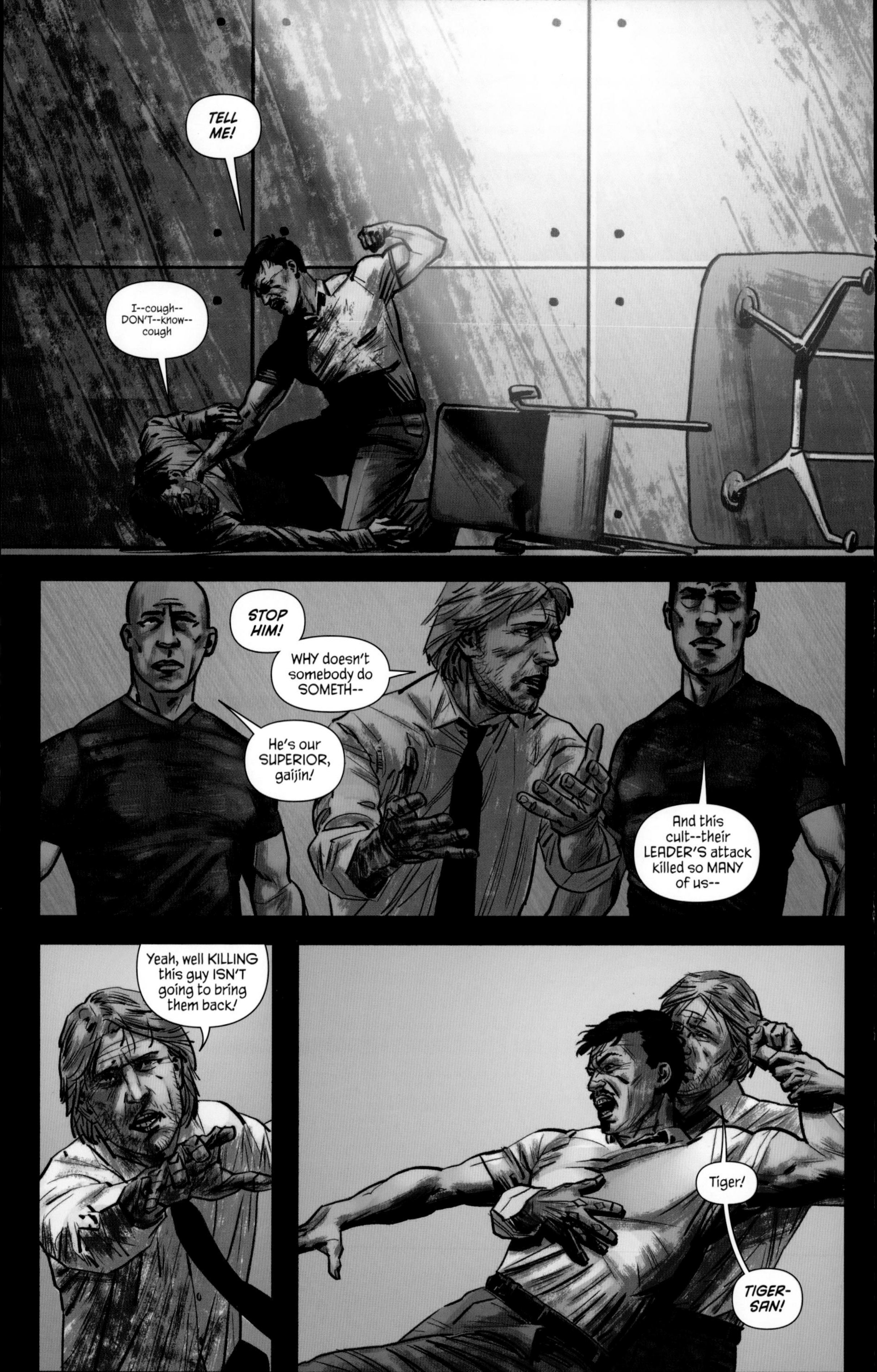
TELL ME!
I--cough--DON'T--know--cough
STOP HIM!
WHY doesn't somebody do SOMETH--
He's our SUPERIOR, gaijin!
And this cult--their LEADER'S attack killed so MANY of us--
Yeah, well KILLING this guy ISN'T going to bring them back!
Tiger!
TIGER-SAN!

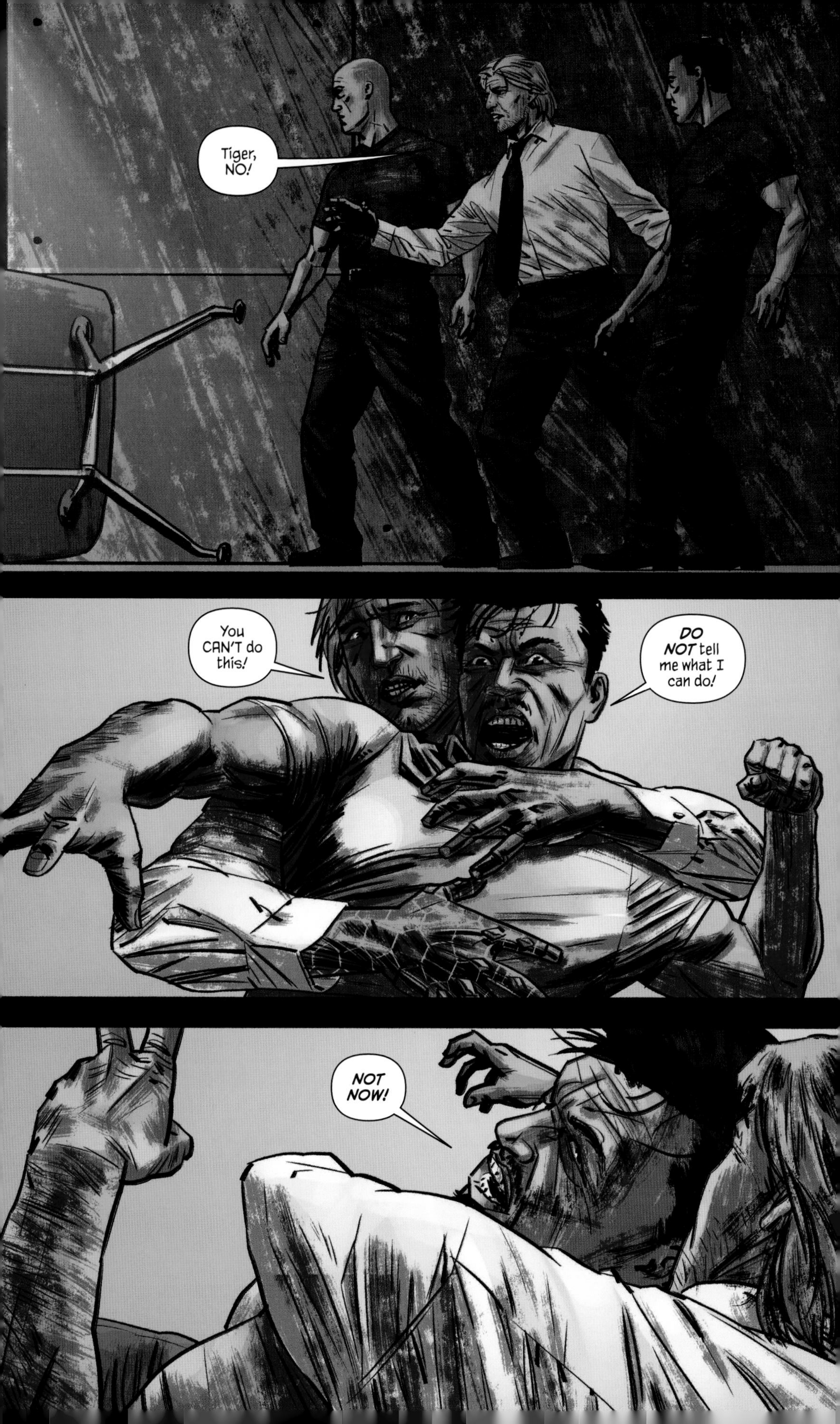
Tiger, NO!
You CAN'T do this!
DO NOT tell me what I can do!
NOT NOW!

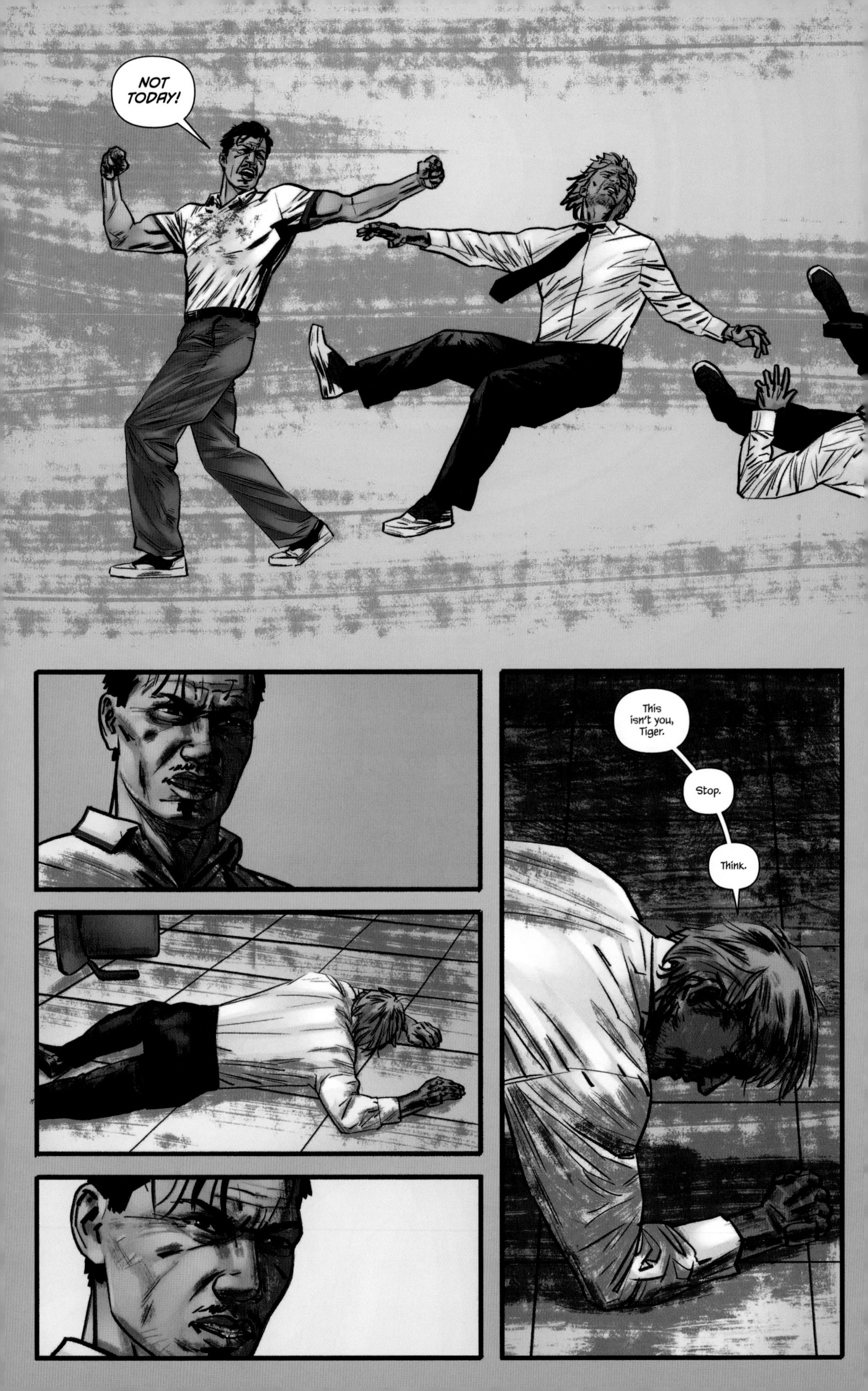
NOT TODAY!
This isn't you, Tiger.
Stop.
Think.

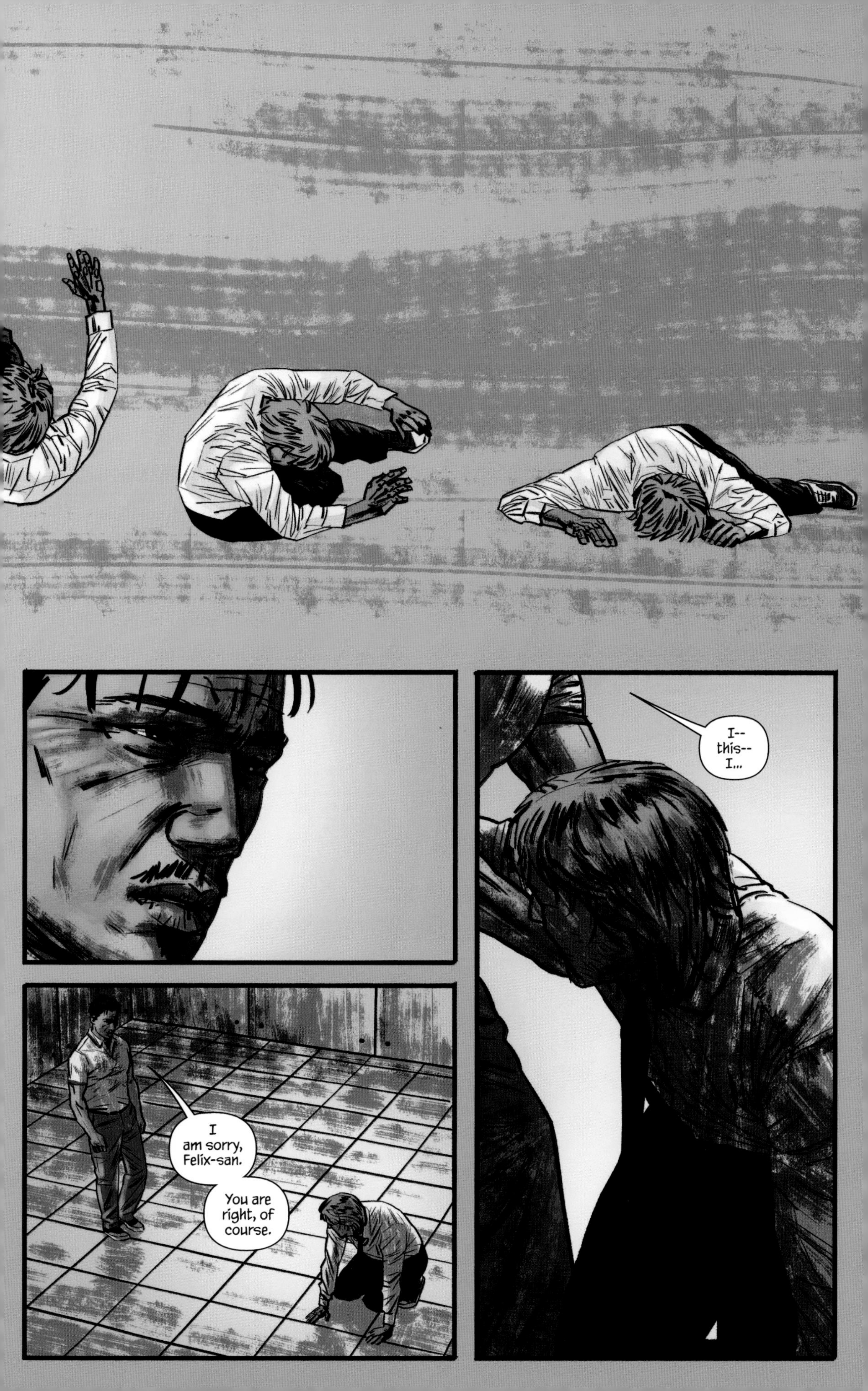
I-- this-- I...
I am sorry, Felix-san.
You are right, of course.

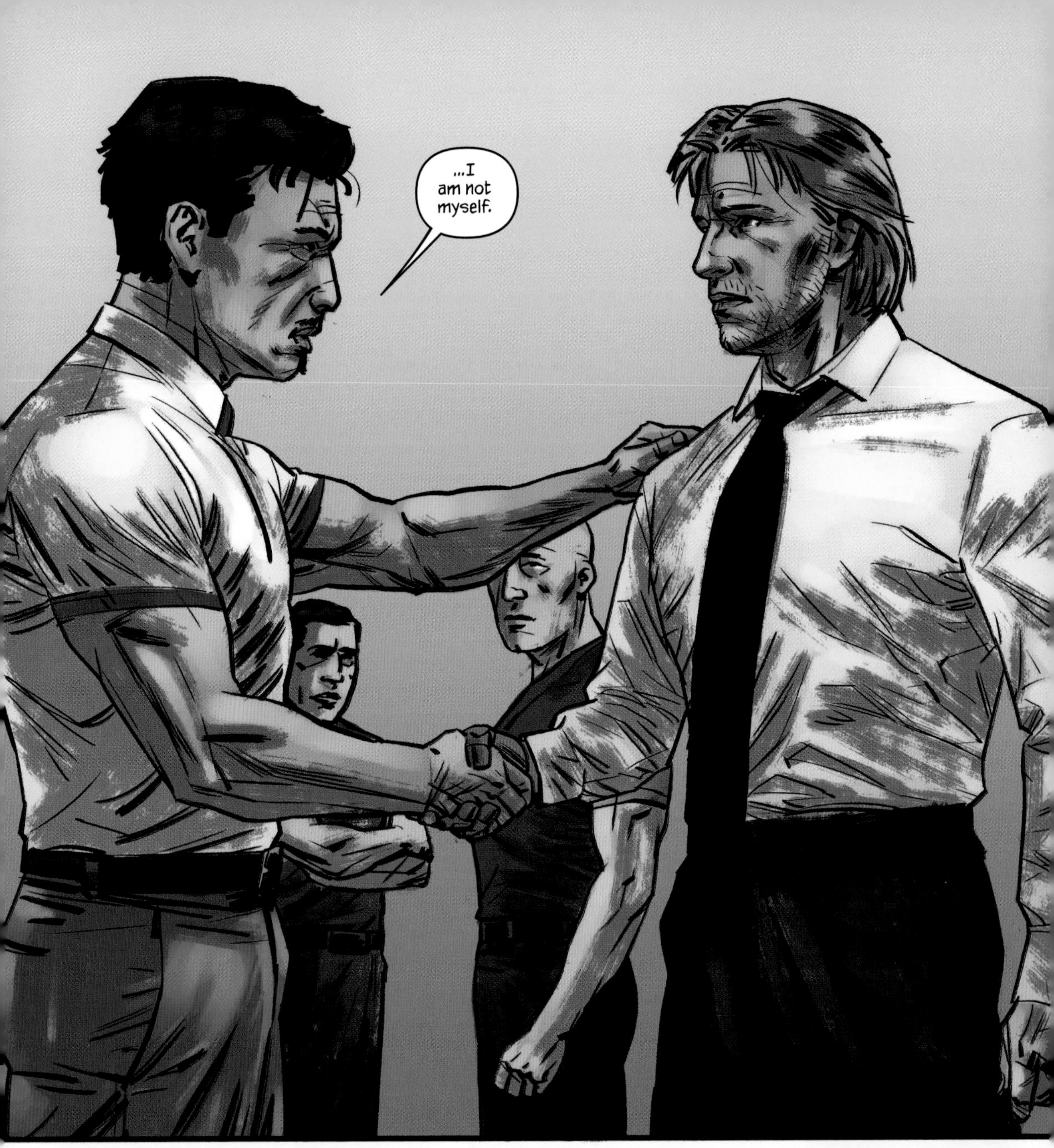
...I am not myself.
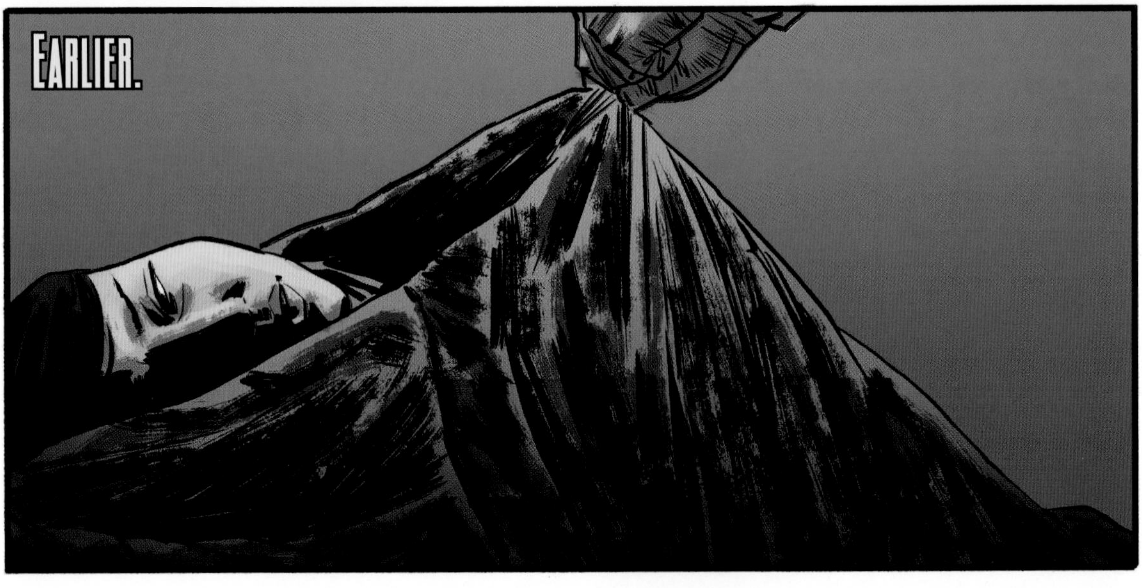
EARLIER.

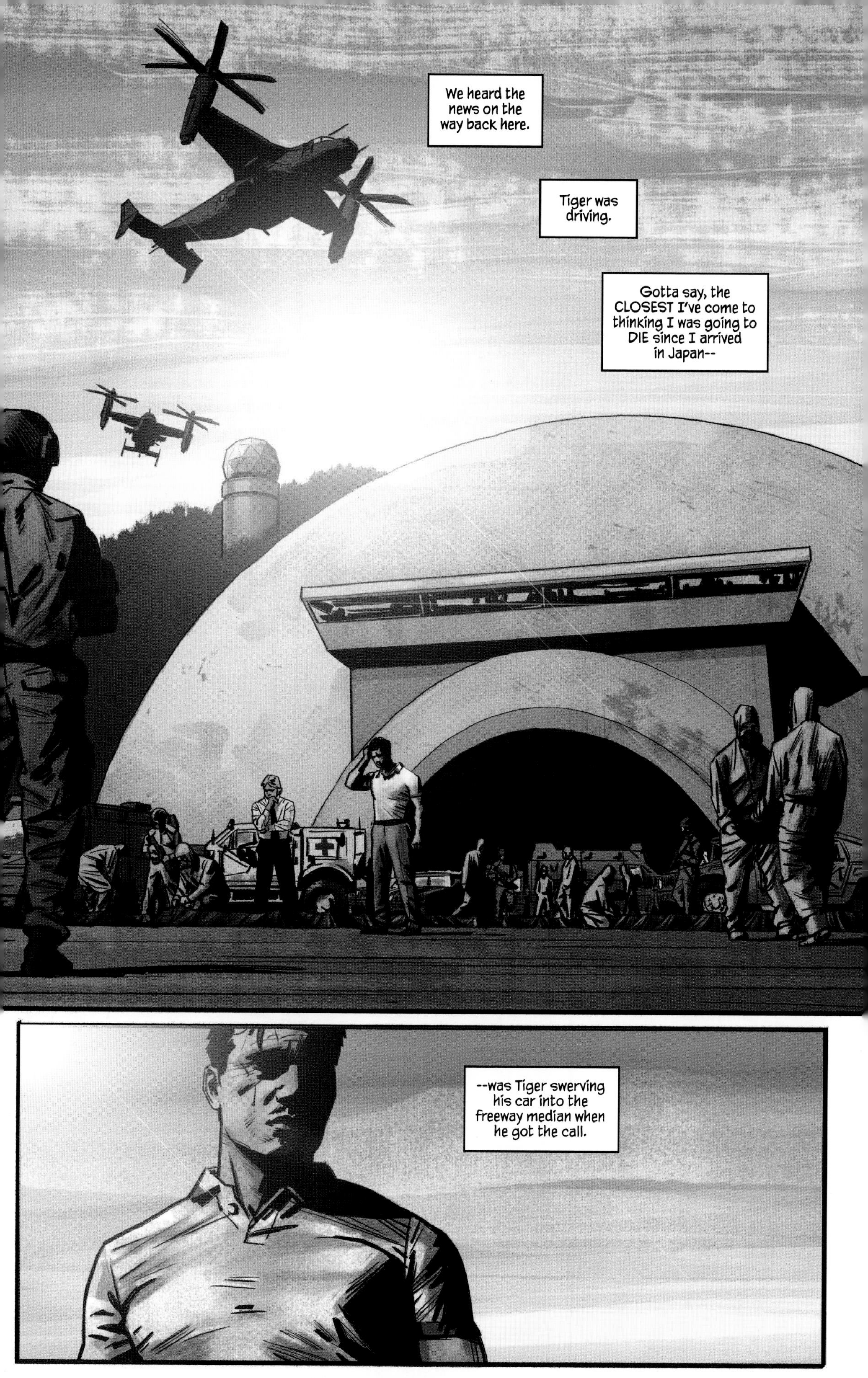
We heard the news on the way back here.
Tiger was driving.
Gotta say, the CLOSEST I've come to thinking I was going to DIE since I arrived in Japan--
--was Tiger swerving his car into the freeway median when he got the call.

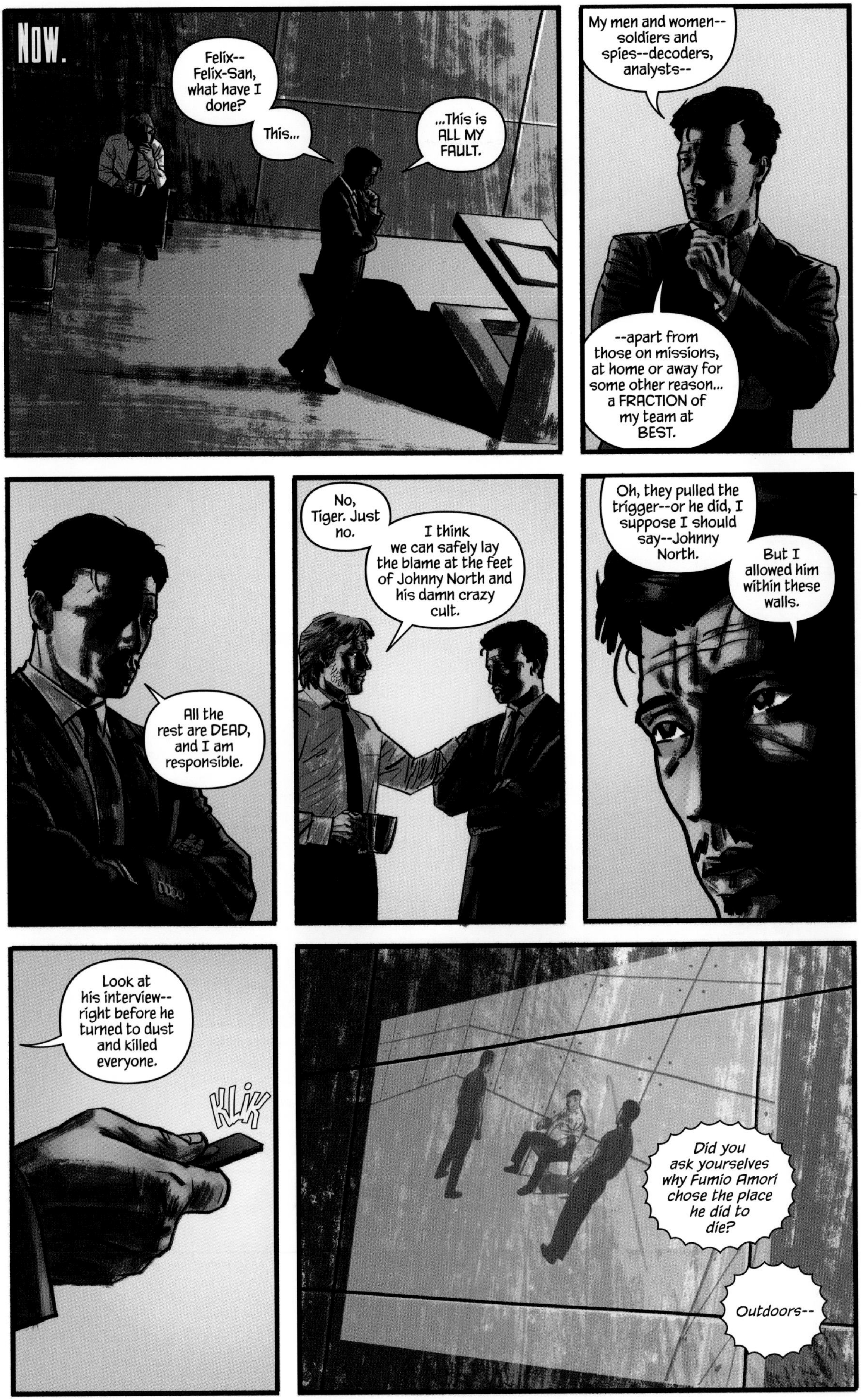
NOW.
Felix--
Felix-San, what have I done?
This...
...This is ALL MY FAULT.
My men and women--soldiers and spies--decoders, analysts--
--apart from those on missions, at home or away for some other reason... a FRACTION of my team at BEST.
All the rest are DEAD, and I am responsible.
No, Tiger. Just no.
I think we can safely lay the blame at the feet of Johnny North and his damn crazy cult.
Oh, they pulled the trigger--or he did, I suppose I should say--Johnny North.
But I allowed him within these walls.
Look at his interview--right before he turned to dust and killed everyone.
KLIK
Did you ask yourselves why Fumio Amori chose the place he did to die?
Outdoors--

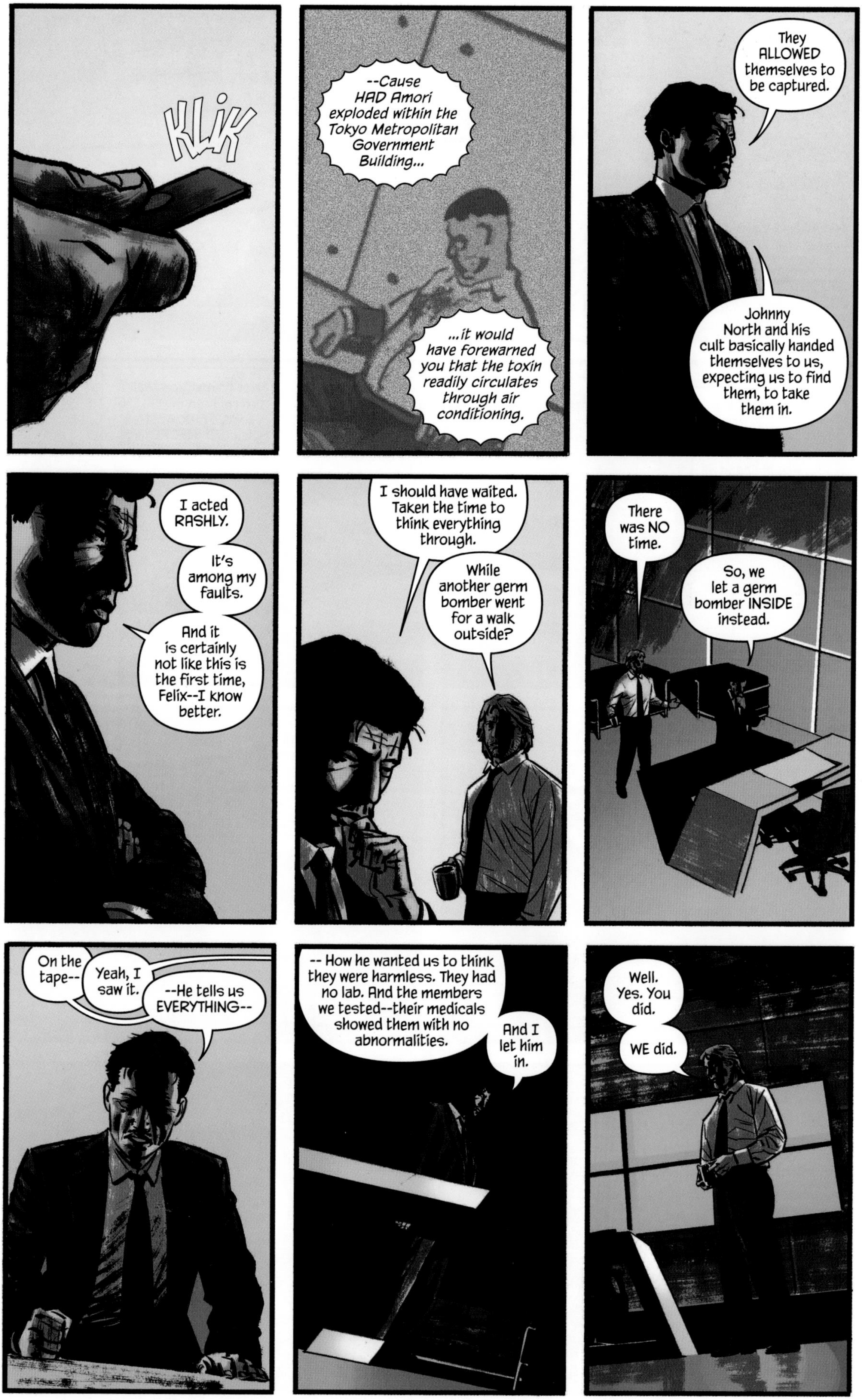
KLIK
--Cause HAD Amori exploded within the Tokyo Metropolitan Government Building...
...it would have forewarned you that the toxin readily circulates through air conditioning.
They ALLOWED themselves to be captured.
Johnny North and his cult basically handed themselves to us, expecting us to find them, to take them in.
I acted RASHLY.
It's among my faults.
And it is certainly not like this is the first time, Felix--I know better.
I should have waited. Taken the time to think everything through.
While another germ bomber went for a walk outside?
There was NO time.
So, we let a germ bomber INSIDE instead.
On the tape--
Yeah, I saw it.
--He tells us EVERYTHING--
-- How he wanted us to think they were harmless. They had no lab. And the members we tested--their medicals showed them with no abnormalities.
And I let him in.
Well. Yes. You did.
WE did.

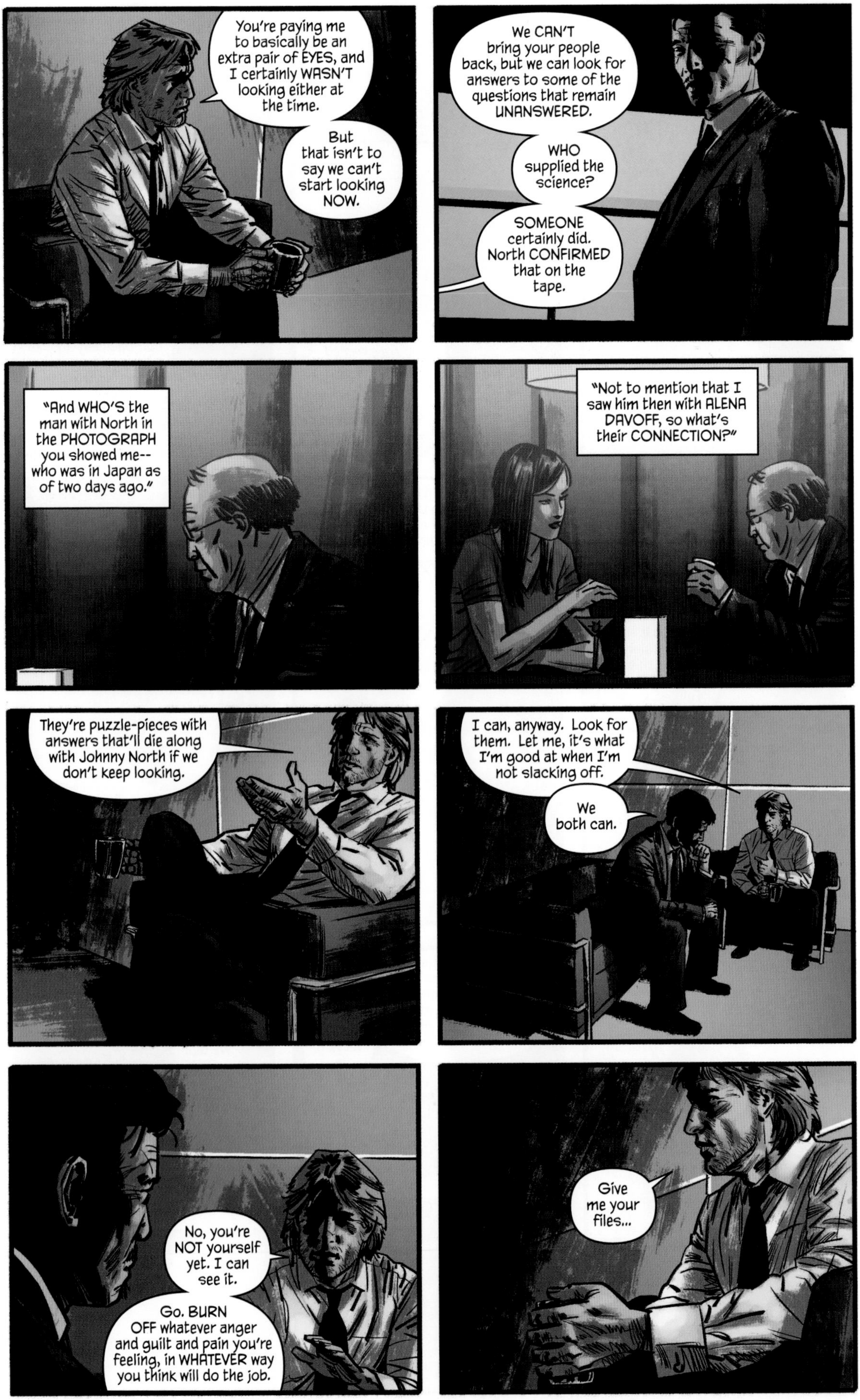
You're paying me to basically be an extra pair of EYES, and I certainly WASN'T looking either at the time.
But that isn't to say we can't start looking NOW.
We CAN'T bring your people back, but we can look for answers to some of the questions that remain UNANSWERED.
WHO supplied the science?
SOMEONE certainly did. North CONFIRMED that on the tape.
"And WHO'S the man with North in the PHOTOGRAPH you showed me--who was in Japan as of two days ago."
"Not to mention that I saw him then with ALENA DAVOFF, so what's their CONNECTION?"
They're puzzle-pieces with answers that'll die along with Johnny North if we don't keep looking.
I can, anyway. Look for them. Let me, it's what I'm good at when I'm not slacking off.
We both can.
No, you're NOT yourself yet. I can see it.
Go. BURN OFF whatever anger and guilt and pain you're feeling, in WHATEVER way you think will do the job.
Give me your files...

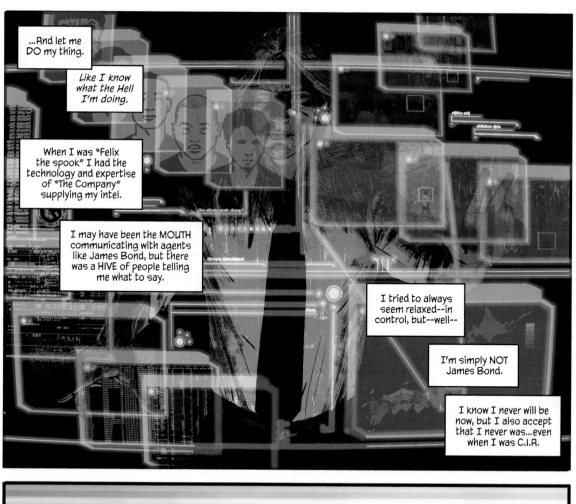

...And let me DO my thing.

Like I know what the Hell I'm doing.

When I was "Felix the spook" I had the technology and expertise of "The Company" supplying my intel.

I may have been the MOUTH communicating with agents like James Bond, but there was a HIVE of people telling me what to say.

I tried to always seem relaxed--in control, but--well--

I'm simply NOT James Bond.

I know I never will be now, but I also accept that I never was...even when I was C.I.A.

At least Tiger isn't here to see how inept I am.

How long it takes me.

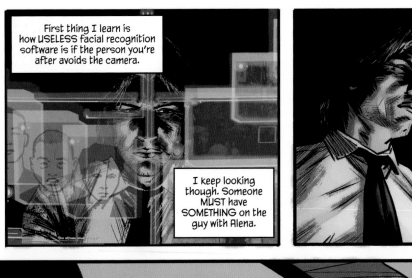

First thing I learn is how USELESS facial recognition software is if the person you're after avoids the camera.

I keep looking though. Someone MUST have SOMETHING on the guy with Alena.

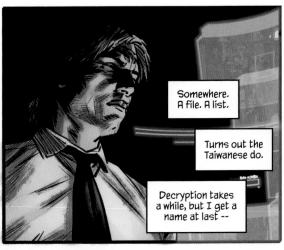

Somewhere. A file. A list.

Turns out the Taiwanese do.

Decryption takes a while, but I get a name at last --

CHOI KI-MOON. North Korean.

And at least according to Taiwanese intel, the man behind murderous acts in many lands.

Foreign agents, politicians, people both at home and abroad viewed as enemies by our chubby friend Kim Jong-Un.

Oh, and get this...last confirmed sighting: Ryanggang Province, North Korea nine months back--same location where a scientist, PARK JU-YUNG, was also last seen.

Although the extent of Ju-yung's work ISN'T known due to North Korea being what it is, he's believed to be the country's leader...

...in the field of BIOLOGICAL WARFARE.

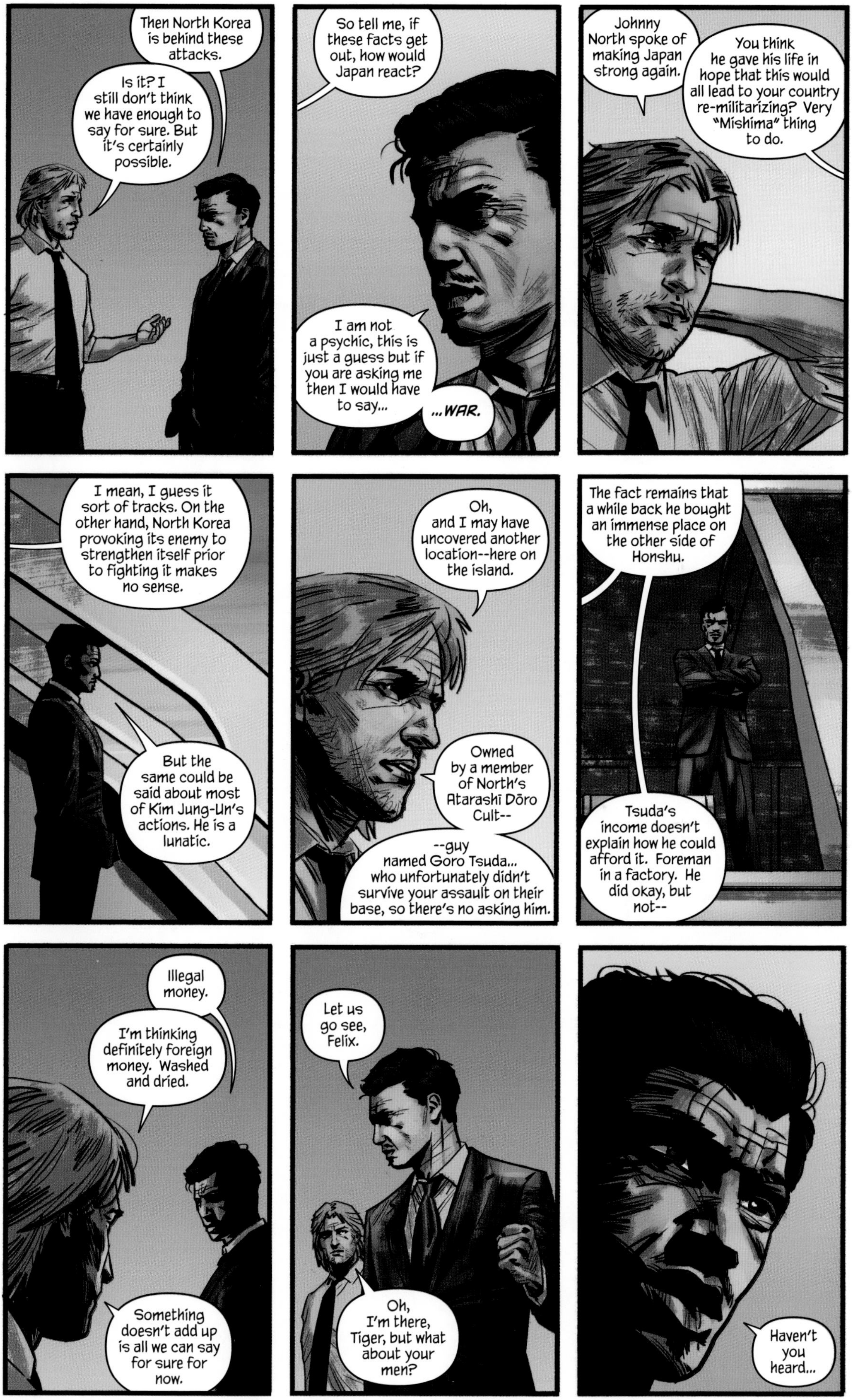

Then North Korea is behind these attacks.
Is it? I still don't think we have enough to say for sure. But it's certainly possible.
So tell me, if these facts get out, how would Japan react?
I am not a psychic, this is just a guess but if you are asking me then I would have to say...
...WAR.
Johnny North spoke of making Japan strong again.
You think he gave his life in hope that this would all lead to your country re-militarizing? Very "Mishima" thing to do.
I mean, I guess it sort of tracks. On the other hand, North Korea provoking its enemy to strengthen itself prior to fighting it makes no sense.
But the same could be said about most of Kim Jung-Un's actions. He is a lunatic.
Oh, and I may have uncovered another location--here on the island.
Owned by a member of North's Atarashī Dōro Cult--
--guy named Goro Tsuda... who unfortunately didn't survive your assault on their base, so there's no asking him.
The fact remains that a while back he bought an immense place on the other side of Honshu.
Tsuda's income doesn't explain how he could afford it. Foreman in a factory. He did okay, but not--
Illegal money.
I'm thinking definitely foreign money. Washed and dried.
Something doesn't add up is all we can say for sure for now.
Let us go see, Felix.
Oh, I'm there, Tiger, but what about your men?
Haven't you heard...

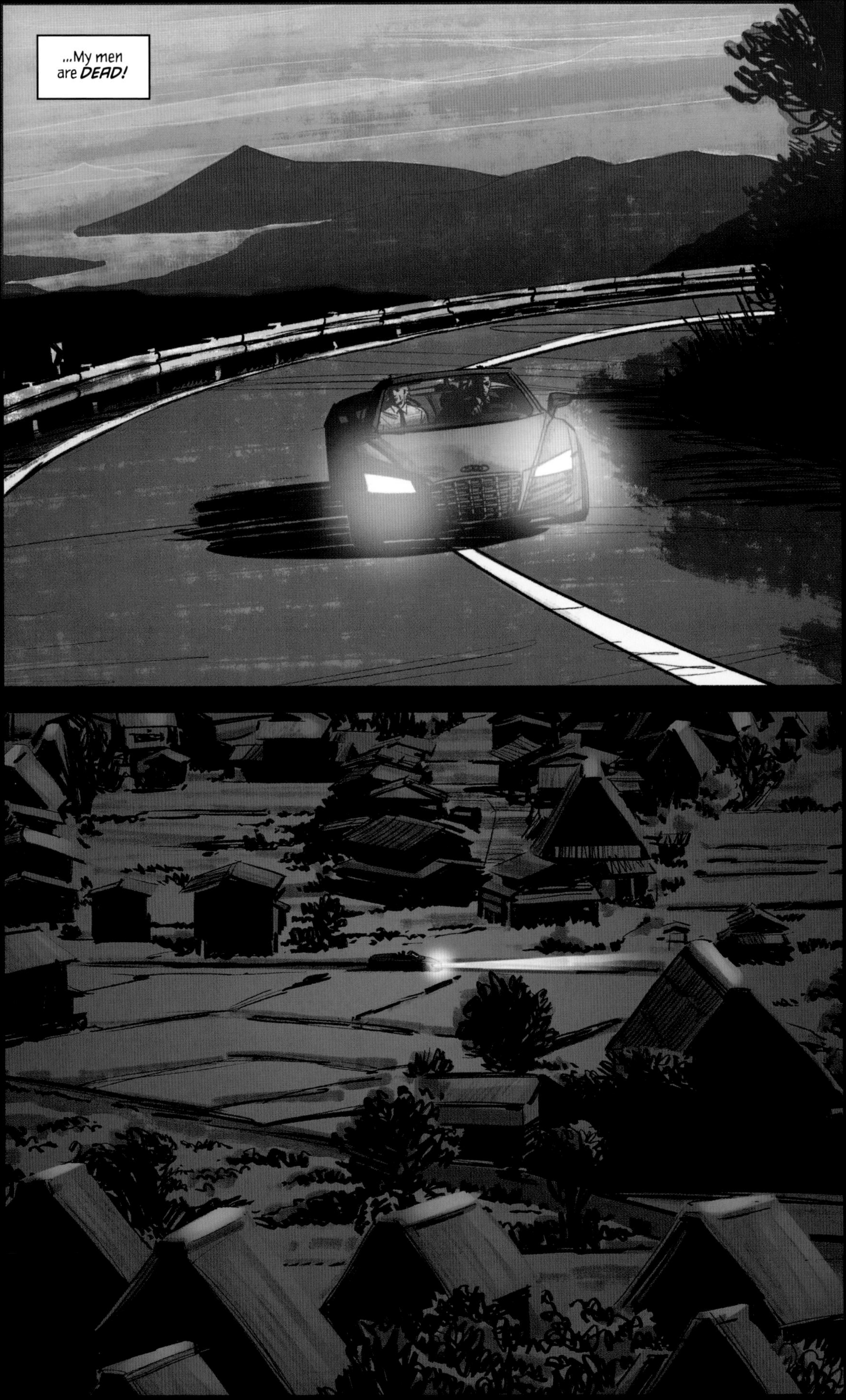
...My men are DEAD!

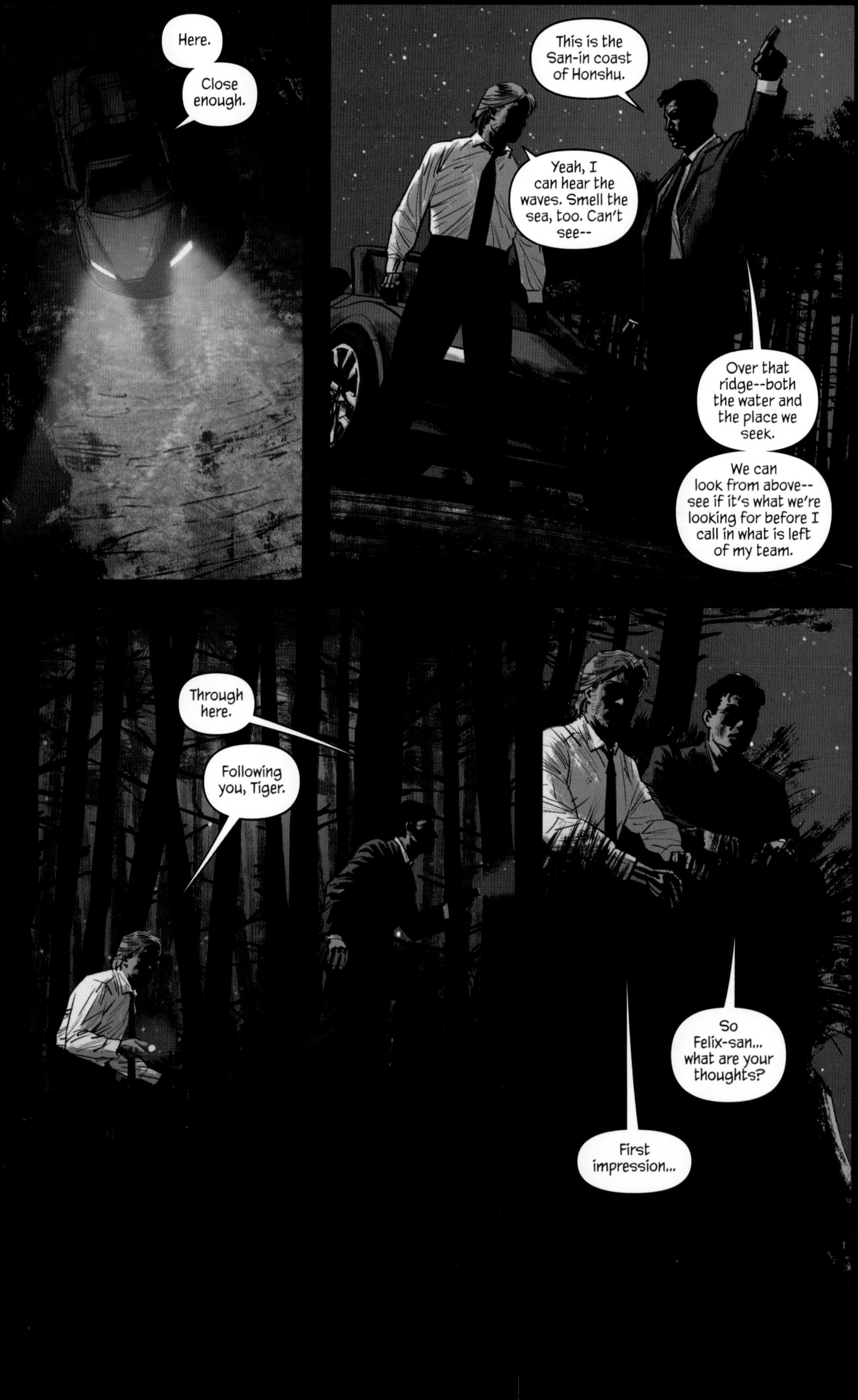
Here.
Close enough.
This is the San-in coast of Honshu.
Yeah, I can hear the waves. Smell the sea, too. Can't see--
Over that ridge--both the water and the place we seek.
We can look from above--see if it's what we're looking for before I call in what is left of my team.
Through here.
Following you, Tiger.
So Felix-san... what are your thoughts?
First impression...

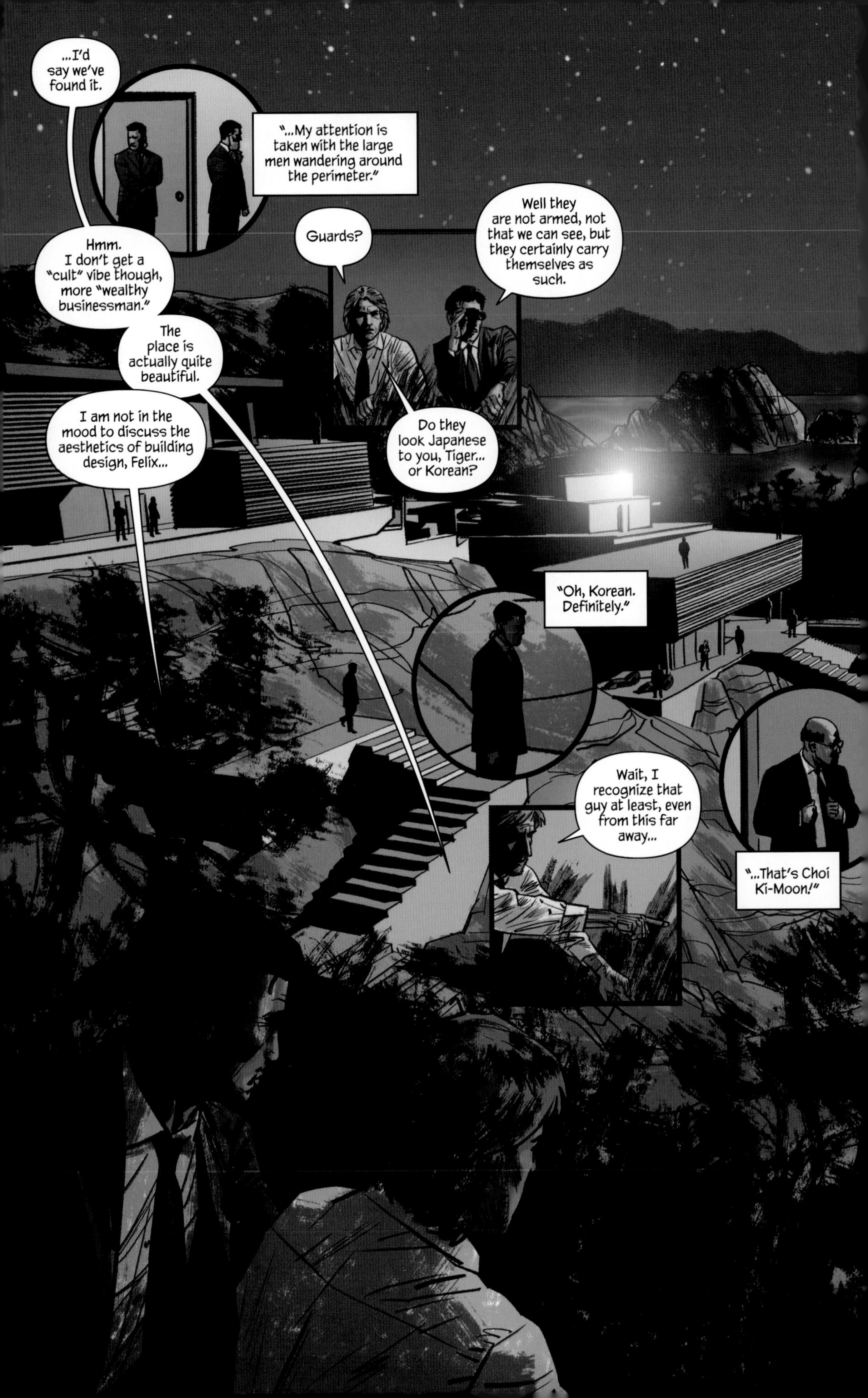
...I'd say we've found it.
"...My attention is taken with the large men wandering around the perimeter."
Hmm. I don't get a "cult" vibe though, more "wealthy businessman."
Guards?
Well they are not armed, not that we can see, but they certainly carry themselves as such.
The place is actually quite beautiful.
I am not in the mood to discuss the aesthetics of building design, Felix...
Do they look Japanese to you, Tiger... or Korean?
"Oh, Korean. Definitely."
Wait, I recognize that guy at least, even from this far away...
"...That's Choi Ki-Moon!"

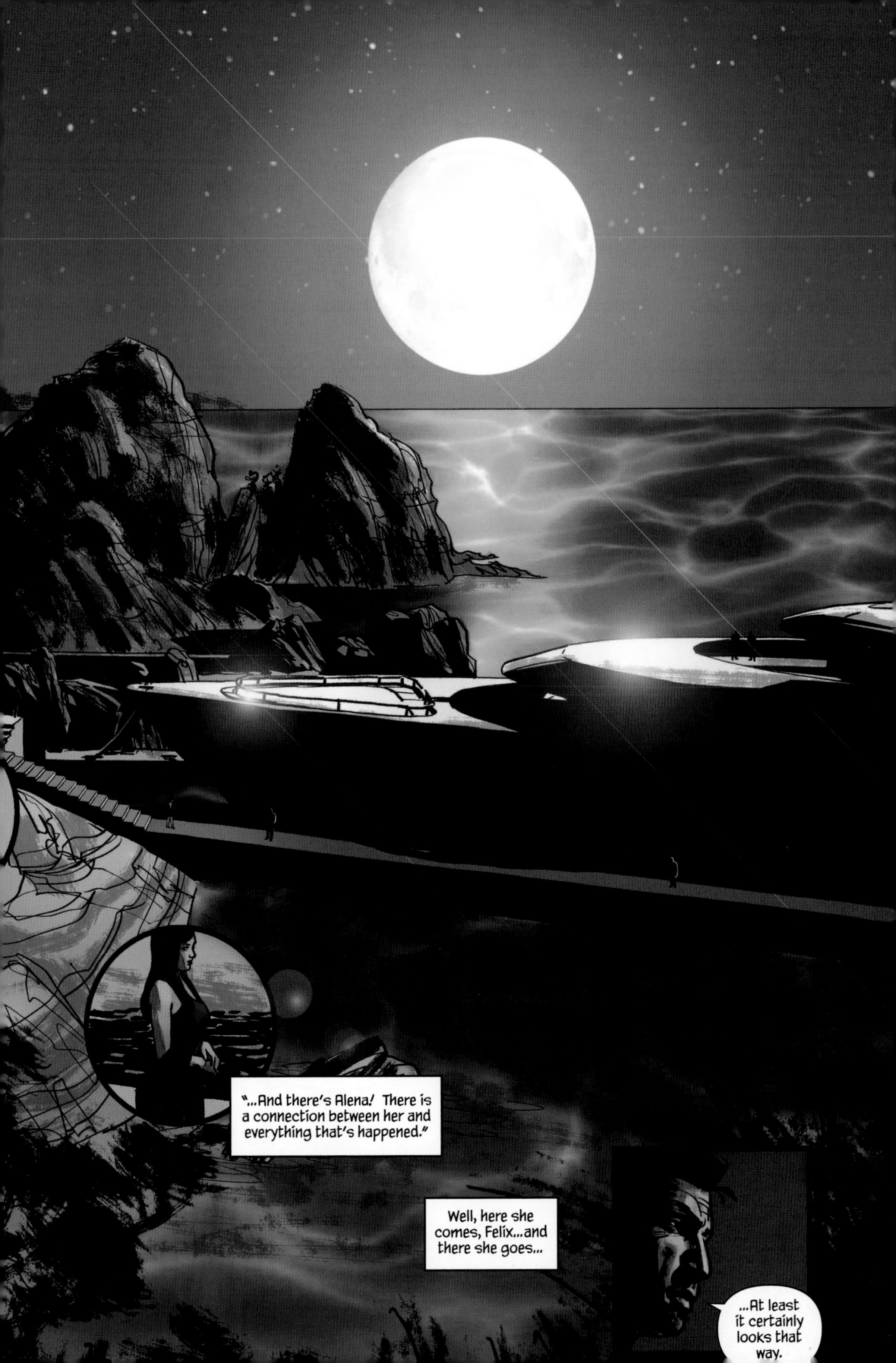
"...And there's Alena! There is a connection between her and everything that's happened."
Well, here she comes, Felix...and there she goes...
...At least it certainly looks that way.

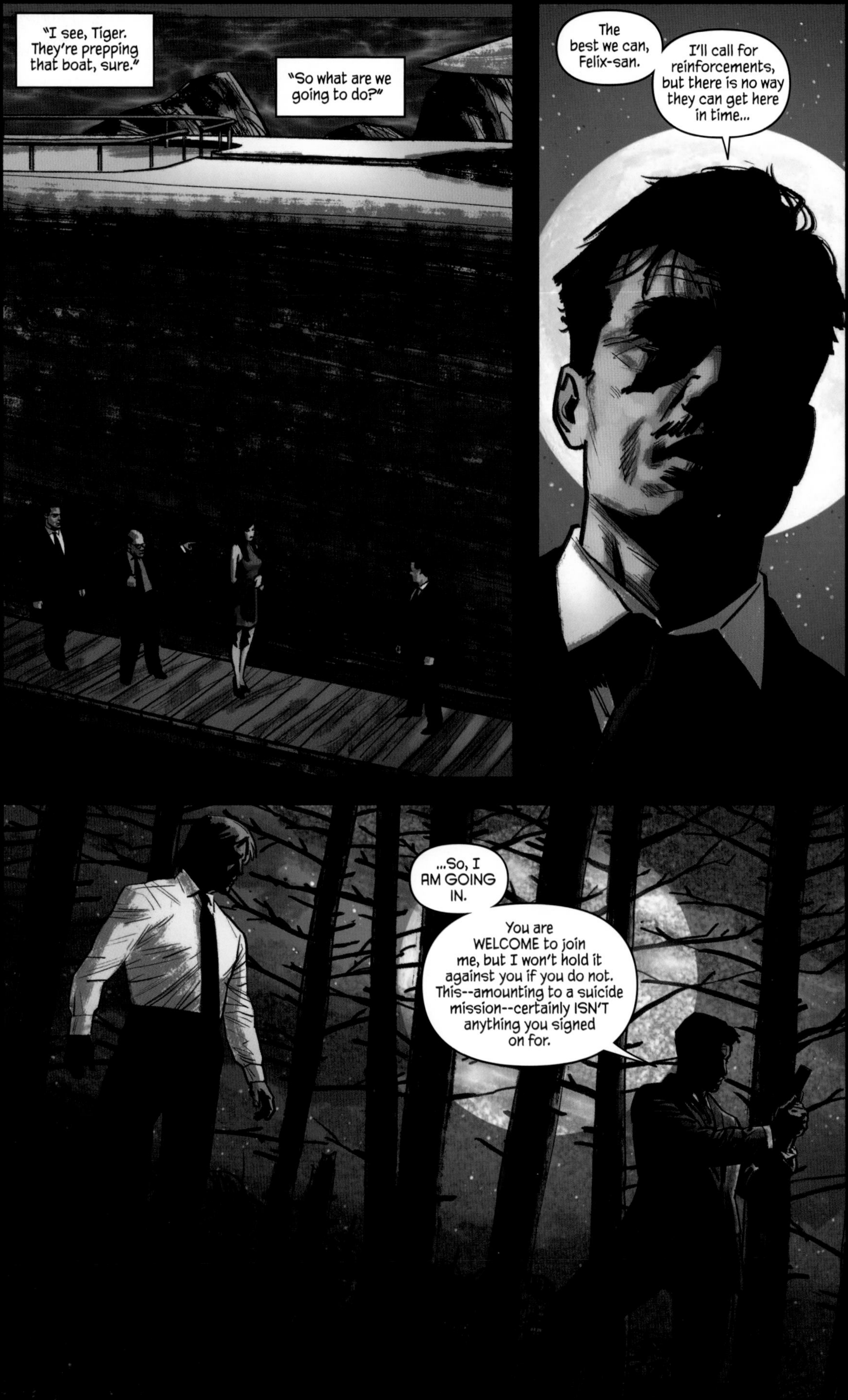
"I see, Tiger. They're prepping that boat, sure."
"So what are we going to do?"
The best we can, Felix-san.
I'll call for reinforcements, but there is no way they can get here in time...
...So, I AM GOING IN.
You are WELCOME to join me, but I won't hold it against you if you do not. This--amounting to a suicide mission--certainly ISN'T anything you signed on for.

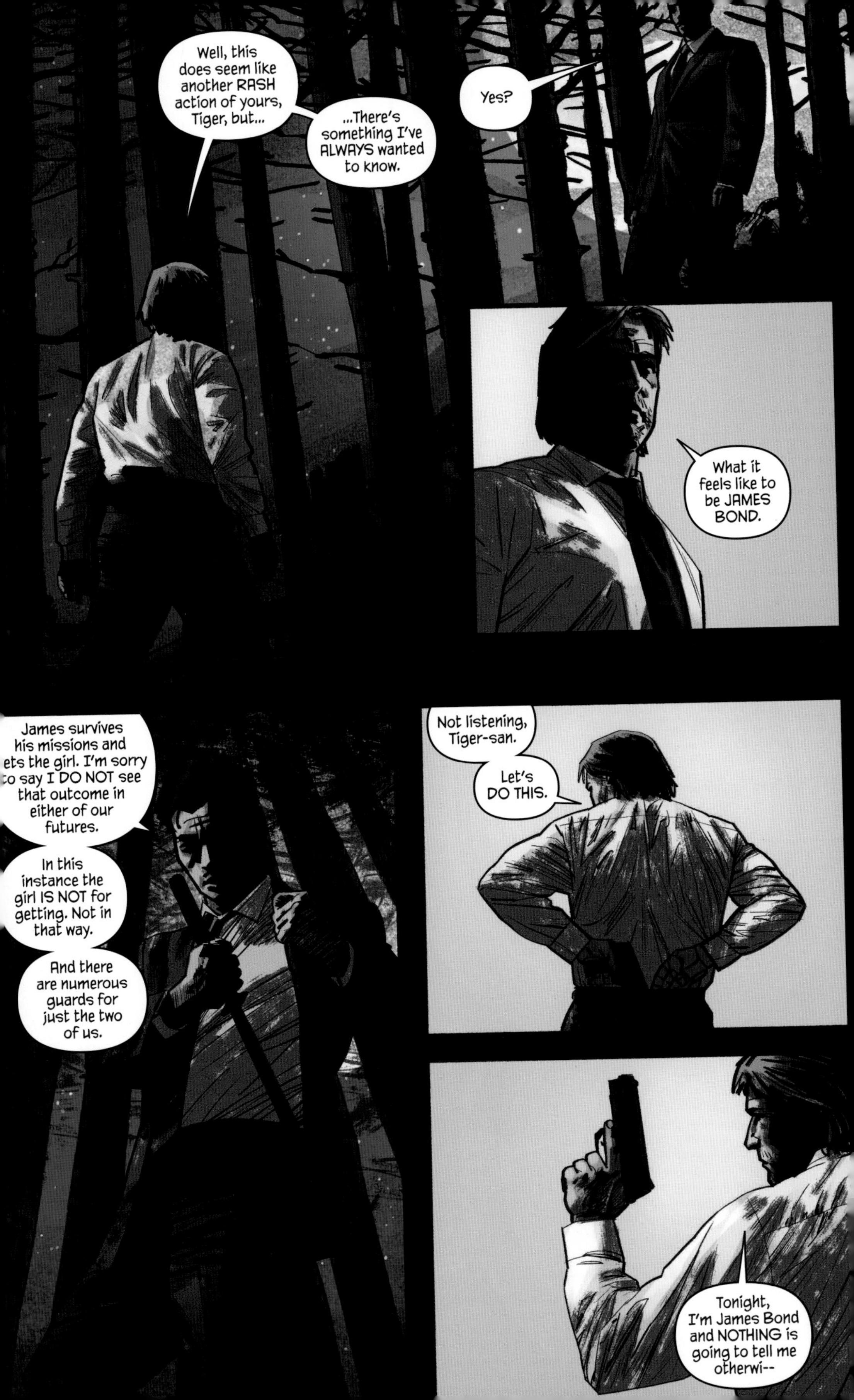
Well, this does seem like another RASH action of yours, Tiger, but...
...There's something I've ALWAYS wanted to know.
Yes?
What it feels like to be JAMES BOND.
James survives his missions and ets the girl. I'm sorry :o say I DO NOT see that outcome in either of our futures.
In this instance the girl IS NOT for getting. Not in that way.
And there are numerous guards for just the two of us.
Not listening, Tiger-san.
Let's DO THIS.
Tonight, I'm James Bond and NOTHING is going to tell me otherwi--

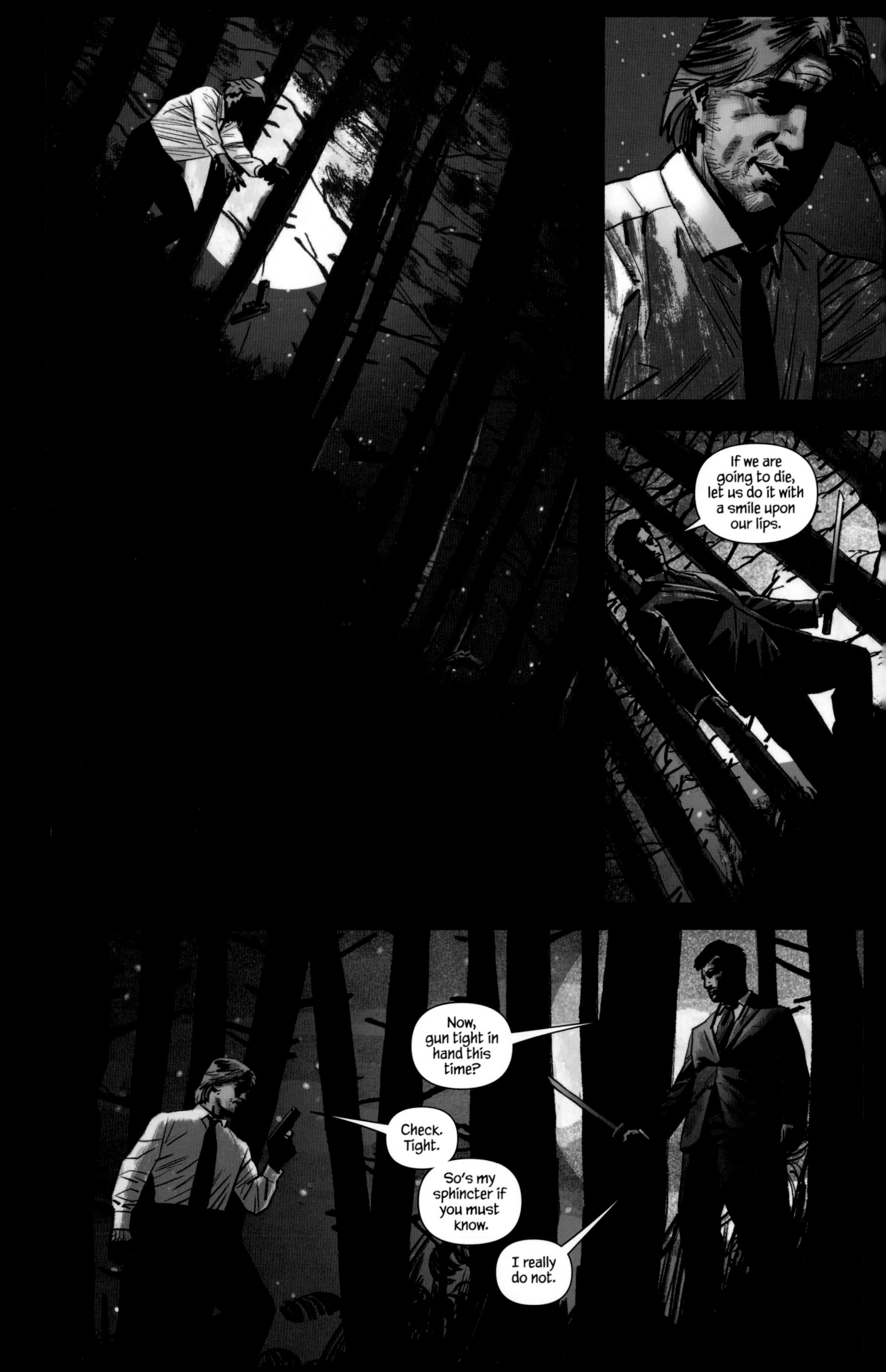
If we are going to die, let us do it with a smile upon our lips.
Now, gun tight in hand this time?
Check. Tight.
So's my sphincter if you must know.
I really do not.

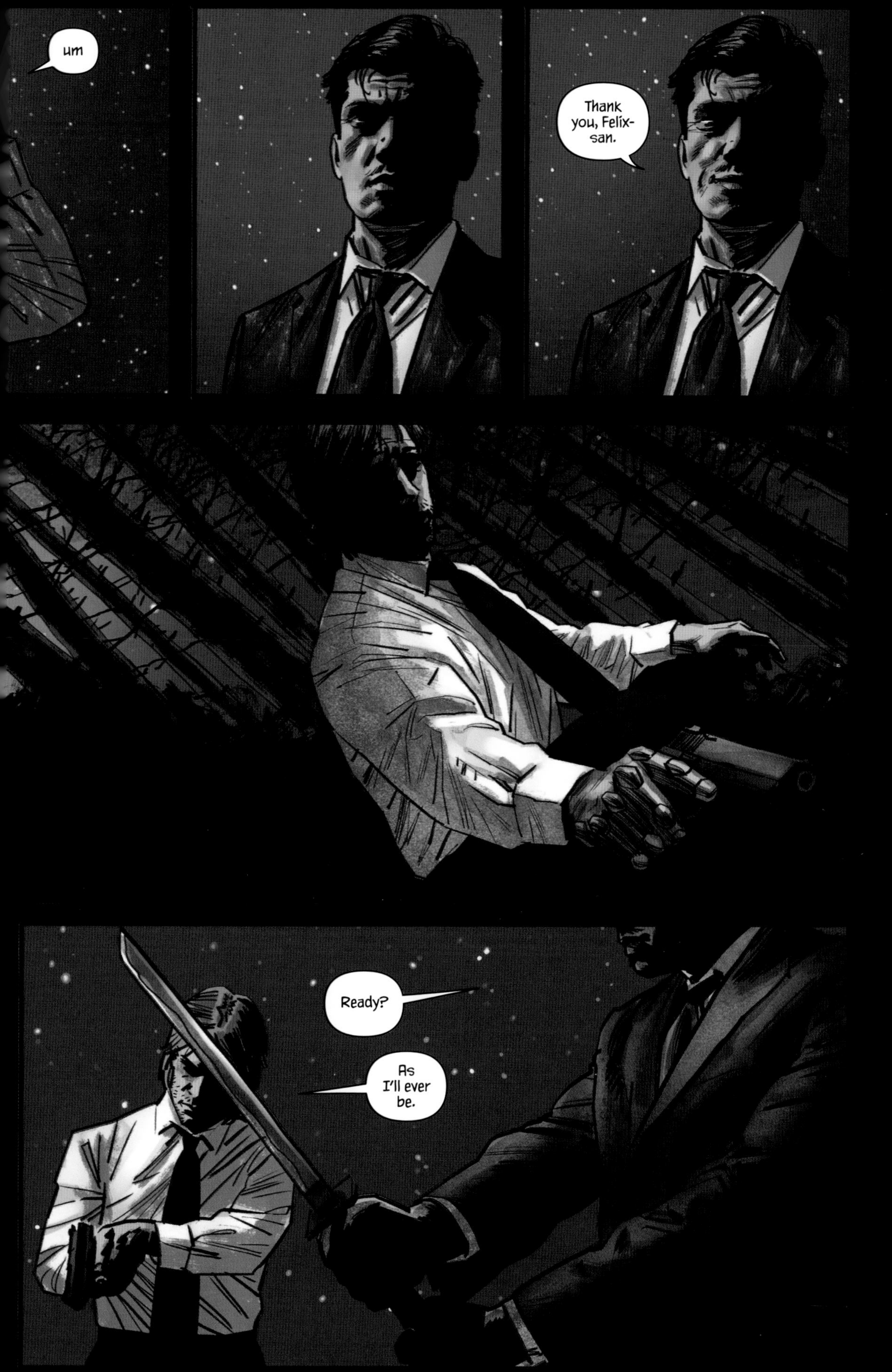
um
Thank you, Felix-san.
Ready?
As I'll ever be.

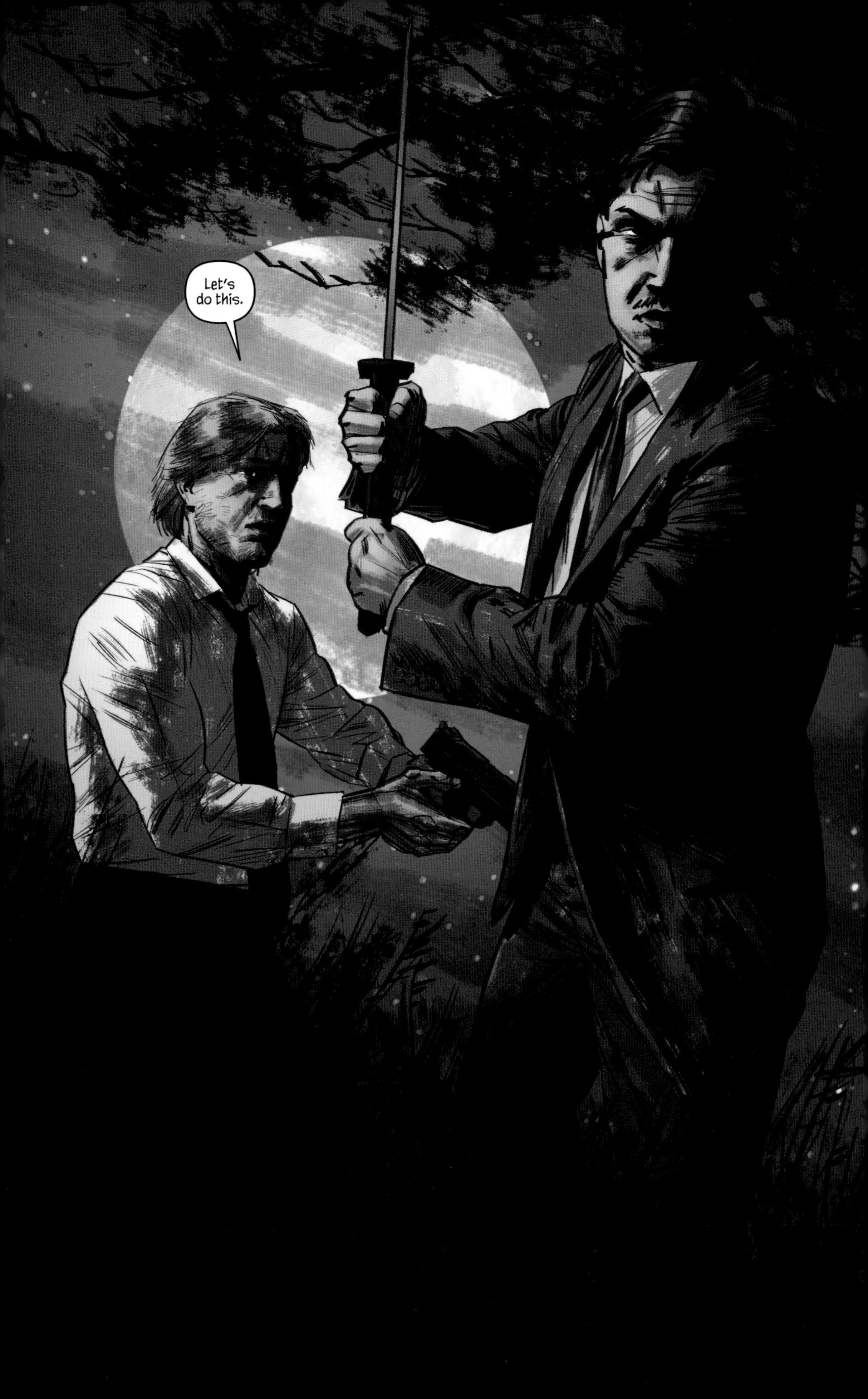
Let's do this.

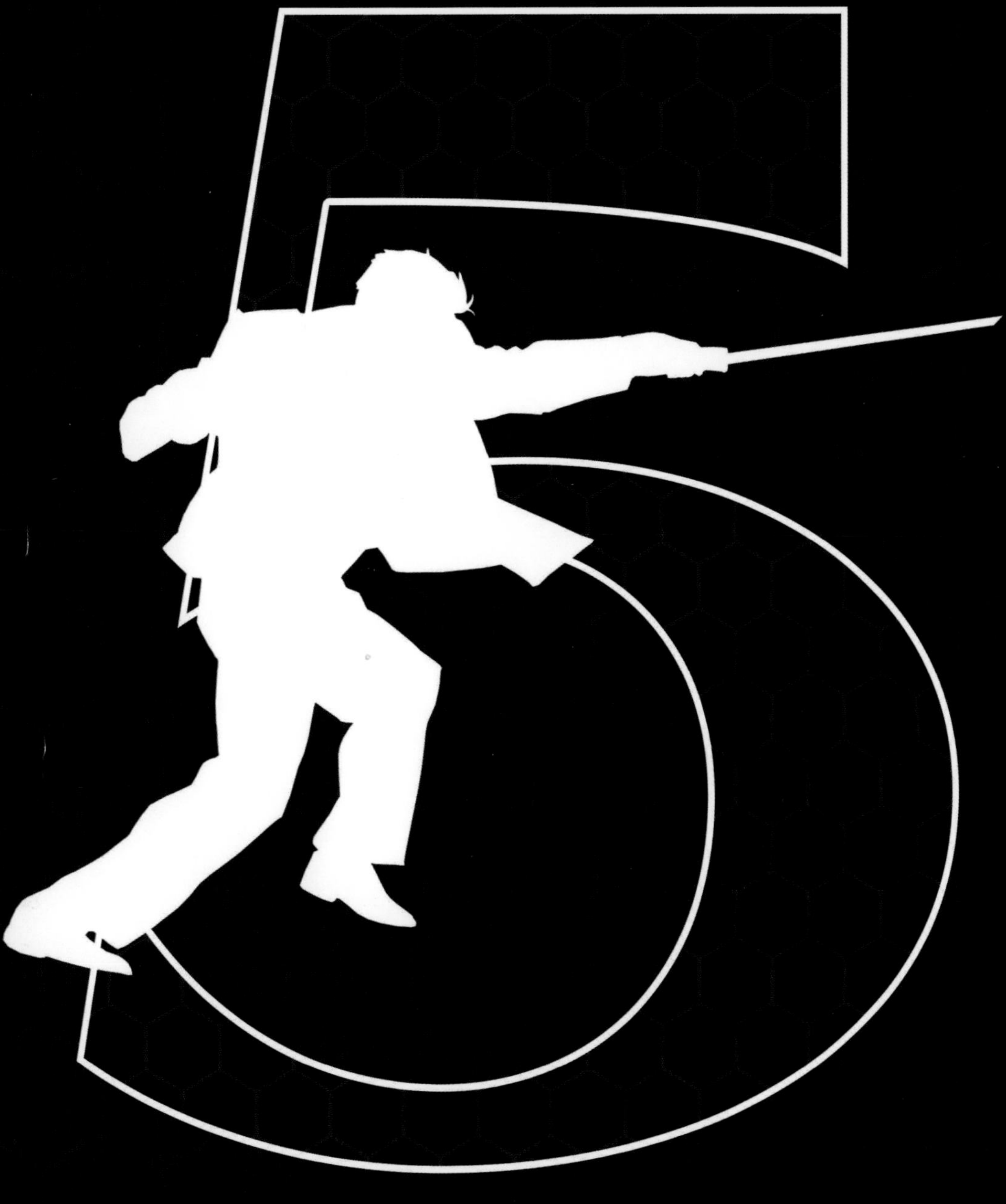
5

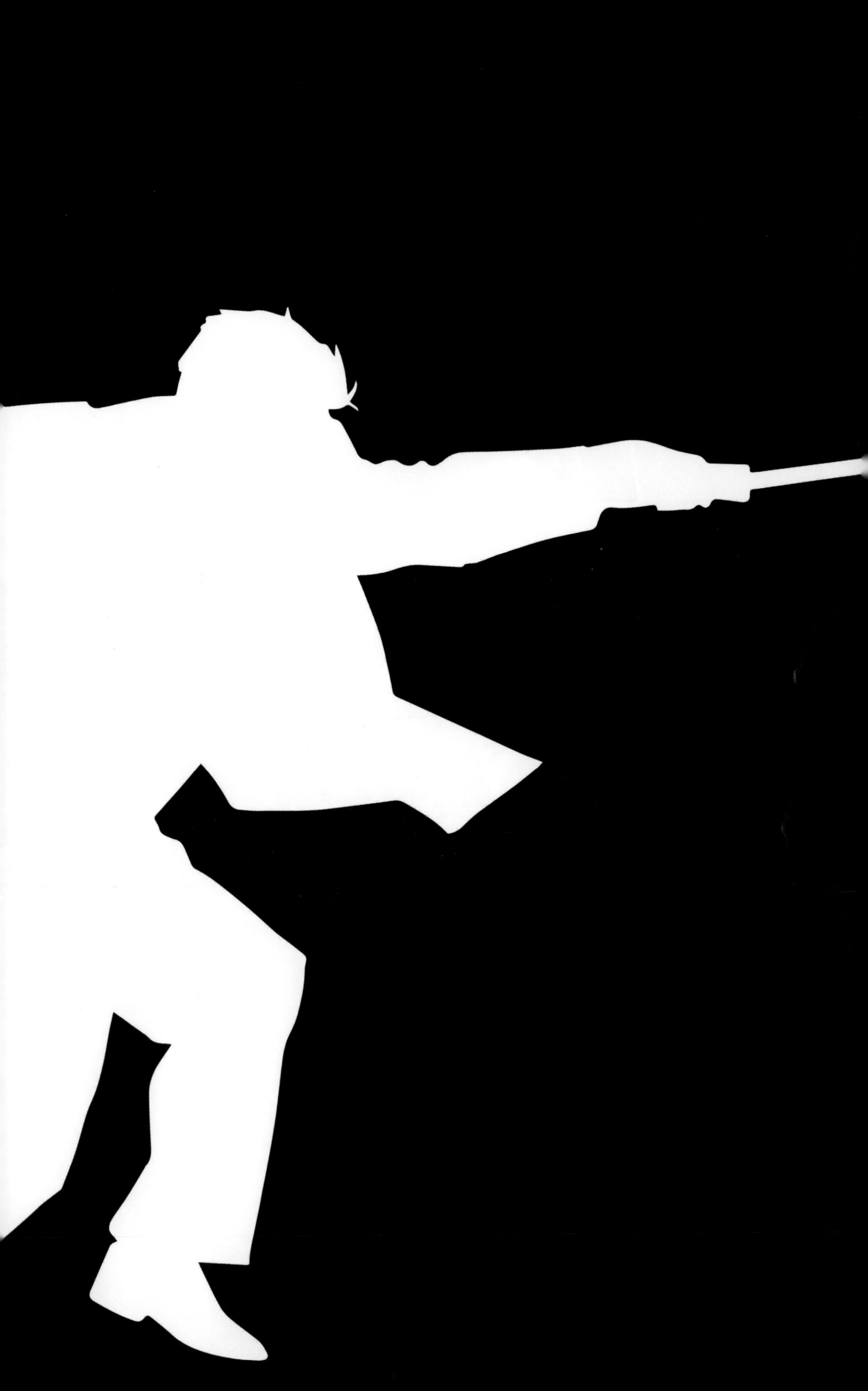

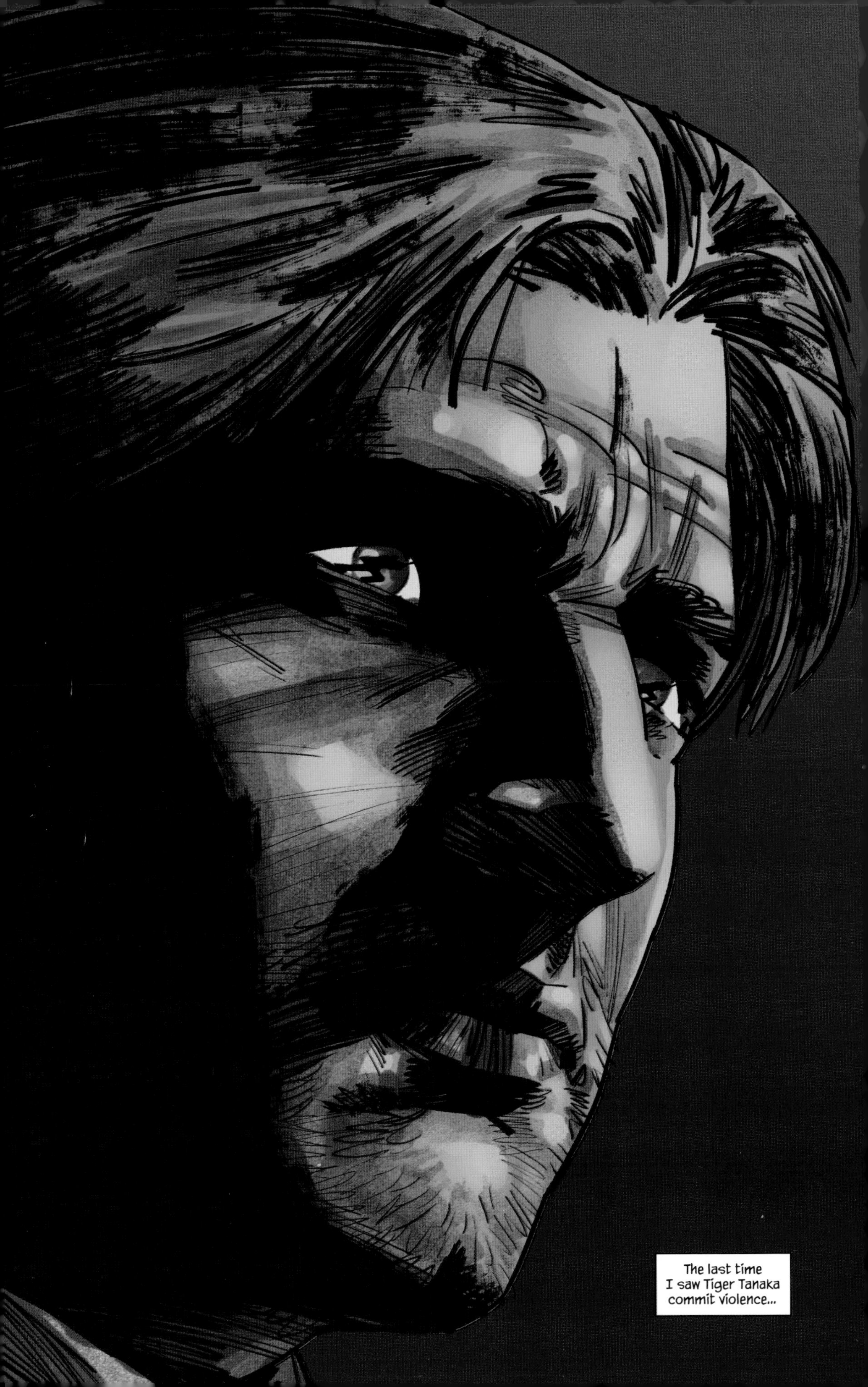
The last time I saw Tiger Tanaka commit violence...

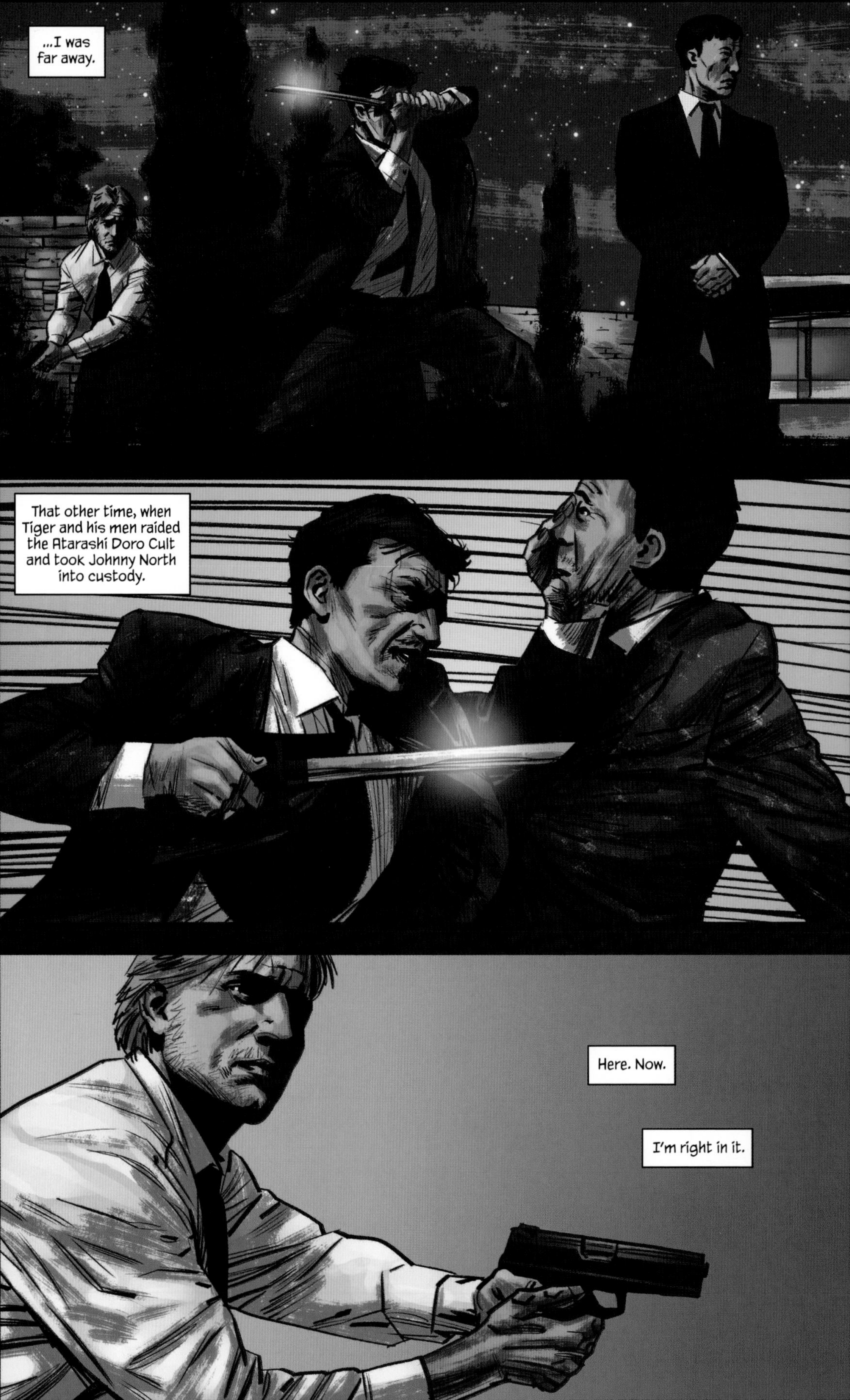
...I was far away.
That other time, when Tiger and his men raided the Atarashi Doro Cult and took Johnny North into custody.
Here. Now.
I'm right in it.

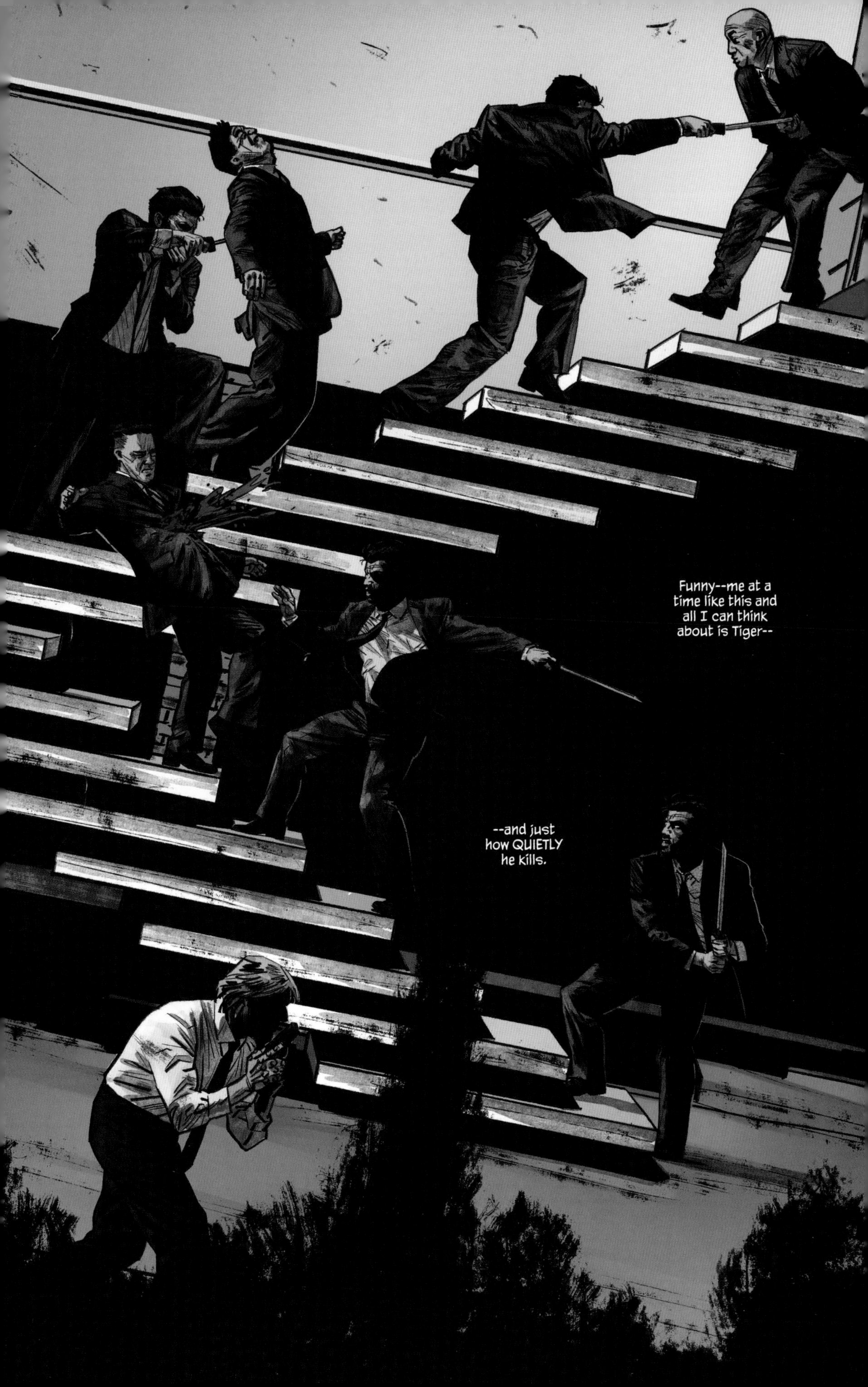
Funny--me at a time like this and all I can think about is Tiger--
--and just how QUIETLY he kills.

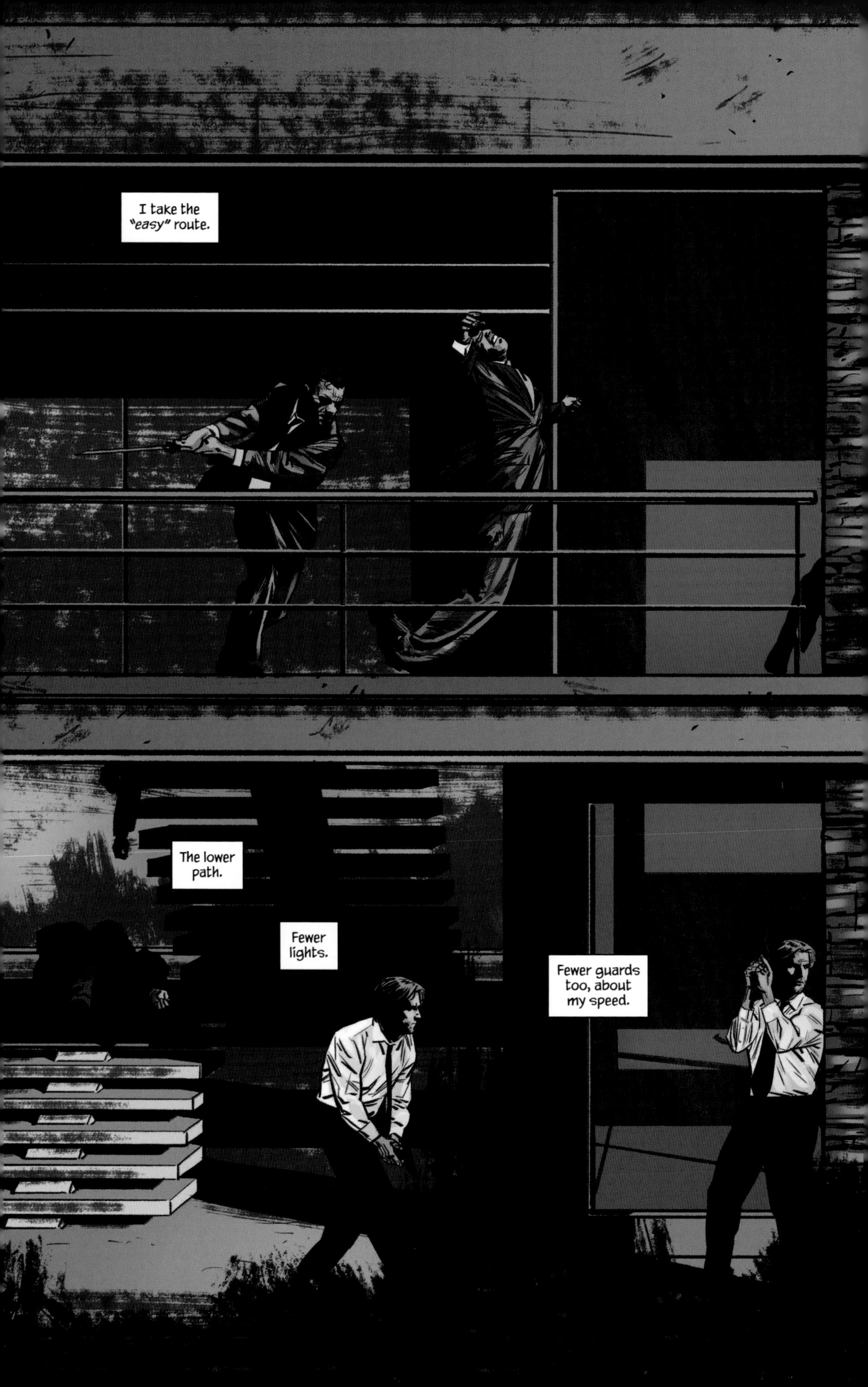
I take the "*easy*" route.
The lower path.
Fewer lights.
Fewer guards too, about my speed.

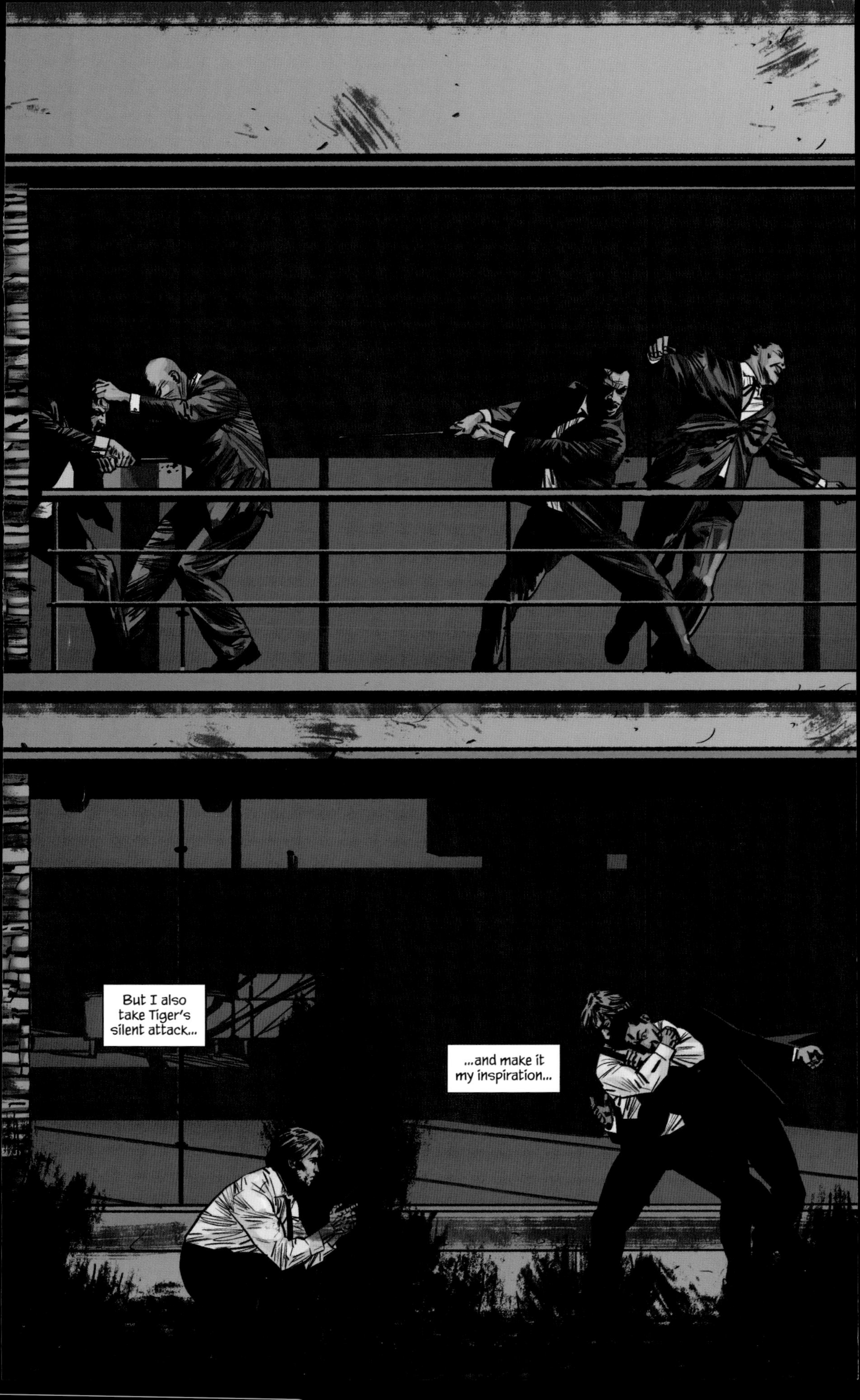
But I also take Tiger's silent attack...
...and make it my inspiration...

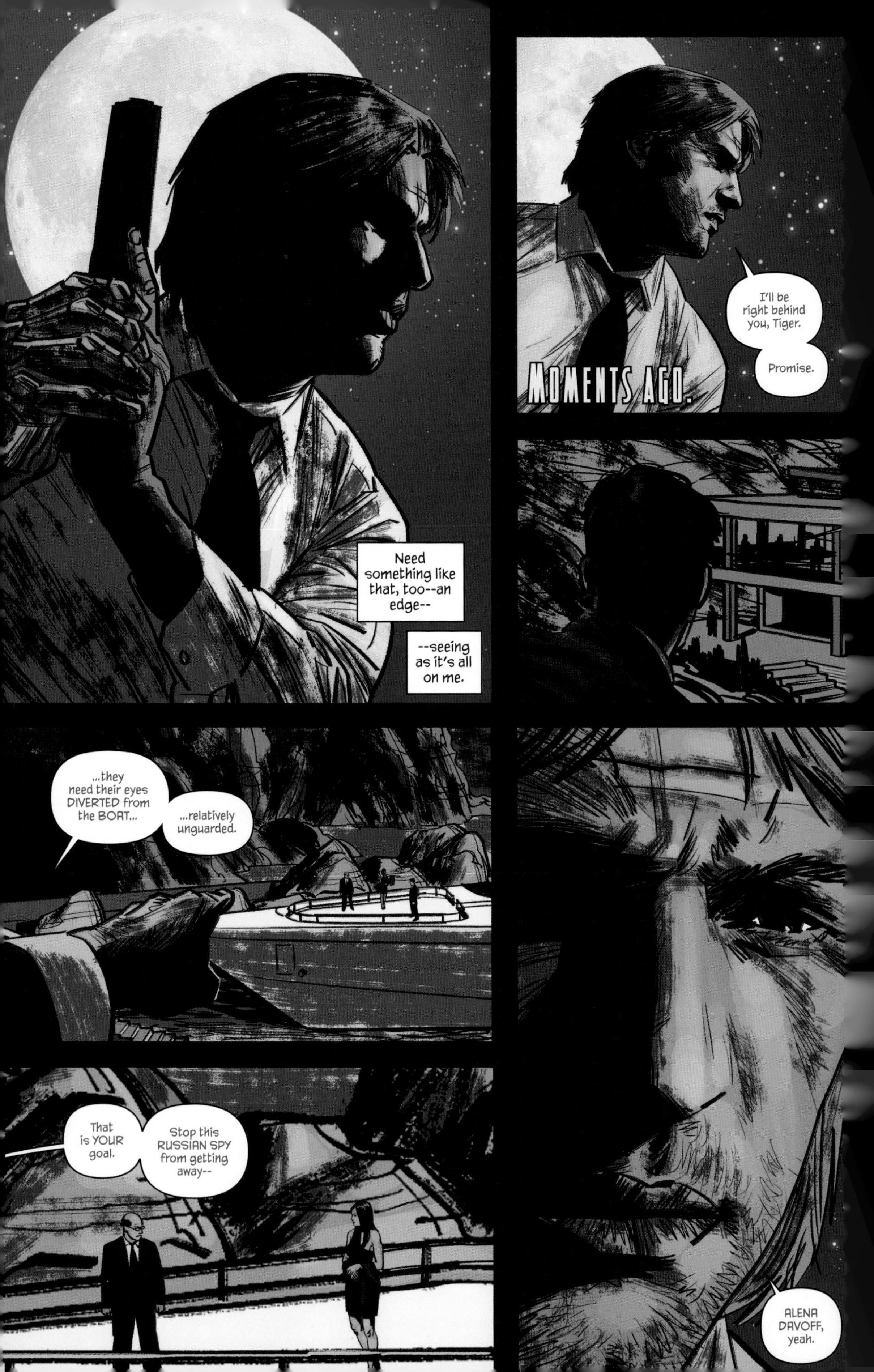

Need something like that, too--an edge--
--seeing as it's all on me.
MOMENTS AGO.
I'll be right behind you, Tiger.
Promise.
...they need their eyes DIVERTED from the BOAT...
...relatively unguarded.
That is YOUR goal.
Stop this RUSSIAN SPY from getting away--
ALENA DAVOFF, yeah.

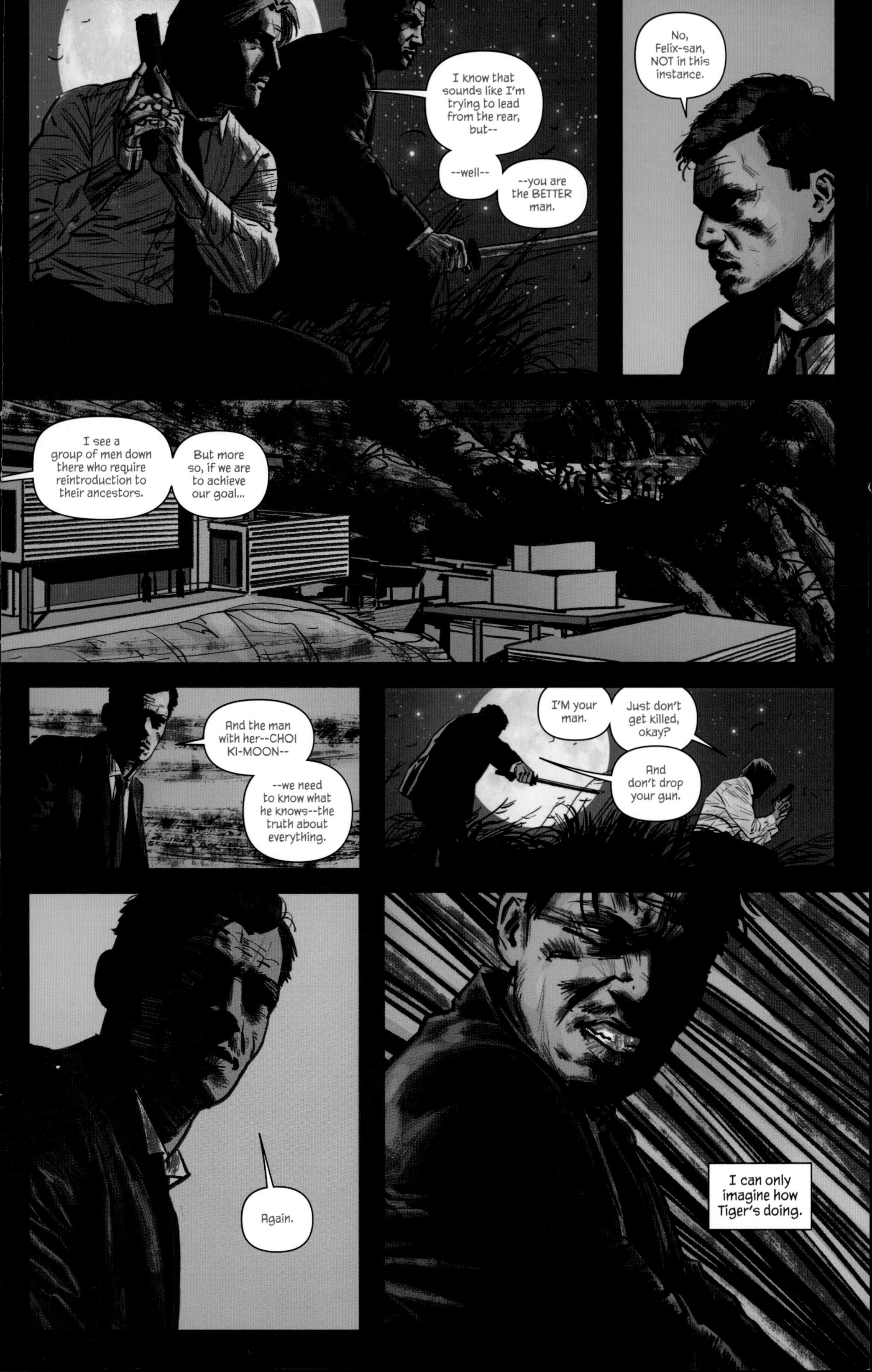
I know that sounds like I'm trying to lead from the rear, but--
--well--
--you are the BETTER man.
No, Felix-san, NOT in this instance.
I see a group of men down there who require reintroduction to their ancestors.
But more so, if we are to achieve our goal...
And the man with her--CHOI KI-MOON--
--we need to know what he knows--the truth about everything.
I'M your man.
Just don't get killed, okay?
And don't drop your gun.
Again.
I can only imagine how Tiger's doing.

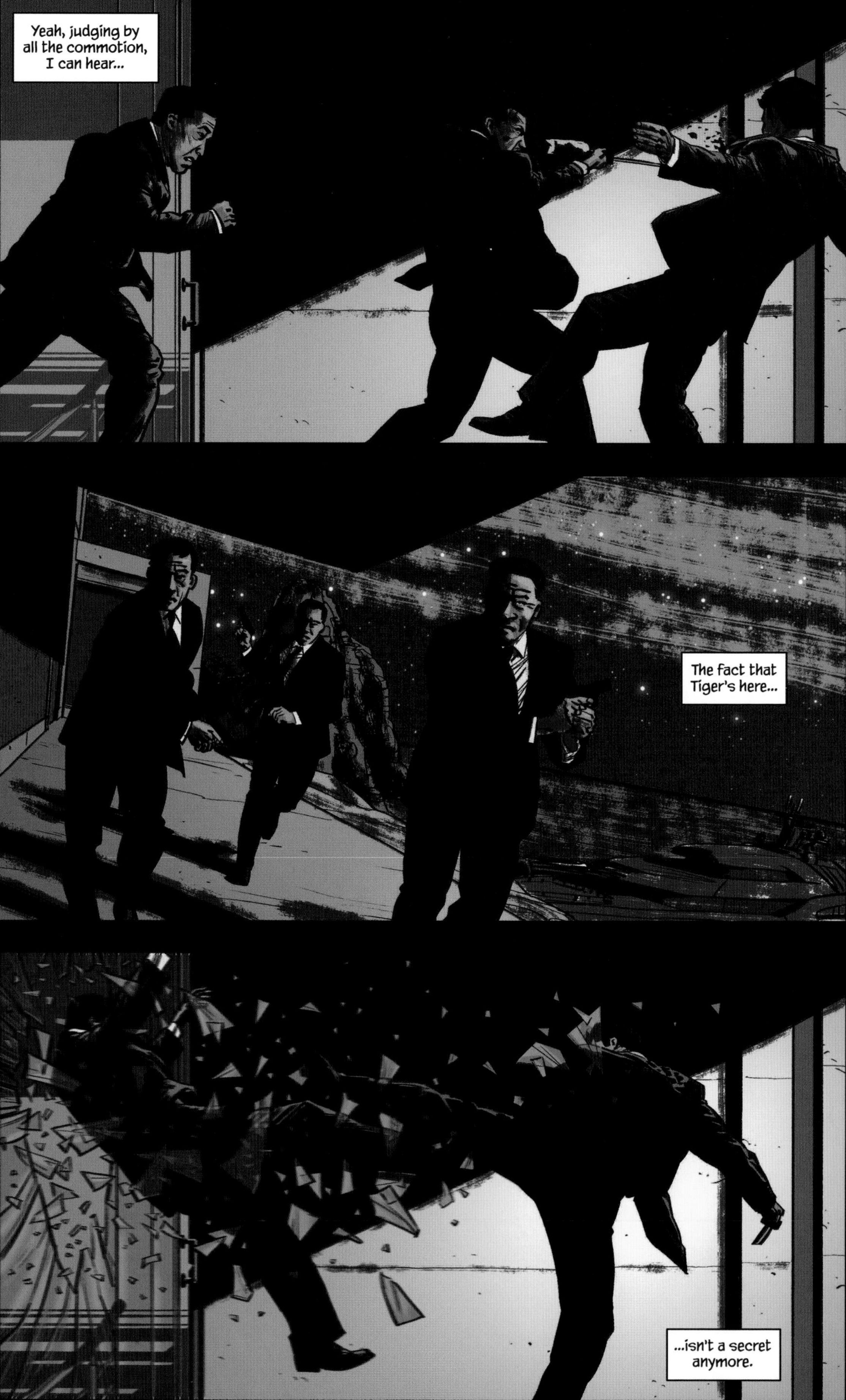
Yeah, judging by all the commotion, I can hear...
The fact that Tiger's here...
...isn't a secret anymore.

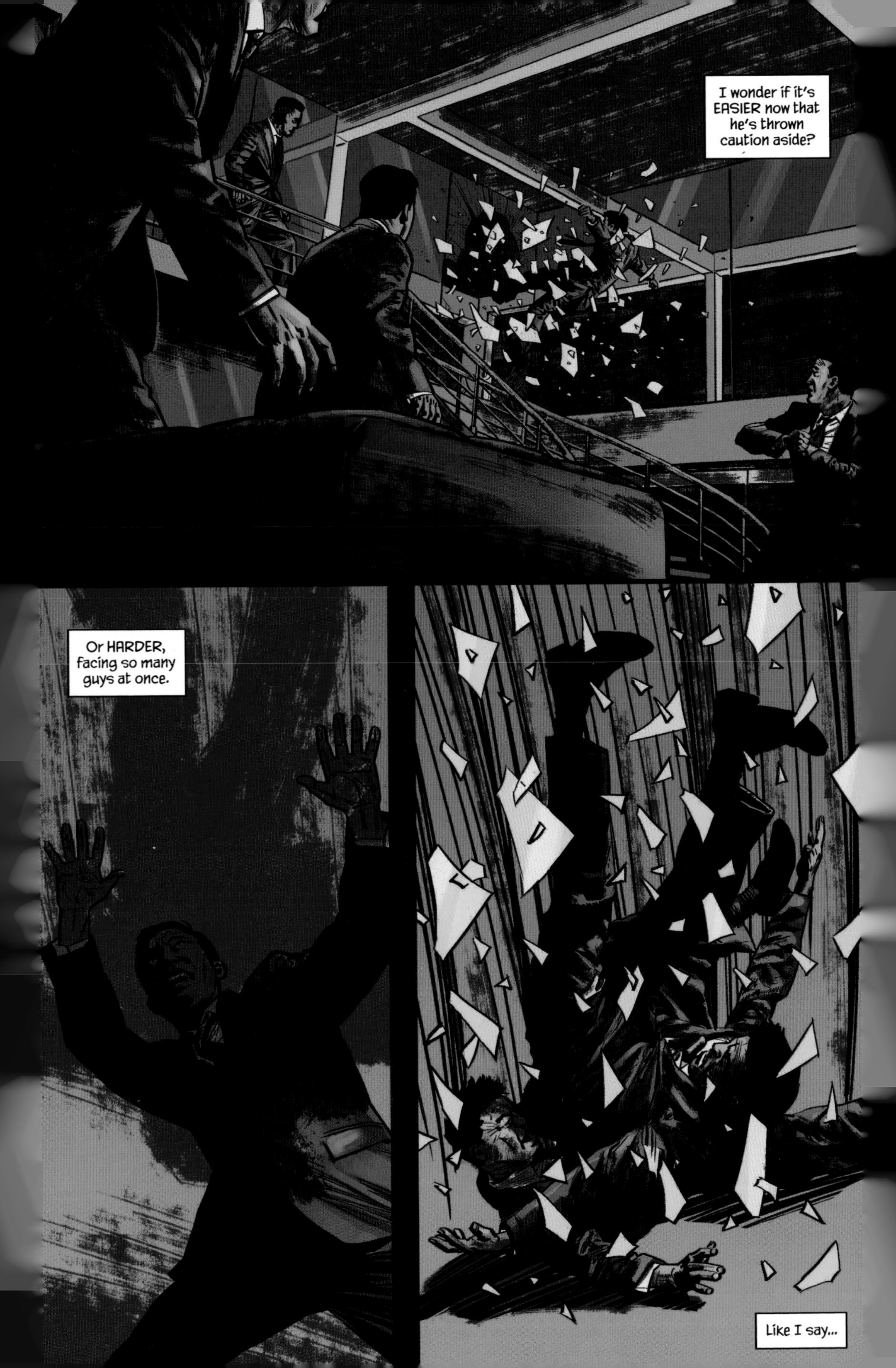
I wonder if it's EASIER now that he's thrown caution aside?
Or HARDER, facing so many guys at once.
Like I say...

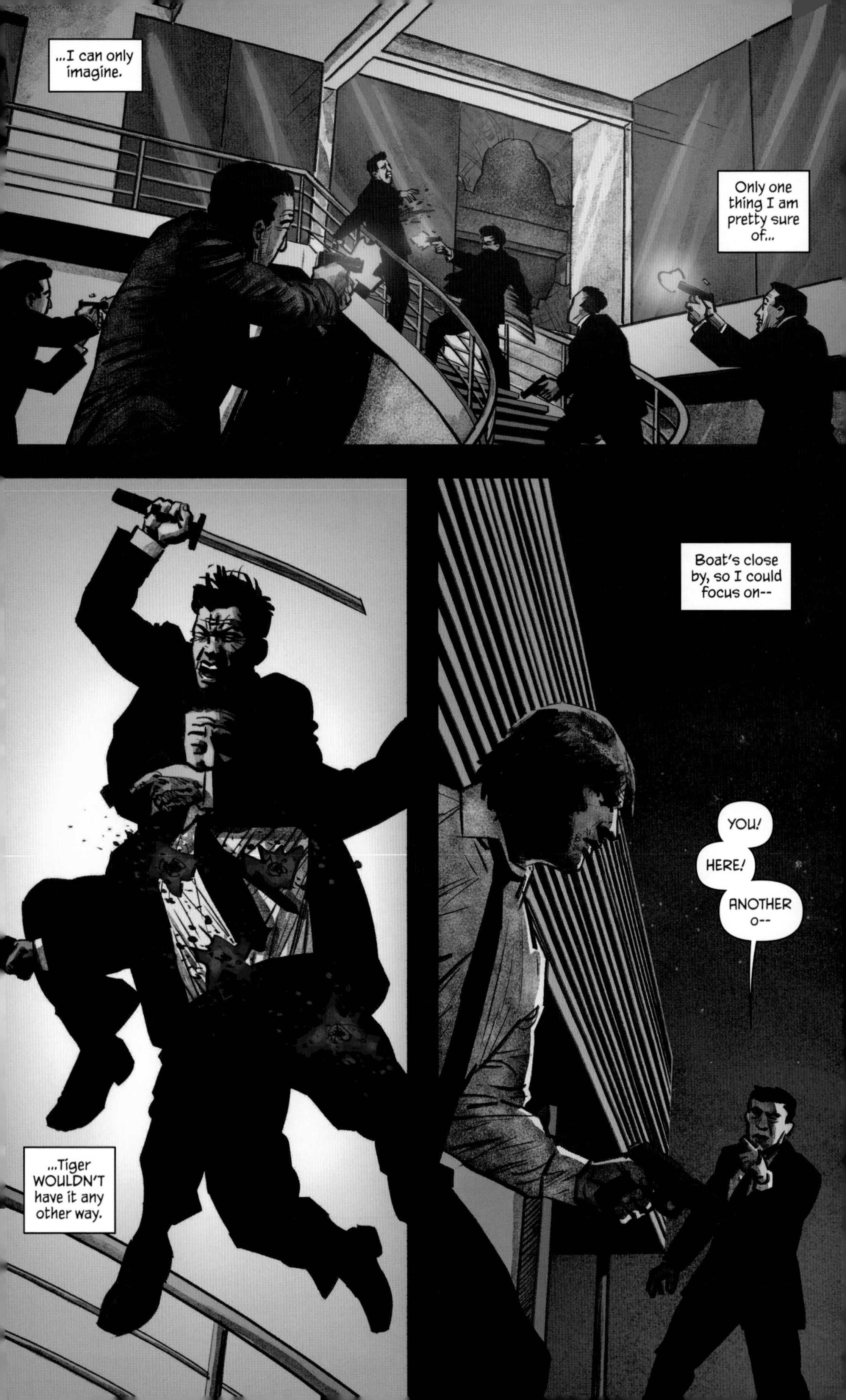
...I can only imagine.
Only one thing I am pretty sure of...
Boat's close by, so I could focus on--
YOU!
HERE!
ANOTHER O--
...Tiger WOULDN'T have it any other way.

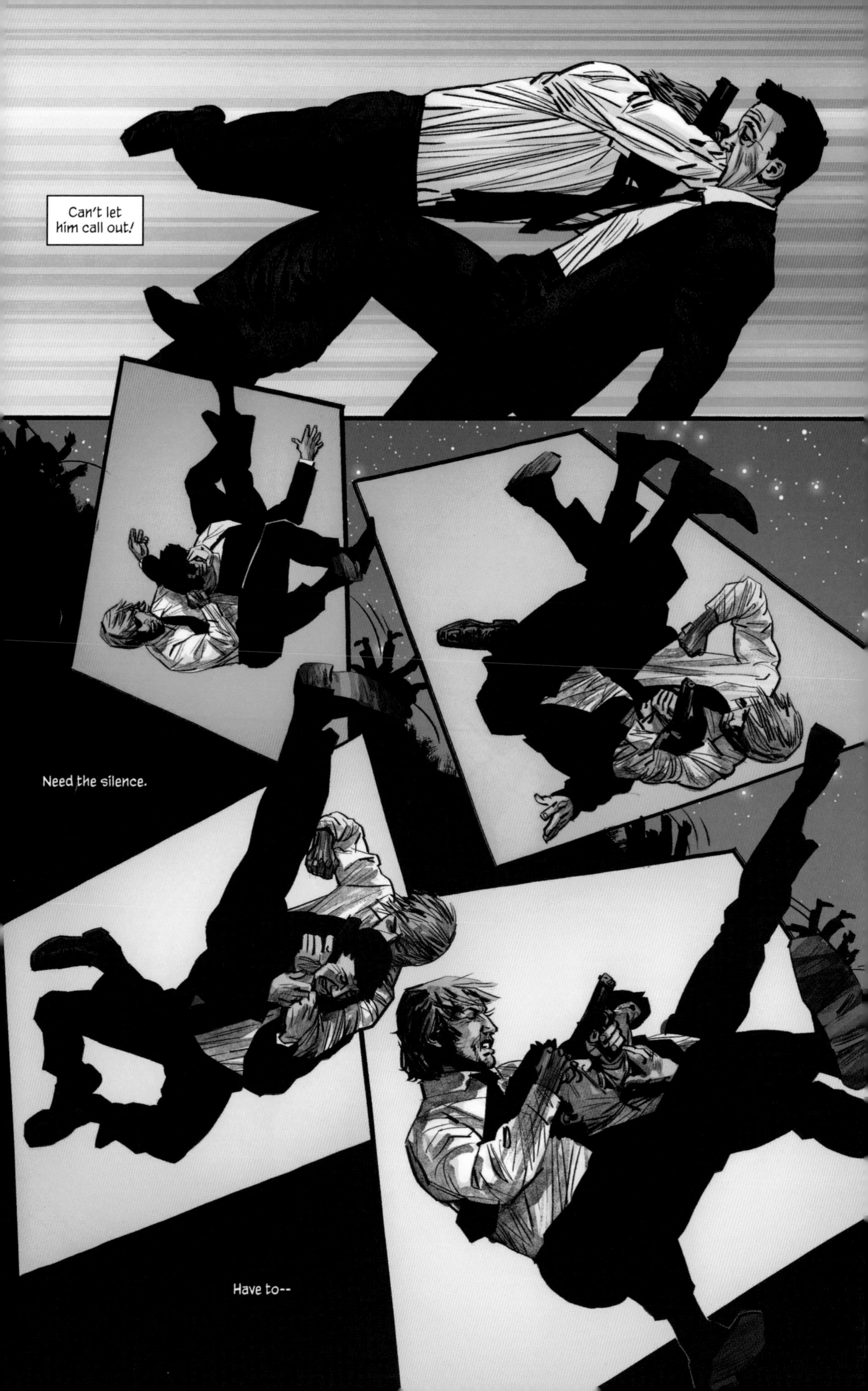
Can't let him call out!
Need the silence.
Have to--

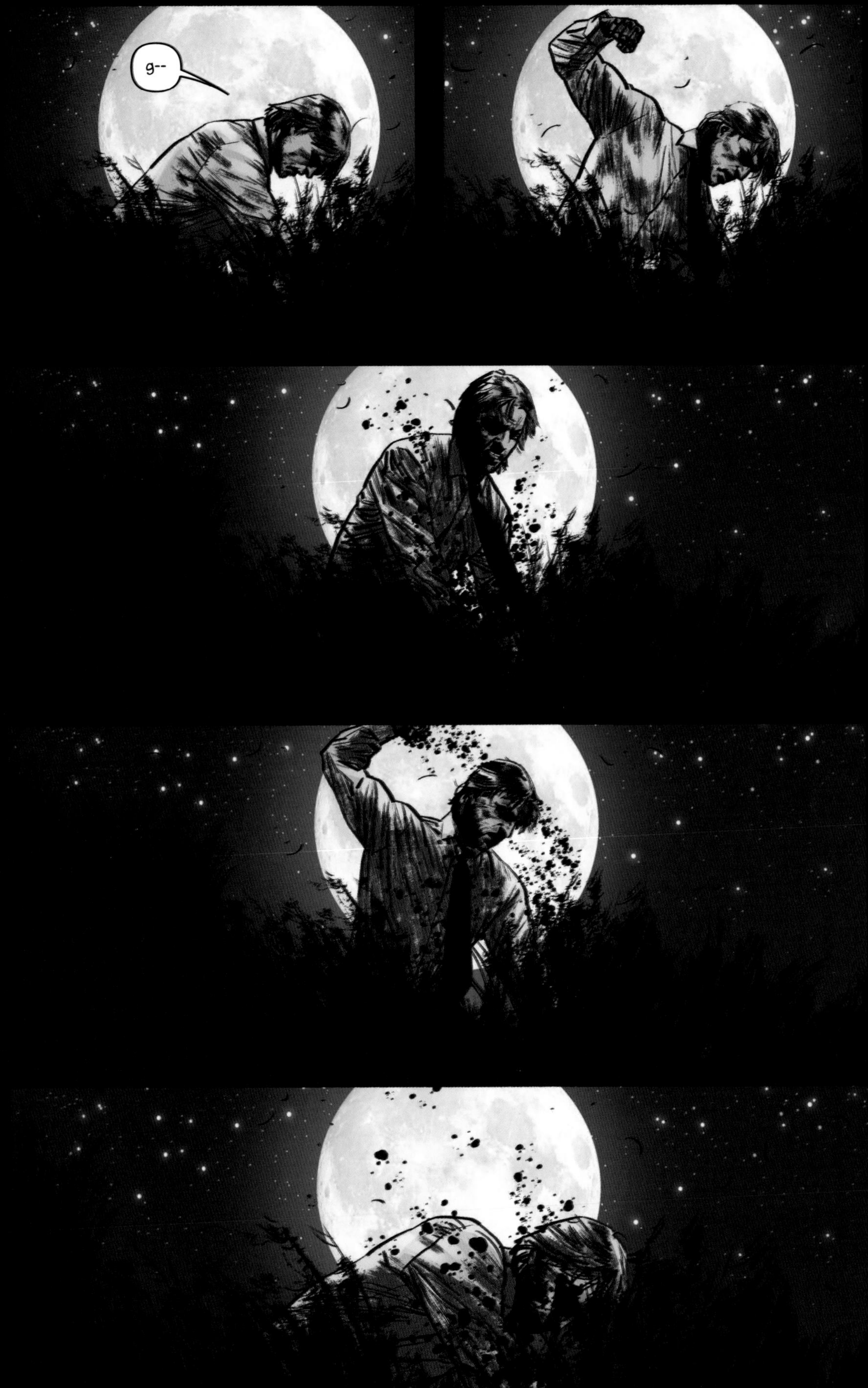
g--

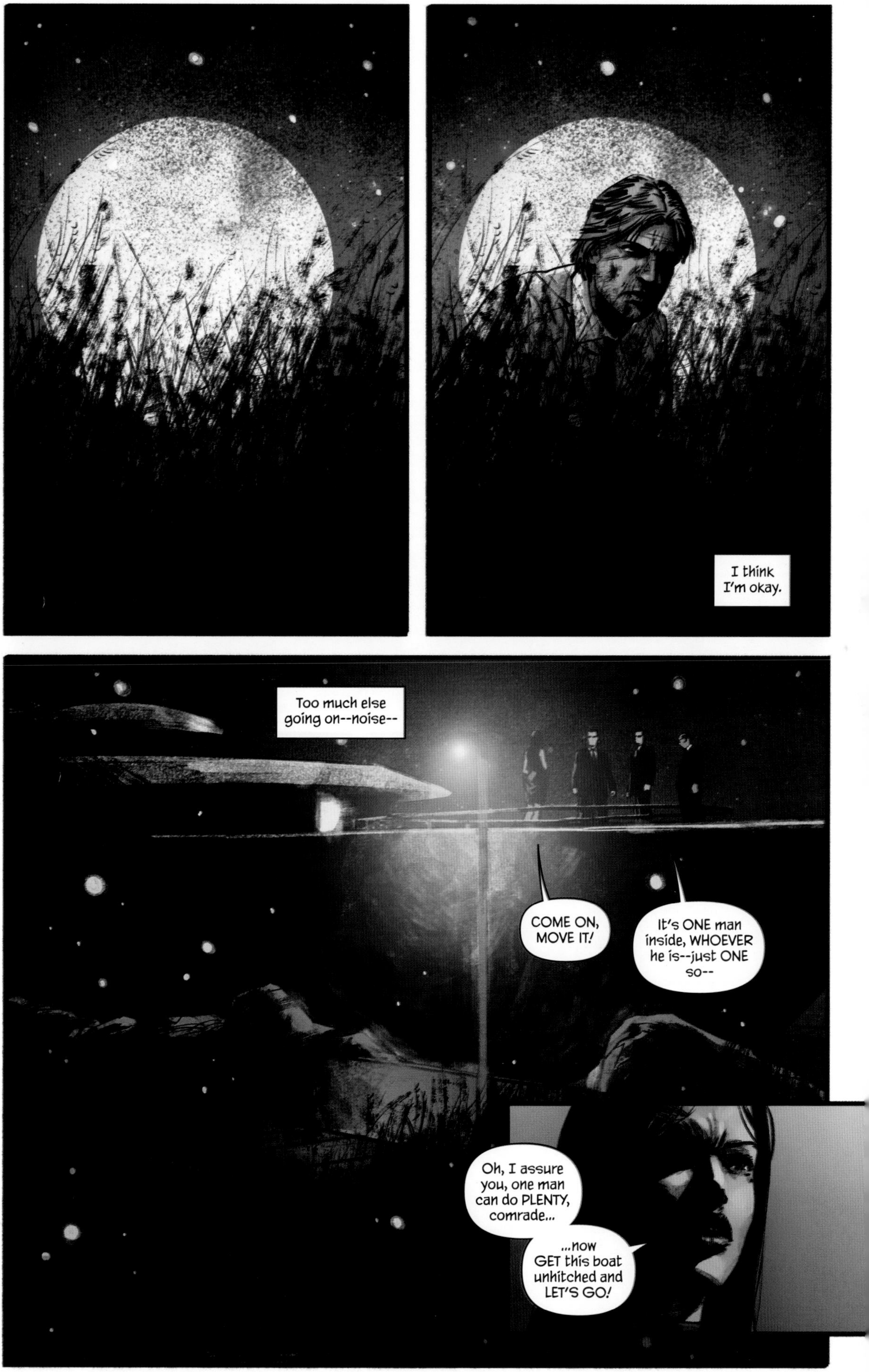
I think I'm okay.
Too much else going on--noise--
COME ON, MOVE IT!
It's ONE man inside, WHOEVER he is--just ONE so--
Oh, I assure you, one man can do PLENTY, comrade...
...now GET this boat unhitched and LET'S GO!

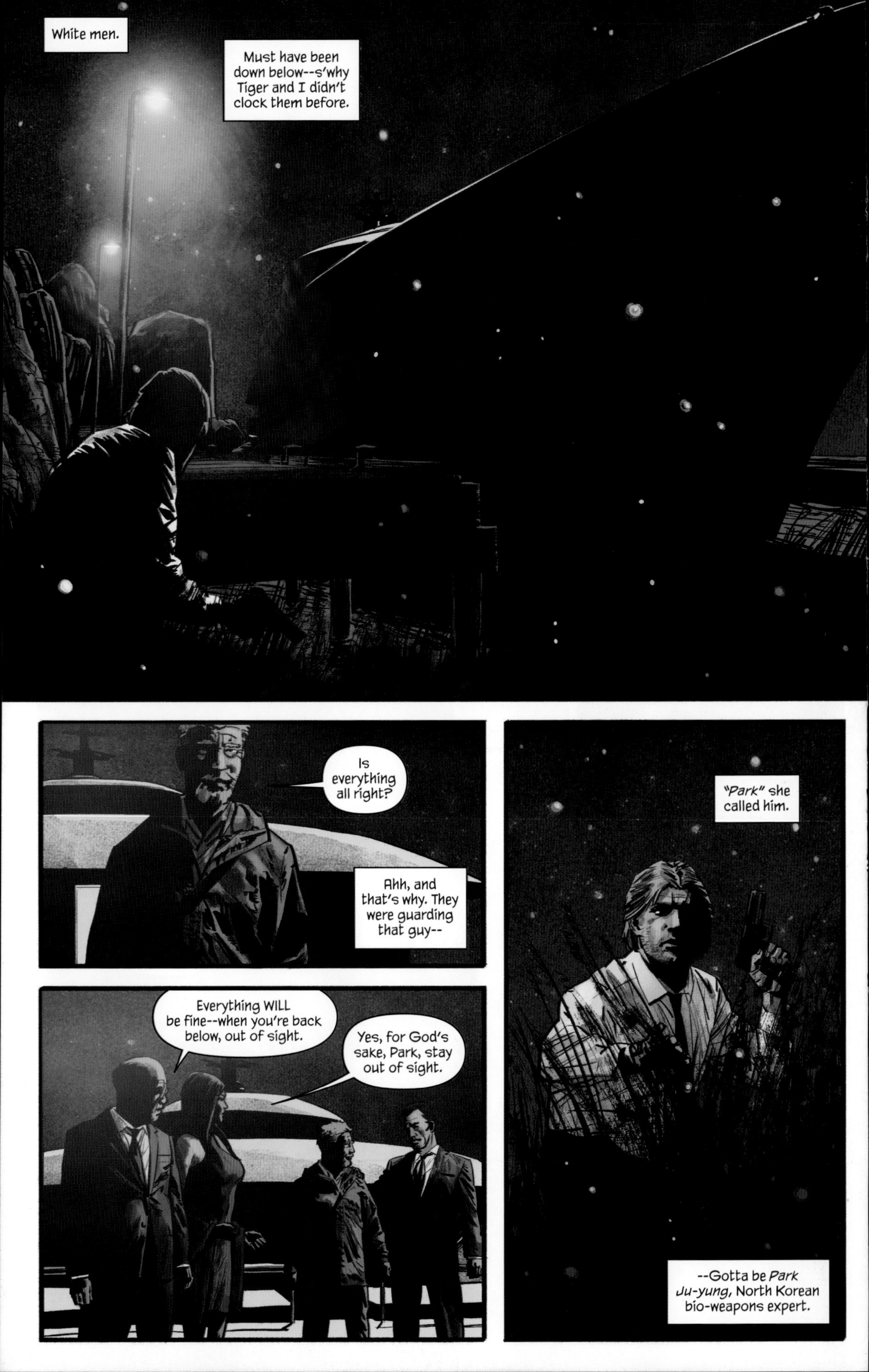

White men.
Must have been down below--s'why Tiger and I didn't clock them before.
Is everything all right?
Ahh, and that's why. They were guarding that guy--
Everything WILL be fine--when you're back below, out of sight.
Yes, for God's sake, Park, stay out of sight.
"Park" she called him.
--Gotta be Park Ju-yung, North Korean bio-weapons expert.

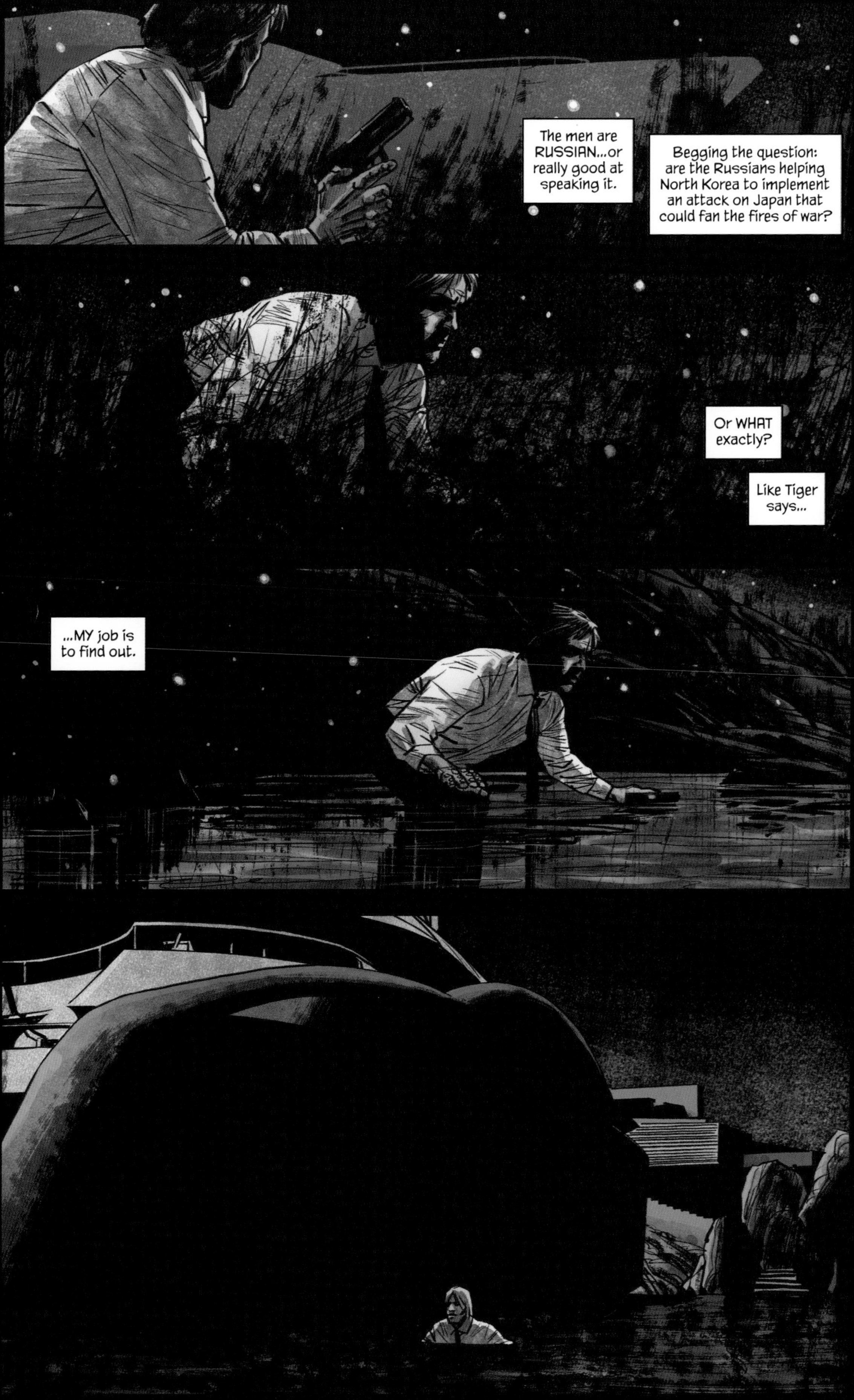

The men are RUSSIAN...or really good at speaking it.
Begging the question: are the Russians helping North Korea to implement an attack on Japan that could fan the fires of war?
Or WHAT exactly?
Like Tiger says...
...MY job is to find out.

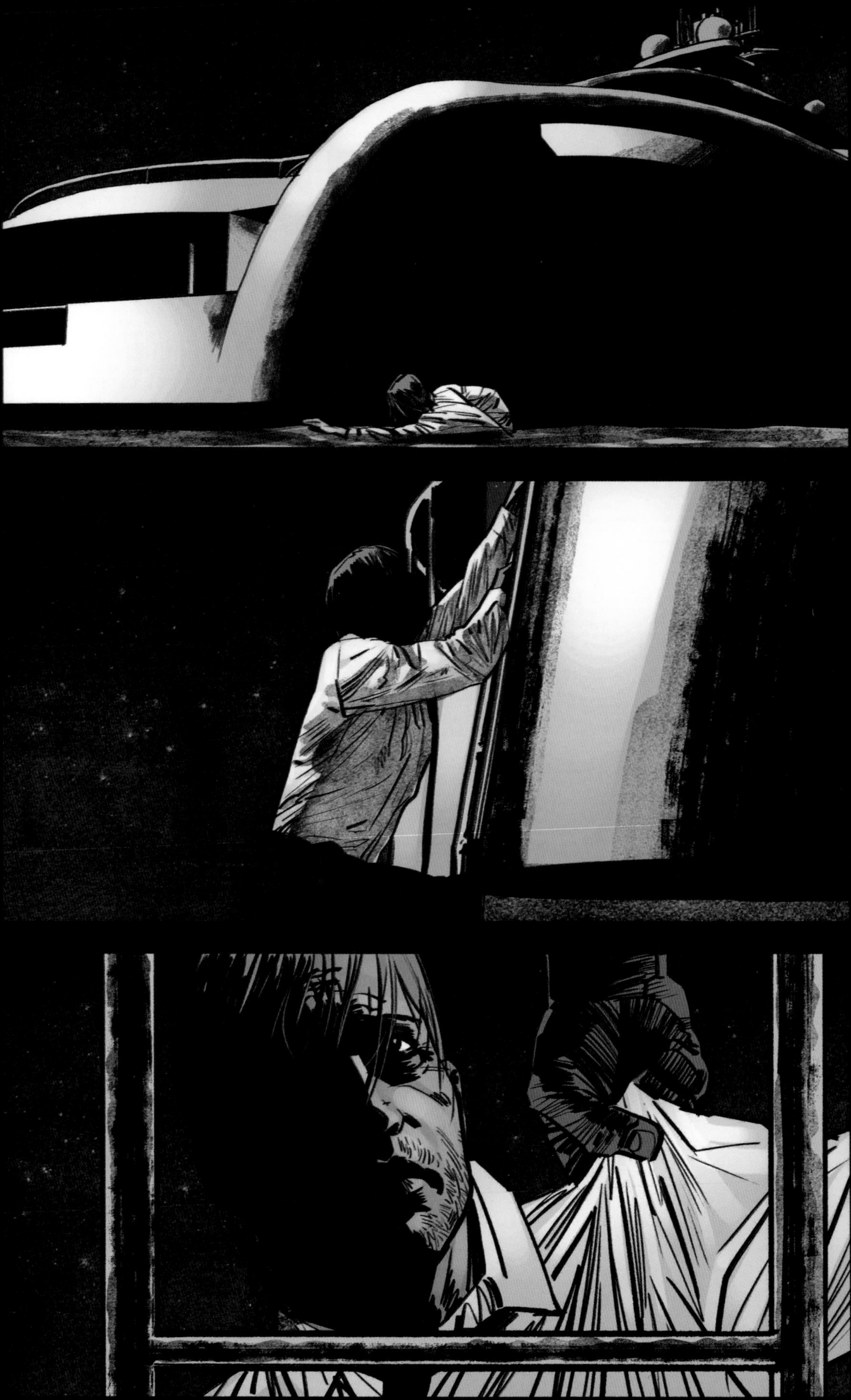

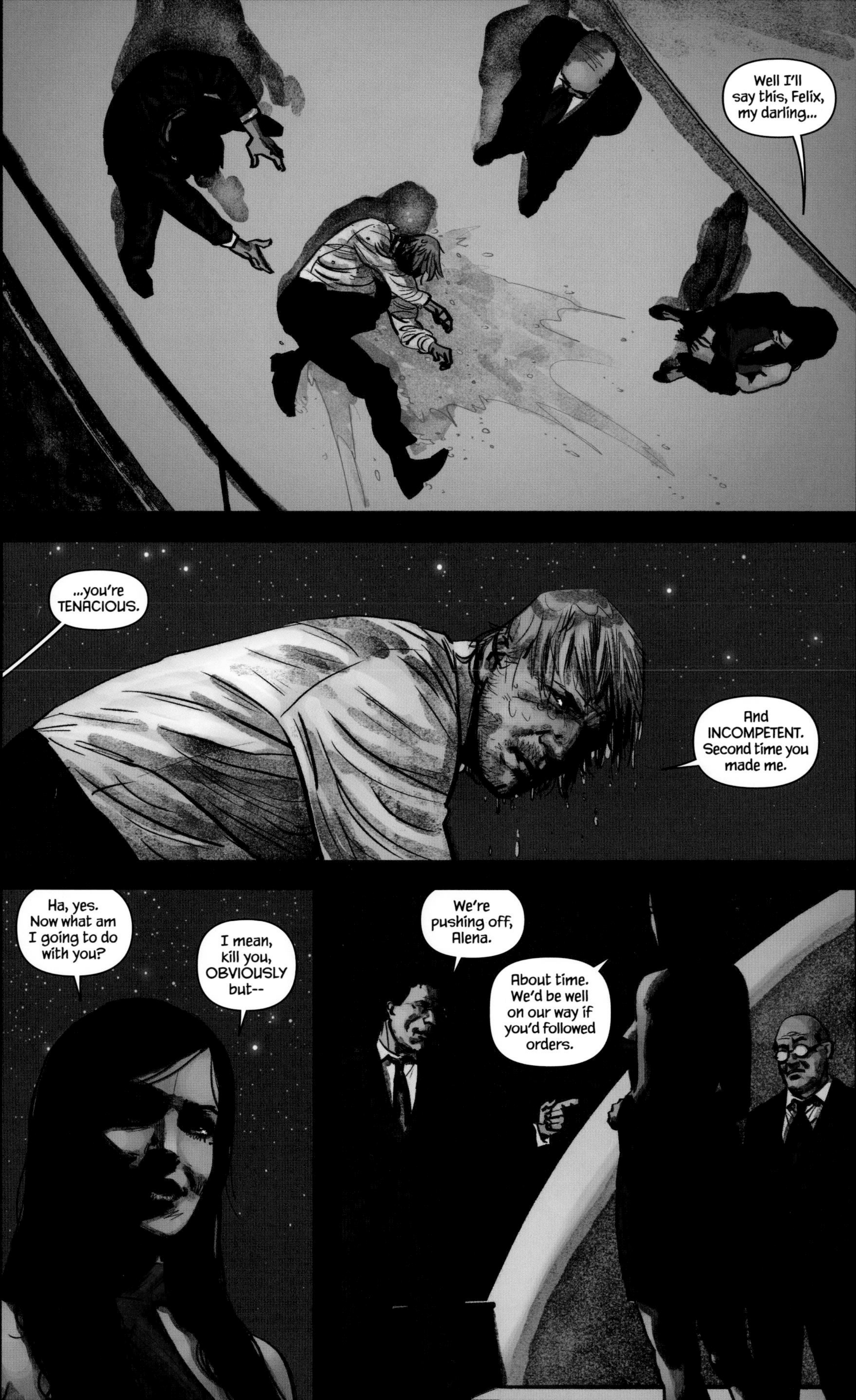
Well I'll say this, Felix, my darling...
...you're TENACIOUS.
And INCOMPETENT. Second time you made me.
Ha, yes. Now what am I going to do with you?
I mean, kill you, OBVIOUSLY but--
We're pushing off, Alena.
About time. We'd be well on our way if you'd followed orders.

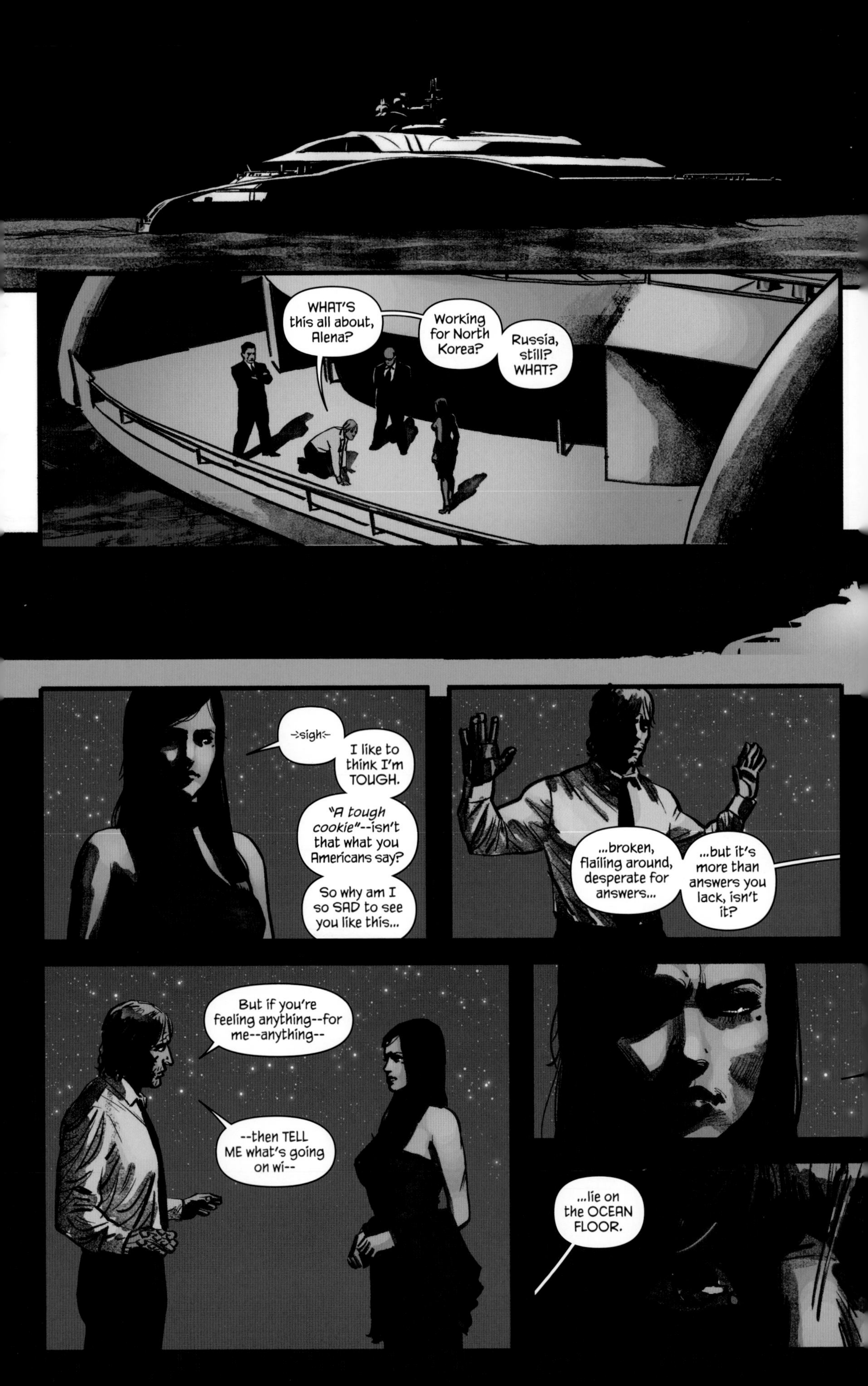
WHAT'S this all about, Alena?
Working for North Korea?
Russia, still? WHAT?
-sigh-
I like to think I'm TOUGH.
"A tough cookie"--isn't that what you Americans say?
So why am I so SAD to see you like this...
...broken, flailing around, desperate for answers...
...but it's more than answers you lack, isn't it?
But if you're feeling anything--for me--anything--
--then TELL ME what's going on wi--
...lie on the OCEAN FLOOR.

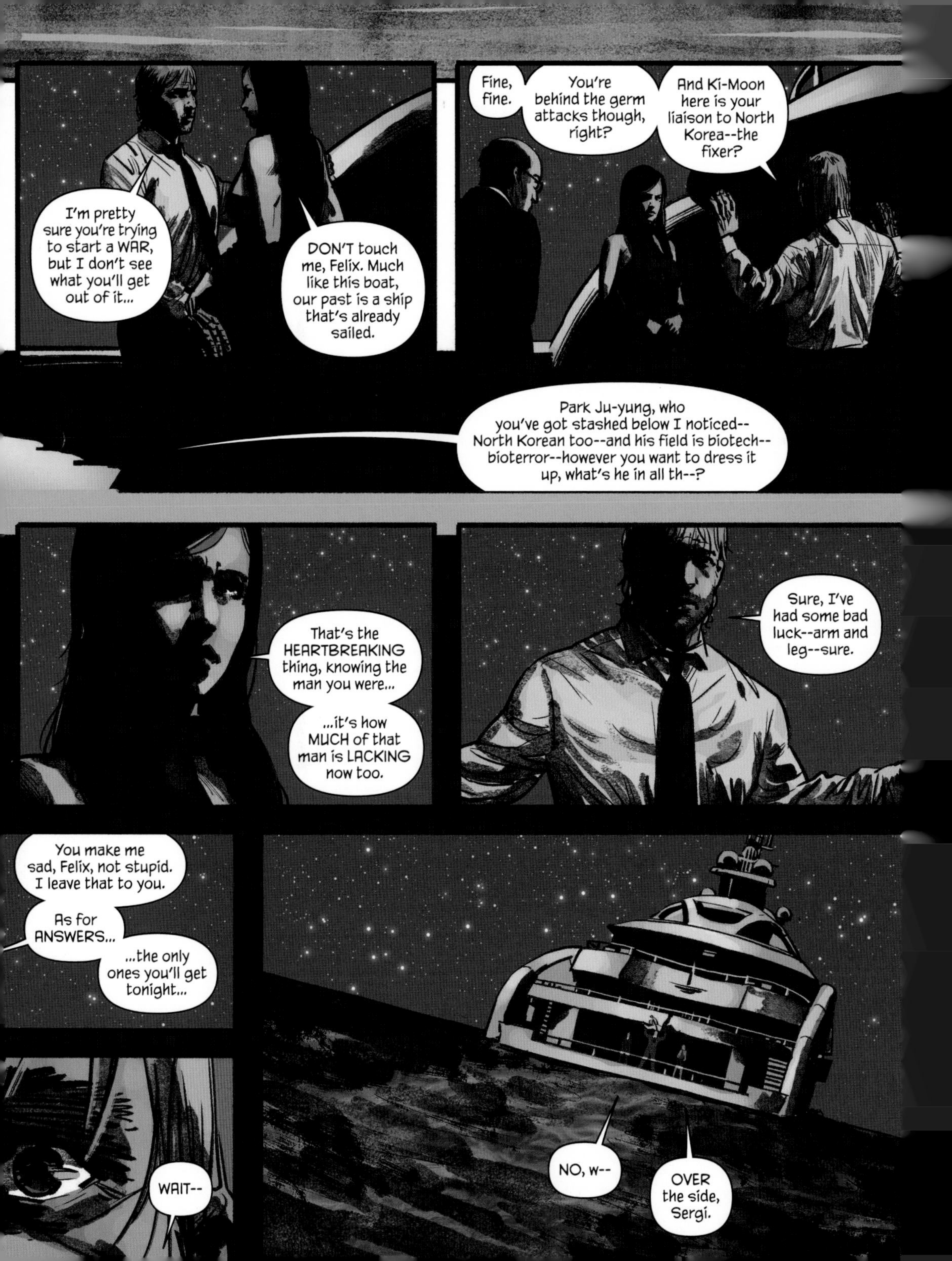
I'm pretty sure you're trying to start a WAR, but I don't see what you'll get out of it...
DON'T touch me, Felix. Much like this boat, our past is a ship that's already sailed.
Fine, fine.
You're behind the germ attacks though, right?
And Ki-Moon here is your liaison to North Korea--the fixer?
Park Ju-yung, who you've got stashed below I noticed--North Korean too--and his field is biotech--bioterror--however you want to dress it up, what's he in all th--?
That's the HEARTBREAKING thing, knowing the man you were...
...it's how MUCH of that man is LACKING now too.
Sure, I've had some bad luck--arm and leg--sure.
You make me sad, Felix, not stupid. I leave that to you.
As for ANSWERS...
...the only ones you'll get tonight...
WAIT--
NO, w--
OVER the side, Sergi.

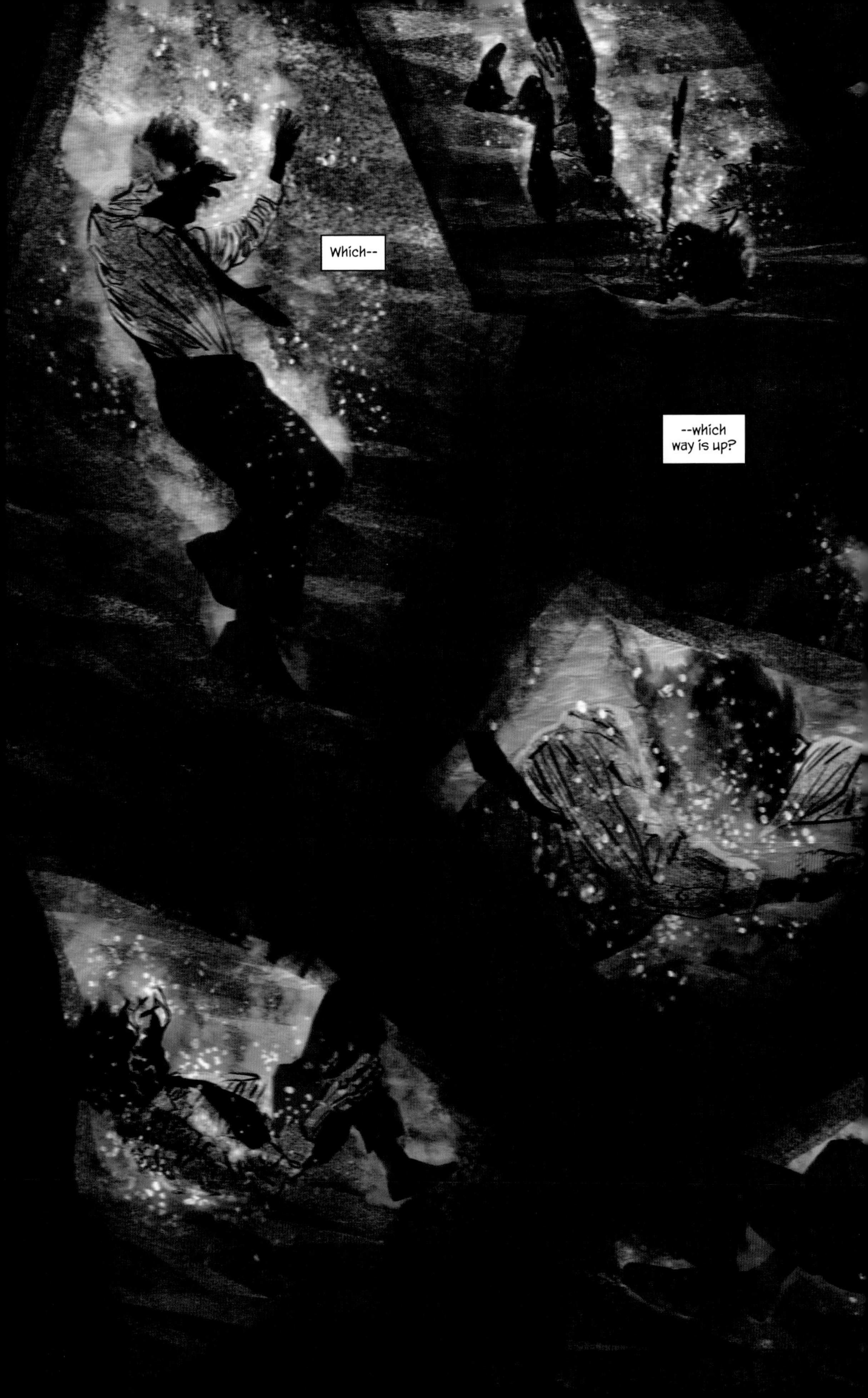
Which--
--which way is up?

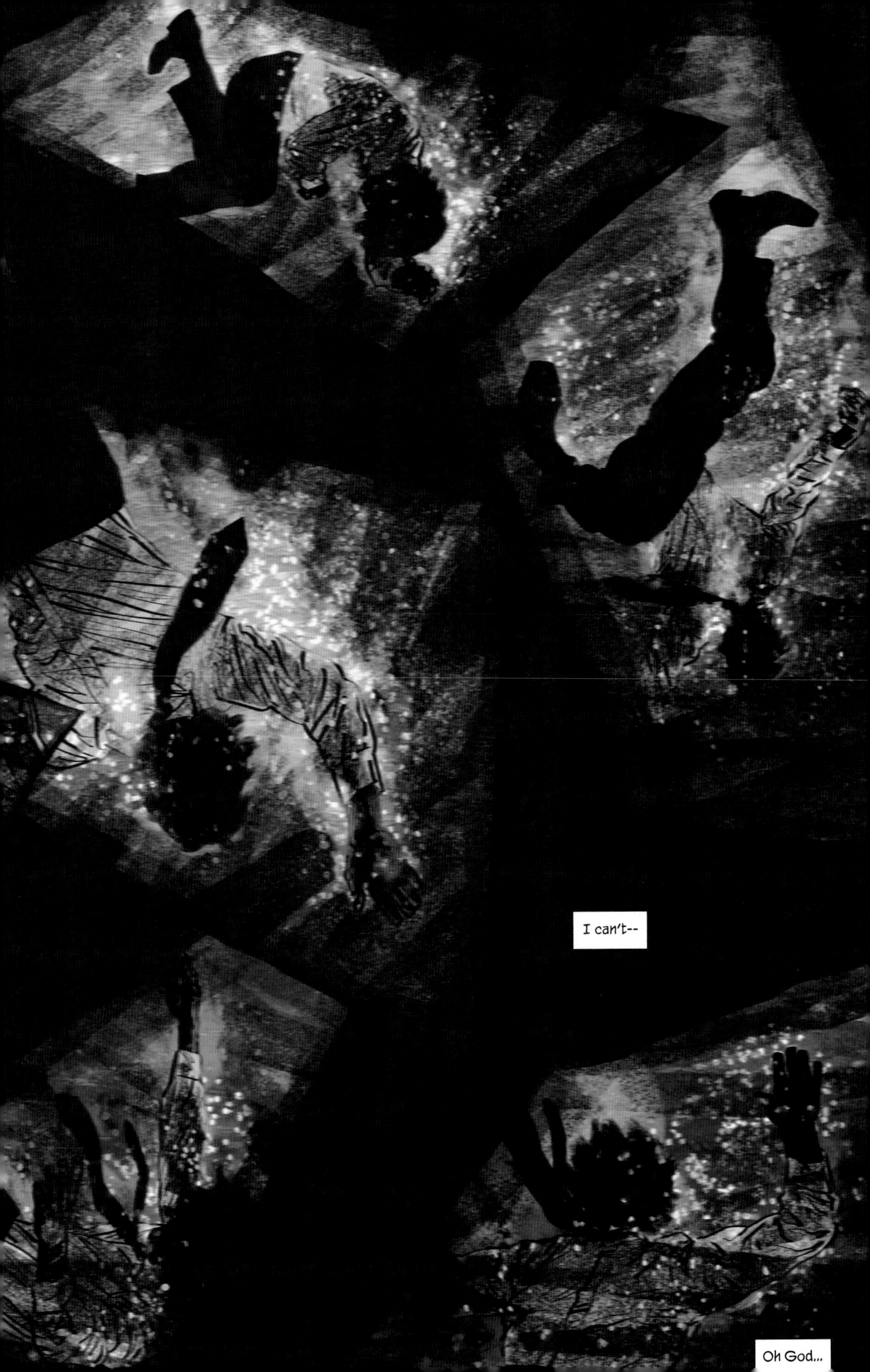
I can't--
Oh God...

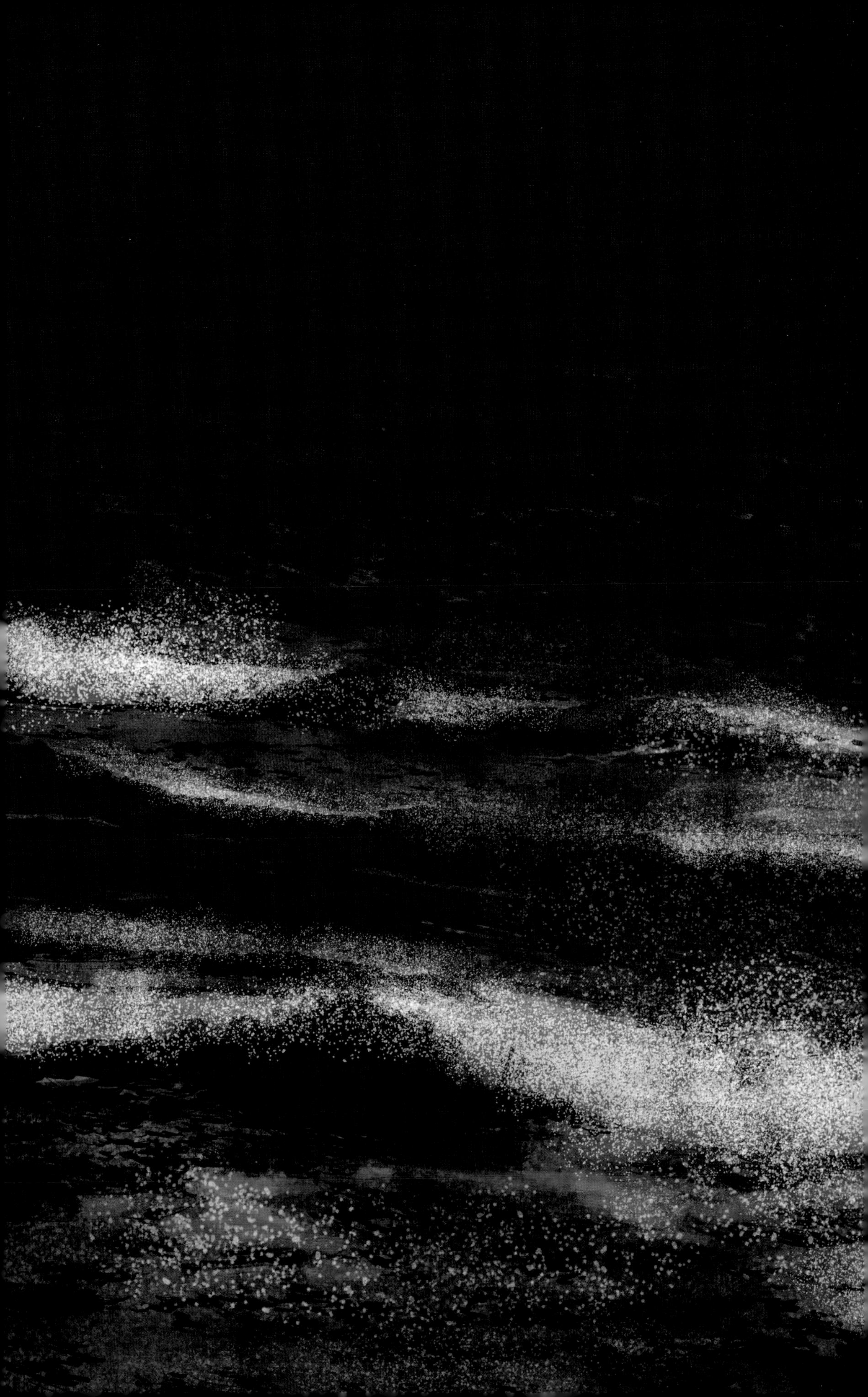

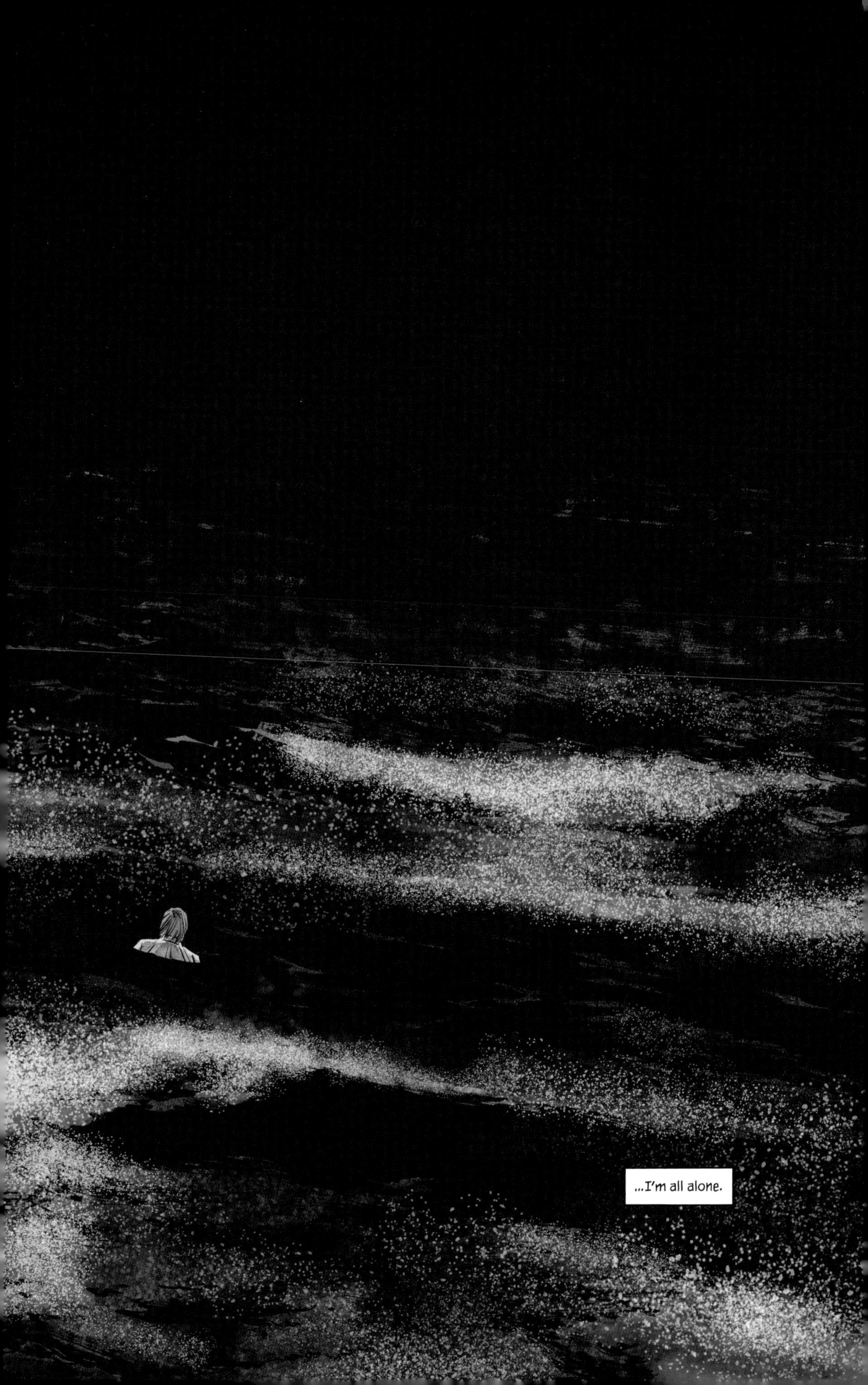
...I'm all alone.

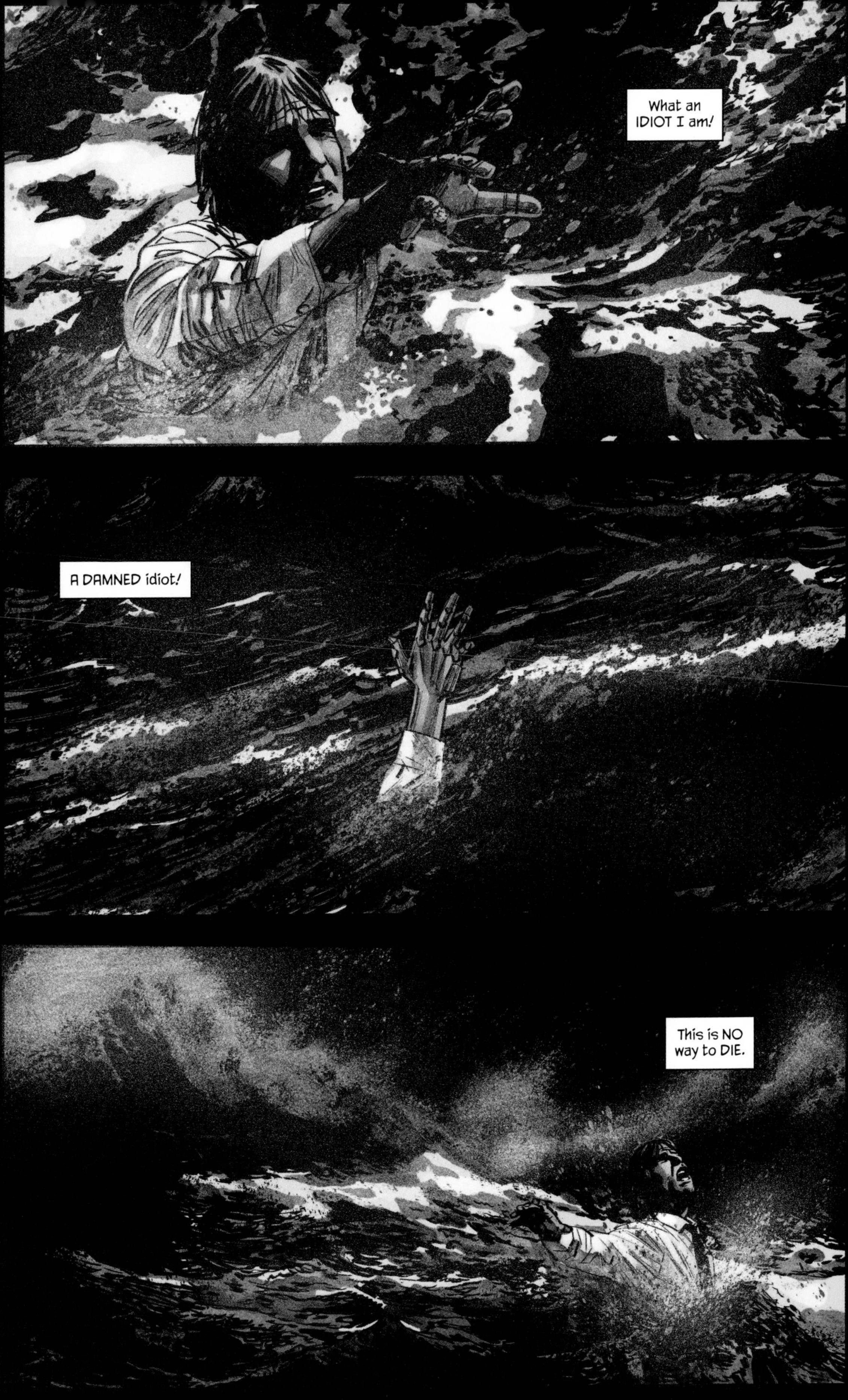
What an IDIOT I am!
A DAMNED idiot!
This is NO way to DIE.

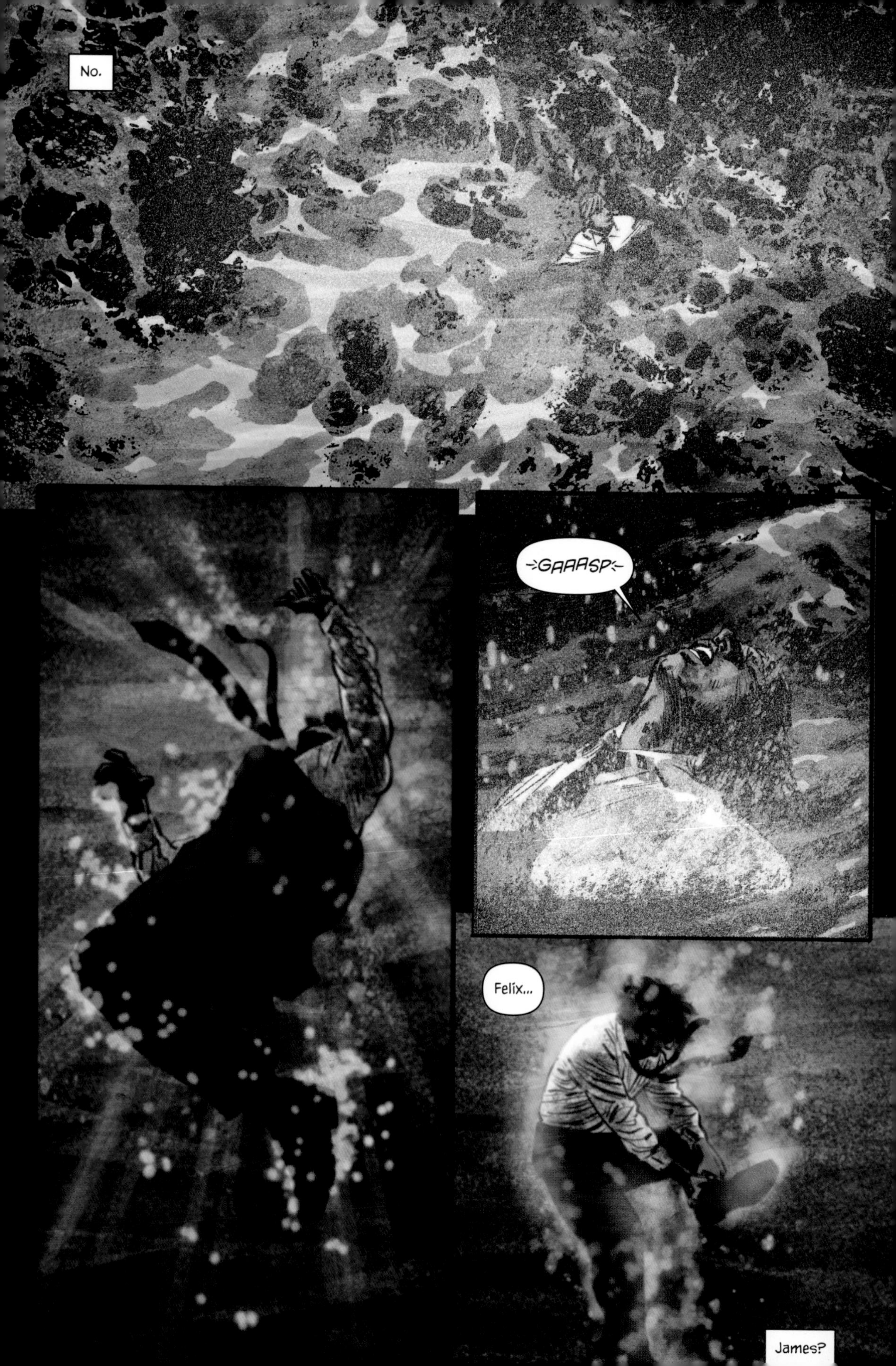
No.
-GAAASP-
Felix...
James?

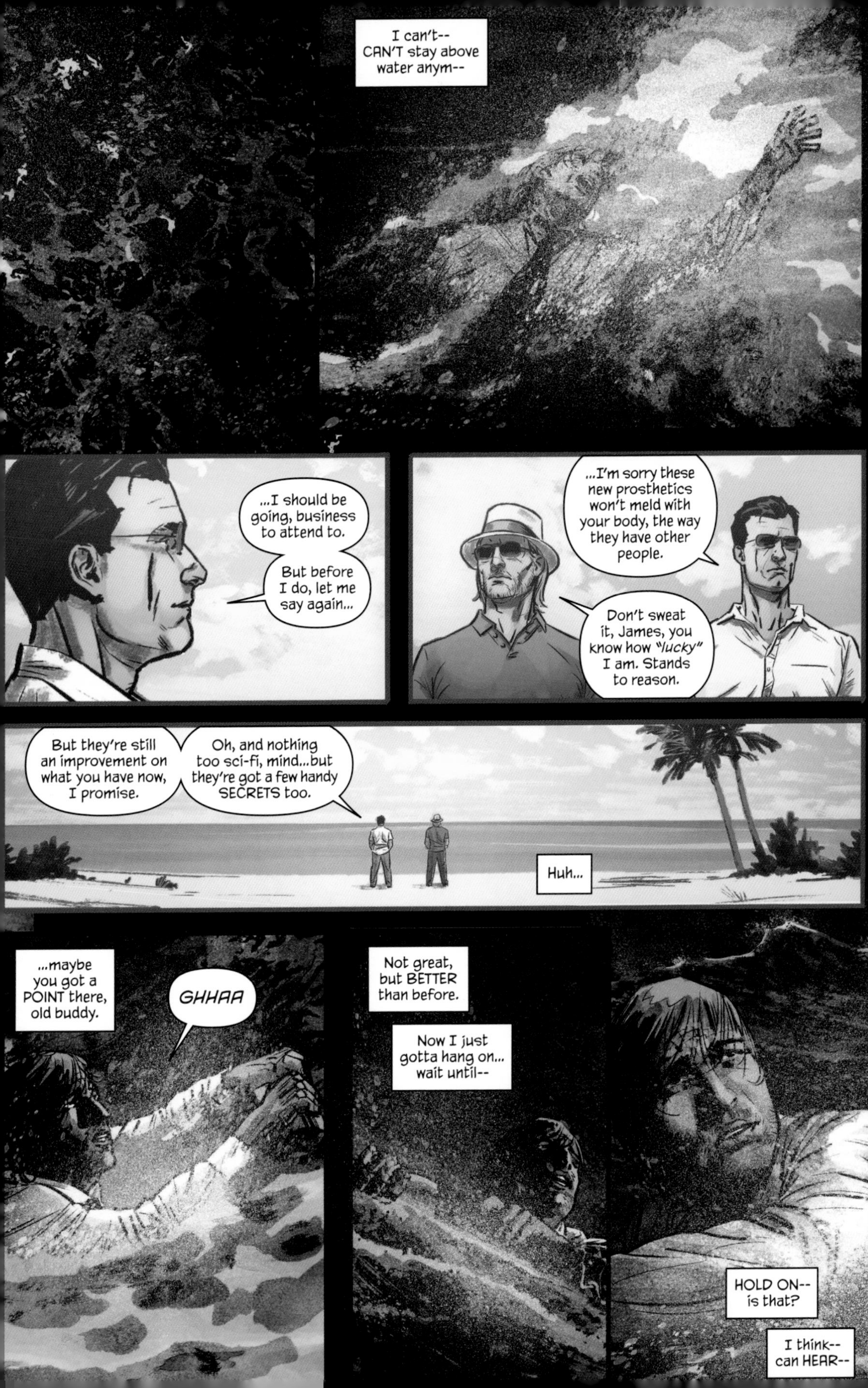
I can't--
CAN'T stay above water anym--
...I should be going, business to attend to.
But before I do, let me say again...
...I'm sorry these new prosthetics won't meld with your body, the way they have other people.
Don't sweat it, James, you know how "lucky" I am. Stands to reason.
But they're still an improvement on what you have now, I promise.
Oh, and nothing too sci-fi, mind...but they're got a few handy SECRETS too.
Huh...
...maybe you got a POINT there, old buddy.
GHHAA
Not great, but BETTER than before.
Now I just gotta hang on... wait until--
HOLD ON-- is that?
I think-- can HEAR--

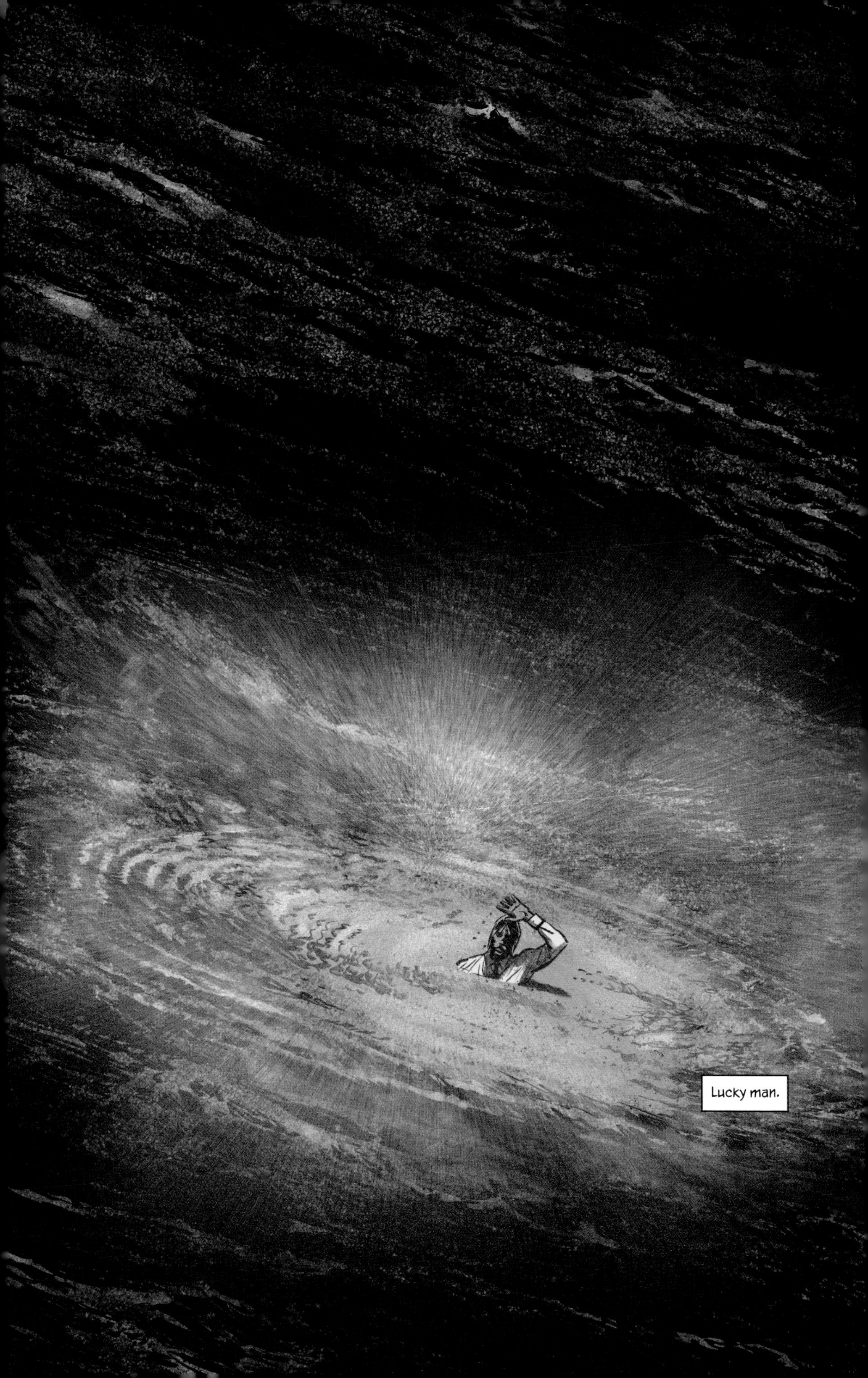
Lucky man.

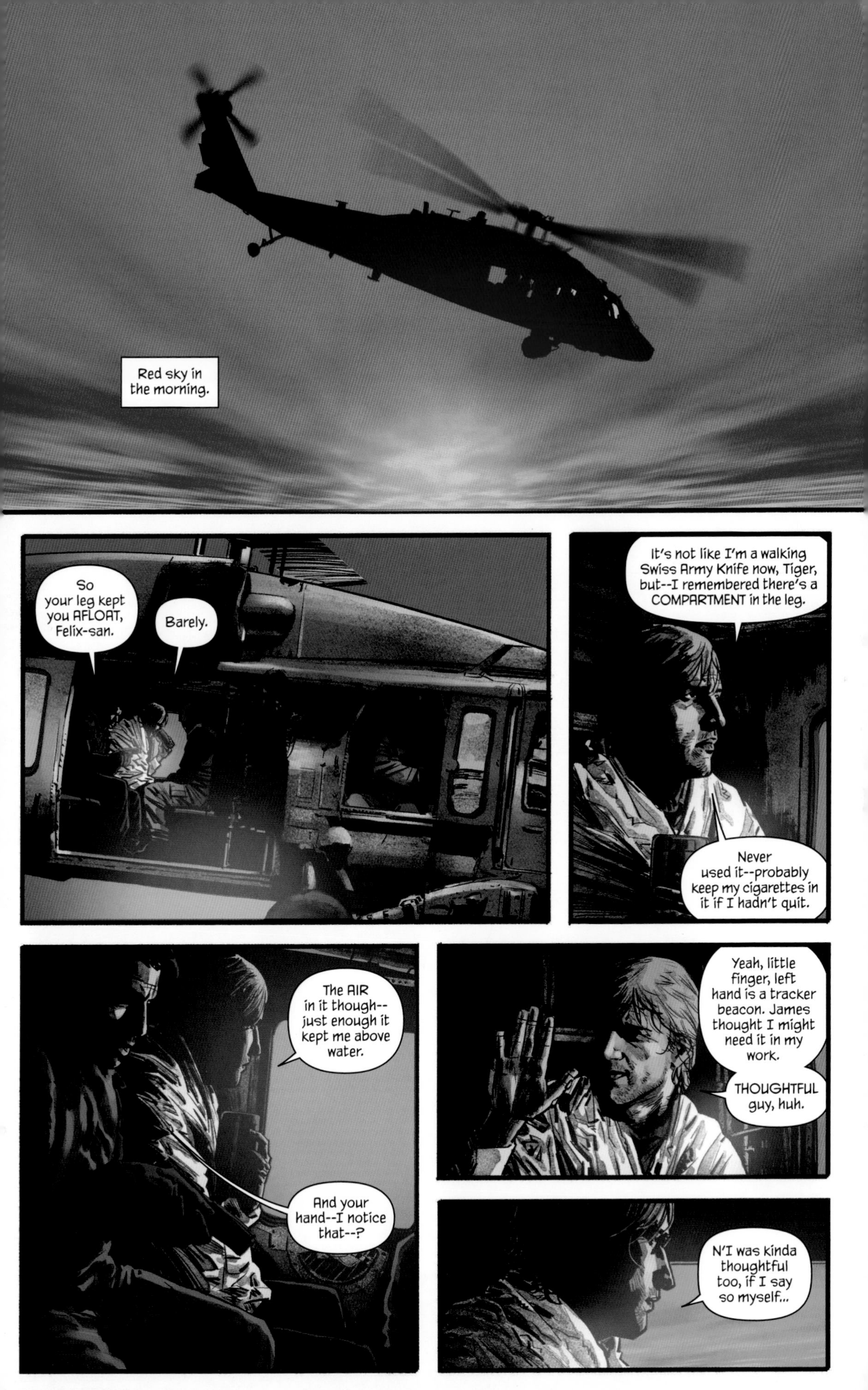
Red sky in the morning.
So your leg kept you AFLOAT, Felix-san.
Barely.
It's not like I'm a walking Swiss Army Knife now, Tiger, but--I remembered there's a COMPARTMENT in the leg.
Never used it--probably keep my cigarettes in it if I hadn't quit.
The AIR in it though--just enough it kept me above water.
And your hand--I notice that--?
Yeah, little finger, left hand is a tracker beacon. James thought I might need it in my work.
THOUGHTFUL guy, huh.
N'I was kinda thoughtful too, if I say so myself...

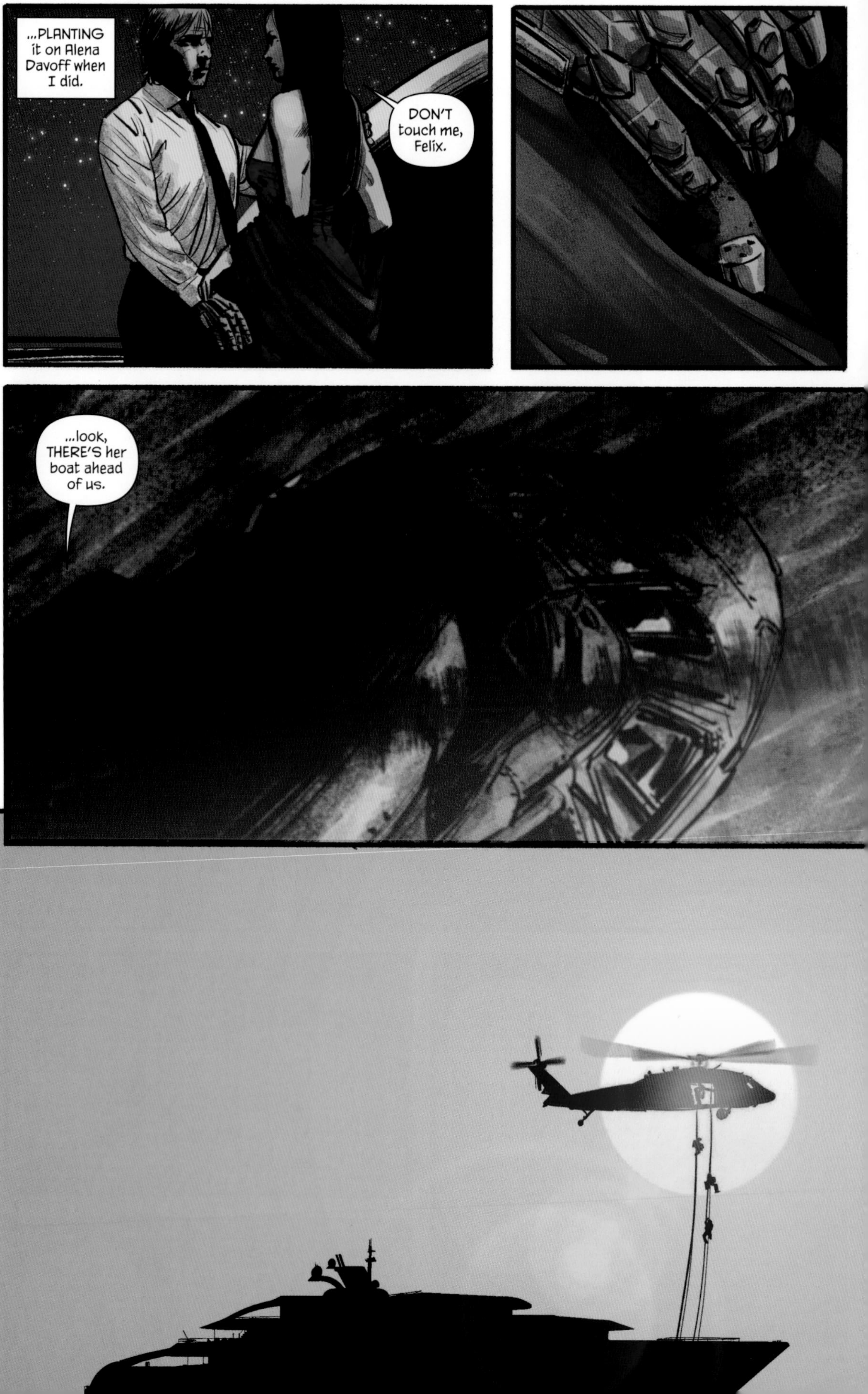

...PLANTING it on Alena Davoff when I did.
DON'T touch me, Felix.
...look, THERE'S her boat ahead of us.

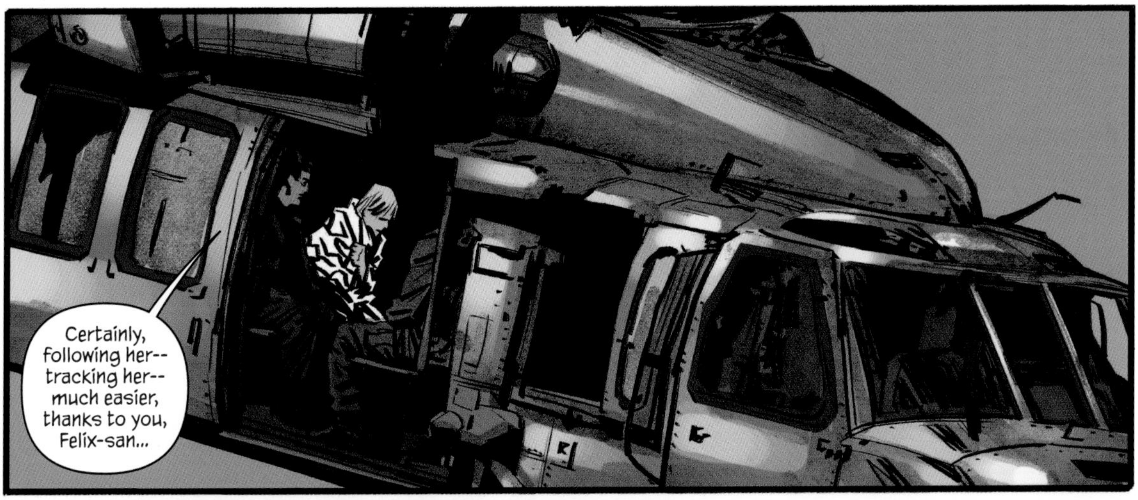
Certainly, following her-- tracking her-- much easier, thanks to you, Felix-san...

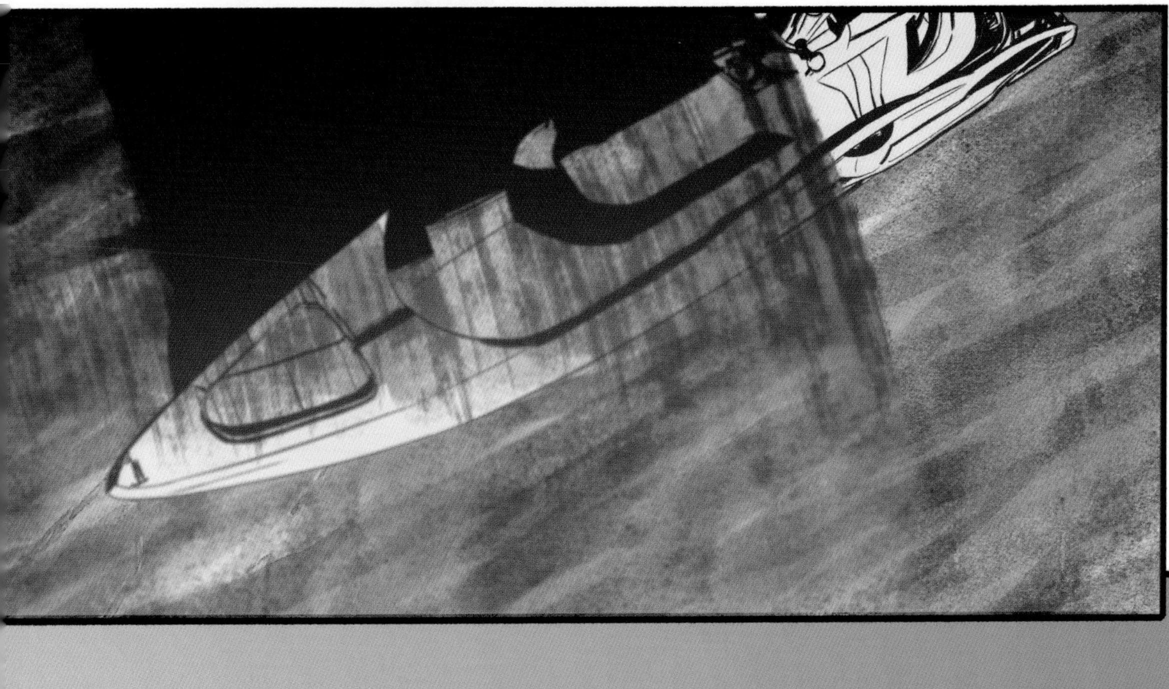

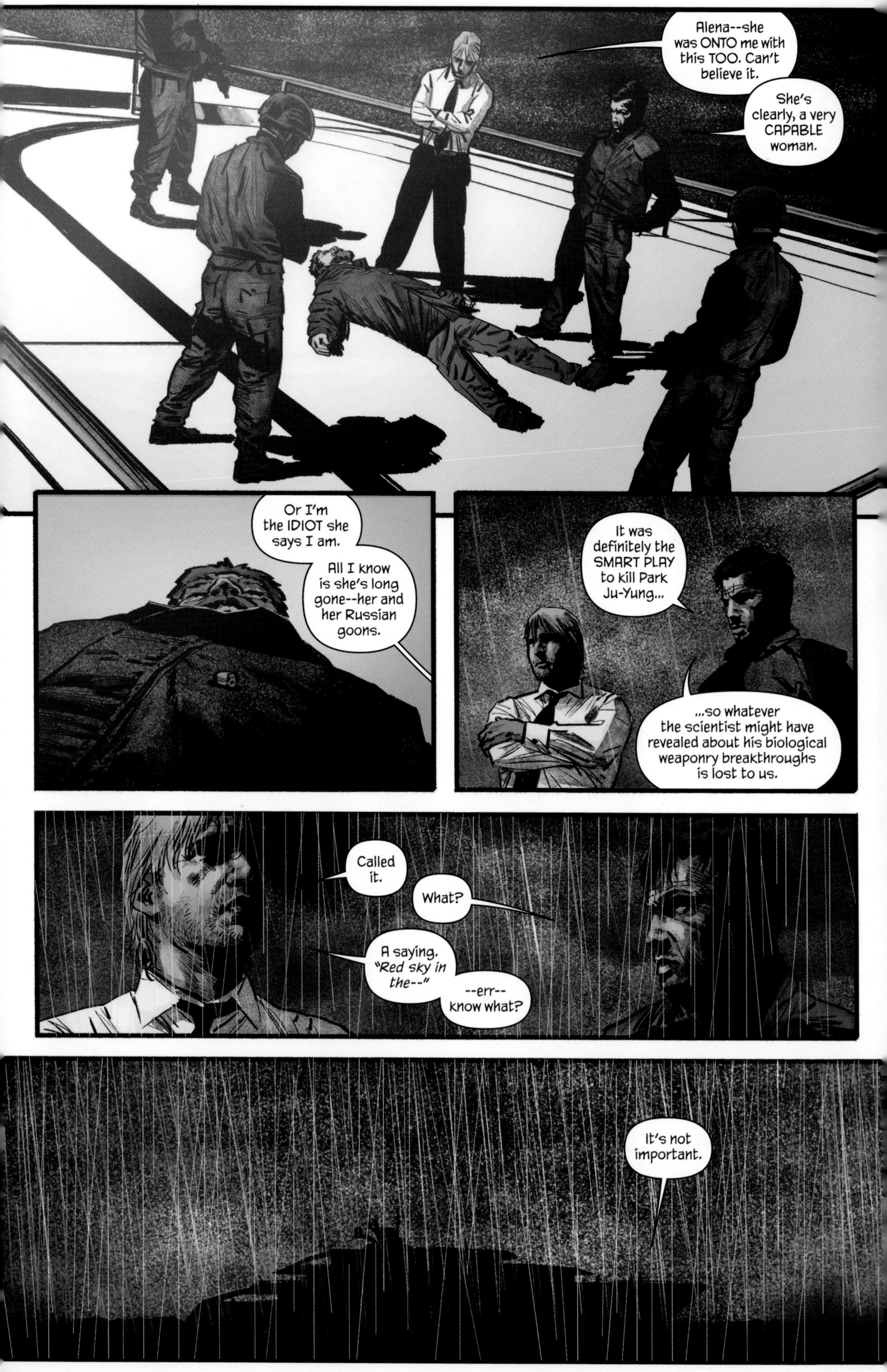
Alena--she was ONTO me with this TOO. Can't believe it.
She's clearly, a very CAPABLE woman.
Or I'm the IDIOT she says I am.
All I know is she's long gone--her and her Russian goons.
It was definitely the SMART PLAY to kill Park Ju-Yung...
...so whatever the scientist might have revealed about his biological weaponry breakthroughs is lost to us.
Called it.
What?
A saying. *"Red sky in the--"*
--err-- know what?
It's not important.

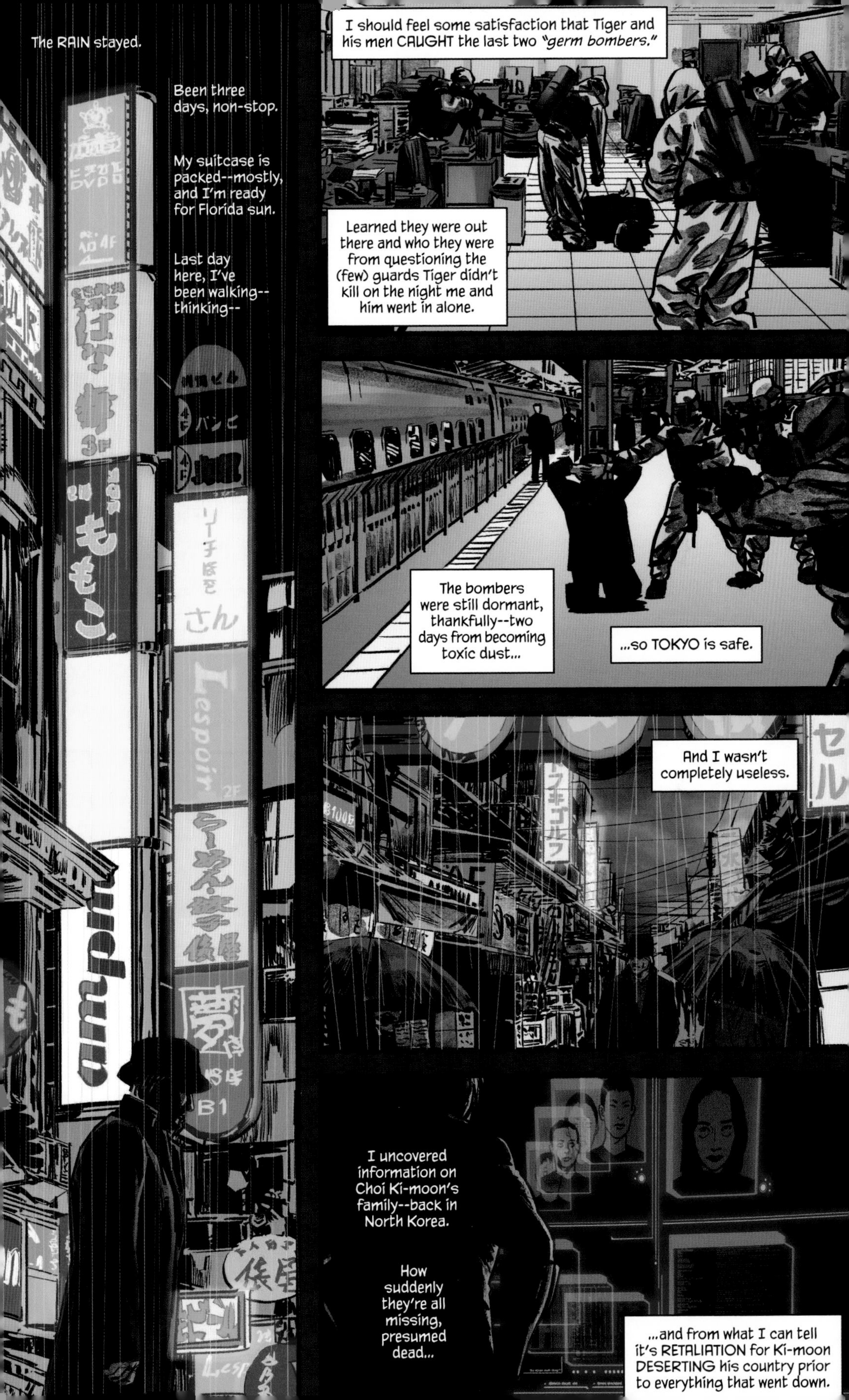
The RAIN stayed.
Been three days, non-stop.
My suitcase is packed--mostly, and I'm ready for Florida sun.
Last day here, I've been walking--thinking--
I should feel some satisfaction that Tiger and his men CAUGHT the last two *"germ bombers."*
Learned they were out there and who they were from questioning the (few) guards Tiger didn't kill on the night me and him went in alone.
The bombers were still dormant, thankfully--two days from becoming toxic dust...
...so TOKYO is safe.
And I wasn't completely useless.
I uncovered information on Choi Ki-moon's family--back in North Korea.
How suddenly they're all missing, presumed dead...
...and from what I can tell it's RETALIATION for Ki-moon DESERTING his country prior to everything that went down.

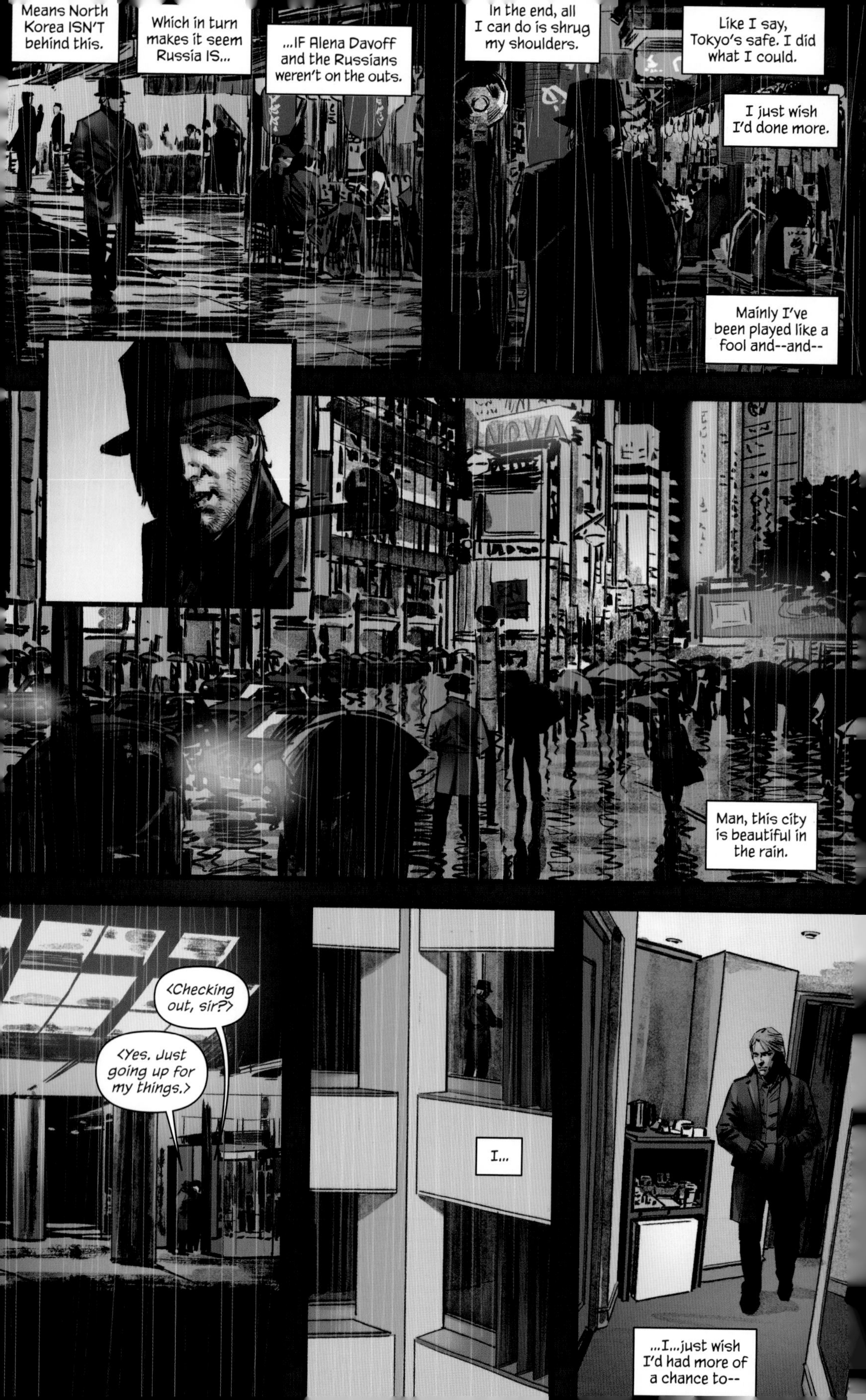
Means North Korea ISN'T behind this.
Which in turn makes it seem Russia IS...
...IF Alena Davoff and the Russians weren't on the outs.
In the end, all I can do is shrug my shoulders.
Like I say, Tokyo's safe. I did what I could.
I just wish I'd done more.
Mainly I've been played like a fool and--and--
Man, this city is beautiful in the rain.
<Checking out, sir?>
<Yes. Just going up for my things.>
I...
...I...just wish I'd had more of a chance to--

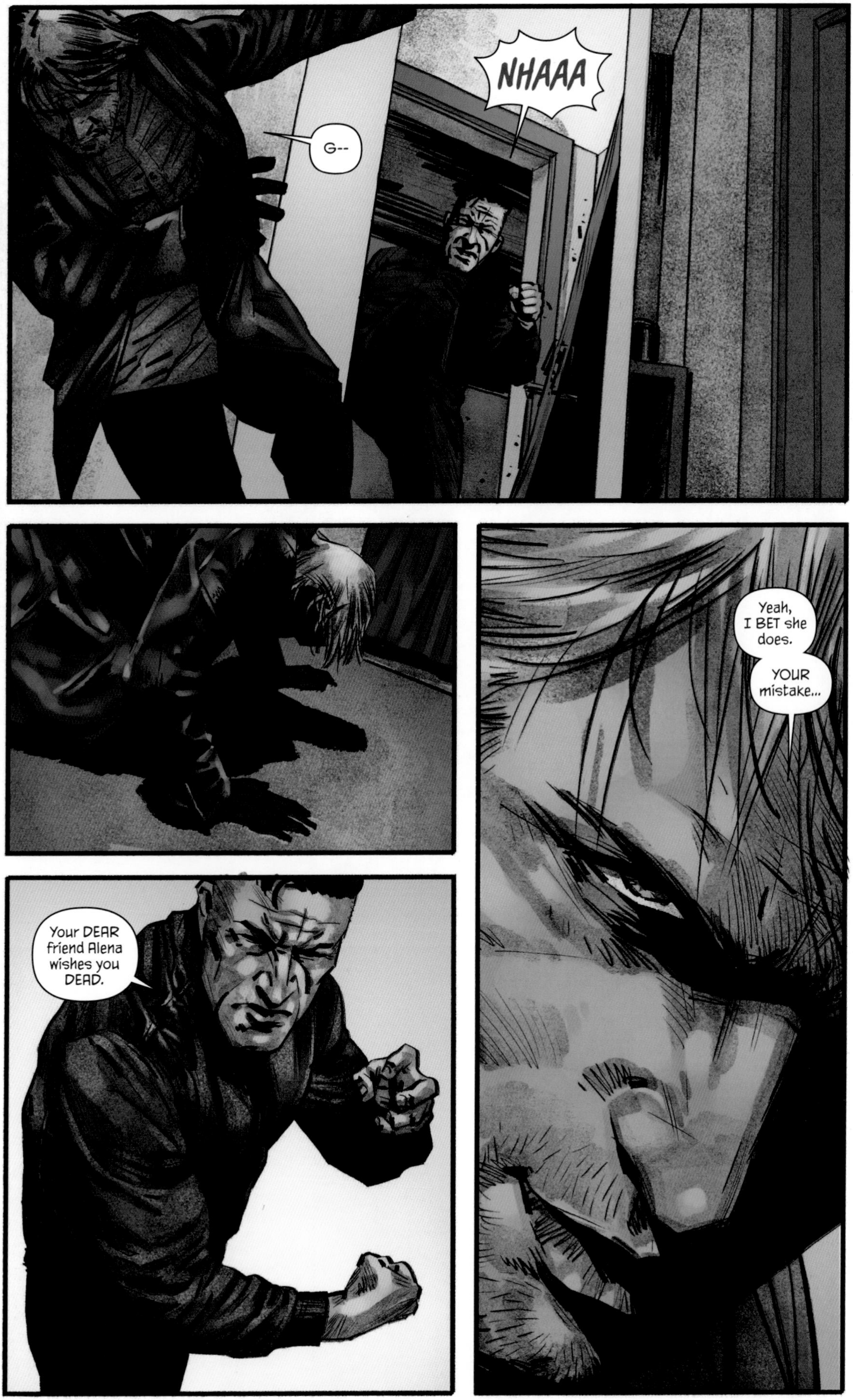
NHAAA
G--
Your DEAR friend Alena wishes you DEAD.
Yeah, I BET she does.
YOUR mistake...

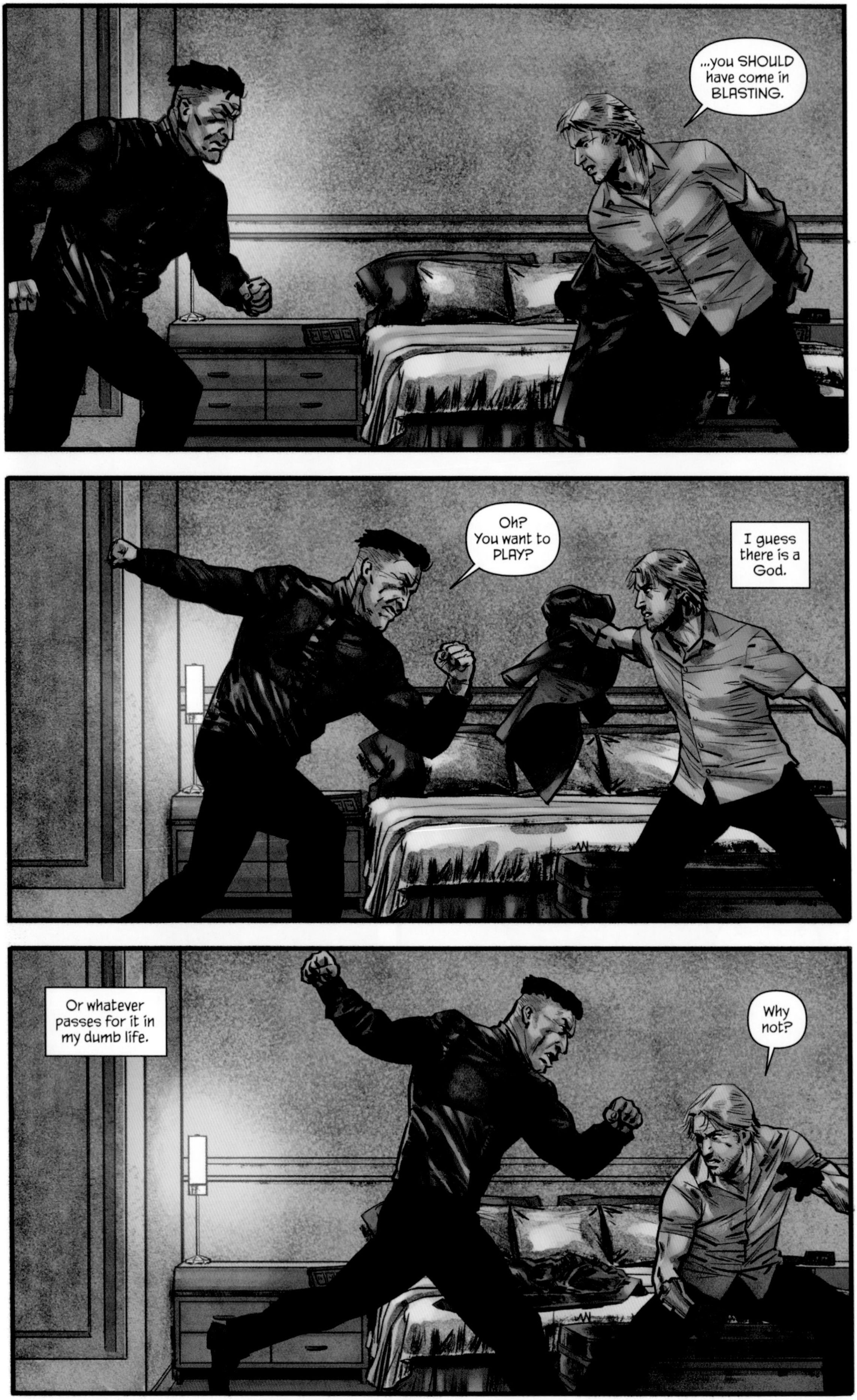
...you SHOULD have come in BLASTING.
Oh? You want to PLAY?
I guess there is a God.
Or whatever passes for it in my dumb life.
Why not?

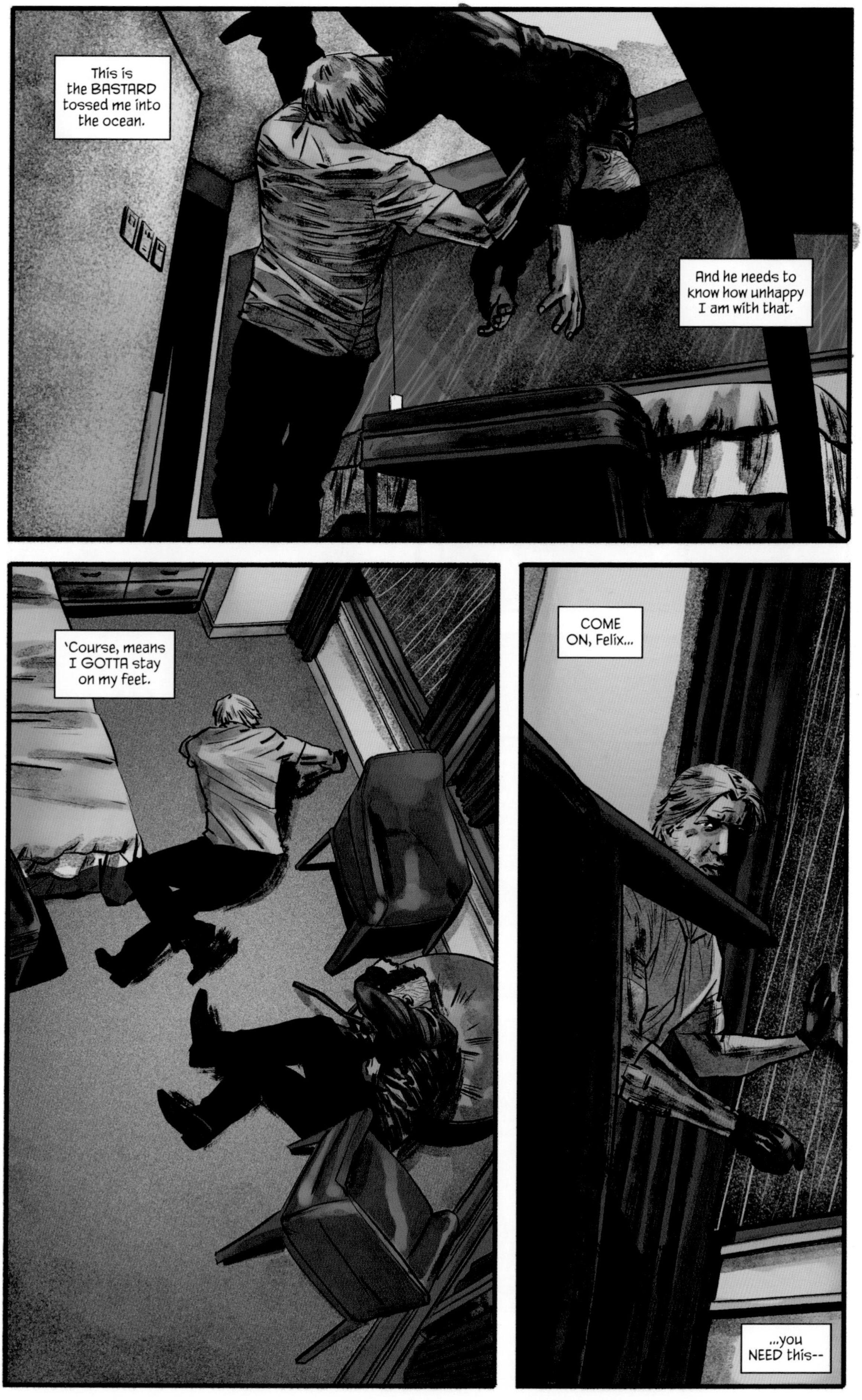
This is the BASTARD tossed me into the ocean.
And he needs to know how unhappy I am with that.
'Course, means I GOTTA stay on my feet.
COME ON, Felix...
...you NEED this--

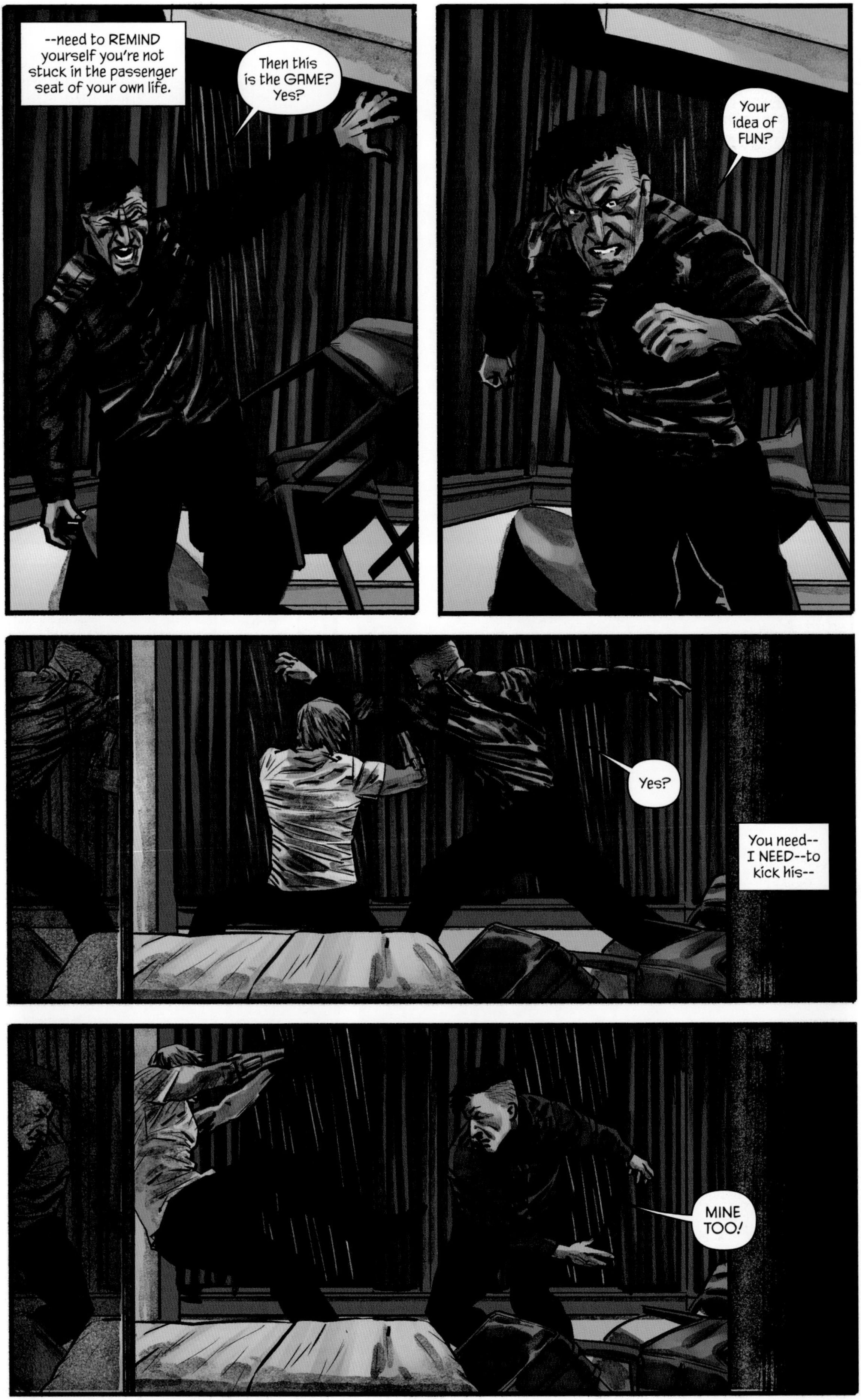
--need to REMIND yourself you're not stuck in the passenger seat of your own life.
Then this is the GAME? Yes?
Your idea of FUN?
Yes?
You need-- I NEED--to kick his--
MINE TOO!

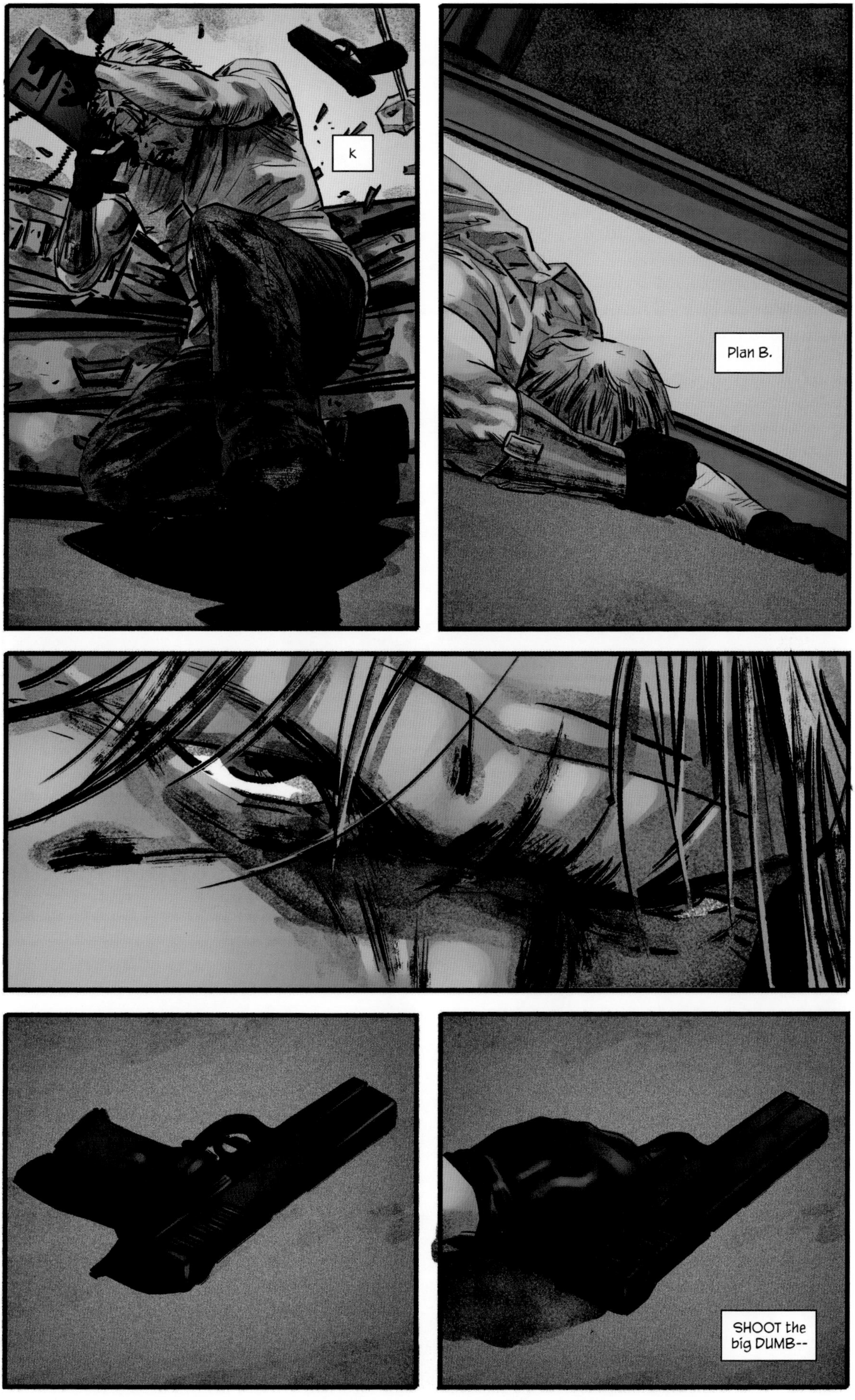
k
Plan B.
SHOOT the big DUMB--

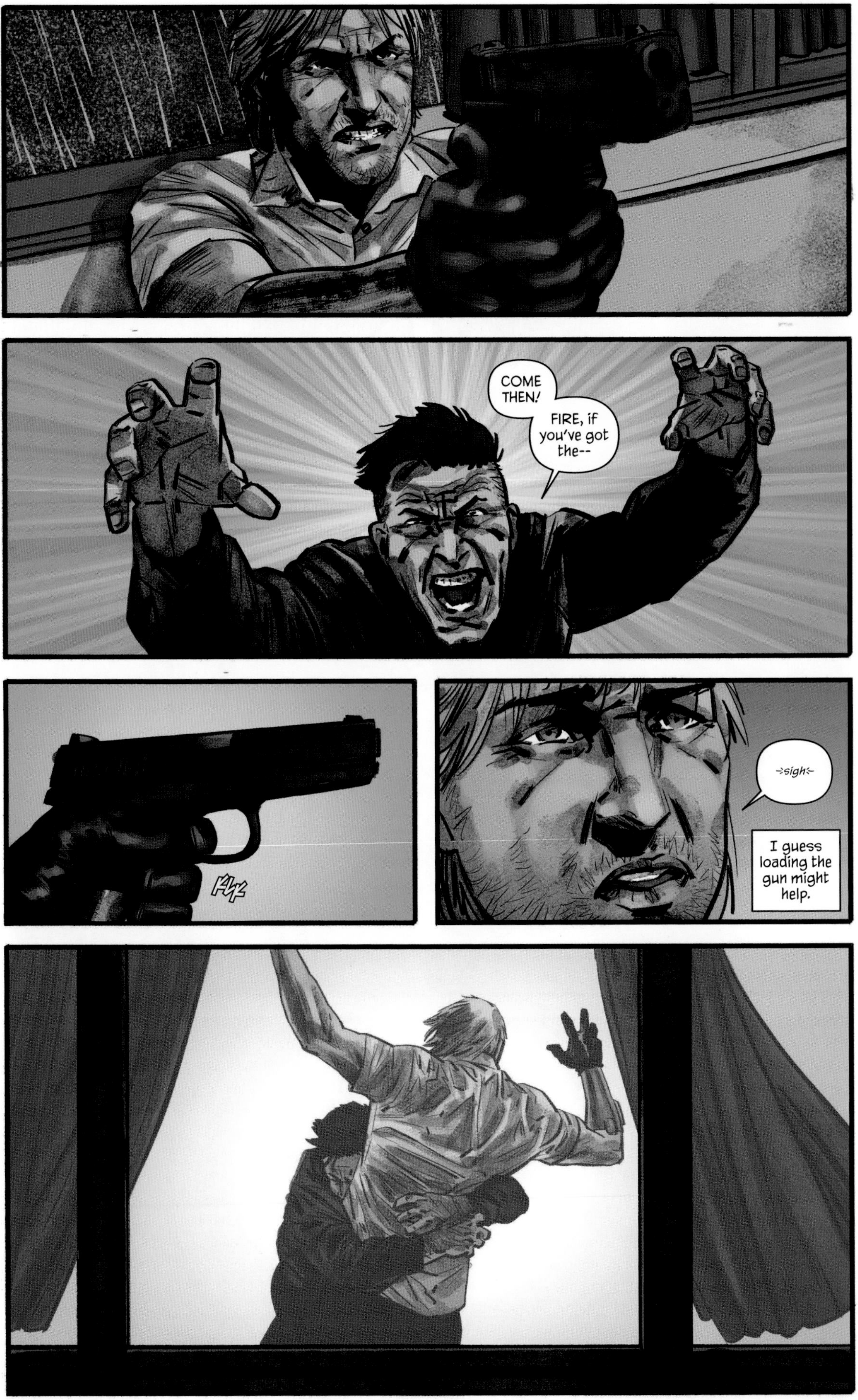
COME THEN!
FIRE, if you've got the--
KLIK
-sigh-
I guess loading the gun might help.

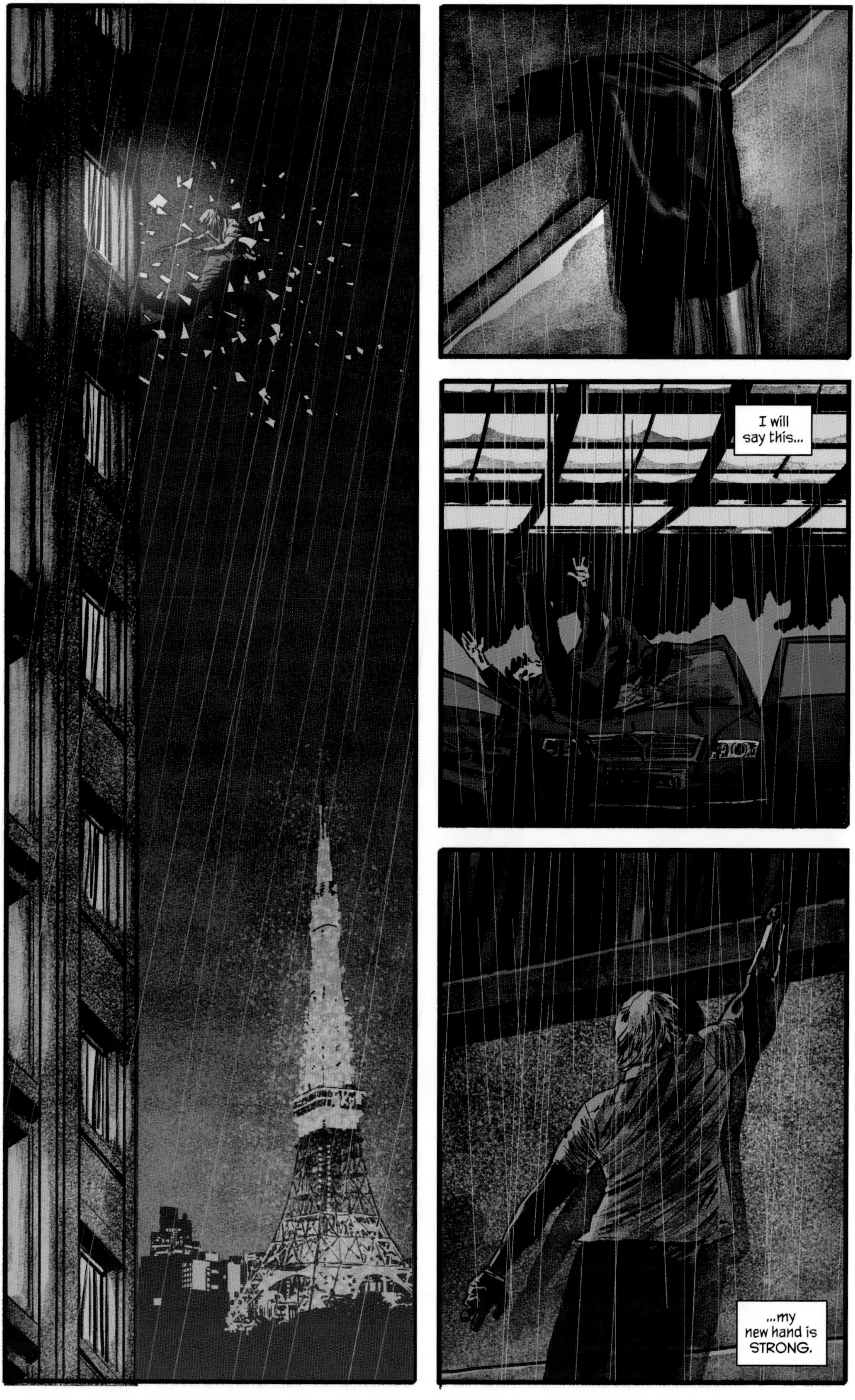
I will say this...
...my new hand is STRONG.

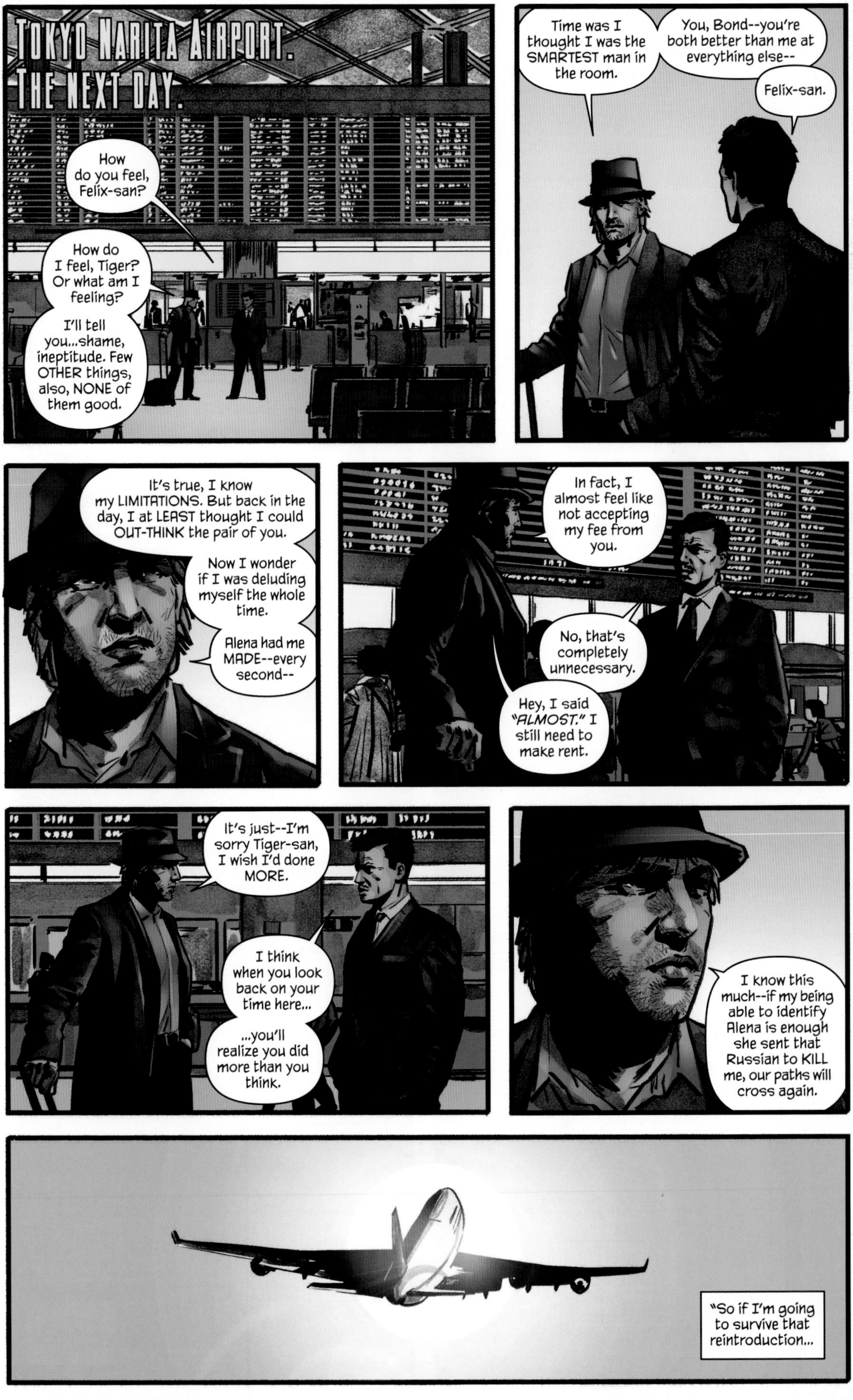
Tokyo Narita Airport. The next day.
How do you feel, Felix-san?
How do I feel, Tiger? Or what am I feeling?
I'll tell you...shame, ineptitude. Few OTHER things, also, NONE of them good.
Time was I thought I was the SMARTEST man in the room.
You, Bond--you're both better than me at everything else--
Felix-san.
It's true, I know my LIMITATIONS. But back in the day, I at LEAST thought I could OUT-THINK the pair of you.
Now I wonder if I was deluding myself the whole time.
Alena had me MADE--every second--
In fact, I almost feel like not accepting my fee from you.
No, that's completely unnecessary.
Hey, I said "ALMOST." I still need to make rent.
It's just--I'm sorry Tiger-san, I wish I'd done MORE.
I think when you look back on your time here...
...you'll realize you did more than you think.
I know this much--if my being able to identify Alena is enough she sent that Russian to KILL me, our paths will cross again.
"So if I'm going to survive that reintroduction...

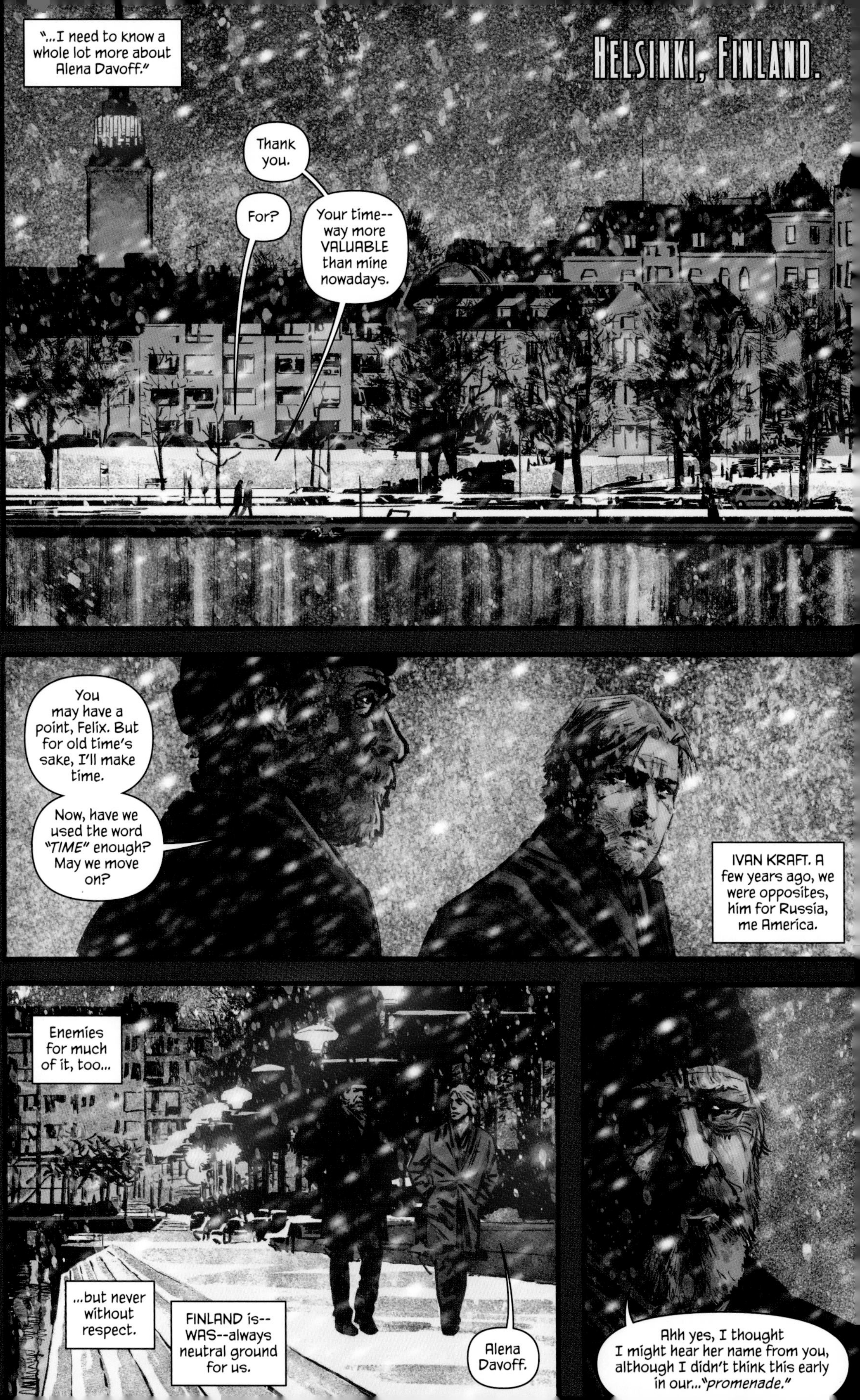
"...I need to know a whole lot more about Alena Davoff."
HELSINKI, FINLAND.
Thank you.
For?
Your time--way more VALUABLE than mine nowadays.
You may have a point, Felix. But for old time's sake, I'll make time.
Now, have we used the word "TIME" enough? May we move on?
IVAN KRAFT. A few years ago, we were opposites, him for Russia, me America.
Enemies for much of it, too...
...but never without respect.
FINLAND is--WAS--always neutral ground for us.
Alena Davoff.
Ahh yes, I thought I might hear her name from you, although I didn't think this early in our..."promenade."

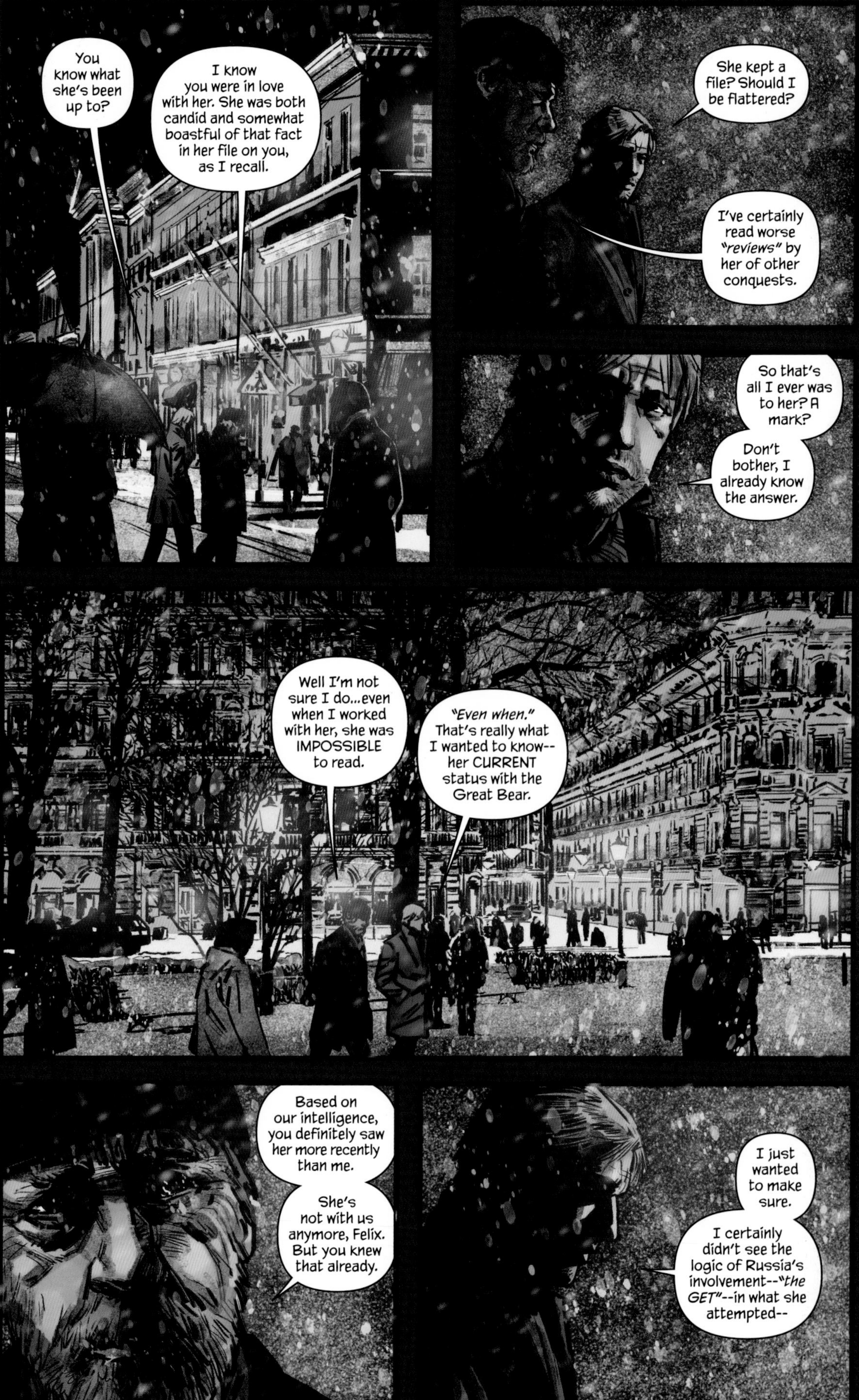

You know what she's been up to?
I know you were in love with her. She was both candid and somewhat boastful of that fact in her file on you, as I recall.
She kept a file? Should I be flattered?
I've certainly read worse "reviews" by her of other conquests.
So that's all I ever was to her? A mark?
Don't bother, I already know the answer.
Well I'm not sure I do...even when I worked with her, she was IMPOSSIBLE to read.
"Even when." That's really what I wanted to know--her CURRENT status with the Great Bear.
Based on our intelligence, you definitely saw her more recently than me.
She's not with us anymore, Felix. But you knew that already.
I just wanted to make sure.
I certainly didn't see the logic of Russia's involvement--"the GET"--in what she attempted--

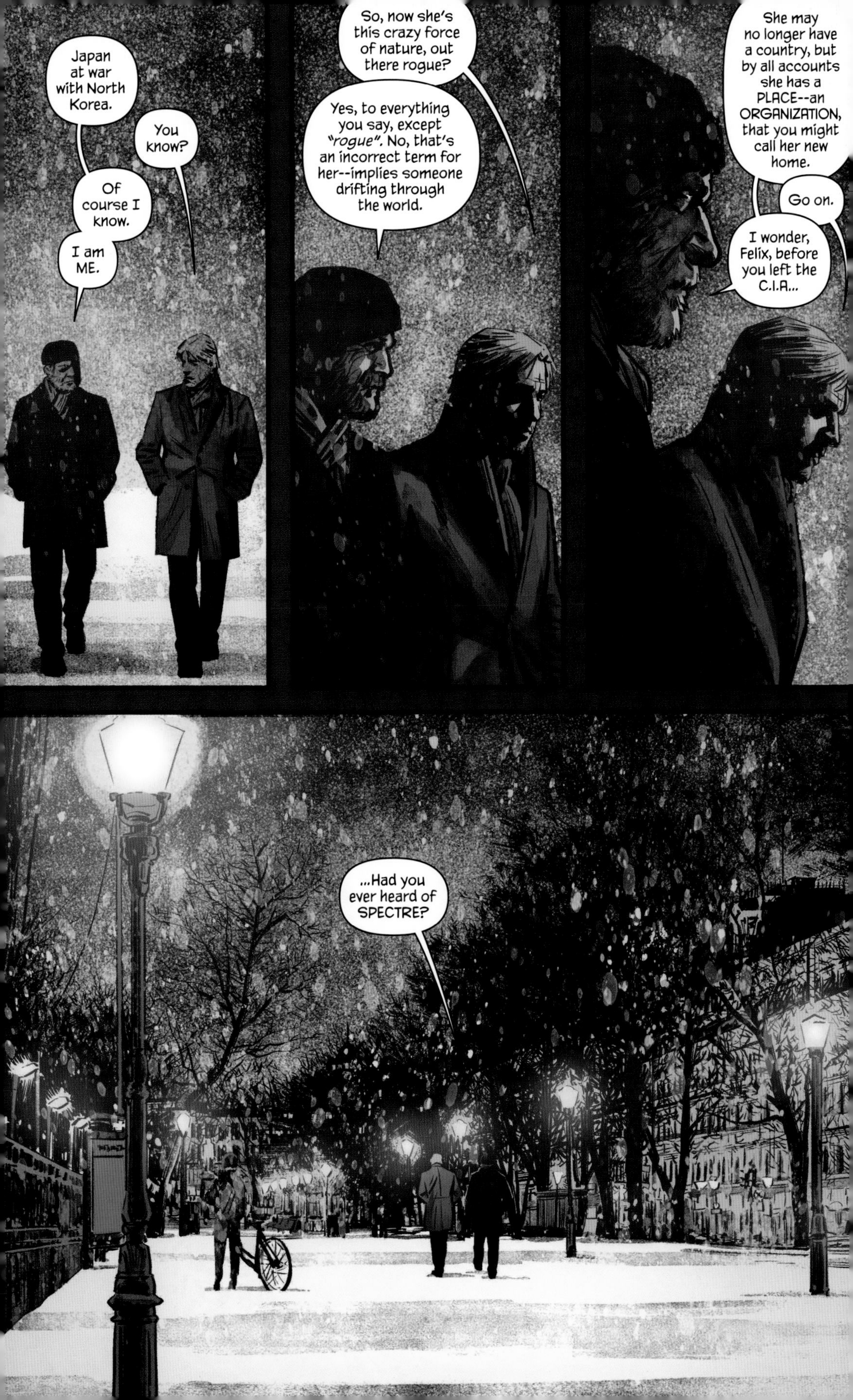
Japan at war with North Korea.
You know?
Of course I know.
I am ME.
So, now she's this crazy force of nature, out there rogue?
Yes, to everything you say, except *"rogue"*. No, that's an incorrect term for her--implies someone drifting through the world.
She may no longer have a country, but by all accounts she has a PLACE--an ORGANIZATION, that you might call her new home.
Go on.
I wonder, Felix, before you left the C.I.A...
...Had you ever heard of SPECTRE?

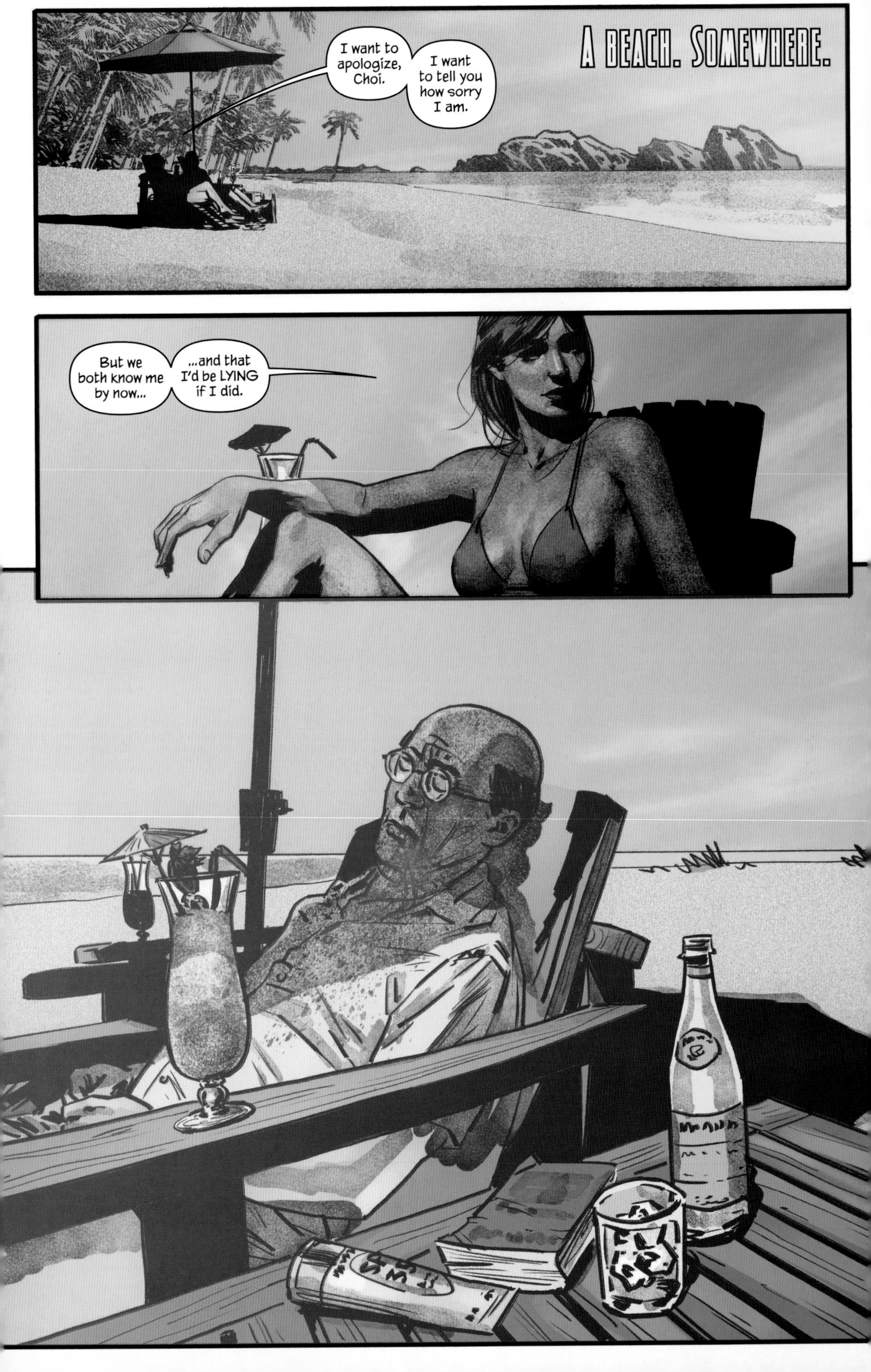
A BEACH. SOMEWHERE.
I want to apologize, Choi.
I want to tell you how sorry I am.
But we both know me by now...
...and that I'd be LYING if I did.

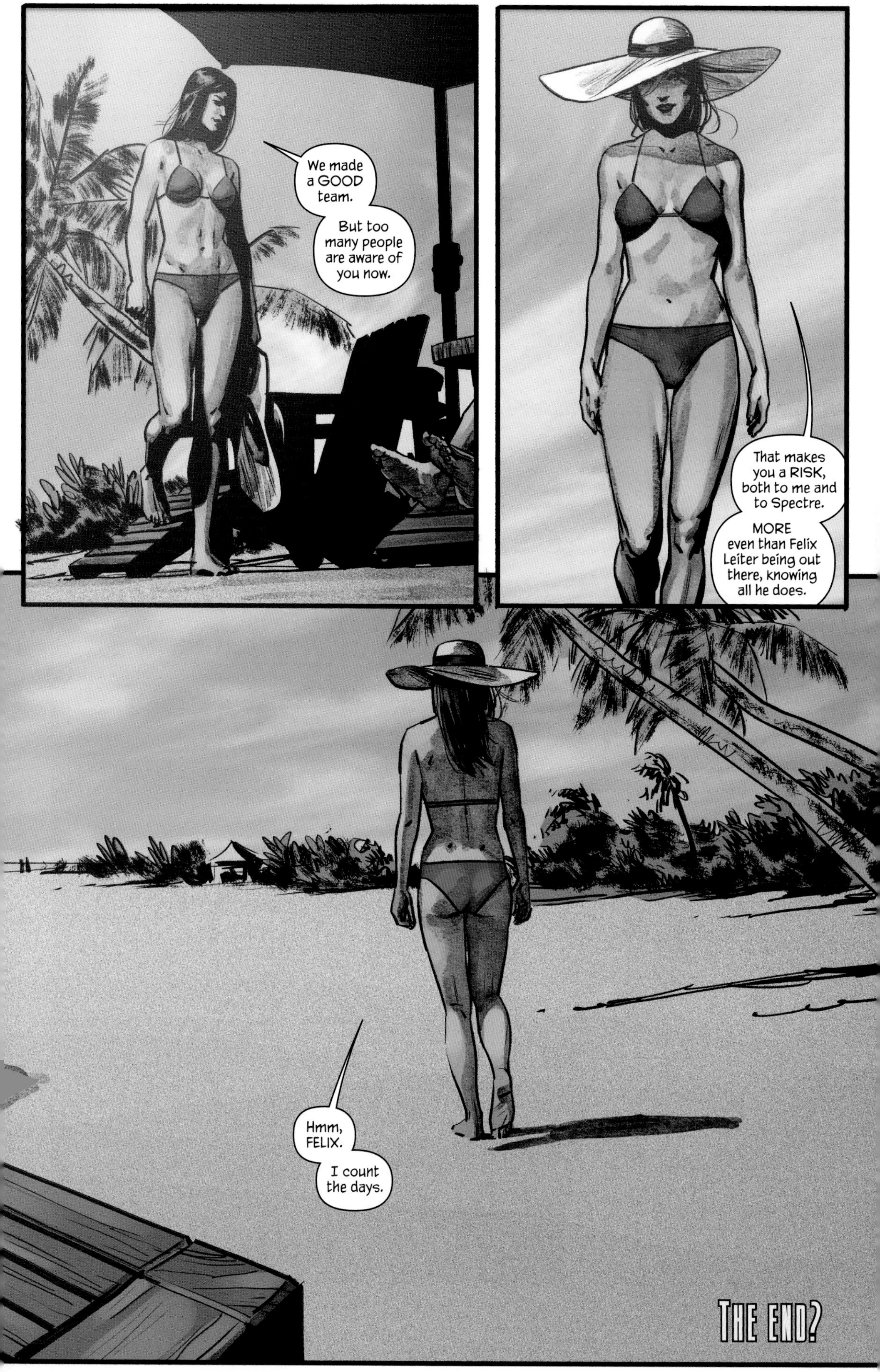

We made a GOOD team.
But too many people are aware of you now.
That makes you a RISK, both to me and to Spectre.
MORE even than Felix Leiter being out there, knowing all he does.
Hmm, FELIX.
I count the days.
THE END?

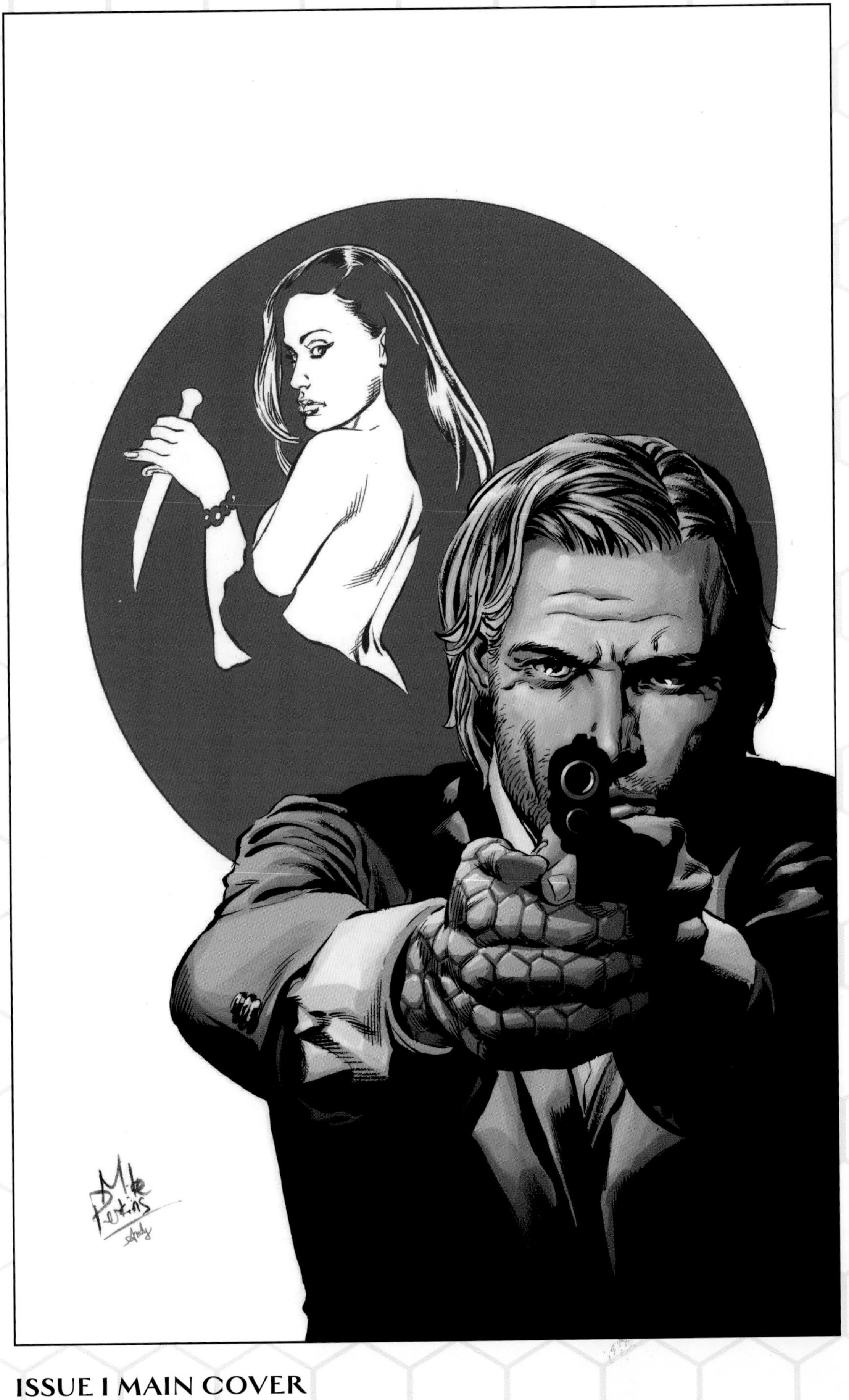

ISSUE 1 MAIN COVER

BY MIKE PERKINS | COLORS BY ANDY TROY

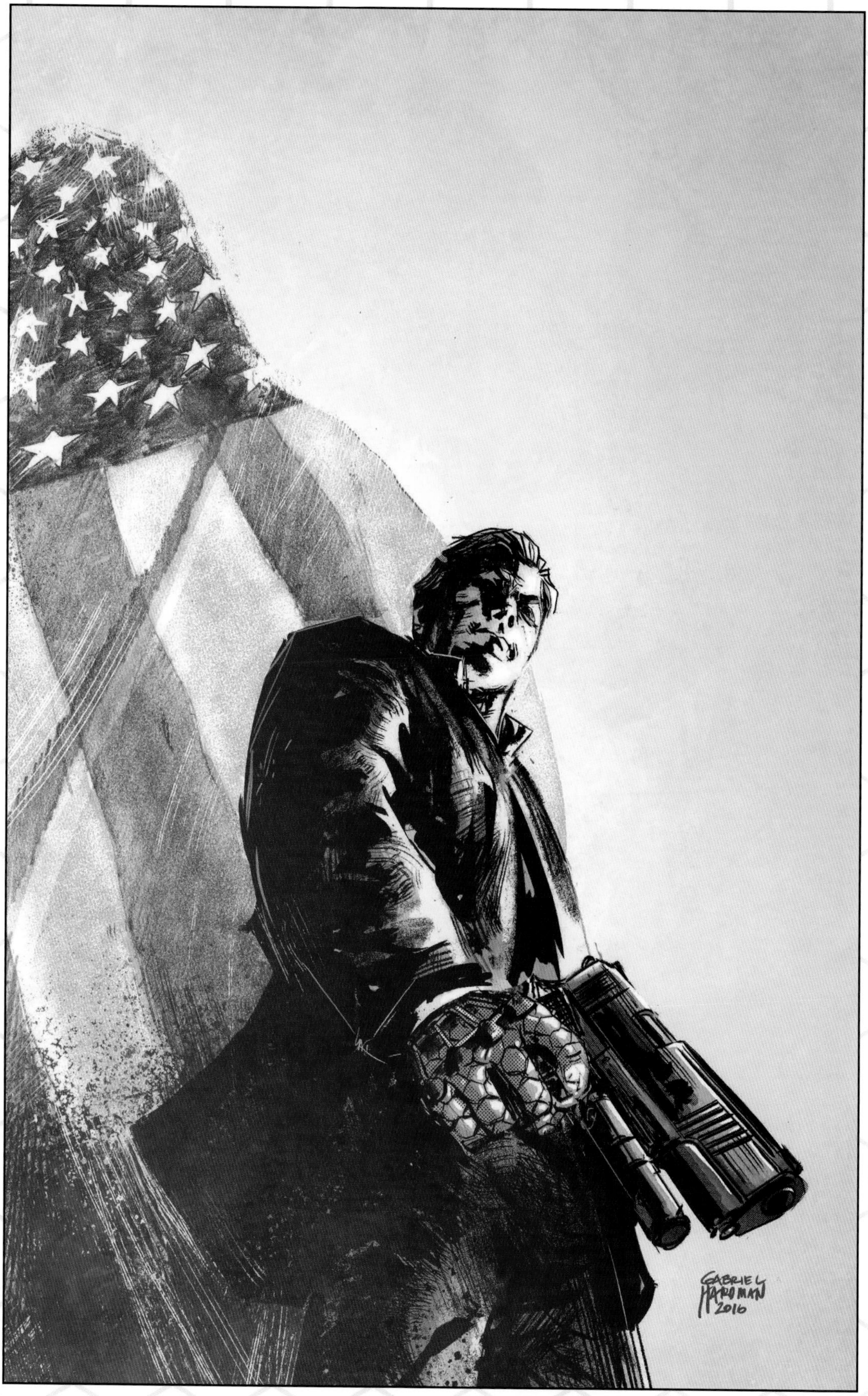
GABRIEL
HARDMAN
2016

ISSUE 1 VARIANT COVER
BY GABRIEL HARDMAN | COLORS BY JORDAN BOYD

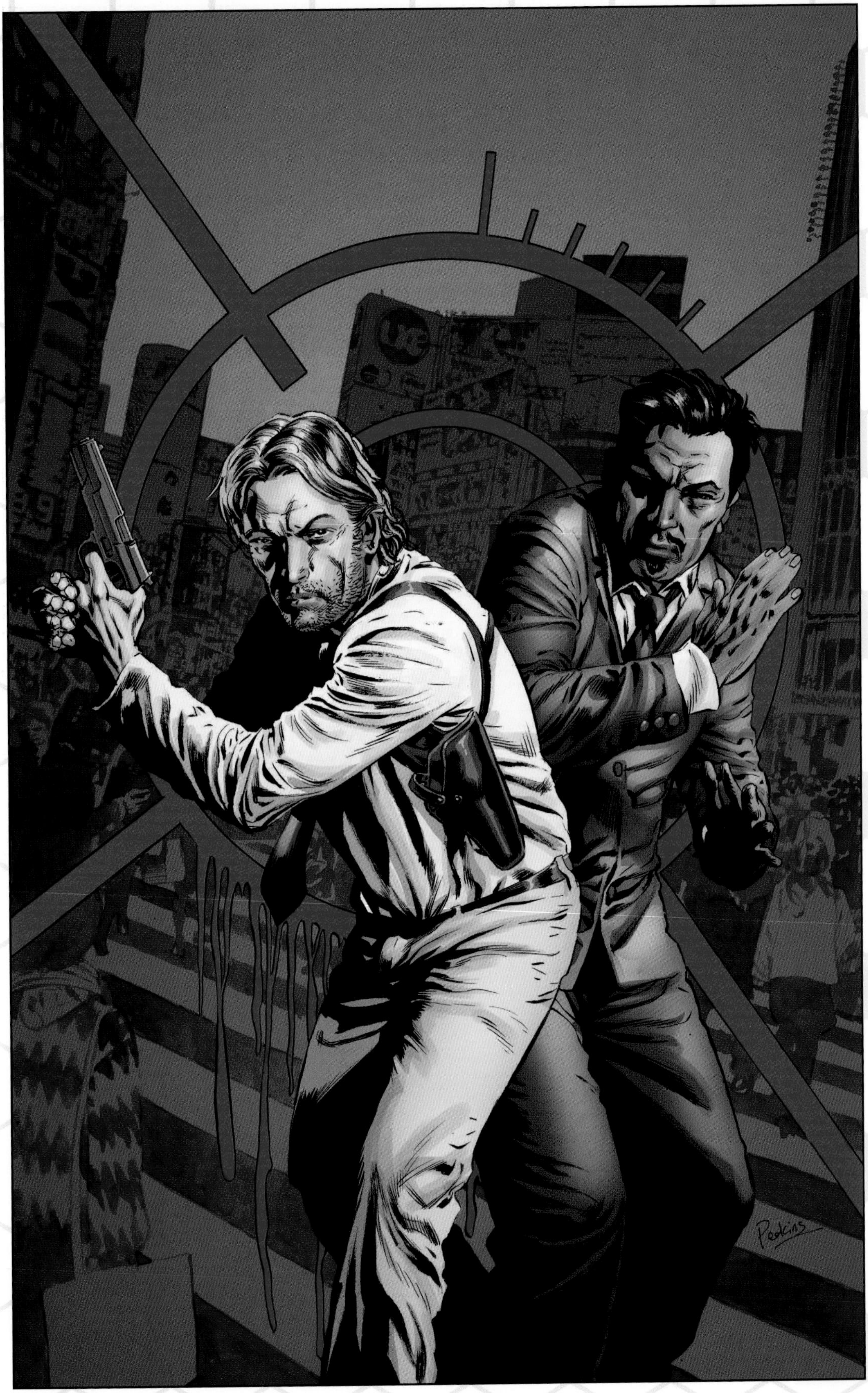
Perkins

ISSUE 2 COVER
BY MIKE PERKINS | COLORS BY ANDY TROY

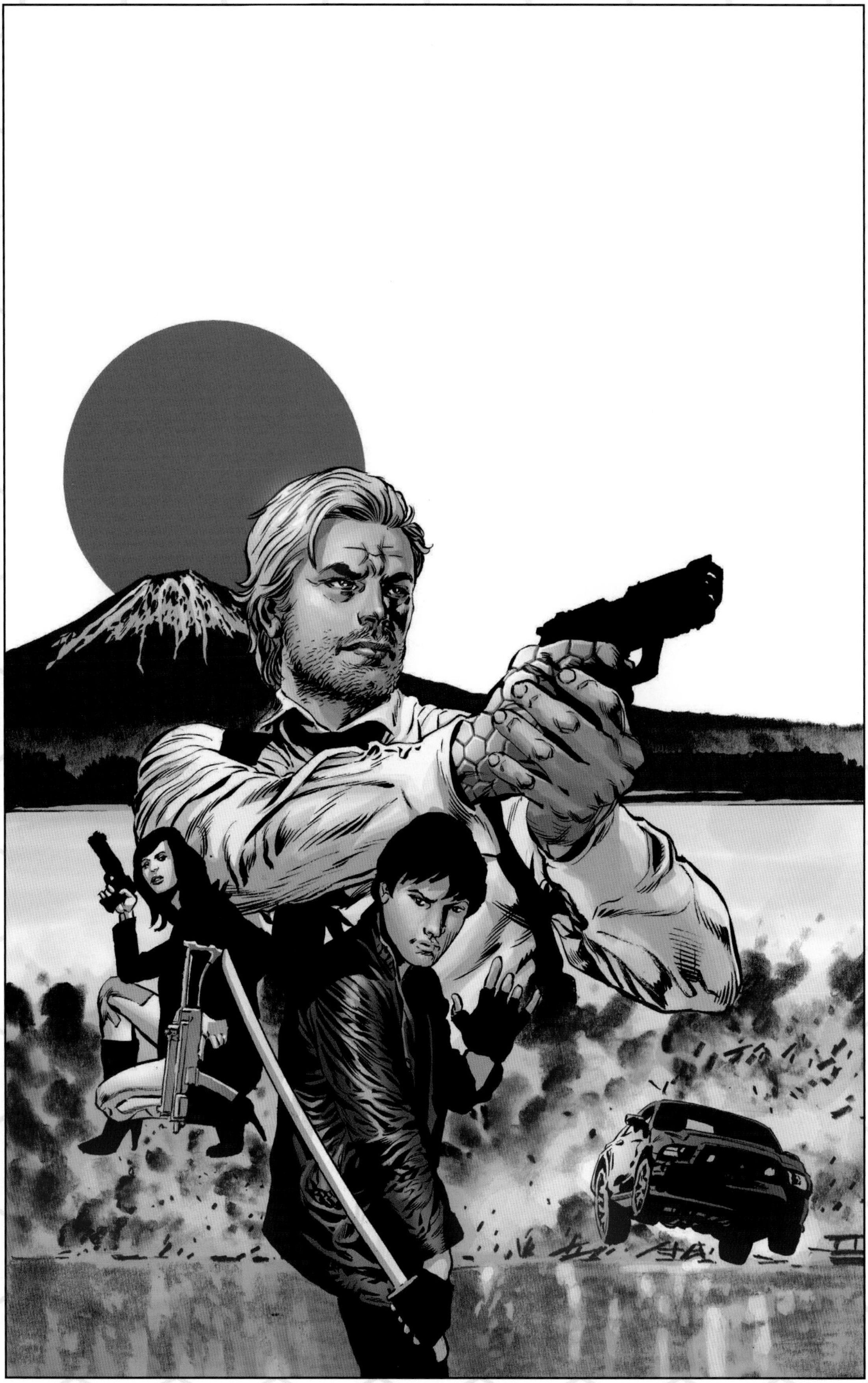

ISSUE 3 COVER

BY MIKE PERKINS | COLORS BY ANDY TROY

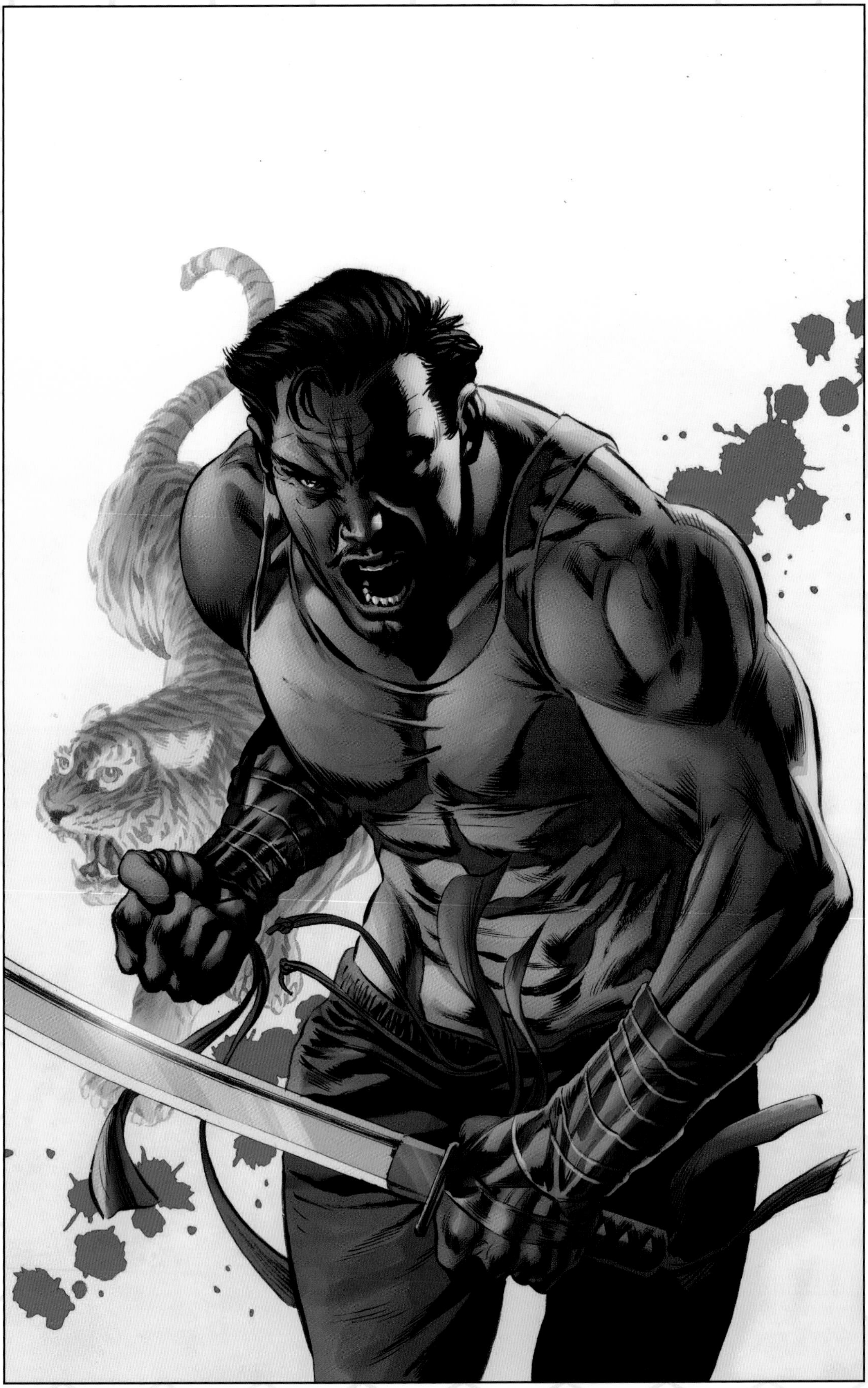

ISSUE 2 COVER

BY MIKE PERKINS | COLORS BY ANDY TROY

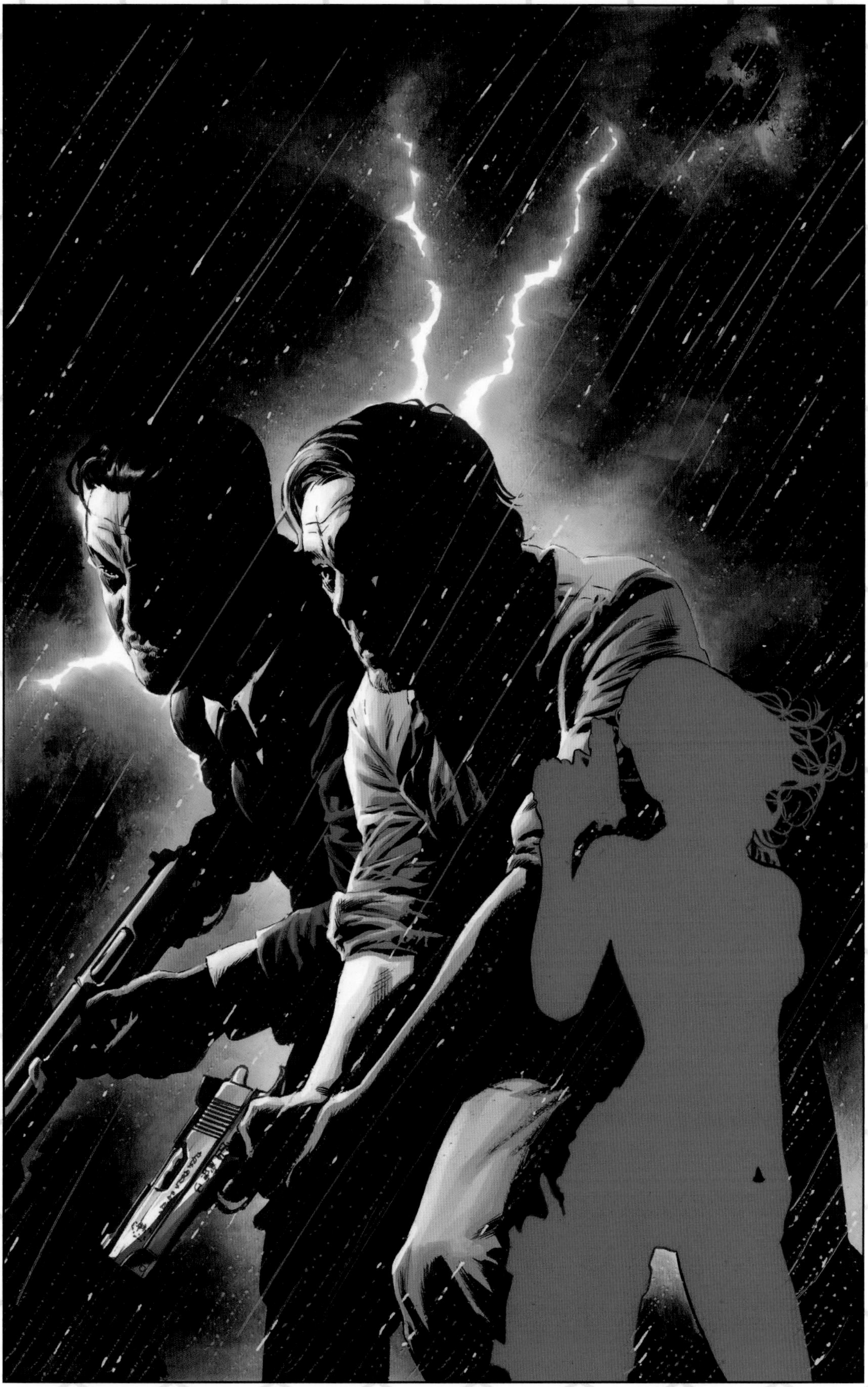

ISSUE 3 COVER

BY MIKE PERKINS | COLORS BY ANDY TROY

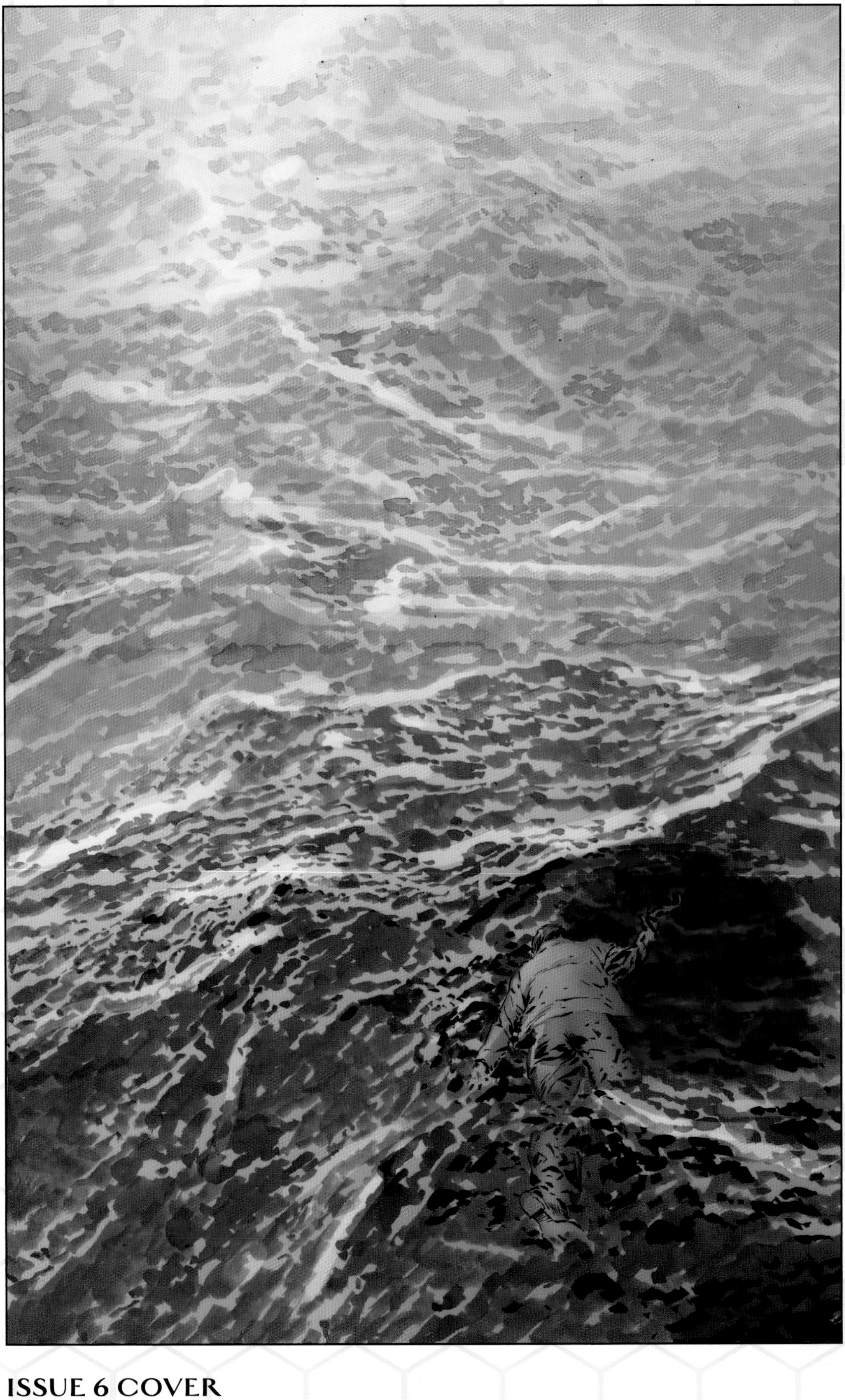

ISSUE 6 COVER
BY MIKE PERKINS | COLORS BY ANDY TROY

James Robinson talks to Byron Brewer about James Bond: Felix Leiter #1

BYRON BREWER: James, as a longtime Bond fan, I cannot tell you how long I have awaited a book featuring Felix Leiter. Tell us how this came about with you and Dynamite.

JAMES ROBINSON: Well, firstly it started because I had a great time working with Dynamite on my own book Grand Passion. (Issue #1 out in two weeks, check it out!) However, even before that, quite a while ago actually, I agreed to do Felix. It seemed like a great fit with me writing a beaten-down P.I. character in the world of Bond. And the pedigree of the main title with Warren Ellis and Andy Diggle meant I was in very lofty company too, which appealed to my vanity. And as a lover of the Bond books, I jumped at the challenge of giving some weight to this somewhat under-utilized supporting character.

BB: In the main James Bond series from Dynamite, Warren Ellis has of course been using the Ian Fleming novels as source material. Will that be true for your take on Leiter as well? Will this be a contemporary iteration?

JR: Well, I'd say Felix is exactly in the same world as Warren's run. It even refers to it, in terms of the advanced prosthetics that Bond encounters in Warren's run. I see Warren's Bond as having the feel of the books, while at the same time it's updated. It isn't the movie Bond, it has the feel of the books, but it's in our world today. There are things that set it apart from the books and movies. The era it's set in isn't the books, but the look and feel of the characters isn't like the movies.

FELIX LEITER
ORIGINAL SKETCHES
BY **AARON CAMPBELL**

I think it's very much its own incarnation of Bond and his world. A world were M is a black man. A world where Felix is a scruffy haired modern guy. It's enough like the books that I've jokingly called the original Bond novels set during the 1950s and 60s as the Bond of Earth 2 and this is the modern Bond but with the same feel, so it's the Bond of Earth 1.

BB: Are there any Bond/Leiter tropes from the movies that might work their way into your adventure as Easter eggs? Are you more a fan of the Bond novels or movies?

JR: Well, I'm following Warren's lead here, so he's more an updated version of the book character. There's a (almost) science fiction element that slips into some of the films. True it also began to enter Fleming's writing too once the movies started to come out, but it was never as much as it was in the films. I'm a fan of a lot of the movies. Most of the Connery, Lazenby, some Brosnan and Dalton. I'm a fan of Daniel Craig too, although I think I may be the one person in the world who didn't like Skyfall. The first half is Bond making too many mistakes. The villain's plot is needlessly complicated and the end felt more like a Jack Higgins adventure than a Bond film.

BB: What can you tell us about the Russian spy Leiter is pursuing as we join the adventure in #1?

JR: Alena Davoff is a woman who has kept her appearance in the shadows. Felix is one of the few people alive who can identify her. She's an old flame from his days in the C.I.A. when he has all his limbs. When he was "whole". She's a spy very much in the femme fatale mold. I have plans for her that go beyond this first series, so buy lots of copies so I'll get to write more Felix adventures after this one.

BB: How much research did you do on Tokyo and other background locales for this book? Ellis has really done a fantastic job of weaving the culture into his scenes so it's not just cookie-cutter globe-hopping. Will your backdrops be important to the adventure Leiter is having?

JR: I did a lot of research. I'm excited to set it there and thereby (in this new Dynamite version of Bond) to also get to reintroduce Tiger Tanaka (from You Only Live Twice.) I think readers will enjoy mine and Aaron Campbell's depiction of Tokyo and Honshu as a whole.

BB: How is it to work with artist Aaron Campbell? He certainly hit it out of the park in the two volumes of Dynamite's Uncanny!

JR: He continues to swing for the fences. The work is wonderful. And his style marrying the everyday with the fantastic so seamless it's perfect for the world of Bond and for Felix especially. I love working with the guy.

BB: So if you can, non-spoilery, what can we expect from James Bond: Felix Leiter going forward?

JR: Felix is in Tokyo for one reason — to identify Alena Davoff. However, a bigger, more deadly threat shows its face and Felix is dragged into that too. Lots of action and wild James Bond-like happenings, but at the same time we get into Felix's head about what it's like to be outside and apart from the C.I.A now. We learn who the guy is. All while he's trying to keep the body parts he hasn't already lost still attached to himself.

TIGER
ORIGINAL SKETCHES
BY **AARON CAMPBELL**

Felix leiter
Issue 1
By James Robinson

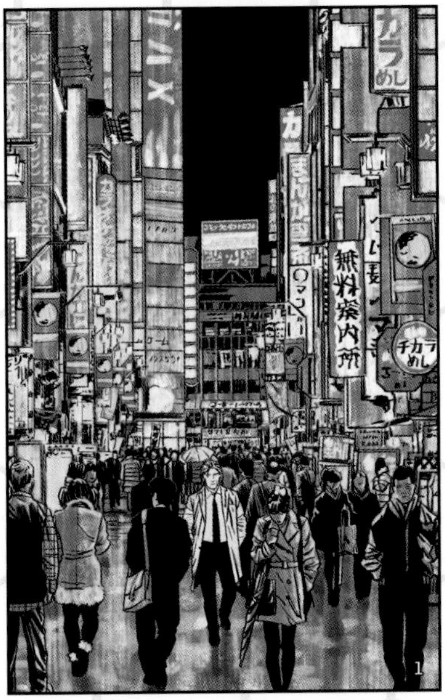
無料案内所
1

Page one.
Full page.

We're above slightly looking down a busy street in tokyo. It's night time

(We should also note that it's rained not that long ago so there are puddles on the ground and roofs and areas of the shot.)

In among the people in the street we see felix leiter. He's in a suit and overcoat, with the tie open. He has a bucket hat on, in lieu of an old fashioned private eye's hat.

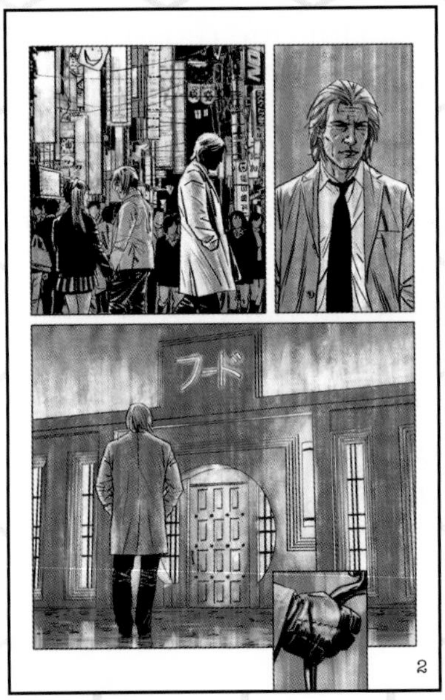
フード
2

Colorist, can you give felix some aspect of his attire that has a brightness to it? He's small here, lost in among the other pedestrians and people.

As to his physical description, there is a style sheet already in existence about his facial features and age. Go with that, unless you need more help in which case i'm obviously available.

Caption: shinjuku area of tokyo, japan.

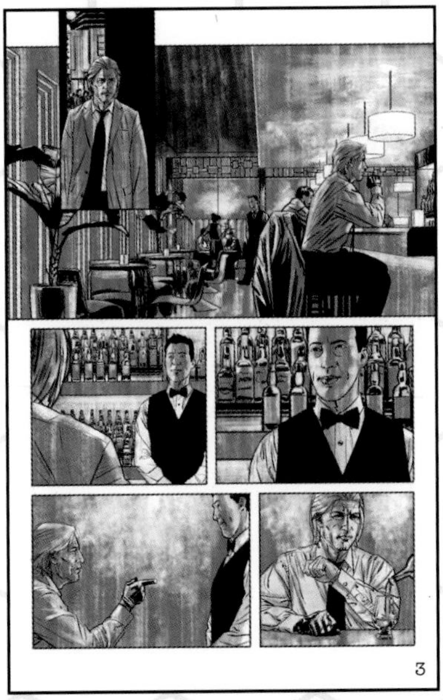
3

Page two.
Panel one.

Felix is side-on to us walking across the street. His head is bowed slightly and his hands are in the pockets of his overcoat. He's a full figure here, walking towards panel right. There is a sad melancholy look to his expression and demeanor.

We see a japanese young couple, who are clearly on a date and/or very happy to be together, with the girl holding onto the man's face and looking up at him with happiness/love. They are walking fast in the other direction towards panel left, a contrast, both in age and in vitality.

Caption (felix): looks like i missed the rain.

Panel two.
Cu of felix walking towards us. We see his melancholy.

Caption (felix): yeah.

Panel three.
Ls of felix as a small figure walking away from us towards a bar/restaurant. The bar has a glitzy, modern exterior.

You know those kind of massive wooden doors, like from an old temple on a new sleek surround/exterior. Where there's a juxtaposition of old and new.

We see some of this scene/shot partially reflected upside down in areas of the ground there are still puddles.

Caption (felix): one good thing, i guess.

Panel four.
Cu of felix's hand pulling the door of the bar open. We see he's wearing a glove, so for the moment, his hand looks human.

No dialogue

Page three.
Panel one.

Felix enters through the door, with some of the street/background still visible.

No dialogue

Panel two.
L/s. Felix sits at the bar. We can see beyond it to see that there are booths and tables further. The interior is actually quite expansive, although it's also dark and intimate at the same time. Lots of shadows affording us more shadow than detail.

I found this image of a bar/restaurant of one of the high-end bar/restaurants in tokyo. I'm imagining something like this, but not exactly.

Felix and the bar he's at it to the fore of panel. With patrons and activity further away.

By making it dark, we can believe that felix could sit at the end of the bar and not be spotted by someone who wasn't actually expecting him.

Panel three.
Felix faces away from us, looking at the back wall of the bar, lined with bottles of booze. Lots of whiskies.

The bartender, a lean, younger japanese man, faces felix/us.

Felix: <<whisky, please.>>

Panel four.
Cu of the bartender looking off panel at felix.

Bartender: <<scotch or irish? You should look at our menu, we've quite a list.>>

Bartender: <<alhough i'm partial to the glenmorangie signet myself.>>

Panel five.
Tight side-on shot of felix and the bartender facing each other, both in profile to us.

Felix: <<actually...is that a nikka taketsuru 17 years, i see behind you?>>

Bartender: <<ahh. You know japanese whiskies?>>

Panel six.
Cu of felix, looking down slightly, as the bartenders hand/bottom comes into shot, pouring the whisky into a glass in the f/g - the bar-top in front of felix.

Felix: <<i know what i like.>>

Felix: <<one ice cube.>>

Bartender: <<of course.>>

Page Four.
Panel one.

Med shot of felix as he sits there, sipping his drink. His eyes are looking up off panel (at a clock on the wall, to the side/top of the bar.)

Caption (felix): last time i was here -- company orders --

Caption (felix): back when i was all of me.

Panel two.
We look past the back of felix's head and thereby show the clock. It's large and a cool design, in among the bottles, but clear and visible, big there

among everything.

We can see that it's a little past 9 o'clock.

Caption (felix): now, this time, it's little more than a favor.

Caption (felix): and gotta say -- how i was raised, when someone does you a favor...

Panel three.
A moment later.

Felix in cu. He is no longer sipping his drink, but rather, is listening to his cell-phone.

Caption (felix): ...it's rude to keep them waiting.

Sfx (small, barely visible): ring ring ring

Panel four.
Tighter c/u as he speaks into the phone.

Felix (smaller, like he's speaking softly): tiger.

Felix (smaller, like he's speaking softly): i hope the reason you're not picking up...

Panel five.
Felix's eyes looking panel right. He's clearly spotted someone/is looking

Felix (smaller, like he's speaking softly): ...is because you're already on your way.

Page Five.
Panel one.

This is a shot of the person (we'll learn in a moment) that felix has been sent to identify.

Alena davoff. She is a beautiful russian woman (about 30). (She's dressed in a tight top and jeans and boots.) She is sitting in a booth further away at the back of the bar. Next to her in the booth is choi ki-moon, her north korean contact. They are talking, both with

a drink in front of them. A wine for her and some kind of liquor for him. They are talking, concentrating on each other, but not in a romantic way. Ki-moon is an older man, balding and with spectacles.

However they still sit relatively close together in the booth, in serious conversation but as if they're trying to keep their voices down and not be overheard.

Caption (felix): alena davoff.

Panel two.
Felix sips his whisky, still looking towards panel right/alena far away out of panel.

Caption (felix): "the unknown woman."

Panel three.
Felix and alena in the afghanistan countryside.

They're in army/guerilla clothing, like special ops or covert forces, might wear in such a terrain (if you look online at shots of british s.A.S or u.S. Special forces in afghanistan, you'll see they often adopt this kind of attire.)

They are together, in a clearing. Standing there. Both have weapons, felix has an assault rifle and alena has a russian revolver. They have the weapons up/at rest having just fired them.

Around them we see several dead afghani/taliban.

Beyond them in the distance we see a field of poppies, stretching away from us far away.

Oh, and don't beat it over the head, but just to further (subtly) illustrate that this is the past, have felix's sleeves rolled up enough we see both of his arms are real.

Caption (felix): except to me.

Panel four.
We're back in the present. Alena now in c/u looking off panel/talking to ki-moon.

Caption (felix): yeah...

Page Six.
Panel one.

Top half of the page.

Another flashback image. We see felix and alena in a bed, having passionate sex. The sheets are tangled up around them and in this way, show skin but keep things pg. They're entwined, kissing, deeply passionate.

I don't know if we want a down-shot or maybe side-on. What do you think will look better?

Also have it tight in on them, don't have too much background.

It's a dark room, but daylight is shining across them from a slatted window to their room.

Caption (felix): ...me and her go way back.

Panel two.
Felix in the present, recalling this. There is a gentle, slight, sad, half small on his face.

No dialogue

Panel three.
Tighter in, more so just his eyes, as he looks sideways. We can see the shock on them.

Caption (felix): dammit, felix --

Panel four.
We cut to the booth of alena and ki-moon and see that the booth is empty. It's very much a felix p.O.V. Shot, so have stuff semi-visible and semi-cropped by the panel edges.

Caption (felix): -- amateur hour.

Panel five.
Felix emerges/rushes out into the street, look-ing around. Some of the people in the street (mainly japanese) are reacting mildly to how felix is rushing in front of them. -No dialogue

Page Seven.
Panel one.

We look down the street (more of less from felix's p.O.V.) Alena and the korean are down the street, semi-obscured by other pedestrians.

We see that alena now has a long camel-colored overcoat on.

Caption (felix): no.

Caption (felix): got her.

Panel two.
Med shot of felix. We see the first drop of returning rain fall/hit his shoulder.

Small sound effect: ptt

Panel three.
L/s looking down somewhat and from the p.O.V. Of across the street. We see that felix is following alena and ki-moon. He's far away from them, pushing through the crowd to get closer to alena.

Alena and ki-moon are oblivious to him walking on, calmly.

The sudden shower is falling away from us in perspective, now covering everything/everyone. Some people are reacting to the rain, pulling their collars up and such, as well as huddling together as they walk.

No dialogue

Panel four.
Alena and the korean turn the corner into a side street/semi-alley way. It's dim and starkly lit. The rain is now falling hard.

No dialogue

Panel five.
Tighter in on felix as he follows, turning into the same corner.

Caption (felix): turned here.

Panel six.
Felix emerges into a clearing/courtyard on the other end of the alley. There are dumpsters to one side. There is more alley beyond it too, with his open area between one alley and the other.
The lighting is such that although felix is just entering the courtyard, his shadows is thrown long and distorted across it.

There are puddles reflecting neon signs from high up, these distorted by the rain falling.

The rain continues to fall hard.

No dialogue

Page Eight.
Panel one.

Alena tight med shot, facing us, with felix in c/u to one side of shot spinning to looking away from us/face her.

We see her standing there in the rain with her overcoat open down the middle.

She looks cool and intense, like she's going to kick felix's ass.

Alena: so this is what counts as your best now, felix?

Panel two.
Big panel. We see alena connecting a spin-kick to the face of felix, sending him flying back off his feet.

The shot is all action and momentum. We see the motion of alena's violent spin-kick to felix's face, with her open overcoat flowing in the trail of her motion like a cape, fanning out dramatically.

Felix is flying backwards, flailing as he falls.

Alena: sad!

Page Nine.
Panel one.

Felix hits the ground hard, sliding along the ground towards the garbage dumpsters. (He's yet to reach them/collide with them here though, that's next panel.)

No dialogue

Panel two.
Ls from far away.

Alena is to one side/left side of panel with felix to the other side/right side as he slams into the dumpsters violently. One of the bins if caving in a bit to one side and rising up a bit too from the impact.

Both alena and felix are small figures here with the rain falling hard around them.

No dialogue

Panel three.
Felix on his hands and knees, attempts to rise/look up. He has a cut on the temple and his nose his bleeding. He looks fucked up and already beaten.

The rain is falling on him.

He looks off panel towards where alena would be.

Felix (small/weak lettering): alena.

Panel four.
Wider shot.

We see felix there still sprawled on his hands and knees, attempting to rise.

Now we see alena's long shadow falling across him and the area of ground in front of him/in the foreground.

The rain falls everywhere too.

Alena (o/s): what, felix?

Alena (o/s): tell me...

Page ten.
This is a two page conversation between alena and felix, with felix stalling for time and by talking and acting helpless. In terms of their eye-lines, she's standing and he's on the

ground looking up. Also have some high lights (street lamps and such) shining down, so when we look at alena, we get some lens flare behind her head and across shot sometimes. And by us looking up at her some shots, throw her into semi-silhouette too.

Panel one.
Top tier of page ten.

We looking at/re-establish the overall layout with alena standing and felix on the ground, looking up at her. We see the rain falling hard and maybe a puddle with a reflection of alena's head/upper torso visible too.

Alena: ...what could you possible have to say to me?

Panel two.
Med shot of felix looking up with a slight smile on his face, like finding mild humor in the absurdity of the situation.

Felix: i confess at this moment, baby.

Felix: i'm lost for words.

Panel three.
Reverse angle med shot of alena looking down at felix coldly.

Alena: do you think i'm enjoying this -- the man you are now.

Alena: pathetic.

Felix: there was a time--

Panel four.
Tighter in shot of alena, looking down at felix with a slight sneer on her face.

Alena: yes, there was -- when i'd never have known you were on me.

Alena: now look at you -- i made you before you'd even entered the bar.

Panel five.
We look past alena down at felix.

Felix: yeah, i'm not the man i used to be.

Felix: but you've done such a good job of destroying all records of yourself...
Panel six.
We see that alena has pulled a gun. It's a small, modern makarov. She aims it down at felix.

Felix: ...what i still am...is one of the few people who knows what you look like.

Alena: not for much longer.

Page Eleven.
Panel one.

Side on shot of alena and felix with the rain and the dumpsters.

Alena: it will be a mercy killing at that. You've already lost what body parts -- a hand?

Felix: more. Arm and a leg.

Alena: and you aren't c.I.A. Anymore, so what am i to you?

Panel two.
Cu of felix.

Felix: apart from a few bitter-sweet recollections?

Felix: you're nothing, alena.

Panel three.
We're looking at felix and alena, upside-down reflected in a puddle.

Some of them is awkwardly cropped due to the erratic shape of the puddle.

Felix: and yeah, the company cut me loose.

Felix: i'm a private detective now.

Alena: i know that.

Panel four.
We look up past the head/shoulder of felix cropped to one side, up towards alena standing there aiming the gun at us.

Felix: you're keeping tabs on me still? I'm flattered.

Alena: don't be.

Alena: not in a while -- since you last mattered at all.
Panel five.
C/u of felix, looking up with a wry "ow, that hurt" expression on his face.

Felix: ouch.

Panel six.
Side on shot to show a l/s of the pair and the overall layout before we go to more action. Alena now pointing her pistol down at felix and him there looking up.

The rain still falls.

Alena: so, you're here to identify me?

Felix: favor. The u.S. "Lent" me to japan, and no, i have no idea why they care so much.

Felix: all i do know is they're paying me, and seeing as the last couple of months haven't been so good, i'm not complain--

Panel seven.
Tight c/u of alena.

Alena: enough.

Alena: i'm bored.

Page Twelve.
Panel one.

Wide shot as felix lunges/tackles alena, grabbing her gun arm by the wrist and yanking up so she fires wild into the air.

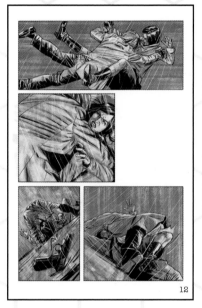

Felix: me too!

Caption (felix): alena davoff --

Panel two.
The pair of them are locked in a struggle. We're tight in on them, with some of their bodies cropped by how tight we're in shot here.

Caption (felix): -- russian agent -- used to be anyway.
Caption (felix): dangerous.

Caption (felix): maybe a little crazy.

Panel three.
Felix rams alena's wrist down hard on the

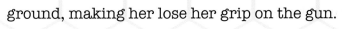

ground, making her lose her grip on the gun.

Caption (felix): the most exciting woman i've ever met.

Panel four.
We're further from them.

We see the gun go skittering across the pavement towards us, splashing in/through a puddle as it does so.

Imagining this as a movie shot, the gun is coming at us in focus with the struggle between alena and felix further from us and murkier/less defined.

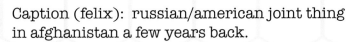

Caption (felix): russian/american joint thing in afghanistan a few years back.

Caption (felix): her and me.

Panel five.
Alena and felix continue to struggle, with felix now on top of alena bringing his weight down on her. However at the same time it is clear that alena now has a leg/knee under felix between them.

Caption (felix): got to know her then.

Page Thirteen.
Panel one.

Ls as alena flips felix high into the air over her body, past her, like a judo move. You know?

The shot shows them in l/s however with the rain and the puddles and the dumpsters around them.

Caption (felix): now she's off the grid apparently -- took herself there.

Caption (felix): destroying all data about her before she went.

Panel two.

Alena rises in a crouch, like an angry, cornered cat. She has a knife in her hand now.

Caption (felix): so suddenly i'm one of the few remaining people alive who can identify
        Her.

Caption (felix): report said she was in japan -- so of course they want to know the who,   where and why of her being here.

Panel three.
Felix on the ground. He's landed awkwardly and is now scrambling to his feet, but clearly he isn't ready for whatever is about to happen.

Caption (felix): i'm not c.I.A. Anymore, like i told her, but the company still "requested" i
        Come here.

Caption (felix): a favor to japan.

Panel four.
Another long shot.

Alena dives at felix, knife raised.

Caption (felix): and like i also just said...at least they're paying me.

Panel five.
Felix, still only semi-raised and backing up slightly in a crab style, raises his hand/arm on reflex.

There is wary/shock/not-quite-fear his face.

Alena's shadow is falling across shot, as if in a moment she will be upon him.

Caption (felix): although at this exact moment in time, it's not nearly enough.

Page Fourteen.
Panel one.

Felix and alena are now in a semi-struggle, semi-embrace, where at the same time we see that alena has rammed the knife into felix's right/prosthetic arm/forearm and that as a result sparks/shows of electricity is flying out into both of their faces.

Felix: ahh

Alena: gh--

Panel two.
Tighter med shot of felix as he falls back/away from the sparks in his face, staggering back more than falling i guess, with his eyes closed/dazzled and his other hand/non-prosthetic arm up to his face a bit.

Caption (felix): can't see --

Caption (felix): my new arm -- shorted --

Caption (felix): -- servos -- maybe --.

Panel three.
Tight c.U. As felix looks about, peering through eyes that are clearly still finding it hard to see.

Caption (felix): or defense?

Caption (felix): dunno.

Caption (felix): can't see --

Panel four.
Felix's p.O.V. Shot. He/we see alena's gun lying there in the rain.

Caption (felix): i'm --

Caption (felix): gun!

Panel five.
Felix's left/non-prosthetic hand/arm as he snatches the gun up.

Caption (felix): now!

Page Fifteen.
Panel one.

Med shot as felix staggers to his feet, still blinking, trying to focus and aiming the gun up to fire at the first sign of movement.

Felix: alena!
Panel two.
Felix aiming the gun in a different direction, turning/spinning frantically to look for alena, aiming to fire is he sees her.

No dialogue

Panel three.
Finally...

...We look down on felix standing there. He's lowered his gun. He/we realize he is alone.

The rain falls down in perspective. It's a very classic noir/asian crime movie type image.

No dialogue

Page Sixteen.
Panel one.

Hotel exterior.

This is the prince park tower in tokyo. Note the small red eiffel tower near it. It's still night.

Caption: later.

Caption (felix): at least the hotel they put me in is nice.

Panel two.
Big panel of felix in a chair in shorts and a t-shirt with his cybernetic prosthetics lying on the floor in front of him. He has a bottle of whisky on the table to the side of the chair and is pouring himself a shot with his one good arm.

He's sitting on the side of the bed. Or maybe on the toilet with the lid down. He's near a surface/side table where he can rest the glass/pour into it.

There are towels all around the area too, like he's dried himself off.

Felix sits there facing us, looking beaten up and exhausted. His face has the signs of his beating, being bruised and a bit cut up.

Felix is sitting there as a tight full-figure facing us, but with his thoughts clearly his own and without him actually looking straight at us.

17

Caption (felix): lots of towels.

(Space between captions here.)

Caption (felix): it was supposed to be easy.

Caption (felix): report said she'd be there -- i pick her out...

Caption (felix): ...easy.

Caption (felix): yeah, except the one thing missing from tonight's recipe for miso soup...

Page Seventeen.
Panel one.

LEITER INVESTIGATIONS
CONFIDENTIAL
AL'S BARBER SHOP
18

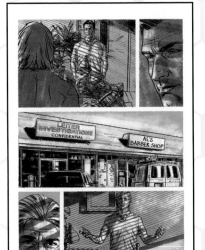

Cu felix resting the cool glass against his forehead.

Caption (felix): ...tiger tanaka and his men.

Panel two.
Felix's p.O.V. Looking at the prosthetics lying there on the floor discarded. We're tight in on the two prosthetic and we can now see that they're the type/design that was first shown in warren ellis' 1st james bond arc.

Caption (felix): and i still don't know what happened with the arm.

Caption (felix): electrical blast when the knife went it.

Panel three.
Felix in c/u. He's a profile here, side-on to us. He's looking off, deep in thought.

Caption (felix): still works okay -- fingers, wrist -- so --
Felix: huh.

Caption (felix): newly designed prosthetics... new, barely out of the box. Yeah...

Panel four.
Same panel/framing of felix in c/u. But now

we see we're in the past, with felix looking off panel at someone. Felix has a fred perry polo shirt on, but has the top button of the shirt/tie open. It's too tight to see anything more than that, we'll show more when we turn the page.

The lighting is different too, as you'll see when we turn the page for the bigger description to come.

Caption (felix): ...that was supposed to be easy too.

Bond (o/s): you were tricky to find, felix.

Page Eighteen.
Panel one.

Full figure of james bond standing there with felix's head/shoulder to one side of panel, looking away from us towards james.

Bond wears stylish clothing for being in a hot place. (The kind of thing daniel craig wore in the tropics at the beginning of the casino royale movie.)

In front of felix between him/us and james bond facing us, we can see some of felix's desk. It's a normal ikea type desk that's covered in files and clutter. A computer too, but not the most modern.

The office has boring filing cabinets and a drab, unsuccessful feel to it.

Light is shining on to one side, throwing the shape of a sunny window across the shapes and objects in the office behind bond.

The office is rundown and messy and cramped.

Caption: key west, florida. The past.

Felix: you're a british agent with double 0 clearance, mister "bond, james bond", so i don't
       Think finding anyone is too "tricky" for you.

Panel two.
Cu bond. He looks down with a wry smile.

Bond: fair enough...

Panel three.

With a generic sign reading "leiter investigations" in large lettering and "confidential" below it in smaller lettering. The sign is over one such shop within the mall. Of an couple of letters in the word "confidential" are either crooked or missing.

Caption (bond): "...then let's just say you were further from the pinkerton agency than i
	Expected to find you."

Panel four.
Reverse angle close up of felix.

Felix: what can i tell you? I outgrew them.

Felix: or them me.

Panel five.
We pull out from panel four.

We see felix behind his cluttered desk, looking up at us/bond. His prosthetic hand is visible here and it's clearly a cruder version than the one that we saw lying on the floor in the page prior.

Seeing felix more clearly now, he's in a fred perry shirt and slacks.

Felix: you know -- my office -- suddenly i don't want to be here, james...

Page Nineteen.
Panel one.

Looking down on car driving along a highway in florida. We're in a vintage convertible t-bird (the 1961-63 model with the spear-like profile.

Bond is the passenger, felix drives.

Caption (felix): "...let's go for a drive."
Panel two.
We see a bit of the car in the f/g parked by the side of a beach. We see bond and felix as small full-figures walking away from us, on the beach towards the sea/water, further off.

Bond: i won't be cloying and sentimental, and say that i miss you, felix...

Bond: ...but damn it, i miss you.
Panel three.
Med shot of the two men side by side. They look out at the bright sun. Maybe they both have sunglasses on now. Bond in tortoise shell classics and felix in aviators.

Bond: you're happy here in key west?

Felix: i don't know that i'm ever happy, you know me.

Felix: i wake up each morning and close my eyes at night.

Felix: i had more of a ready smile when i still had all my fingers and toes, i'm admit that.

Panel four.
C/u of bond, glancing to his side/at bond.

Bond: ah well, maybe i'm here at an opportune time then...

Page Twenty.
[Need to massage timeline of prosthetic as he had it while active in cia and this is after that. Could be showing up to provide repairs as the manufacturer was destroyed during first ellis arc]
Panel one.

L/s of bond and felix standing on the beach looking at the sea.

Bond: the case i put in the trunk of your car -- any idea what's in it?

Felix: i assumed it was suits and a martini shaker.

Felix: or some state-of-the art weapon. One or the other, with you.

Bond: well you got "state-of-the-art" at least.

Panel two.
We're looking at felix's parked car, looking more/focusing more on the trunk. As we're looking at the trunk, so we're actually seeing a cutaway section of it, showing the prosthetic arm and leg in the trunk. We see their high-tech design, akin to what was shown in the ellis james bond series.

Caption (bond): "-- advanced prosthetics."

Caption (bond): "better than anything out there -- certainly an improvement on what you
Have."

Caption (bond): "let's call it spoils of war."

Panel three.
Med shot of bond and felix. Felix is turning to look at bond with surprise.

Bond: i took the liberty of getting your medical specs, so q's team could
have them pre-fitted.

Bond: i'd say that they could be grafted onto you so they're part of your
body --

Felix: you're kidding?

Panel four.
C.U. Of felix as he looks off, momentarily subdued by what he's learning.

Bond: except...in some cases -- one in ten, when they simply won't take --

Felix: and seeing as you've run my records, let me guess where i fall.

Panel five.
Ls of the two men with the sand around them and the sea beyond.

Felix: huh.

Felix: i heard a rumor, that now in the c.I.A., When a mission hits a run of
bad luck...

Felix: ...they say it's "gone felix."

Panel six.
Med shot of bond and felix. Bond looks at him with a calm, ever-so-slightly
gentle expression.

Bond: you can still wear the prosthetic, felix. They are amazing.

Felix: better than nothing.

Felix: thanks, james.

Panel seven.
Cu of felix back in the present. He's clearly recalling the flashback we just
witnessed. The lighting is back to how it was in the hotel prior to the flashback too. Sound effect (off panel): brrr brrr brrr

Page Twenty-One.
This is a very basic nine panel page. We close in on felix panel by panel, but we leave the shot very tight in on tiger tanaka, although we angle around a bit at the same time, so it isn't just a repetition of the same image.
Panel one.
Felix in med c/u on the phone. There's a questioning look on his face. Felix now has his cell phone up to his face.

Tiger (phone): felix-san.

Felix: tiger?

Panel two.
C/u of tiger, looking calm and without much expresson.

Tiger: alena davoff? Did you i.D. Her?

Panel three.
Close in slightly on felix and angle around a little bit too.

Felix: let's just say we found each other.

Felix: found her and lost her, as far as my end goes.

Felix: now, where the hell were you? 'Cause the whole thing could have gone better...

Panel four.
Another c/u of tiger. He's the same distance away, but like with felix in the panel prior we've angled around a bit.

Felix (phone): ...if...you and your men being in place like we arranged.

Tiger: yes, yes, apologizes. Sincerely. Unfortunately the night could have gone better for
        Both of us.

Tiger: you have seen the news i'm sure.

Panel five.

Felix again, closing in on him from panel three.

Felix: after my little jaunt down memory lane with alena, it hurts to move, let alone turn on
	The tv.

Felix: what's wrong?

Tiger (phone): in a word, everything.

Panel six.
C/u of tiger.

Tiger: terrorist attack.

Tiger: a nerve gas of some kind.

Felix (phone): like before -- 95' -- the sarin gas thing on the subway?

Panel seven.
Another c/u of tiger, angling around and closing in a bit, finally.

Tiger: hmm. No, i would not say it is like before.

Tiger: the attack tonight was even more ambitious...and singular.

Panel eight.
C/u of felix acting with surprise.

Tiger: of course you are familiar with the tokyo metropolitan government offices in west Shinjuku?

Panel nine.
Tight c/u of tiger, with a grim expression.

Tiger: let us just say...

Page Twenty-Two/Twenty-Three.
Double page spread

To one side is a grim looking (but still impeccable in a suit) is Tiger Tanaka. Think chow yun fat when he was younger (like when he was in hard boiled or the killer.) He has a cell phone to his ear. He faces us, with a grim expression.

Behind him, and to the rest of the double page spread, we see bodies and bodies stretching away from is, filling the entire double page spread.
We're outside in the courtyard --

With bodies of people, young and old, mainly japanese but some white too, all over the place, near and far covering the whole area in perspective, to so a scene of devastation.

These people are mainly in the kind of clothing you'd imagine office workers and daytime workers to be wearing.

Tiger: ...you might not recognize how it looks at the moment.

Caption: to be continued...

JAMES BOND HARDCOVER COLLECTION
FEATURING WARREN ELLIS, BEN PERCY, AND ANDY DIGGLE

ELLIS · MASTERS
IAN FLEMING'S
JAMES BOND 007
VARGR
DYNAMITE

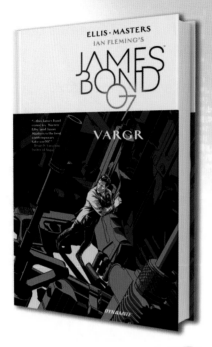

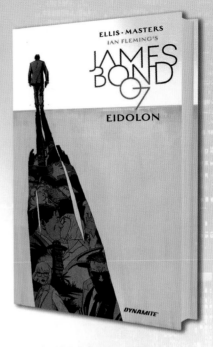

JAMES BOND: VARGR
HARDCOVER | 978-1-60690-901-0
SOFTCOVER | 978-1-5241-0480-1

ELLIS · MASTERS
IAN FLEMING'S
JAMES BOND 007
EIDOLON
DYNAMITE

JAMES BOND: EIDOLON
HARDCOVER | 978-1-5241-0272-2

PERCY · LOBOSCO
IAN FLEMING'S
JAMES BOND 007
BLACK BOX
DYNAMITE

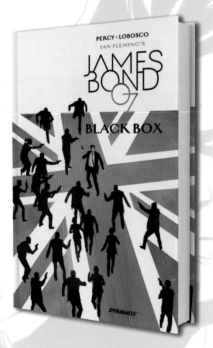

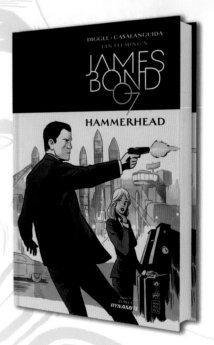

JAMES BOND: BLACK BOX
HARDCOVER | 978-1-5241-0409-2
FINAL COVER MAY VARY

DIGGLE · CASALANGUIDA
IAN FLEMING'S
JAMES BOND 007
HAMMERHEAD
DYNAMITE

JAMES BOND: HAMMERHEAD
HARDCOVER | 978-1-5241-0409-2

DYNAMITE
dynamite.com

IAN FLEMING PUBLICATIONS LIMITED

/Dynamitecomics | Facebook /Dynamitecomics | Instagram dynamitecomics.tumblr.com @dynamitecomics | Twitter